PREFACE

The origin of this book can be traced to lovely Stratford-upon-Avon, where in 1964 I was asked to explain to executives of Turner and Newall Ltd., the essence of linear programming. Linear algebra, which I had used so far when teaching linear programming was of no avail, so that I had to start from scratch. The result can be found, not greatly changed, in Chapter 2. Later on, I extended the same approach in lectures for nonspecialist classes in Operations Research, which served as a basis of this book.

The book is designed as an introductory text for students in economics and business administration. It is my opinion that linear programming is an indispensable tool for the economist. Firstly, it provides economists with a very useful decision technique; since economics is mainly analytically orientated this serves as a necessary complement. Students in economics are frequently frustrated by the surfeit of analysis in economics. Secondly, linear programming can also be used in economic analysis as is shown in Chapter 10. One of the advantages is that in this case numerical examples can be easily worked out. For students of business administration linear programming stands apart from other techniques of operations research by giving an evaluation of the values of machines, plants, sales constraints and other bottlenecks, so that these can be directly related to the values used in the accounting system.

The methods presented in this book are not new and the number of books on the same subject is not exactly small. The main advantage of this book is thought to consist in the approach used for the explanation of the various methods. Linear programming is explained in such a manner that the essentials are covered without use of linear algebra. I hope to have demonstrated in this book that this is possible. Furthermore, transportation methods, network methods and integer programming are treated in a manner which follows naturally from general linear programming; in this respect the book can claim some novelty.

It is obvious that the book relies on developments of the subject as they are found in the literature. However, in a book of this kind it is of great importance to have examples and exercises which are both nontrivial and manageable. Whereas most of the examples and exercises of this book are new, some have been taken from other sources.

The material of the book is suitable for a half year course or a full year course. In the first case it is likely that some material such as that on integer programming must be left out. It is my experience that, in order to obtain a full understanding of the methods, it is indispensable that the students work out a reasonable number of problems manually. Usually students find at first the material difficult and the problems time-consuming, but before the course is finished they usually agree that the methods are not difficult but merely complicated.

Thanks are due to students in Birmingham, Groningen, Lafayette (Ind.) and Calgary who, having to go through this material, improved it by their comments, and to my secretaries in the places aforementioned, who typed various versions of the manuscript. Finally, I am grateful to Mr. Victor G. Taylor on whose thesis the example of crude oil distribution is based.

Calgary, December 1970

LINEAR PROGRAMMING AND RELATED TECHNIQUES

C. van de PANNE

University of Calgary, Alberta, Canada

1971

NORTH-HOLLAND PUBLISHING COMPANY – AMSTERDAM · LONDON

Library of Congress Catalog Card Number 75-157018

International Standard Book Number 0 7204 2049 0

Publishers:

NORTH-HOLLAND PUBLISHING COMPANY — AMSTERDAM

NORTH-HOLLAND PUBLISHING COMPANY, LTD. — LONDON

Printed in The Netherlands

CONTENTS

PART 1

BASIC METHODS OF LINEAR PROGRAMMING

1. INTRODUCTION

1.1. Linear Programming in Historical Perspective

Consider a company having at its disposal given capacities on various types of machines, a given labor force, and given limited supplies of raw materials. It can produce a range of products for each of which is known the selling price, the variable costs, its capacity requirements, its labor requirements, and its raw material requirements. What is the production program which maximizes profits? This is a linear programming problem.

It is a fundamental problem in general economics as well as in business economics and it remained basically unsolved until the late 1940's. Before this, economists analyzed the properties of the optimal solution of such a problem, but left the actual finding of this optimal solution to private or public enterprise. In business economics the problem was never completely solved and the solutions suggested were not completely valid.

The basic method to solve linear programming problems was developed by G.B. Dantzig in 1947 and is called the *simplex method*. It is a mathematical technique though a straightforward economic interpretation can be given to it. The main reason why such a relatively easy mathematical problem was not solved before is that it was never properly formulated. Once a problem is properly formulated and its importance recognized, there is generally no lack of effort spent on its solution.

It is of course possible to point to various precursors. The French mathematician Fourier has formulated linear programming problems for use in mechanics and probability theory and suggested a way of solution as early as 1826. In mathematics, systems of linear inequalities were studied before the development of linear programming. The Russian mathematician Kantorovich published in 1939 a book entitled *Mathematical Methods of Organizing and Planning of Production* [10] in which he formulated production problems as linear programming problems, emphasized their importance and suggested a solution method. However, his work went unnoticed both in the Soviet Union and the West.

3

The Second World War has done much to create interest in the study of interdependent activities. Large-scale military operations required careful planning of logistic support. Systematic study of these problems led to the start of development of a number of mathematical techniques for solving these problems. These techniques were called *Operations Research Techniques*. After the war these techniques were found useful in industrial applications and were greatly developed. Linear programming can be considered as one of the techniques of operations research and its development can also be traced to World War influences.

In 1947 Dantzig developed the simplex method. In 1949 T.C. Koopmans, who during the war worked with transportation models, which are a special case of general linear programming models, organized in Chicago the Cowles Commission conference on linear programming where economists, mathematicians, and statisticians presented papers on linear programming; these papers were collected by Koopmans in the book *Activity Analysis of Production and Allocation* (1951) [11] which formed a start of a rapidly increasing literature on linear programming. In the 1950's the industrial use of linear programming expanded rapidly. Charnes and Cooper, who with Henderson wrote the first textbook on linear programming [4] have been very active in this field.

Linear programming can be applied to almost any industrial operation. Oil refinery operations is the largest single field of application; it is almost universally used here and companies in this field spend large amounts of money to formulate accurate models and solve and implement them. Other very well-known applications are in cattle-feed mixing, the steel industry, the paper industry and the dairy industry. Since linear programming is concerned with the basic problem of allocation of resources to various uses, it is applicable to almost any economic activity. The cases in which it is of not much use are those in which the problem is so trivial that the solution is obvious or cases in which the model is complicated by constraints which do not fit into the linear programming model; other methods have been and are being developed to cope with these problems.

The calculations needed in linear programming are very simple but for more realistic problems they have to be performed so many times that it is very tedious to do them by hand or desk calculator. However, all calculations can be performed on a computer which can handle problems of a size which could not be solved otherwise. Modern computers can handle linear programming problems in thousands of variables with hundreds or sometimes thousands of equations. Computer programs and packages of computer programs have been developed which allow the user to limit himself to feeding in the data and reading off the resulting solution.

Though the actual computations are performed by the computer, it is still desirable to know and understand the methods used. Firstly, understanding the methods will give an insight into the nature of the problem. Secondly, small or larger variations and modifications can easily be made if the method is known. Thirdly, anybody working with these models should have an understanding of how they are solved.

1.2. Economic Decisions and Linear Programming

Let us consider the following case. A company produces two products, Product A and Product B. For Product A the selling price is $15 per unit and variable costs (raw materials, labor, etc.) are $10 per unit. For Product B, the selling price is $25 per unit and variable costs are $17 per unit. We assume that the plant which produces these products has a limited capacity of 100,000 hours per year. Product A requires 1 hour of capacity per unit and Product B, 2 hours of capacity per unit; this means that at most 100,000 units of Product A can be produced per year or 50,000 units of Product B, or an equivalent combination of both. What should be the quantities to be produced per year of Product A and Product B?

Two decisions can be distinguished, the decision for Product A and the decision for Product B. Each of these decisions is not simply a choice between two alternatives, but, since the quantities produced are continuous, between an infinite number of alternatives. We could try to find out the optimal quantity to be produced for each product separately. The profit per unit is for Product A: $15 − $10 = $5. The maximum quantity to be produced is 100,000 units, profit is maximized by producing the maximum amount; then total profit for Product A is $500,000. Turning now to the decision for Product B, we find that the profit per unit is $25 − $17 = $8 per unit. Profit for Product B is maximized by producing the maximum 50,000 units, so that profit on Product B is $400,000. It is obvious that these two decisions are not compatible since the available capacity is used twice over. Because the products use the same capacity, the decisions for production of the two products are obviously dependent, so that they should be considered simultaneously.

Since decisions involve continuous quantities, it is not possible to combine the alternatives of both decisions in an easy manner. It is much better to give a mathematical formulation of the problem. Let x_1 be the quantity to be produced of Product A and x_2 the quantity to be produced of Product B; let total profit be f. Then

(2.1) $f = 5x_1 + 8x_2$.

There is a capacity restriction on both products. Since Product A requires one hour of capacity per unit and Product B 2 hours per unit, the total required annual capacity is $x_1 + 2x_2$ hours. This should not exceed the available capacity, 100,000 hours. Hence x_1 and x_2 should satisfy

(2.2) $x_1 + 2x_2 \leqq 100,000$.

Since the quantities produced can never be negative, we have

(2.3) $x_1 \geqq 0 , \quad x_2 \geqq 0$.

The decision problem is now to maximize f as given in (2.1), subject to (2.2) and (2.3). This is a *linear programming problem,* now in a mathematical formulation. Since the problem is so simple, its solution is obvious (see also Exercise 1):

$$x_1 = 100,000, \quad x_2 = 0 , \quad f = 500,000 .$$

However, if there are more restrictions and more variables, the solutions to these problems are not obvious.

Coming back to independence of decisions, it should be realized that even though capacity restrictions like (2.2) exist, decisions for different products may be independent. Suppose that at most 25,000 units of Product A can be sold and at most 30,000 units of Product B. Then taking these constraints into account, we shall not need more than $25,000 + 2 \cdot 30,000 = 85,000$ hours, so that limited capacity cannot make the decisions for these products dependent.

Another and more general kind of independence is achieved in the following way. Suppose that instead of having the capacity constraint (2.2) we have a certain cost per hour of capacity and that these capacity costs are used in the evaluation of profit per unit. We shall later see that a value for these costs exists such that if profit per unit of product is determined taking these costs into account, these profits may be used for each product separately in order to determine whether it should be produced or not. For instance if these "imputed costs" of capacity are $5 per hour, Product A has a profit per unit

$$15 - 10 - 1 \cdot 5 = 0 ;$$

it just breaks even, so it can be produced. For Product B we find

$$25 - 17 - 2 \cdot 5 = -2 ;$$

it yields a loss, so it should not be produced.

This is, of course, the way a market economy works. Decisions which are dependent because they use the same resources of which there is only a limited quantity are made independent by charging costs for these resources in such a manner that the available quantity is distributed among its users in an optimal manner. Any internal decision problem is, as we shall see in Chapter 2, solved essentially in the same manner.

In old-fashioned business economics the same method is used, but the capacity costs are based on fixed costs and overhead costs which are allocated in a certain manner to the product. The decisions reached in this manner are not necessarily optimal. Only if imputed costs of capacity are computed as indicated in Chapters 2 and 3, this leads to the optimal solution.

1.3. The Linear Programming Problem

The problem which linear programming solves is, strictly formulated, a mathematical problem. A linear function of a number of variables should be maximized, subject to a number of linear restrictions. The linear function to be maximized is called the *objective function*; it can be written in the following manner:

$$(3.1) \qquad f = p_1 x_1 + p_2 x_2 + ... + p_n x_n ;$$

f is the function to be maximized, the x's are variables, the values of which should be determined in such a way that f is maximized, and the p's are given fixed coefficients. For instance f may stand for total profit, x_1 for the quantity to be produced of Product 1, p_1 for the profit per unit of Product 1, x_2 and p_2 refer to the same concept for Product 2, and so on.

If f is maximized without any restriction, then if all p's are not equal to zero, the value of f can be raised indefinitely. For instance, if $p_1 > 0$, a very large value can be chosen for x_1 while all other x-variables are given a value zero; this results in a high value of f, which can be increased indefinitely by increasing x_1. If $p_1 < 0$, a negative value for x_1 can be chosen and f can be increased indefinitely by decreasing x_1 indefinitely. Hence the maximization of a linear function is meaningful only if there are constraints on the values which the x-variables can take. If all p's are equal to zero, the value of f remains the same for all values of the x-variables, so that maximization has no purpose.

The objective function in (3.1) is not a completely general linear function;

a completely general linear function in the variables $x_1, x_2, ..., x_n$ would be

(3.2) $f^* = p_0 + p_1 x_1 + p_2 x_2 + ... + p_n x_n$.

However, this function may be written in terms of f as given in (3.1) as follows

(3.3) $f^* = p_0 + f$;

if f is maximized by some values of the x-variables, then according to (3.3), f^* will be maximized by maximizing f.

Suppose that f^* stands for profits and p_0 is negative and stands for minus fixed and overhead costs. We just saw that instead of maximizing f^* we may maximize f, since the same solution is obtained. Hence fixed and overhead costs are irrelevant for the determination of the optimal production program.

Instead of maximizing f as given in (3.1), $-f$ could be minimized:

(3.4) $-f = -p_1 x_1 - p_2 x_2 - .... - p_n x_n$.

If f is maximized for certain values of the x-variables, $-f$ is minimized for the same values. This meant that it is irrelevant whether f is maximized or $-f$ is minimized. Hence the definition of a linear programming problem may be slightly generalized by defining it as the *maximization or minimization* of a linear function subject to linear constraints.

The constraints subject to which the objective function is maximized or minimized can be distinguished in equality constraints and inequality constraints. The general form of a linear inequality constraint is

(3.5) $a_1 x_1 + a_2 x_2 + ... + a_n x_n \leqq b$,

where the a's and b are given fixed coefficients. For instance, it could be that b stands for the total available production capacity and $a_1, a_2, ..., a_n$ for the capacities required to produce one unit of the products $1, 2, ..., n$, respectively.

If both sides in (3.5) are multiplied by -1, the following relation which is equivalent with (3.5) is obtained:

(3.6) $-a_1 x_1 - a_2 x_2 - ... - a_n x_n \geqq -b$.

From this, it is obvious that any inequality with a $\leq$-sign can easily be transformed into an inequality with a $\geq$-sign and *vice versa*.

Nearly always in a linear programming problem all variables except f are required to be nonnegative. If x_1 stands for production of Product 1, it is obvious that production cannot be negative. In the following we shall always require nonnegativity of the variables:

(3.7) $x_1, x_2, ..., x_n \geq 0$.

The constraints may also be in the form of a linear equality:

(3.8) $a_1 x_1 + a_2 x_2 + ... + a_n x_n = b$.

This form is equivalent to a linear inequality constraint, which may be shown as follows. Let a_1 be nonzero; then (3.8) may be written as

(3.9) $x_1 = a_1^{-1} b - a_1^{-1} a_2 x_2 - ... - a_1^{-1} a_n x_n$.

We may substitute for x_1 in the objective function and all other constraints so that x_1 is eliminated from the problem. Substituting (3.9) in the equality $x_1 \geq 0$, we find

(3.10) $a_1^{-1} x_2 + ... + a_1^{-1} a_n x_n \leq a_1^{-1} b$.

Hence each equality constraint can by means of elimination of a variable be transformed into an inequality constraint.

On the other hand, each inequality constraint can be transformed into an equality constraint by the introduction of a new variable. For instance constraint (3.5) can be replaced by

(3.11) $a_1 x_1 + a_2 x_2 + ... + a_n x_n + y = b$,

(3.12) $y \geq 0$.

The y-variable is in this case called the *slack variable* of the inequality. If the inequality is

(3.13) $a_1 x_1 + a_2 x_2 + ... + a_n x_n \geq b$,

it may be replaced by

(3.14) $a_1 x_1 + a_2 x_2 + \ldots + a_n x_n - y = b$,

(3.15) $y \geqq 0$.

From this it may be concluded that inequality constraints other than non-negativity constraints may be converted into equalities and *vice versa.* Note that in each case the number of inequalities including nonnegativity constraints remains the same.

Since linear programming deals with a linear objective function and linear constraints, we would expect that linear programming techniques should be similar to the solution of a number of linear equations for a number of variables. This is indeed true, but there are two important differences. The first is that in linear programming we maximize or minimize a linear function. The second is that instead of or in addition to linear equations we have linear inequality constraints. It turns out that all effective linear programming methods are variants of the complete elimination method for the solution of linear equations with modifications related to the maximization or minimization and to the nonnegativity constraints.

The values of the x-variables which maximize (or minimize if the problem is a minimization problem) the objective function subject to the constraints are called the *optimal solution.* Values of the x-variables which satisfy the constraints but which do not necessarily maximize the objective function are called *feasible solutions.* It may be that no values of the x-variables exist which satisfy all constraints; in that case the problem is said to have *no feasible* solution; obviously, it then does not have an optimal solution either. On the other hand, it may be that the objective function can be increased indefinitely by increasing the values of some x-variables indefinitely in a certain way; the problem is then said (perhaps somewhat improperly) to have an *infinite solution.*

In the analysis of some mathematical problems, a geometrical presentation is useful. For linear programming, the use of geometrical presentations turns out to be limited, mainly because so many variables are involved while geometrical presentations only allow two or three variables. A geometrical presentation of a small linear programming problem is given in order to give a partial insight into the nature of the linear programming problem; however, it should be remembered that geometrical considerations play a very small part in linear programming. As an example, let us consider the following problem. Maximize

(3.16) $f = 2x_1 + 3x_2$

subject to

(3.17) $-x_1 + x_2 \leqq 1\tfrac{1}{2}$,

(3.18) $-x_1 + 2x_2 \leqq 4$,

(3.19) $x_1 + x_2 \leqq 6\tfrac{1}{2}$,

(3.20) $x_1, x_2 \geqq 0$.

This is a problem in two variables (if f is not counted as a variable) so that a two-dimensional graph can be used.

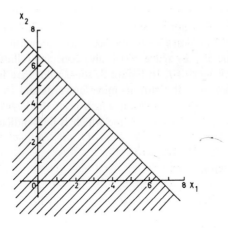

Fig. 1.

The constraint (3.19) is indicated in Figure 1. The points on the line represent solutions for which $x_1 + x_2 = 6\tfrac{1}{2}$, the points below and to the left of this line, the shaded area, are solutions for which $x_1 + x_2 < 6\tfrac{1}{2}$. Hence the shaded area including the line includes the solutions which are feasible for this constraint. The points above and to the right of this line are solutions for which $x_1 + x_2 > 6\tfrac{1}{2}$, which are therefore infeasible for constraint (3.19). Other constraints can be indicated in the same manner. For instance, the feasible

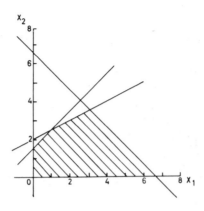

Fig. 2.

solutions to the constraint $x_1 \geqq 0$ are the points on the x_2-axis and to the right of this axis. The points which are situated on or at the right side of all constraints are contained in a polygon which is called the *feasible region*. In Figure 2 the feasible region for constraints (3.17)–(3.20) is shaded.

The objective function f does not occur as a dimension in the figure, but the points in the x_1, x_2 space which give constant values of f may be indicated for a few values of f. In Figure 3, some values are indicated for f. It is obvious that f increases if solutions move upwards and to the left. The optimal direction, that is the direction which gives the largest increase of f per unit of movement, is given by a line which is perpendicular to the lines of

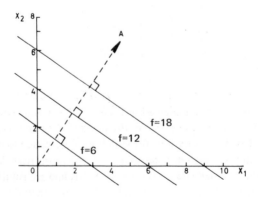

Fig. 3.

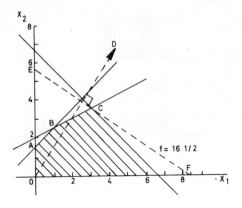

Fig. 4.

constant values of f; this direction is called the *gradient* of the objective function. In Fig. 3, OA is the gradient for the objective function (3.16).

The linear programming problem can now be stated geometrically as follows. Find a point within the feasible region which is situated on the line of constant values of f with the highest value or, what amounts to the same, is situated farthest in the direction of the gradient. In Fig. 4 this point is easily found by inspection; it is point C. EF is the line of constant f-values for $f = 16\frac{1}{2}$.

Let us now consider a linear programming problem which has the following constraints:

$$(3.21) \qquad x_1 + x_2 \leqq 6\frac{1}{2},$$

$$(3.22) \qquad x_2 \geqq 8,$$

$$(3.23) \qquad x_1 \geqq 0, \quad x_2 \geqq 0.$$

Figure 5 gives a geometrical presentation of this problem. The horizontally shaded area gives solutions which are feasible for constraints (3.21) and (3.23) and the vertically shaded area gives solutions which are feasible for constraints (3.22) and (3.23). Obviously, there are no solutions which are feasible for all constraints; this can also be seen immediately from the constraints (3.21)– (3.23). Note that the constraint $x_2 \geqq 8$ makes the constraint $x_2 \geqq 0$ redundant.

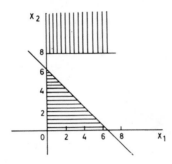

Fig. 5.

Consider the following problem. Maximize

(3.24) $f = 2x_1 + 3x_2$

subject to

(3.25) $x_1 + x_2 \geqq 6\tfrac{1}{2}$,

(3.26) $x_2 \leqq 8$,

(3.27) $x_1 \geqq 0$, $x_2 \geqq 0$.

Figure 6 gives a geometrical presentation of this problem with the feasible region being shaded. It is obvious that this problem has an infinite solution; by taking $x_2 = 8$ and $x_1 \to \infty$, f can be increased indefinitely.

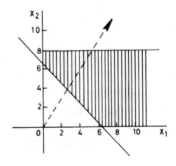

Fig. 6.

For problems in two variables all these properties are found by inspection. The methods presented in later chapters will find for any linear programming problem the optimal solution or indicate that no feasible solution exist or indicate that there is an infinite optimal solution.

Linear programming techniques have developed considerably since the discovery of the simplex method. Chapter 2 contains an exposition of the simplex method and as such constitutes the core of this book. In the remainder of the book further developments, alternative methods, methods for problems of a special type, applications and related techniques are discussed.

Exercises

1. Solve the problem of the two products in Section 1.2, considering production quantities for Product A of 0, 25,000, 50,000, 75,000, and 100,000 units and for Product B of 0, 25,000, and 50,000 units. Combine the two decisions with 5 and 3 alternatives into one decision with 15 alternatives (of which a number are not feasible), and determine the optimal decision.

2. (a) Transform the following problem into a maximization problem with inequality constraints only having a $\leq$ -sign: Minimize

$$f = 4x_1 + 3x_2 + 5x_3$$

subject to

$$x_1 + x_2 + x_3 = 1 \, ,$$

$$x_1 + x_2 \geq \tfrac{1}{2} \, ,$$

$$x_1 + x_3 \geq \tfrac{1}{2} \, ,$$

$$x_2 + x_3 \geq \tfrac{1}{2} \, ,$$

$$x_1, x_2, x_3 \geq 0 \, .$$

(b) Solve the resulting problem graphically.

3. (a) Solve algebraically and graphically: Maximize

$$f = 4x_1 + 5x_2$$

subject to

$$x_1 + x_2 = 1 \, ,$$

$$-2x_1 + 3x_2 = 2 \, ,$$

$$x_1, x_2 \geqq 0 \, .$$

Comment on the nature of the solution you have obtained.

(b) Solve the same problem algebraically and graphically if there is a $\leqq$ - sign in the second constraint.

(c) Do the same for a $\geqq$ -sign.

4. Solve graphically: Minimize

$$f = x_1 + x_2$$

subject to

$$x_1 \geqq 1 \, ,$$

$$x_2 \leqq 5 \, ,$$

$$x_1 + x_2 \geqq 2 \, ,$$

$$x_1, x_2 \geqq 0 \, .$$

Indicate all solutions to the problem.

2. THE SIMPLEX METHOD FOR LINEAR PROGRAMMING

2.1. Production Planning With One Resource Limitation

In linear programming a number of methods may be used, but the *simplex method* is the most important one; it is virtually the only method used in practical applications. In this chapter, the simplex method for linear programming will be explained using a simple example of production planning. The economic aspects of linear programming will be stressed, which is done by first presenting the simplex method in its economic interpretation, after which its equivalents in terms of equations and tableaux are given.

Let us consider an integrated textile company which produces four products: two yarns, Yarn A and Yarn B, and two fabrics, Fabric A and Fabric B. It is supposed that these products can be sold at given prices in unlimited quantities; these prices are given in the first row of Table 1. The variable costs per unit of product, such as cost of raw material, some labor costs, etc., are also known; they are given in the second row of Table 1. Subtracting variable costs from the selling price, we obtain net revenue per unit of product; this is given in the third row of Table 1. Fixed costs are not taken into account, since they are not affected by a decision about the production program.

The company uses various installations for the production of the four commodities; all installations have given fixed capacities. The capacities we

Table 1
Data for production planning problem

	Yarn A	Yarn B	Fabric A	Fabric B
Selling Price ($/unit)	12	10	75	29
Direct Costs ($/unit)	3.	2	25	10
Net Revenue ($/unit)	9	8	50	19
Spinning Time (h/unit)	3	2	10	4
Loom Time (h/unit)	–	–	2	½

are considering here are spinning and loom capacity. In this section we shall assume that there are available 18,000 hours of spinning capacity per week and enough loom capacity for any production program using not more than 18,000 hours of spinning capacity. Hence we assume that spinning capacity is the only resource limitation or bottleneck.

Let us now find the optimal production program in this situation, that is the production program with the maximum profit. At the very first sight we would perhaps take the product with the maximum selling price, Fabric A, but it is obvious that net revenue which is found by subtraction of direct costs from the selling price is more relevant. At this point it should again be noted that fixed costs play no role in choosing the optimal production program with existing facilities, since our decisions will not affect fixed costs.

In this situation Fabric A has the highest net revenue per unit, $50. But we soon realize that, since spinning time is the only limiting factor, the relevant criterion for the product to be produced is net revenue *per unit of spinning time* required for that product. The net revenue for Yarn A is $9, it uses 3 hours of spinning time so that its net revenue per hour of spinning time is $3. In the same way we find for Yarn B $4 per spinning hour, for Fabric A $5 per spinning hour, and for Fabric B $4.75 per spinning hour. Hence Fabric A has the highest net revenue per spinning hour, and should therefore be produced, using up the available spinning capacity. Total profits can be computed in two ways. First, we may take the number of units of Fabric A which can be produced with the available spinning capacity times the net revenue per unit:

$$\frac{18,000}{10} \cdot \$50 = \$90,000 \ .$$

Secondly, it may be computed as spinning capacity times net revenue per spinning hour:

$$18,000 \cdot \$5 = \$90,000 \ .$$

The net revenue per spinning hour may be called the *imputed costs* of spinning capacity, because it may be used to evaluate the profitability of other products. Hence we find for Yarn A which has a net revenue of $9 per unit and uses 3 hours of spinning capacity per unit:

$$9 - 3 \cdot 5 = -6 \ .$$

This may be called the *reduced revenue* of Yarn A. Since it is negative, Yarn A should not be taken into production. For Yarn B we find

$$8 - 2 \cdot 5 = -2 \ ,$$

which is also negative. For Fabric A we find

$$50 - 10 \cdot 5 = 0 \, ,$$

which is, of course, explained by the fact that the imputed cost of spinning capacity was computed from Fabric A. For Fabric B we find

$$19 - 4 \cdot 5 = -1 \, ,$$

which is again negative.

That the reduced revenues for products other than Fabric A are negative is because this product had the highest net revenue per spinning hour. If there is only one limiting factor, the product with the highest net revenue per unit of this limiting factor may be chosen, but if there are more limiting factors, this cannot be done. We shall therefore consider also for the case with one limiting factor a procedure which differs slightly from the above.

Let us take a product with a positive net revenue, say Yarn A. Using this product, the following imputed cost of spinning capacity can be computed:

$$\$9/3 = \$3 \, .$$

Total profits are $6,000 \cdot \$9 = \$54,000 = 18,000 \cdot \$3$. The imputed cost may be used to evaluate the other products. For the reduced revenues of Yarn B we find

$$8 - 2 \cdot 3 = 2 \, ,$$

for Fabric A:

$$50 - 10 \cdot 3 = 20 \, ,$$

and for Fabric B:

$$19 - 4 \cdot 3 = 7 \, .$$

All other products give positive reduced revenues, so that any of them may replace Yarn A in the production program. Let us take Yarn B. The imputed costs of spinning capacity are now

$$\$8/2 = \$4 \, ,$$

and total profits are

$$9,000 \cdot \$8 = \$72,000 = 18,000 \cdot \$4 \, .$$

The imputed costs may again be used to evaluate the other products. For the reduced revenues of Yarn A and Fabric A and B we find

$$9 - 3 \cdot 4 = -3 \, , \quad 50 - 10 \cdot 4 = 10 \, , \quad 19 - 4 \cdot 4 = 3 \, .$$

Hence Fabric A and B both have positive net revenues, so that either one of them may replace Yarn B. Let us take Fabric A. For the imputed costs of spinning capacity we find now

$$\$50/10 = \$5 \ ,$$

and total profits are

$$1{,}800 \cdot \$50 = \$90{,}000 = 18{,}000 \cdot \$5 \ .$$

Now the reduced revenues for the other products are all negative, as we have seen before. Hence the optimal production program is to produce 1,800 units of Fabric A which yield $90,000 in profits.

   In the procedure indicated above, the reduced revenue of each of the products was computed, given the imputed costs of the limiting factor derived from the product in the production program. If the reduced revenue for a product is negative, it is not able to bear as costs the imputed costs, so that it is not profitable to enter it into the production program. If, on the other hand, the reduced revenue for a product is positive, it is able to bear the imputed costs and have some additional revenue above that, so that this product may replace the product in the production program which only just breaks even with the present imputed costs (which were, of course, derived from that product). The procedure uses a number of steps and seems therefore more cumbersome than a straightforward computation of imputed costs per spinning hour for all products, from which the maximum may be taken. However, it will be seen in the next section that the stepwise procedure can be readily generalized for more than one production factor, which is not possible for the other procedure.

2.2. Production Planning with Two Resource Limitations

   The loom capacity necessary for the production of 1,800 units of Fabric A is 3,600 hours. If the available loom capacity is less than 3,600 hours per week, the production program of 1,800 units of Fabric A is not feasible. Let us assume that 3,000 hours of loom capacity are available; the spinning capacity is still 18,000 hours. A somewhat generalized version of the procedure of the last section will be applied.

   Let us take a product with a positive net revenue, say Fabric A. The production of Fabric A now faces two bottlenecks; if all spinning capacity is used, at most

$$\frac{18{,}000}{10} = 1{,}800$$

units can be produced and if all loom capacity is used, at most

$$\frac{3,000}{2} = 1,500$$

units can be produced. This means that in this situation the loom capacity limitation is more strict than the spinning capacity limitation. Hence for loom capacity the following imputed costs are computed:

$$\frac{50}{2} = 25 \ .$$

At this point all loom capacity is completely used, but there are still $18,000 - 1,500 \cdot 10 = 3,000$ hours of free spinning capacity. Hence the imputed cost of spinning capacity is taken as zero. Total profits can be computed in two ways:

$$1,500 \cdot \$50 = \$75,000 = 3,000 \cdot \$25 + 18,000 \cdot 0 \ .$$

For the reduced revenues of other products we find for Yarn A, Yarn B, and Fabric B:

$$9 - 0 \cdot 25 = 9 \ , \quad 8 - 0 \cdot 25 = 8 \ , \quad 19 - \frac{1}{2} \cdot 25 = 6\frac{1}{2} \ .$$

All other products have a positive reduced revenue. Let us take Yarn A into the production program.

Yarn A does not use any loom capacity; it only uses spinning capacity of which there was a surplus of 3,000 hours in the previous production program. Hence a quantity of $3,000/3 = 1,000$ units of Yarn A may be produced together with the same quantity of Fabric A. The computation of imputed costs is now somewhat more complicated. The imputed costs are the values of the limited resources which are derived from the values of the products which use these resources. Let us denote the imputed cost of one hour spinning capacity u_1 and the imputed cost of one hour loom capacity u_2. Then, since 3 hours of spinning capacity and no loom capacity are required for Yarn A, the following equation may be formulated:

$$3u_1 + 0u_2 = 9 \ .$$

For Fabric A, 10 hours of spinning capacity and 2 hours of loom capacity are required; its net revenue is 50, so that the following equation is obtained:

$$10u_1 + 2u_2 = 50 \ .$$

From the first equation we obtain $u_1 = 3$, and then from the second $u_2 = 10$. The imputed costs of spinning and loom time are therefore 3 and 10, respectively. Total profits may again be found in two ways, units of products produced times net revenue or quantities of resources times imputed costs:

$$1,000 \cdot 9 + 1,500 \cdot 50 = \$84,000 = 18,000 \cdot 3 + 3,000 \cdot 10 .$$

The imputed costs can be used to evaluate the profitability of the products not in the production program. For the reduced revenue of Yarn B we find

$$8 - 2 \cdot 3 - 0 \cdot 10 = 2 ,$$

and Fabric B

$$19 - 4 \cdot 3 - \tfrac{1}{2} \cdot 10 = 2 .$$

Hence total profits can be increased by taking Yarn B or Fabric B into the production program. Let us take Yarn B first. If this product is produced, it will use spinning capacity but no loom capacity. If both spinning capacity and loom capacity are to remain fully occupied, Yarn B should replace Yarn A. If this is done, 1,500 units of Yarn B are produced and an unchanged quantity of Fabric A, also 1,500 units. The imputed costs of capacity now are found from the equations for Yarn B and Fabric A:

$$2u_1 + 0u_2 = 8 ,$$

$$10u_1 + 2u_2 = 50 .$$

Hence $u_1 = 4$ and $u_2 = 5$. It should be noted that, though loom capacity hardly seemed to be involved, its imputed costs are changed. Total profits of the new production program are, as usual, found in two ways:

$$1,500 \cdot 8 + 1,500 \cdot 50 = 87,000 = 18,000 \cdot 4 + 3,000 \cdot 5 .$$

The imputed costs are used to evaluate the profitability of the products not in the production program. For the reduced revenue of Yarn A we have

$$9 - 3 \cdot 4 - 0 \cdot 5 = -3 ,$$

and for that of Fabric B

$$19 - 4 \cdot 4 - \tfrac{1}{2} \cdot 5 = \tfrac{1}{2} .$$

It is therefore profitable to take Fabric B into the production program. Which product should it replace if the entire production capacity is used? If it replaces Yarn B, the quantities produced of the products in the production program, Fabric A and Fabric B should be determined. Let these be denoted by x_3 and x_4. Since both spinning and loom capacity are completely used, the following equations in spinning capacity and loom capacity are valid:

$$18,000 = 10x_3 + 4x_4$$

$$3,000 = 2x_3 + \tfrac{1}{2}x_4 .$$

From these two equations we find $x_3 = 1,000$ and $x_4 = 2,000$. If Fabric B has replaced Fabric A, we would have the following equations in x_2, the quantity of Yarn B produced and x_4, the quantity of Fabric B produced:

$$18,000 = 2x_2 + 4x_4 ,$$

$$3,000 = 0x_2 + \tfrac{1}{2}x_4 .$$

We find $x_4 = 6,000$ and $x_2 = -3,000$. Since it is not feasible to produce a negative quantity of a product, the previous solution with Fabric A and Fabric B in the production program is considered.

The imputed costs are found from equations in u_1 and u_2 for Fabric A and Fabric B. These equations are

$$10u_1 + 2u_2 = 50 ,$$

$$4u_1 + \tfrac{1}{2}u_2 = 19 .$$

The solution of this equation system is $u_1 = 4\tfrac{1}{3}$ and $u_2 = 3\tfrac{1}{3}$. Total profits are

$$1,000 \cdot 50 + 2,000 \cdot 19 = \$88,000 = 18,000 \cdot 4\tfrac{1}{3} + 3,000 \cdot 3\tfrac{1}{3} .$$

The profitability of other products, Yarn A and Yarn B, is evaluated by computing their reduced revenues using the imputed costs. For Yarn A we find

$$9 - 3 \cdot 4\tfrac{1}{3} - 0 \cdot 3\tfrac{1}{3} = -4$$

and for Yarn B

$$8 - 2 \cdot 4\tfrac{1}{3} - 0 \cdot 3\tfrac{1}{3} = -\tfrac{2}{3} .$$

Neither of these products is profitable. Another possibility of changing the production program would be to leave some of the spinning capacity or some of the loom capacity unused. However, this would result in lower profits, since both these capacities have positive imputed costs. Hence the production program maximizing profits must have been found.

The procedure described above is equivalent to the simplex method; it generates the same successive solutions. The procedure gives an illustration of an economic interpretation of the simplex method. In particular, it stresses the role which imputed costs play in that method. In other respects, the procedure was cumbersome, because at each step a number of equation systems had to be solved. It will be seen in the next section that the proper simplex method does not have these computational difficulties.

2.3. Production Planning Using the Simplex Method

The production planning problem can conveniently be formulated in terms of some equations and inequalities. Let x_1 be the amount produced of Yarn A, x_2 the amount produced of Yarn B, and x_3 and x_4 the similar amounts of Fabric A and B. Since Yarn A uses 3 hours of spinning capacity, Yarn B, 2 hours, Fabric A, 10 hours and Fabric B, 4 hours, the total spinning capacity used by a production program x_1, x_2, x_3, x_4 is

$$3x_1 + 2x_2 + 10x_3 + 4x_4 .$$

For any feasible production program, this should be less than the available spinning capacity, which is 18,000 hours. Hence any feasible production program should satisfy the inequality

(3.1) $\qquad 3x_1 + 2x_2 + 10x_3 + 4x_4 \leq 18,000 .$

The loom capacity used by any feasible production program should not exceed the available loom capacity of 3,000 hours; we may therefore formulate the inequality

(3.2) $\qquad 0x_1 + 0x_2 + 2x_3 + \frac{1}{2}x_4 \leq 3,000 .$

Furthermore, in any feasible production program, the quantities produced cannot be negative; hence we have the following four inequalities

(3.3) $\qquad x_1 \geq 0 , \quad x_2 \geq 0 , \quad x_3 \geq 0 , \quad x_4 \geq 0 .$

The company wants to maximize profits, which are equal to net revenue per unit of product times the number of products produced of the product, summed over all products. Let us call total profits f. We then have the following equation for total profits:

(3.4) $\qquad f = 9x_1 + 8x_2 + 50x_3 + 19x_4 .$

The problem can now be formulated in mathematical terms as that of finding values $x_1, x_2, x_3,$ and x_4 which satisfy the inequalities (3.1), (3.2), and (3.3) and for which f as given by (3.4) is maximized. This problem has all characteristics of a linear programming problem; in a general linear programming problem a linear function [such as (3.4)] is maximized subject to a number of linear inequalities and equations [such as (3.1), (3.2), and (3.3)].

The simplex method will now be explained using the production planning example. For an application of the simplex method the inequalities other than the nonnegativity requirements such as then in (3.3) should be formulated as equalities. In (3.1) this is done by the introduction of a *slack variable* y_1 which can be interpreted as hours of unused spinning capacity; for a feasible solution of the problem y_1 should be nonnegative. Hence (3.1) can be replaced by

$$3x_1 + 2x_2 + 10x_3 + 4x_4 + y_1 = 18,000 \, ,$$

(3.5)

$$y_1 \geqq 0 \, .$$

In the same way (3.2) can be replaced by

(3.6) $$0x_1 + 0x_2 + 2x_3 + \tfrac{1}{2}x_4 + y_2 = 3,000 \, ,$$

$$y_2 \geqq 0 \, ;$$

y_2 can be interpreted as the unused loom capacity.

Now the equations of (3.5), (3.6) and (3.4) can be written as the following equation system:

$$18,000 = 3x_1 + 2x_2 + 10x_3 + 4x_4 + y_1 \, ,$$

(3.7) $$3,000 = 0x_1 + 0x_2 + 2x_3 + \tfrac{1}{2}x_4 + y_2 \, .$$

$$0 = -9x_1 - 8x_2 - 50x_3 - 19x_4 + f \, .$$

This is a system of three equations in seven variables. Generally, such an equation system will have many solutions. Let us consider the particular solution in which the variables x_1, x_2, x_3, and x_4 are zero. The corresponding terms in (3.7) may then be deleted, so that the system becomes

$$18,000 = y_1 \, ,$$

(3.8) $$3,000 = y_2 \, ,$$

$$0 = f \, .$$

This gives us a solution to the equation system. It is also a solution of the linear programming problem which is feasible, since all variables are nonnegative. It is not necessarily a solution which maximizes total profits. In fact, the solution is far from optimal, since all x-variables, which stand for the amounts produced, are zero, and the y-variables, which represent idle capacity, are equal to the available capacity. Profits then are of course zero, as is indicated by the last equation of (3.8).

We want to improve this situation, which can be done by considering the effect of increases in the amounts produced of the four commodities. How will our present solution change if we have a positive amount of Yarn A instead of an amount of zero? This can be found from the system (3.7) if the terms in x_1 are moved to the other side of the equation signs and x_2, x_3 and x_4 are put equal to zero as before. We obtain

$$18{,}000 - 3x_1 = y_1 \,,$$

(3.9) $$3{,}000 = y_2 \,,$$

$$9x_1 = f \,.$$

From the last equation, $f = 9x_1$, it can be seen that if x_1 increases, f increases. From this we conclude that x_1 should be increased as much as possible. We could also consider an increase of x_2 instead of x_1; we would then obtain $f = 8x_2$. For an increase in x_3 we would obtain $f = 50x_3$, and for an increase in x_4 we would obtain $f = 19x_4$. Hence increasing the production of any of the products would boost profits. Since the factor of x_3 is the largest, let us decide to increase x_3 as much as possible, keeping x_1, x_2, and x_4 at zero.

The equation system (3.7) may then be written as

$$18{,}000 - 10x_3 = y_1 \,,$$

(3.10) $$3{,}000 - 2x_3 = y_2 \,,$$

$$50x_3 = f \,.$$

We would like to increase x_3 as much as possible, but the first two equations indicate that as x_3 increases, the values of y_1 and y_2 diminish. Since the final solution should be feasible, we should take care that the y-variables do not become negative. From the first equation it is found that y_1 becomes zero for $x_3 = 1{,}800$ and from the second that y_2 becomes zero for $x_3 = 1{,}500$; hence y_2 becomes zero first. This means that the maximum value which x_3 can take without making the solution negative is 1,500. Now a new solution to the system is found which is $x_3 = 1{,}500$; the values of y_1, y_2 and f are found by substitution of this in (3.10):

$$18,000 - 10 \cdot 1,500 = 3,000 = y_1 \, ,$$

(3.11) $\qquad 3,000 - 2 \cdot 1,500 = \qquad 0 = y_2 \, ,$

$$50 \cdot 1,500 = 75,000 = f.$$

The values of x_1, x_2, and x_4 are zero. The production program implied by this solution is the same as was found in the previous section.

Let us return for a moment to system (3.7). The solution (3.8) with the x-variables equal to zero was so easily obtained because y_1 occurred only in the first equation of (3.7) with a unit coefficient, y_2 occurred only in the second equation with a unit coefficient, and f occurs only in the third equation with a unit coefficient. y_1, y_2, and f are in this case called the *basic variables* of the system, the x-variables of (3.7) are called the *non-basic variables*. (3.8) is called the *basic solution* of the system (3.7). Nonbasic variables are always zero in a basic solution; basic variables are equal to the constant term of the equations. The new solution (3.11) is not a basic solution of the system (3.7) because x_3 is positive but is a nonbasic variable in (3.7), while y_2 is zero in (3.11) but is a basic variable in (3.7). However, the system (3.7) may be transformed into another system of which (3.11) is a basic solution. This can be done by transforming the system in such a way that x_3 has a unit coefficient in the second equation and zero coefficients in the other equations; this means that x_3 should replace y_2 as basic variable for the second equations. Since $y_2 = 0$ for the new solution, it may be considered as a nonbasic variable in the new system.

A system of equations is transformed by multiplying or dividing an equation of the system by a nonzero constant or by adding a multiple of one equation to another. We wish x_3 to have a unit coefficient in the second equation of (3.7), so we divide this equation by 2. The result is

(3.12) $\qquad 1,500 = 0x_1 + 0x_2 + x_3 + \tfrac{1}{4}x_4 + \tfrac{1}{2}y_2 \, .$

In order to make the coefficient 10 of x_3 in the first equation of (3.7) vanish, we may subtract 10 times (3.12) from this equation. The result is

$$3,000 = 3x_1 + 2x_2 + 1\tfrac{1}{2}x_4 + y_1 - 5y_2 \, .$$

The coefficient -50 of x_3 in the third equation of (3.7) may be reduced to zero by subtracting -50 times (3.12) from this equation, which results in

$$75,000 = -9x_1 - 8x_2 - 6\tfrac{1}{2}x_4 + 25y_2 + f.$$

The last three equations may be written as the new equation system

$$3,000 = 3x_1 + 2x_2 + 1\tfrac{1}{2}x_4 + y_1 - 5y_2 \,,$$

(3.13) $$1,500 = 0x_1 + 0x_2 + x_3 + \tfrac{1}{4}x_4 + \tfrac{1}{2}y_2 \,,$$

$$75,000 = -9x_1 - 8x_2 - 6\tfrac{1}{2}x_4 + 25y_2 + f \,.$$

This equation system has y_1, x_3, and f as basic variables. Its basic solution is

$$3,000 = y_1 \,,$$

(3.14) $$1,500 = x_3 \,,$$

$$75,000 = f \quad,$$

with the nonbasic variables x_1, x_2, x_4, and y_2 equal to zero. This is the same solution as (3.11).

Using the system (3.13), we try to increase profits further. Considering an increase in x_1, keeping the other nonbasic variables at zero, we find for the values of basic variables

$$3,000 - 3x = y_1 \,,$$

(3.15) $$1,500 \qquad = x_3 \,,$$

$$75,000 + 9x_1 = f \,.$$

Hence f, and therefore profits increase for an increase in x_1 by $9x_1$. In the same way we find that if x_2 or x_4 are increased from zero, profits increase by $8x_2$ or $6\tfrac{1}{2}x_4$, respectively. A positive value of y_2 leads to the following solution:

$$3,000 + 5y_2 = y_1 \,,$$

(3.16) $$1,500 + \tfrac{1}{2}y_2 = x_3 \,,$$

$$75,000 - 25y_2 = f \,.$$

Hence we see that an increase in y_2 from zero leads to a decrease of profits of $25y_2$.

This means that if in this situation a unit of loom capacity is left unused, \$25 is lost. This is the same as the imputed costs of loom capacity. We see that the imputed costs of the limited resources can be found as the coefficient of the y-variables in the f-equation.

Since x_1 has the most negative coefficient in the f-equation of (3.13) we decide to make it a basic variable and increase it as much as possible. From (3.15) it is found that y_1 decreases for increasing x_1; for $x_1 = 1,000$, $y_1 = 0$.

x_3 is not affected by an increase of x_1. Hence x_1 is made a basic variable while y_1 becomes nonbasic. The equation system (3.13) is transformed accordingly, which is done by dividing its first equation by 3, which results in

(3.17) $1,000 = x_1 + \frac{2}{3}x_2 + \frac{1}{2}x_4 + \frac{1}{3}y_1 - 1\frac{2}{3}y_2$.

The second equation of (3.13) has a zero coefficient of x_1. The coefficient of x_1 in the third equation, -9, is reduced to zero by subtracting -9 times (3.17) from it. The transformed equation system is

$$1,000 = x_1 + \frac{2}{3}x_2 \qquad + \frac{1}{2}x_4 + \frac{1}{3}y_1 - 1\frac{2}{3}y_2 \text{ ,}$$

(3.18) $$1,500 = \qquad 0x_2 + x_3 + \frac{1}{4}x_4 + 0y_1 + \frac{1}{2}y_2 \text{ ,}$$

$$84,000 = \qquad -2x_2 \qquad - 2x_4 + 3y_1 + 10y_2 + f \text{ .}$$

The basic solution of this system is

$$1,000 = x_1 \text{ ,}$$

(3.19) $$1,500 = x_3 \text{ ,}$$

$$84,000 = f \text{ .}$$

This is the same solution as was found in the previous section. The imputed costs of spinning and loom capacity can be found as the coefficients of y_1 and y_2 in the f-equation, which are 3 and 10.

From this f-equation we also see that profits can be increased by increasing x_2 and x_4 from zero. Let us increase x_2; this results in

$$1,000 - \frac{2}{3}x_2 = x_1 \text{ ,}$$

(3.20) $$1,500 = x_3 \text{ ,}$$

$$84,000 + 2x_2 = f \text{ .}$$

x_1 decreases with increasing x_2; from

$$1,000 - \frac{2}{3}x_2 = 0$$

we find that x_1 becomes zero for $x_2 = 1,500$, x_3 is not affected. x_2 therefore replaces x_1 as basic variable. The equation system (3.18) is transformed accordingly, the result is

$$1,500 = 1\frac{1}{2}x_1 + x_2 + \qquad \frac{3}{4}x_4 + \frac{1}{2}y_1 - 2\frac{1}{2}y_2 \text{ ,}$$

(3.21) $$1,500 = 0x_1 \qquad + x_3 + \frac{1}{4}x_4 + 0y_1 + \frac{1}{2}y_2 \text{ ,}$$

$$87,000 = 3x_1 \qquad - \frac{1}{2}x_4 + 4y_1 + 5y_2 + f \text{ .}$$

The corresponding basic solution is obvious from the system. Profits have increased to \$87,000; imputed costs are 4 and 5 for spinning and loom capacity, respectively. Since x_4 has a coefficient of $-\frac{1}{2}$ in the f-equation, profits can be increased if x_4 is increased. We find

$$1{,}500 - \tfrac{3}{4}x_4 = x_2 \, ,$$

(3.22)
$$1{,}500 - \tfrac{1}{4}x_4 = x_3 \, ,$$

$$87{,}000 + \tfrac{1}{2}x_4 = f \, .$$

x_2 becomes zero for $x_1 = 1{,}500/\tfrac{3}{4} = 2{,}000$ and x_3 becomes zero for $x_4 = 1{,}500/\tfrac{1}{4} = 6{,}000$. Hence x_4 replaces x_2 as basic variable. The system (3.21) is therefore transformed into the system

$$2{,}000 = \quad 2x_1 + 1\tfrac{1}{3}x_2 \qquad + x_4 + \quad \tfrac{2}{3}y_1 - 3\tfrac{1}{3}y_2 \, ,$$

(3.23)
$$1{,}000 = -\tfrac{1}{2}x_1 - \tfrac{1}{3}x_2 + x_3 \qquad - \quad \tfrac{1}{6}y_1 + 1\tfrac{1}{3}y_2 \, ,$$

$$88{,}000 = \quad 4x_1 + \quad \tfrac{2}{3}x_2 \qquad\qquad + 4\tfrac{1}{3}y_1 + 3\tfrac{1}{3}y_2 + f \, .$$

Since none of the coefficients of the nonbasic variables is negative, no further increase in profits is possible; the optimal solution must have been reached. This can be proved rigorously by writing the last equation of (3.23) as

(3.24) $f = 88{,}000 - 4x_1 - \tfrac{2}{3}x_2 - 4\tfrac{1}{3}y_1 - 3\tfrac{1}{3}y_2 \, .$

Any feasible solution must satisfy the original equation system (3.7) and therefore also its transformed system (3.23); furthermore it must be non-negative in all variables. Suppose that there is another solution which has a higher value of f than 88,000. Let the values of x_1, x_2, y_1, and y_2 be $\bar{x}_1, \bar{x}_2$, $\bar{y}_1$, and $\bar{y}_2$; these values must be nonnegative and at least one of them must be positive, because if not, the solution would be the same as the basic solution of (3.23), since in order to satisfy the equation system, the basic variables are determined by the nonbasic ones. From (3.24) it is then clear that the corresponding value of f must be less than 88,000.

The imputed costs of spinning and loom capacity are for the optimal solution $4\tfrac{1}{3}$ and $3\tfrac{1}{3}$. This means that if an extra hour of spinning capacity became available, profits would increase by $4\tfrac{1}{3}$ and if an extra hour of loom capacity became available, profits would increase by $3\tfrac{1}{3}$. The equations by which the imputed costs were derived in the previous section can also be derived from the equation system. Let us consider a direct transformation of system (3.7) into system (3.23). Since x_3 and x_4 are basic in (3.23) they should have zero coefficients in the last row. These coefficients are made zero by adding to the last equation of (3.7) u_1 times the first equation, and u_2 times the second equation of (3.7). For the coefficients of x_3 we obtain the equation

(3.25)
$$-50 + u_1 \cdot 10 + u_2 \cdot 2 = 0 ,$$

$$-19 + u_1 \cdot 4 + u_2 \cdot \tfrac{1}{2} = 0 .$$

The solution is, of course, $u_1 = 4\,{}^1/_3$, $u_2 = 3\,{}^1/_3$. The coefficient of y_1 in (3.7) was zero and now becomes u_1; that of y_2 was zero and now becomes u_2. Total profits, the constant term in the f-equation of (3.7) becomes

$$0 + u_1 \cdot 18{,}000 + u_2 \cdot 3{,}000 .$$

For $u_1 = 4\,{}^1/_3$, $u_2 = 3\,{}^1/_3$ we find $f = 88{,}000$. For the coefficient of x_1 in the f-equation we find

$$-9 + u_1 \cdot 3 + u_2 \cdot 0 = 4 ,$$

which corresponds to the expression for the reduced revenue for Yarn A in the last section. There is a complete correspondence between the procedure of the last section and the simplex method, but the computations of the simplex method are much easier to perform.

Instead of writing down the complete systems of equations, only the coefficients of the systems may be written down; the variables are mentioned in column headings. The results are so-called simplex tableaux. Table 2 gives the successive tableaux corresponding to the systems (3.7), (3.13), (3.18), (3.21), and (3.23). The second column of these tableaux gives the basic variables and the third one gives values in the basic solution which are, of course, the constant terms in the equations. Each of the rows of the tableaux should be interpreted as the coefficients of an equation. The coefficient of the variable which is to become basic in the equation of the basic variable which is to become nonbasic, is underlined in each tableau; it is called the *pivot* of the transformation which transforms this tableau into the next tableau.

In Table 2, the columns of basic variables of each tableau are entirely redundant, since we know that any such column should have a one in its row and zero's elsewhere. Then columns may therefore be deleted. If in a transformation a nonbasic variable becomes basic, its column is used for the basic variable which becomes nonbasic. We should therefore in each column indicate the nonbasic variable to which it belongs. In this way a compact form of the simplex tableaux is obtained. Table 3 gives the compact simplex tableaux for our example. For the sake of simplicity all values of basic variables have been divided by 1,000.

Table 2
Simplex tableaux for production planning problem

Tableau	Basic Variables	Values Basic Variables	x_1	x_2	x_3	x_4	y_1	y_2	f
0	y_1	18,000	3	2	10	4	1	0	0
	y_2	3,000	0	0	2	½	0	1	0
	f	0	−9	−8	−50	−19	0	0	1
1	y_1	3,000	3	2	0	1½	1	−5	0
	x_3	1,500	0	0	1	¼	0	½	0
	f	75,000	−9	−8	0	−6½	0	25	1
2	x_1	1,000	1	²/₃	0	½	¹/₃	−1²/₃	0
	x_3	1,500	0	0	1	¼	0	½	0
	f	84,000	0	−2	0	−2	3	10	1
3	x_2	1,500	1½	1	0	¾	½	−2½	0
	x_3	1,500	0	0	1	¼	0	½	0
	f	87,000	3	0	0	−½	4	5	1
4	x_4	2,000	2	1¹/₃	0	1	²/₃	−3¹/₃	0
	x_3	1,000	−½	−¹/₃	1	0	−¹/₆	1¹/₃	0
	f	88,000	4	²/₃	0	0	4¹/₃	3¹/₃	1

Table 3
Compact simplex tableaux for example

Tableau	Basic Variables	Values Basic Variables	Nonbasic Variables			
			x_1	x_2	x_3	x_4
0	y_1	18	3	2	10	4
	y_2	3	0	0	2	½
	f	0	−9	−8	−50	−19
			x_1	x_2	y_2	x_4
1	y_1	3	3	2	−5	1½
	x_3	1½	0	0	½	¼
	f	75	−9	−8	25	6½
			y_1	x_2	y_2	x_4
2	x_1	1	¹/₃	²/₃	−1²/₃	½
	x_3	1½	0	0	½	¼
	f	84	3	−2	10	−2

Table 3 (continued)

Tableau	Basic Variables	Values Basic Variables	Nonbasic Variables			
			y_1	x_1	y_2	x_4
3	x_2	1½	½	1½	$-2½$	¾
	x_3	1½	0	0	½	¼
	f	87	4	3	5	$-½$
			y_1	x_1	y_2	x_2
4	x_4	2	⅔	2	$-3⅓$	$1⅓$
	x_3	1	$-⅙$	$-½$	$1⅓$	$-⅓$
	f	88	$4⅓$	4	$3⅓$	⅔

2.4. A general treatment of the Simplex Method

Let us consider the following general linear programming problem: Maximize

$$(4.1) \qquad f = p_1 x_1 + p_2 x_2 + ... + p_n x_n ,$$

subject to

$$(4.2) \quad \begin{cases} a_{11}x_1 + a_{12}x_2 + ... + a_{1n}x_n \leqq b_1 , \\ a_{21}x_1 + a_{22}x_2 + ... + a_{2n}x_n \leqq b_2 , \\ ... \\ a_{m1}x_1 + a_{m2}x_2 + ... + a_{mn}x_n \leqq b_m , \end{cases}$$

and

$$(4.3) \qquad x_1, x_2, ..., x_n \geqq 0 .$$

This is a problem in n variables with m constraints. It could be a production planning problem with n products and m scarce resources.

The inequalities of (4.2) may be converted into equations by the introduction of nonnegative y-variables, which stand for unused capacities in the production planning case. Hence instead of (4.2) we may write

$$(4.4) \quad \begin{cases} a_{11}x_1 + a_{12}x_2 + ... + a_{1n}x_n + y_1 = b_1 \,, \\[2mm] a_{21}x_1 + a_{22}x_2 + ... + a_{2n}x_n + y_2 = b_2 \,, \\[2mm] ... \\[2mm] a_{m1}x_1 + a_{m2}x_2 + ... + a_{mn}x_n + y_m = b_m \,, \end{cases}$$

$$(4.5) \quad y_1, y_2, ..., y_m \geqq 0 \,.$$

Now we consider the equation system consisting of (4.1) and (4.4). This may be written as

$$(4.6) \quad \begin{cases} 0 = -p_1x_1 - p_2x_2 - ... - p_nx_n + f \,, \\[2mm] b_1 = a_{11}x_1 + a_{12}x_2 + ... + a_{1n}x_n + y_1 \,, \\[2mm] b_1 = á_{21}x_1 + a_{22}x_2 + ... + a_{2n}x_n + y_2 \,, \\[2mm] ... \\[2mm] b_m = a_{m1}x_1 + a_{m2}x_2 + ... + a_{mn}x_n + y_m \,. \end{cases}$$

This is an equation system in which f and the y-variables are basic variables; the basic solution is

$$(4.7) \quad f = 0 \,, \quad y_1 = b_1 \,, \quad y_2 = b_2, ..., y_n = b_m \,.$$

This is a feasible solution if all b's are nonnegative. The simplex method requires as starting point an equation system with a basic solution which is feasible. If no such equation system is immediately available, it may be found in certain ways, as will be explained later.

It is convenient to change to notation of system (4.6) in the following manner:

$$a_{00} = 0 \,, \quad a_{01} = -p_1 \,, \quad a_{02} = -p_2, ..., a_{0n} = -p_n \,,$$

$$a_{10} = b_1 \,,$$

$$a_{20} = b_2 \,,$$

$$.$$

$$a_{m0} = b_m \,.$$

The equation system may now be written as

$$(4.7) \begin{cases} a_{00} = a_{01}x_1 + a_{02}x_2 + \dots + a_{0n}x_n + f, \\ a_{10} = a_{11}x_1 + a_{12}x_2 + \dots + a_{1n}x_n + y_1, \\ a_{20} = a_{21}x_1 + a_{22}x_2 + \dots + a_{2n}x_n + y_2 \\ \dots \\ a_{m0} = a_{m1}x_1 + a_{m2}x_2 + \dots + a_{mn}x_n + y_m. \end{cases}$$

All equation systems generated in an application of the simplex method may be represented in this manner by simply rearranging the equations and variables of the system. Hence a step or iteration of the simplex method may be indicated using the system (4.7), for which it is given that the constants $a_{10}, a_{20}, \dots, a_{m0}$ are nonnegative.

In (4.7), the present value of the objective function is a_{00}. The objective function may be increased by increasing a nonbasic variable with a negative coefficient in the f-equation. It is usual, but by no means necessary, to select the nonbasic variable with the most negative coefficient. If there are no nonbasic variables with negative coefficients, the maximum solution has been obtained, as has been proved before. Suppose then that the new basic variable is x_k, which is to be increased as much as possible. For the corresponding values of basic variables we find

$$(4.8) \begin{cases} a_{00} - a_{0k}x_k = f, \\ a_{10} - a_{1k}x_k = y_1, \\ a_{20} - a_{2k}x_k = y_2, \\ \dots \\ a_{m0} - a_{mk}x_k = y_m. \end{cases}$$

The y-variables have to remain nonnegative. If $a_{1k} \leq 0$, an increase in x_k does not decrease y_1, but if $a_{1k} > 0$, y_1 will become zero for $a_{10} - a_{1k}x_k = 0$ or $x_k = a_{10}/a_{1k}$. For other y-variables similar upper bounds for x_k are found. The maximum value of x_k is equal to the minimum of the upper bounds:

$$x_k = \text{Min}\left[\frac{a_{10}}{a_{1k}} \text{ if } a_{1k} > 0, \frac{a_{20}}{a_{2k}} \text{ if } a_{2k} > 0, \dots, \frac{a_{m0}}{a_{mk}} \text{ if } a_{mk} > 0\right],$$

Table 4

A transformation of a simplex tableau

	Basic Variables	Values Basic Variables	x_1	x_2	x_3	x_4	f	y_1	y_2	y_3
I	f	a_{00}	a_{01}	a_{02}	a_{03}	a_{04}	1	0	0	0
	y_1	a_{10}	a_{11}	$\boxed{a_{12}}$	a_{13}	a_{14}	0	1	0	0
	y_2	a_{20}	a_{21}	a_{22}	a_{23}	a_{24}	0	0	1	0
	y_3	a_{30}	a_{31}	a_{32}	a_{33}	a_{34}	0	0	0	1
II	f	$a_{00}-a_{02}a_{12}^{-1}a_{10}$	$a_{01}-a_{02}a_{12}^{-1}a_{11}$	0	$a_{03}-a_{02}a_{12}^{-1}a_{13}$	$a_{04}-a_{02}a_{12}^{-1}a_{14}$	1	$-a_{02}a_{12}^{-1}$	0	0
	x_2	$a_{12}^{-1}a_{10}$	$a_{12}^{-1}a_{11}$	1	$a_{12}^{-1}a_{13}$	$a_{12}^{-1}a_{14}$	0	a_{12}^{-1}	0	0
	y_2	$a_{20}-a_{22}a_{12}^{-1}a_{10}$	$a_{21}-a_{22}a_{12}^{-1}$	0	$a_{23}-a_{22}a_{12}^{-1}a_{13}$	$a_{24}-a_{22}a_{12}^{-1}a_{14}$	0	$-a_{22}a_{12}^{-1}$	1	0
	y_3	$a_{30}-a_{32}a_{12}^{-1}a_{10}$	$a_{31}-a_{32}a_{12}^{-1}a_{11}$	0	$a_{33}-a_{32}a_{12}^{-1}a_{13}$	$a_{34}-a_{32}a_{12}^{-1}a_{14}$	0	$-a_{32}a_{12}^{-1}$	0	1

or in shorter notation

$$(4.9) \qquad x_k = \underset{i}{\text{Min}} \left[\frac{a_{i0}}{a_{ik}} \;\middle|\; a_{ik} > 0 \right].$$

If all a_{ik}, $i = 1, ..., m$, are nonpositive, x_k, and therefore f, can be increased indefinitely; this means that there is an *infinite optimal solution.* Since in reality it simply does not happen that profits can be increased indefinitely, usually the problem formulation has been incorrect when an unbounded solution is found. Let the minimum in (4.9) be found in the r-th equation; if this minimum is not unique but is found in two or even more equations, any of these equations may be taken. [1]

The equation system should be transformed in such a way that x_k replaces y_r as a basic variable. The pivot of the transformation is a_{rk}. The r-th equation is transformed by dividing it by a_{rk}:

$$(4.10) \qquad a_{rk}^{-1} a_{r0} = a_{rk}^{-1} a_{ri} x_1 + ... + x_k + ... + a_{rk}^{-1} a_{rm} x_m + a_{rk}^{-1} y_r .$$

The other equations are transformed by subtraction of multiples of (4.10) in such a way that terms in x_k vanish; the i-th equation $(i \neq r)$ is transformed by a subtraction of a_{ik} times (4.10). The result is

$$(4.11) \qquad a_{i0} - a_{ik} a_{rk}^{-1} a_{r0} = (a_{i1} - a_{ik} a_{rk}^{-1} a_{r1}) x_1 + ...$$

$$+ 0 x_k + ... + (a_{im} - a_{ik} a_{rk}^{-1} a_{rm}) x_m - a_{ik} a_{rk}^{-1} y_r .$$

This is a new equation system with a basic solution $x_k = a_{rk}^{-1} a_{r0}$, $y_i = a_{i0} - a_{ik} a_{rk}^{-1} a_{r0}$, $i = 1, ..., m$, $i \neq r$, and $f = a_{00} - a_{0k} a_{rk}^{-1} a_{r0}$. The value of the objective function has increased by $-a_{0k} a_{rk}^{-1} a_{r0}$, which is nonnegative since $a_{0k} < 0$, $a_{rk} > 0$, and $a_{r0} \geq 0$. The increase in f is zero only if a_{r0}, the value of y_r in the previous solution, is zero. The new equation system has the same structure as that in (4.7), except that its basic variables are not necessarily the last ones as in (4.7), but this is not essential. Another step or iteration of the simplex method may be performed, and so on, until all coefficients a_{0j}, $j = 1, ..., n + m$, are nonnegative; in the latter case the optimal solution has been obtained.

As indicated before, it is easier to deal with the equation systems in detached coefficient form or tableau form. Tableau I of Table 4 represents a

---

[1] This is sufficient for all practical purposes. In Section 5.1 a definite choice which is theoretically satisfactory is indicated.

Table 5

A transformation of a compact simplex tableau

	Basic Variables	Values Basic Variables	x_1	x_2	x_3	x_4
I	f	a_{00}	a_{01}	a_{02}	a_{03}	a_{04}
	y_1	a_{10}	a_{11}	$\underline{a_{12}}$	a_{13}	a_{14}
	y_2	a_{20}	a_{21}	a_{22}	a_{23}	a_{24}
	y_3	a_{30}	a_{31}	a_{32}	a_{33}	a_{34}
			x_1	y_1	x_3	x_4
II	f	$a_{00}-a_{02}a_{12}^{-1}a_{10}$	$a_{01}-a_{02}a_{12}^{-1}a_{11}$	$-a_{02}a_{12}^{-1}$	$a_{03}-a_{02}a_{12}^{-1}a_{13}$	$a_{04}-a_{02}a_{12}^{-1}a_{14}$
	x_2	$a_{12}^{-1}a_{10}$	$a_{12}^{-1}a_{11}$	a_{12}^{-1}	$a_{12}^{-1}a_{13}$	$a_{12}^{-1}a_{14}$
	y_2	$a_{20}-a_{22}a_{12}^{-1}a_{10}$	$a_{21}-a_{22}a_{12}^{-1}a_{11}$	$-a_{22}a_{12}^{-1}$	$a_{23}-a_{22}a_{12}^{-1}a_{13}$	$a_{24}-a_{22}a_{12}^{-1}a_{14}$
	y_3	$a_{30}-a_{32}a_{12}^{-1}a_{10}$	$a_{31}-a_{32}a_{12}^{-1}a_{11}$	$-a_{32}a_{12}^{-1}$	$a_{33}-a_{32}a_{12}^{-1}a_{13}$	$a_{34}-a_{32}a_{12}^{-1}a_{14}$

general equation system with $m = 3$ and $n = 4$. If x_2 replaces y_1 as basic variable, the underlined element a_{12} is the *pivot* of the transformation which transforms Tableau I into Tableau II. First the pivot row, which is the row of y_1, is transformed by dividing each element of this row by the pivot; the resulting row is called the *transformed pivot row*. The column of x_2 in Tableau I is called the *pivot column;* all the elements of this column, except the one in the pivot row, have to become zero, since x_2 becomes a basic variable. The other rows are therefore transformed by a subtraction of the transformed pivot row multiplied by the corresponding element of the (old) pivot column. For instance, the element a_{31} is transformed as

$$a_{31} - a_{32}(a_{12}^{-1}a_{11}) \, .$$

It is somewhat more convenient to use compact simplex tableaux, in which the columns of basic variables have been deleted. Table 5 gives a transformation of a general compact simplex tableau. The transformation of all elements is the same as for the complete tableau except for the pivot column. The pivot is transformed by taking its inverse and the other elements of the pivot column are found by dividing them by minus the pivot. The rules for a step or iteration of the simplex method using compact tableaux may be stated as follows:

Selection of the new basic variable:
    Select

(4.12) $\underset{j=1,\ldots,n}{\text{Min}} \ (a_{0j}) = a_{0k}$

If $a_{0k} \geqq 0$, the present solution is optimal.

Selection of the leaving basic variable:
    Select

(4.13) $\underset{i=1,\ldots,m}{\text{Min}} \ (\frac{a_{i0}}{a_{ik}} \,|\, a_{ik} > 0 \,) = \frac{a_{r0}}{a_{rk}} \ ;$

if all a_{ik} are nonpositive, there is an infinite optimal solution.

Transformation of the tableau:

(4.14) $\begin{cases} a_{rk}^* = a_{rk}^{-1} \, , \\[2mm] a_{rj}^* = a_{rk}^{-1}a_{rj} \, , & j \neq k \, , \\[2mm] a_{ik}^* = -a_{ik}a_{rk}^{-1} \, , & i \neq r \, , \\[2mm] a_{ij}^* = a_{ij} - a_{ik}a_{rk}^{-1}a_{rj} = a_{ij} - a_{ik}a_{rj}^* \, , & i \neq r, \ j \neq k \, . \end{cases}$

As another example of application of the simplex method, let us consider the following problem.

Maximize

$$f = 2x_1 + x_2 + \tfrac{1}{2}x_3 + 2x_4 + 2x_5$$

subject to

$$4x_1 + 3x_2 + x_3 + 2x_4 \leqq 100 ,$$

$$x_1 \qquad\quad + x_4 + 2x_5 \leqq 40 ,$$

$$2x_1 + 4x_2 \qquad + x_4 + 2x_5 \leqq 60 ,$$

$$x_1, x_2, x_3, x_4, x_5 \geqq 0 .$$

After the introduction of the slack variables y_1, y_2, and y_3, the resulting equation system may be formulated as in Tableau 0 of Table 6. The simplex method is applied as indicated and in three iterations the optimal solution with $f = 90$, $x_1 = 20$, $x_4 = 10$, and $x_5 = 5$ is found. For the imputed costs of the first, second, and third scarce resource we find $\tfrac{1}{2}$, 1, and 0, respectively. An imputed cost of zero means that the scarce resource is not a bottleneck at all; in fact the nonbasic variable y_3 may be increased to 20 without changing the value of f, though the values of x_1, x_4, and x_5 change. In this case a number of optimal solutions can be found, all having the same amount of profits.

If $a_{r0} > 0$, the objective function increases in each iteration. It can be proved that each set of basic variables has a unique solution, that is has unique values of basic variables and therefore also a unique value of f. Since the value of f increases for $a_{r0} > 0$ in each iteration, a solution with the same set of basic variables cannot recur in the course of the iterations. Since there is only a finite number of different sets of basic variables [an upper bound is $\binom{m+n}{m}$, the number of ways in which m basic variables can be chosen out of the total number of $m + n$ variables], the simplex method must terminate in a finite number of iterations if all a_{r0} involved are positive. The a_{r0} will be positive if all values of basic variables of a solution are positive. A solution with nonzero values of basic variables is called a *nondegenerate solution;* a solution in which one or more of the values of basic variables are zero is called a *degenerate solution.* Hence it may be concluded that if no degenerate solutions occur, the simplex method terminates in a finite number of iterations. Theoretically it is possible that a problem with degenerate solutions is not solved by a finite number of iterations of the simplex method,

Table 6
Example of the simplex method

Tableau	Basic Variables	Values Basic Variables	Nonbasic Variables				
			x_1	x_2	x_3	x_4	x_5
0	f	0	-3	-1	$-\frac{1}{2}$	-2	-2
	y_1	100	<u>4</u>	3	1	2	0
	y_1	40	1	0	0	1	2
	y_3	60	2	4	0	1	2
			y_1	x_2	x_3	x_4	x_5
1	f	75	¾	1¼	¼	$-\frac{1}{2}$	-2
	x_1	25	¼	¾	¼	½	0
	y_2	15	¼	$-¾$	$-¼$	½	2
	y_3	10	$-\frac{1}{2}$	2½	$-\frac{1}{2}$	0	<u>2</u>
			y_1	x_2	x_3	x_4	y_3
2	f	85	¼	3¾	$-¼$	$-\frac{1}{2}$	1
	x_1	25	¼	¾	¼	½	0
	y_2	5	¼	$-3¼$	¼	<u>½</u>	1
	x_5	5	$-¼$	1¼	$-¼$	0	½
			y_1	x_2	x_3	y_2	y_3
3	f	90	½	½	0	1	0
	x_1	20	0	4	0	-1	1
	x_4	10	½	$-6½$	½	2	-2
	x_5	5	$-¼$	1¼	$-¼$	0	½

unless the simplex method is modified in a certain manner. Section 5.1 deals with this matter.

Computational practice with the simplex method indicates that the number of iterations of the simplex method is rather independent of the number of variables n but is dependent on the number of equations m; it is said that the number of iterations varies from m to $3m$.

In most computer programs, special forms of the simplex method are used. One of these is known as the *revised simplex method* or *explicit inverse method* and another is known as the *product form of the inverse method.* It should be stressed that these methods only differ from the simplex method as explained in this chapter in the way in which tableau-elements are computed.

2.5. A Geometrical Interpretation of the Simplex Method

The treatment of the simplex method in the previous section was entirely algebraic. It is interesting to find out how the successive solutions generated by the simplex method move in a geometrical presentation of the problem. In order to demonstrate this, the same example will be used as in Section 1.3. The problem was: Maximize

(5.1) $\qquad f = 2x_1 + 3x_2$

subject to

(5.2) $\qquad -x_1 + x_2 \leqq 1\frac{1}{2}$,

(5.3) $\qquad -x_1 + 2x_2 \leqq 4$,

(5.4) $\qquad x_1 + x_2 \leqq 6\frac{1}{2}$,

(5.5) $\qquad x_1, x_2 \geqq 0$.

In Table 7 the simplex method is applied to this problem; Tableau 3 contains the optimal solution.

Let us now find out how the simplex method works in terms of the geometrical presentation of this problem given in Figure 1. The starting point is the point (0,0) in Figure 1. Since an increase in x_2 gives the maximum increase in f, x_2 is increased until constraint (5.2) (in the Figure AB) becomes binding. Then A is found, which corresponds with the solution of Tableau 1 of Table 6. Now x_1 is increased, which means moving along AB. In B, constraint (5.3) becomes binding; point B corresponds to the solution of Tableau 2. Here y_1 is introduced into the basis, which means that constraint (5.2) is not binding anymore. The solution moves from B to C, where constraint (5.4) becomes binding. It turns out that C is the optimal solution.

In geometrical terms, the simplex method moves along the edges of the feasible region until the optimal solution is found. This does not seem to be a

Table 7
An application of the simplex method to the example

Tableau	Basic Variables	Values Basic Variables	Non-basic Variables	
			x_1	x_2
0	f	0	-2	-3
	y_1	1½	-1	$\underline{1}$
	y_2	4	-1	2
	y_3	6½	1	1
			x_1	y_1
1	f	4½	-5	3
	x_2	1½	-1	1
	y_2	1	$\underline{1}$	-2
	y_3	5	2	-1
			y_2	y_1
2	f	9½	5	-7
	x_2	2½	1	-1
	x_1	1	1	-2
	y_3	3	-2	$\underline{3}$
			y_2	y_3
3	f	16½	$1/3$	$2^1/_3$
	x_2	3½	$1/3$	$1/3$
	x_1	3	$-1/3$	$2/3$
	y_1	1	$-2/3$	$1/3$

very efficient procedure, since in this manner solutions such as A and B are found for which a constraint, in this case (5.2), is binding which is not binding for the optimal solution. It could be argued that a method which moves directly into the feasible region, for instance along the gradient $0D$, is more efficient because it may avoid constraint (5.2). However, such arguments

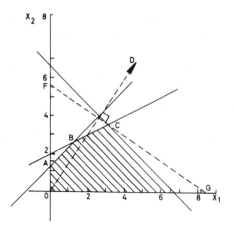

Fig. 1

based on geometrical considerations can be quite misleading. It can be shown that in most realistic cases, in which there are more variables than constraints, such a gradient method is less efficient than the simplex method.

Exercises

1. A company has two kinds of machines. The joint capacity of the first kind of machines is 12,000 hours per week; that of the second kind of machines is 5,000 hours per week. Three products can be produced; the net revenue for each of these is $20, $40, and $25 per unit, respectively. On the first kind of machine, these products require 3, 2, and 4 hours per unit, and on the second kind of machine 1, 2, and 1 hours per unit.

   (a) Determine the optimal production program without using the simplex method if the capacity of the second kind of machines is so large that it can never be a bottleneck, given a capacity of the first kind of machine of 12,000 hours. Give total revenue both as a function of the net revenue of the product in the optimal programme and as a function of the capacity of the first kind of machines. How large should the capacity on the second kind of machine at least be?

   (b) Determine the optimal production programme by the simplex method with the capacities as given. What are the imputed costs of one hour of capacity on the first kind of machine and on the second kind of machine? Write the resulting total revenue as a function of net revenues and quantities to be produced and also as a function of imputed costs of a unit of capacity in each of the machines times available capacities. What is the decrease in profits if in deviation from the optimal production program one unit of the first product was produced? How would the production programme change as a result of this?

2. The production of a company is limited by the capacities of its three departments which are the parts manufacturing department, the assemblage department and the finishing department. The available production capacity per week for these departments are 2,600, 500, and 1,600 hours respectively. Six products are produced, the data for which can be found in the following table.

		Product					
		1	2	3	4	5	6
Selling Price	$/unit	15	12	15	18	43	30½
Direct Cost	$/unit	6	4	5	6	34	23½
Parts manufacturing department	h/unit	6	4	2	2	2	1½
Assemblage department	h/unit	0	0	1½	2	1	1
Finishing department	h/unit	0	0	0	0	3	2

(a) Find the optimal weekly production program by means of the method indicated in Section 2. What are the imputed costs of the capacities of the three departments?

(b) Solve the same problem by means of the simplex method using compact simplex tableaux.

(c) Suppose a new product is proposed, with a selling price of $45 per unit, direct costs of $20 per unit and using 3, 2 and 2 hours per unit of the production capacity of the three departments. Indicate, without including the data for this product in the tableaux, whether this product should be introduced in the production program.

3. For a certain plant the following data are known.

	Product A	Product B	Product C	Product D
Machine X hours/unit	4 hours	1 hour	9 hours	5 hours
Machine Y hours/unit	1 hour	2 hours	6 hours	8 hours
Selling price/unit	$3,550	$2,280	$3,775	$3,750
Direct costs/unit	$3,150	$2,005	$2,825	$2,550

(a) Suppose that the capacities on both machine X and Y are bottlenecks in the production program and that products A and B are produced. Determine the imputed costs (shadow prices, opportunity costs) per hour capacity of these machines. Use the imputed costs to find out whether it is profitable to produce products C and D.

(b) If the capacity available on machine X is 150 hours per week and that on machine Y, 260 hours per week, determine the optimal production program by the simplex method. What are the imputed values in this situation? What is the minimum increase in selling price of products not in the production program which would make production of these products profitable?

4. A car plant can produce both automobiles and trucks. It has four departments: metal stamping, engine assembly, automobile assembly and truck assembly. The net revenue (sales price minus variable costs) for an automobile are $300 and for a truck $250. The following data are known:

Department	Capacity h/year	Automobile requirements h/unit	Truck requirements h/unit
Metal stamping	100,000	4	$2^6/_7$
Engine assembly	64,000	2	3
Automobile assembly	60,000	3	–
Truck assembly	37,500	–	$2^1/_2$

(a) Find the optimal production program for this plant using the simplex method.

(b) Interpret every element in the final tableau.

(c) Solve the same problem graphically.

5. Solve the following linear programming problem by means of the simplex method. Maximize

$$f = 2x_1 + 4x_2 + x_3 + x_4$$

subject to

$$x_1 + 3x_2 + x_4 \leq 4,$$

$$2x_1 + x_2 \leq 3,$$

$$x_1 + 4x_3 + x_4 \leq 3,$$

$$x_1, x_2, x_3, x_4, \geqq 0 .$$

6. Solve the following linear programming problem by means of the simplex method. Maximize

$$f = 3x_1 + 5x_2 + 4x_3$$

subject to

$$2x_1 + 3x_2 \leqq 8 ,$$

$$2x_2 + 5x_3 \leqq 10 ,$$

$$3x_1 + 2x_2 + 4x_3 \leqq 15 ,$$

$$x_1, x_2, x_3 \geqq 0 .$$

7. A farmer has 3000 acres of land, on which he can grow wheat or graze cattle. Three persons are working on the farm, sharing its profits; together they can work 6000 hours per year. They have a working capital of $90,000. It is assumed that both wheat growing and cattle raising requires no fixed capital, but a working capital of $4 per acre of wheat and $250 per head of cattle. One head of cattle requires 10 acres of grazing land. The average annual number of hours worked per acre of wheat planted is $3^1/_3$ hours and per head of cattle is $13^1/_3$ hours. The average net revenue of wheat is $15 per acre and growing $125 per head of cattle.
(a) What is the farmer's optimal production plan? What are the imputed values of land, capital, and labor?
(b) What are the consequences of one man leaving the farm, which reduces the amount of available labor by 2000 hours and the working capital by $45,000?
(c) What is the maximum price the farmer would be prepared to pay for another 1000 acres of land?
(d) Indicate in which respects the model used is unrealistic. Try to modify the model to make it more realistic.

3. RELATED PROBLEMS AND METHODS

3.1. The Composition of Minimum-Cost Cattlefeed

Though minimization problems can easily be converted into problems of maximization and different forms of constraints can be shown to be equivalent, it is nevertheless useful to consider a typical minimization problem in some more detail, since minimization problems have in general properties and interpretations which differ from typical maximization problems. The example to be used is that of the least-cost composition of cattlefeed from a number of raw materials; the feed must satisfy a number of nutritional requirements. For the human diet the same problem can be formulated; this problem is known as the *diet problem,* but its formulation is obviously much more complicated than the cattle feed problem.

We consider the case in which the daily feed of an animal must be determined in such a way that costs are minimal and certain nutritional requirements are met. In order to keep the example as simple as possible, only four raw materials are considered, namely barley, oats, sesame flakes, and groundnut meal. The number of nutritional requirements is limited to two, the first one being that the feed should contain at least 20 units of protein and the second that it should contain at least 5 units of fat. The protein and fat content per unit of each of the raw materials and the costs per unit are given in Table 1. [1]

$$(1.1) \qquad 12x_1 + 12x_2 + 40x_3 + 60x_4 \geqq 20 \, ,$$

$$(1.2) \qquad 2x_1 + 6x_2 + 12x_3 + 2x_4 \geqq 5 \, .$$

---

[1] In most cases all units are weight units, such as tons, pounds or grams. Other measures may occur, and should then be converted in weight units if these are the main units used.

Table 1

Protein and fat content, and cost of raw materials

	Protein Content	Fat Content	Cost per Unit
Barley	12	2	24
Oats	12	6	30
Sesame flakes	40	12	40
Groundnut meal	60	2	50

After introduction of nonnegative slack variables y_1 and y_2, which stand for the overfulfillment of the protein and fat requirements, the inequalities can be formulated as equalities:

$$(1.3) \qquad 12x_1 + 12x_2 + 40x_3 + 60x_4 - y_1 = 20 \ ,$$

$$(1.4) \qquad 2x_1 + 6x_2 + 12x_3 + 2x_4 - y_2 = 5 \ .$$

The objective is to minimize the costs of the feed, so that we have for the equation of the objective function:

$$(1.5) \qquad f = 24x_1 + 30x_2 + 40x_3 + 50x_4 \ .$$

The equations (1.3), (1.4), and (1.5) may be put into a form with y_1, y_2, and f as basic variables by multiplication of (1.3) and (1.4) by -1 and by moving the terms in the x-variables in (1.5) to the other side of the equality sign. Then the following system is obtained:

$$(1.6) \qquad \begin{cases} 0 = -24x_1 - 30x_2 - 40x_3 - 50x_4 + f \ , \\ -20 = -12x_1 - 12x_2 - 40x_3 - 60x_4 + y_1 \ , \\ -5 = - 2x_1 - 6x_2 - 12x_3 - 2x_4 + y_2 \ . \end{cases}$$

This system may be put into a simplex tableau, see Tableau 0 of Table 2.

The difficulty is now that the solution of Tableau 0 is not a feasible one since the basic variables y_1 and y_2 are negative. Since the simplex method requires a feasible solution to start with, such a solution must first be found. A general method to find a feasible solution of a problem will be treated in the next section. Here it will be shown that if a basic feasible solution to the problem is known, this solution may be generated using simplex tableaux by

Table 2
Simplex tableaux for minimum-cost cattlefeed problem

Tableau	Basic Variables	Values Basic Variables	x_1	x_2	x_3	x_4
0	f	0	-24	-30	-40	-50
	y_1	-20	-12	-12	$\underline{-40}$	-60
	y_2	-5	-2	-6	$\underline{-12}$	-2
			x_1	x_2	y_1	x_4
1	f	20	-12	-18	-1	10
	x_3	$1/2$	$3/10$	$3/10$	$-1/40$	$1\,1/2$
	y_2	1	$1\,3/5$	$-2\,2/5$	$-3/10$	$\underline{16}$
			x_1	x_2	y_1	y_2
2	f	$19\,3/8$	-13	$-16\,1/2$	$-1\,3/16$	$-5/8$
	x_3	$1\,3/32$	$3/20$	$21/40$	$1/320$	$-3/32$
	x_4	$1/16$	$1/10$	$-3/20$	$3/160$	$1/16$

introducing the variables of this solution one by one into the basis. Once this solution is generated, the simplex method may be applied as described before.

Finding a basic feasible solution for our example is very simple. Half a unit of sesame flakes will precisely meet the protein requirement; it contains 6 units of fat which is more than the requirement of 5 units. The corresponding basic solution is one in which the quantity of sesame flakes, x_3, is non-zero and hence a nonbasic variable and in which the slack variable for protein y_1, is made zero and is hence a basic variable. This solution is generated from Tableau 0 by pivoting on the element in the row of y_1 and the column of x_3. The result is Tableau 1 which contains the desired feasible solution. The simplex method may now be applied, but it must be kept in mind that we are *minimizing* the objective function. Hence the variable corresponding with the most *positive* element in the first row is chosen as the new basic variable; this is immediately clear by writing the equation corresponding with the first row of Tableau 1 of Table 2 as

$$20 + 12x_1 + 18x_2 + y_1 - 10x_4 = f.$$

x_4 is therefore introduced into the basis and y_2 leaves it.

The result is Tableau 2, the first row of which does not contain any positive elements. The minimum-cost solution must therefore have been found, which is $x_3 = {}^{13}\!/_{32}$ and $x_4 = {}^1\!/_{16}$; the cost of this solution is $19^3\!/_8$.

In the production planning problem an economic interpretation of the simplex method was possible, in which the profitability of all products was evaluated using the imputed costs of products in the production program. For the present problem a similar interpretation can be given. Let us consider the solution indicated by Tableau 2 of Table 2, where the third and the fourth raw materials are used in the cattlefeed. A value u_1 may be assigned to a unit of protein and a value of u_2 to a unit of fat. These values, which may be called the *imputed values* of protein and fat, can be derived from the costs of the raw materials of the cattlefeed. Since a unit of sesame flakes contains 40 units of protein and 12 units of fat and costs 40 per unit, we have the equation

(1.7) $\qquad 40u_1 + 12u_2 = 40$.

In a similar way the following equation is derived for groundnut meal:

(1.8) $\qquad 60u_1 + 2u_2 = 50$.

Solving these equations for u_1 and u_2, we find

$$u_1 = {}^{13}\!/_{16} , \qquad u_2 = {}^5\!/_8 .$$

Hence the imputed value of protein is ${}^{13}\!/_{16}$ per unit of protein and that of fat ${}^5\!/_8$ per unit of fat. Note that these figures appear with a minus-sign in the f-row in the columns of y_1 and y_2 in Tableau 2. The total costs of the present solution may also be evaluated in terms of these imputed values:

$$19^3\!/_8 = 20 \cdot {}^{13}\!/_{15} + 5 \cdot {}^5\!/_8 .$$

The imputed values may be used to find the *reduced costs* of the raw materials not in the product mix, since we should subtract from the costs of a raw material its value in terms of protein and fat. For the reduced costs of the first product, barley, we find

$$24 - 12 \cdot {}^{13}\!/_{16} - 2 \cdot {}^5\!/_8 = 13 ,$$

and for the reduced costs of oats,

$$30 - 12 \cdot {}^{13}\!/_{16} - 6 \cdot {}^5\!/_8 = 16^1\!/_2 .$$

Since these reduced costs are positive, both barley and oats should not be introduced into the feed mix. Note that the reduced costs are found with a minus-sign in the f-row and the columns of x_1 and x_2 of Tableau 2.

The minimum cattlefood problem is typical of the minimization problems in linear programming. These problems usually involve either the blending of a number of ingredients such that the mixture satisfies certain minimum requirements with least costs or materials of the manufacture of a product satisfying given requirements with least costs. Typical minimization problems can be formulated as follows. Minimize

$$(1.9) \qquad f = c_1 x_1 + c_2 x_2 + ... + c_n x_n$$

subject to

$$(1.10) \quad \begin{cases} a_{11} x_1 + a_{12} x_2 + ... + a_{1n} x_n \geq b_1 , \\ \vdots \\ a_{m1} x_1 + a_{m2} x_2 + ... + a_{mn} x_n \geq b_m , \end{cases}$$

with all x-variables being nonnegative; all coefficients in this problem are usually nonnegative. This means that the slack variables which can be introduced in (1.10) cannot be used as basic variables for an initial solution of the simplex method, so that, if this method is to be used, first a basic feasible solution to the problem should be found.

3.2. The Use of Artificial Variables for an Initial Basic Feasible Solution

In the previous section, an initial basic feasible solution was generated by making a certain variable basic; it was known that the resulting basic solution would be feasible. In simple problems, an initial solution may be generated in this manner, but in large or complicated problems this is usually not possible. Hence a general method for finding an initial basic feasible solution is needed. Once such a solution is found, the simplex method may be applied as indicated before.

Let us consider the equation system for the minimum-cost cattlefeed problems, (1.3), (1.4), and (1.5):

$$(2.1) \quad \begin{cases} 0 = -24x_1 - 30x_2 - 40x_3 - 50x_4 + f , \\ 20 = 12x_1 + 12x_2 + 40x_3 + 60x_4 - y_1 , \\ 5 = 2x_1 + 6x_2 + 12x_3 + 2x_4 - y_2 . \end{cases}$$

The first equation has a basic variable, namely f, but the other two equations have none. y_1 and y_2 could be made basic variables in these equations by a multiplication by -1 of these equations, but the resulting basic solution would be infeasible. Let us therefore introduce a variable z_1 in the second equation, so that we have

$$(2.2) \qquad 20 = 12x_1 + 12x_2 + 40x_3 + 60x_4 - y_1 + z_1 .$$

z_1 does not occur in the first or third equation, so that it is a basic variable in the second equation with a value $z_1 = 20$. In the same way a variable z_2 can be introduced into the third equation of (2.1):

$$(2.3) \qquad 5 = 2x_1 + 6x_2 + 12x_3 + 2x_4 - y_2 + z_2 ,$$

with the value $z_2 = 5$. Both z_1 and z_2 should be nonnegative. The variables z_1 and z_2 do not belong to the original system of equations and are therefore called *artificial variables*. They are used for finding an initial feasible solution, but they should be eliminated from the solution as soon as possible. For this reason the objective function (1.5) is changed into

$$(2.4) \qquad f = 24x_1 + 30x_2 + 40x_3 + 50x_4 + M(z_1 + z_2) .$$

where M stands for a very large positive number (say, million). If f is minimized, the z-variables will be decreased as much as possible until they have the value zero; in most cases they have then become nonbasic and are replaced as basic variables by other variables. Once a solution is reached in which all z-variables are nonbasic, a feasible basic solution is obtained, so that the simplex method in its usual formulation may be employed. Hence, if no initial basic feasible solution is available, the simplex method is used in *two phases,* the first of which serves to eliminate the artificial variables in order to obtain a basic feasible solution; the second phase consists of the proper optimization of the objective function.

Consider now the equation system consisting of (2.4), (2.2), and (2.3):

$$(2.5) \quad \begin{cases} 0 = -24x_1 - 30x_2 - 40x_3 - 50x_4 \qquad + f - Mz_1 - Mz_2 , \\[2mm] 20 = 12x_1 + 12x_2 + 40x_3 + 60x_4 - y_1 \qquad + z_1 , \\[2mm] 5 = 2x_1 + 6x_2 + 12x_3 + 2x_4 \quad - y_2 \qquad + z_2 . \end{cases}$$

In this equation system, z_1 and z_2 are not yet basic variables, since they both occur in the first equation. In order to have a system with f, z_1, and z_2 as basic variables, M times the second and the third equation is added to the first equation. The result is

(2.6)
$$\begin{cases} 25M = (-24 + 14M)x_1 + (-30 + 18M)x_2 + (-40 + 52M)x_3 + \\ \qquad\quad + (-50 + 62M)x_4 - My_1 - My_2 + f, \\ 20 = 12x_1 + 12x_2 + 40x_3 + 60x_4 - y_1 + z_1, \\ 5 = 2x_1 + 6x_2 + 12x_3 + 2x_4 - y_2 + z_2. \end{cases}$$

This is a system with a basic feasible solution to which the simplex method can be applied. Since M is a very large number, the coefficients with M always dominate other coefficients. Hence the first variable to enter the basis in this minimization problem is the one with the largest positive coefficient of M, which is x_4. The leaving basic variable is determined as usual.

Again it is more convenient to use simplex tableaux. In this case the coefficients of the first equation are written down in two rows, the first of which is called f_c and contains the coefficients without M and the second of which is called f_M and contains the coefficients to be multiplied by M. The result is Tableau 0 of Table 3. Since the most positive element in the f_M-row is 62, x_4 is the new basic variable. The leaving basic variable is found by comparing the ratios

$$^{20}/_{60} = {}^1/_3 \quad \text{and} \quad {}^5/_2 = 2{}^1/_2,$$

so that z_1 leaves the basis. The entire tableau is transformed using 60 as a pivot; this results in Tableau 1. The z_1-column is deleted because we do not want to have z_1 as basic variable again.

The most positive element in the f_M-row of Tableau 1 is $10^2/_3$, so that x_3 enters the basis. It is found that z_2 leaves the basis, so that the underlined element $10^2/_3$ is the pivot of the transformation which results in Tableau 2; the column of z_2 is deleted because we do not want this variable to become basic again. Tableau 2 does not have basic artificial variables, so that it has a basic feasible solution. The f_M-row can be deleted; the proper optimization can begin.

Now the f_c-row is used for finding the new basic variable. Since all elements of this row are nonnegative, no further iterations can decrease f, so that the minimum-cost solution is obtained. In most problems a number of further iterations is necessary after the artificial variables have been eliminated in order to obtain the optimal solution.

In this example, the choice of new basic variables according to positive elements in the f_M-row led to a basic feasible solution without z-variables.

Table 3
Generation of basic feasible solution using artificial variables

Tableau	Basic Variables	Values Basic Variables	x_1	x_2	x_3	x_4	y_1	y_2
0	f_c	0	-24	-30	-40	-50	0	0
	f_M	25	14	18	52	62	-1	-1
	z_1	20	12	12	40	60	-1	0
	z_2	5	2	6	12	2	0	-1
			x_1	x_2	x_3		y_1	y_2
1	f_c	$16^2/_3$	-14	-20	$-6^2/_3$		$-5/_6$	0
	f_M	$4^1/_3$	$1^3/_5$	$5^3/_5$	$10^2/_3$		$1/_{30}$	1
	x_4	$1/_3$	$1/_5$	$1/_5$	$2/_3$		$-1/_{60}$	0
	z_2	$4^1/_3$	$1^3/_5$	$5^3/_5$	$\underline{10^2/_3}$		$1/_{30}$	-1
			x_1	x_2			y_1	y_2
2	f_c	$19^3/_8$	-13	$-16^1/_2$			$-1^3/_{16}$	$-5/_8$
	f_M	0	0	0			0	0
	x_4	$1/_{16}$	$1/_{10}$	$-3/_{20}$			$-3/_{160}$	$1/_{16}$
	x_3	$1^3/_{32}$	$3/_{20}$	$21/_{40}$			$1/_{320}$	$-3/_{32}$

This is not necessarily so. It may be that after a number of iterations a tableau is obtained with an f_M-row having nonpositive elements (except the first). If the solution of this tableau contains basic z-variables with a nonzero value, no basic feasible solution of the original problem exists, since if such a solution exists, it should be found by an application of the simplex method to the system (2.5). If the tableau has a solution with basic z-variables having the value zero, all z-variables may be replaced by other variables; any nonzero element in the rows of the z-variables may be used as a pivot.

3.3. The Outsider's Point of View or the Dual Problem

Let us consider once more the production planning problem of the integrated textile company. This company has available per period 18,000 hours of spinning capacity and 3,000 hours of loom capacity, which it can use for the production of four commodities. Suppose now that there is somebody, whom we may call the *outsider,* who wishes to take over the spinning and loom capacity of the textile company for one period. He therefore makes an offer to the textile company for the units of spinning and loom capacity. Let u_1 denote the amount he offers for one hour of spinning capacity and u_2 the amount he offers for one hour of loom capacity. The outsider, of course, wants to pay as little as possible for what he wishes to buy. Hence he wants to minimize this amount, which we denote by g:

(3.1) $\qquad g = 18{,}000u_1 + 3{,}000u_2 \,.$

On the other hand, he wishes to be sure that his bid is acceptable, which means that it should not be profitable for the textile company to keep the capacities for production. None of the products of the company should therefore show a profit if the amounts offered for spinning and loom capacity are taken into account. From the net revenue of Yarn A we therefore subtract the value of spinning and loom capacity evaluated at the outsider's prices:

$$9 - 3u_1 - 0u_2 \,;$$

the outsider should offer prices u_1 and u_2 such that this expression is not positive because otherwise the textile company would rather produce Yarn A than sell its capacity. Hence we have

(3.2) $\qquad 9 - 3u_1 - 0u_2 \leqq 0 \,.$

For the other products, similar considerations are valid. This results in the following relations:

(3.3) $\qquad \begin{cases} 8 - 2u_1 - 0u_2 \leqq 0 \,, \\[2mm] 50 - 10u_1 - 2u_2 \leqq 0 \,, \\[2mm] 19 - 4u_1 - \tfrac{1}{2}u_2 \leqq 0 \,. \end{cases}$

Of course the prices offered, u_1 and u_2, should be nonnegative, because a negative price will never be acceptable to the textile company. Hence we have

(3.4) $\qquad u_1 \geqq 0 \,, \quad u_2 \geqq 0 \,.$

The outsider's problem of finding suitable bids u_1 and u_2 for one hour of spinning capacity and one hour of loom capacity can therefore be formulated as follows. Minimize

(3.5) $$g = 18{,}000\, u_1 + 3{,}000 u_2$$

subject to

(3.6)
$$\begin{cases} 3u_1 + 0u_2 \geqq 9\,, \\ 2u_1 + 0u_2 \geqq 8\,, \\ 10u_1 + 2u_2 \geqq 50\,, \\ 4u_1 + {}^1\!/_2 u_2 \geqq 19\,, \end{cases}$$

(3.7) $$u_1 \geqq 0\,, \quad u_2 \geqq 0\,.$$

This is a linear programming problem. It can be solved as indicated in previous sections. It is interesting to compare this problem with the production planning problem of the textile company, which was as follows. Maximize

(3.8) $$f = 9x_1 + 8x_2 + 50x_3 + 19x_4\,.$$

subject to

(3.9)
$$\begin{cases} 3x_1 + 2x_2 + 10x_3 + 4x_4 \leqq 18{,}000\,, \\ 0x_1 + 0x_2 + 2x_3 + {}^1\!/_2 x_4 \leqq 3{,}000\,, \end{cases}$$

(3.10) $$x_1 \geqq 0\,, \quad x_2 \geqq 0\,, \quad x_3 \geqq 0\,, \quad x_4 \geqq 0\,.$$

These two problems have a certain relation to each other. The outsider's problem (3.5)–(3.7) is called the *dual problem* of the production planning problem (3.8)–(3.10) which may be called the *primal problem* to distinguish it from the dual problem.

Let us now look at the relations between the solutions of the two problems. In the primal problem, the optimal solution was to include Fabric A and Fabric B in the production program. The imputed costs of spinning and loom capacity were computed from the net revenue of these products and the quantities used of these capacities:

(3.11)
$$\begin{cases} 10u_1 + 2u_2 = 50\,, \\ 4u_1 + {}^1\!/_2 u_2 = 19\,. \end{cases}$$

The solution is optimal only if the reduced revenue of the other products is nonpositive

$$(3.12) \quad \begin{cases} 9 - 3u_1 - 0u_2 \leqq 0 \, , \\ \\ 8 - 2u_1 - 0u_2 \leqq 0 \, . \end{cases}$$

Comparing (3.11) and (3.12) with (3.6), we find that the imputed costs corresponding with the optimal solution of the primal problem satisfy the constraints of the dual problem.

It may be shown that it is also the optimal solution of the dual problem. For the problem at hand, this will be done by generating the simplex tableau (which stands for an equation system) corresponding with this solution. In the inequalities of the constraints (3.6), nonnegative slack variables v_1, v_2, v_3, and v_4 may be introduced so that the following equations are obtained:

$$(3.13) \quad \begin{cases} 3u_1 + 0u_2 - v_1 = 9 \, , \\ \\ 2u_1 + 0u_2 - v_2 = 8 \, , \\ \\ 10u_1 + 2u_2 - v_3 = 50 \, , \\ \\ 4u_1 + \frac{1}{2}u_2 - v_4 = 19 \, . \end{cases}$$

These equations may, together with (3.5), be written as the following system:

$$(3.14) \quad \begin{cases} 0 = -18{,}000u_1 - 3{,}000u_2 + g \, , \\ \\ -9 = 3u_1 - 0u_2 + v_1 \, , \\ \\ -8 = -2u_1 - 0u_2 + v_2 \, , \\ \\ -50 = -10u_1 - 2u_2 + v_3 \, , \\ \\ -19 = -4u_1 - \tfrac{1}{2}u_2 + v_4 \, . \end{cases}$$

This system may be put into a simplex tableau format as in Tableau 0 of Table 4. Note that the corresponding basic solution is infeasible, since all basic variables are negative; if the solution was not infeasible, it would be optimal, since the coefficients of u_1 and u_2 in the first row are nonpositive.

The desired solution is one in which u_1 and u_2 are basic variables and,

Table 4
Generation of the optimal solution of the dual problem

Tableau	Basic Variables	Values Basic Variables	u_1	u_2
	g	0	−18,000	−3,000
0	v_1	−9	−3	0
	v_2	−8	−2	0
	v_3	−50	−10	−2
	v_4	−19	−4	−$^1/_2$
			v_3	u_2
	g	90,000	−1,800	600
1	v_1	6	−$^3/_{10}$	$^3/_5$
	v_2	2	−$^1/_5$	$^2/_5$
	u_1	5	−$^1/_{10}$	$^1/_5$
	v_4	1	−$^2/_5$	$^3/_{10}$
			v_3	v_4
	g	88,000	−1,000	−2,000
2	v_1	4	$^1/_2$	−2
	v_2	$^2/_3$	$^1/_3$	−$1^1/_3$
	u_1	$4^1/_3$	$^1/_6$	−$^2/_3$
	u_2	$3^1/_3$	−$1^1/_3$	$3^1/_3$

since the third and the fourth inequalities of (3.6) should hold as equalities, v_3 and v_4 are nonbasic variables. The desired solution may therefore be generated by two transformations, in the first of which u_1 replaces v_3 and in the second of which u_2 replaces v_4 as basic variable. Tableau 2 of Table 4 results. In its solution we have $u_1 = 4^1/_3$ and $u_2 = 3^1/_3$, which is the same as the imputed costs of spinning and loom capacity. $v_1 = 4$ which is equal to minus the reduced revenue for Yarn A and $v_2 = {}^2/_3$ which is equal to minus the reduced revenue for Yarn B. The coefficients of v_3 and v_4 in the first row are −1,000 and −2,000; both are nonpositive, so that we have obtained the optimal solution to the dual problem. It is no coincidence that the coefficient of v_3, −1,000, is, apart from the minus-sign, equal to the value of x_3 is the optimal solution of the production planning problem; we also find that the coefficient of v_4 in the first row, $-2,000$, is equal to minus the value of x_4 in the optimal solution of the primal problem.

Quite generally, the elements in the objective function row of the tableau of the optimal solution to the primal problem, are equal to the values of basic variables of the optimal solution to the dual problem. Hence imputed costs and reduced revenues are in fact dual variables. Furthermore, the elements in the objective function row of the optimal solution of the dual problem are equal to the values of basic variables of the optimal solution to the primal problems. The value of the objective function for the optimal solution of both problems is the same, 88,000. The other elements of Tableau 4 of Table 3 and Tableau 2 of Table 4 are the same, apart from a minus-sign and a different arrangement.

From the above, it may be concluded that while solving the primal problem, we implicitly solve the dual problem and *vice versa*. In this case the minimum offer that the outsider can make with a chance of acceptance is $88,000, which is exactly equal to the maximum profits of the textile company.

Also for the minimum-cost cattlefeed problem a dual problem can be constructed. In this case the outsider offers to *supply* to the cattle-owner in some way, at prices to be determined, the required 20 units of protein and 5 units of fat. Let the prices he charges per unit of protein and fat be denoted by u_1 and u_2. He wants to determine these prices in such a way that he maximizes his revenue, which is

$$(3.15) \qquad g = 20u_1 + 5u_2 .$$

His offer will not be accepted unless the value of the raw materials in terms of protein and fat, evaluated at u_1 and u_2 per unit is not more than the cost of the raw material; otherwise the animal owner will rather use the raw material instead of the outsider's supply. Hence u_1 and u_2 have to be determined in such a way that for barley the following equation is valid:

$$(3.16) \qquad 12u_1 + 2u_2 \leqq 24 .$$

For other raw materials we find

$$(3.17) \qquad \begin{cases} 12u_1 + \ 6u_2 \leqq 30 , \\ 40u_1 + 12u_2 \leqq 40 , \\ 60u_1 + \ 2u_2 \leqq 50 . \end{cases}$$

u_1 and u_2 have to be nonnegative because otherwise large quantities will be

Table 5
An application of the simplex method to the dual of the minimum-cost cattlefeed problem

Tableau	Basic Variables	Values Basic Variables	u_1	u_2
	g	0	-20	-5
0	v_1	24	12	2
	v_2	30	12	6
	v_3	40	40	12
	v_4	50	$\underline{60}$	2
			v_4	u_2
	g	$16^2/_3$	$^1/_3$	$-4^1/_3$
1	v_1	14	$-^1/_5$	$1^3/_5$
	v_2	20	$-^1/_5$	$5^3/_5$
	v_3	$6^2/_3$	$-^2/_3$	$\underline{10^2/_3}$
	u_1	$^5/_6$	$^1/_{60}$	$^1/_{30}$
			v_4	v_3
	g	$19^3/_8$	$^1/_{16}$	$1^3/_{32}$
2	v_1	13	$-^1/_{10}$	$-^3/_{20}$
	v_2	$16^1/_2$	$^3/_{20}$	$-^{21}/_{40}$
	u_2	$^5/_8$	$-^1/_{16}$	$^3/_{32}$
	u_1	$1^3/_{16}$	$^3/_{160}$	$-^1/_{320}$

ordered and left unused. [2] This is the dual problem. It may be solved by the simplex method, which is in this case very easy, since an initial basic feasible solution is immediately available by making the slack variables basic. After introduction of nonnegative slack variables v_1, v_2, v_3, and v_4 in (3.16) and (3.17) the following equation system which also includes (3.15) is found:

---

[2] If the required quantities of protein and fat had been *exactly* 20 and 5 units (and not *at least* 20 and 5 units), this nonnegativity condition would not be necessary. The variables u_1 and u_2 would then be unrestricted.

$$
(3.18) \quad
\begin{cases}
0 = -20u_1 - 5u_2 + g \,, \\
24 = 12u_1 + 2u_2 + v_1 \,, \\
30 = 12u_1 + 6u_2 + v_2 \,, \\
40 = 40u_1 + 12u_2 + v_3 \,, \\
50 = 60u_1 + 2u_2 + v_4 \,.
\end{cases}
$$

This system is put into simplex tableau format, see Tableau 0 of Table 5. In two iterations of the simplex method the optimal solution is obtained, see Tableau 2 of Table 5. This tableau should be compared with Tableau 2 of Table 2, which is the tableau of the optimal solution of the primal problem.

First note that the value of the objective function is the same in both cases, $19^{3}/_{8}$. The imputed values of protein and fat, $^{13}/_{16}$ and $^{5}/_{8}$, which are in the f-row and the columns of y_1 and y_2 in the tableau of the primal problem, are equal to the values of u_1 and u_2 in the dual problem. The reduced costs of the raw materials not used, barley and oats, which are 13 and $16^{1}/_{2}$, are found as the values of the slack variables v_1 and v_2 in the dual problem. The values of basic variables of the primal problem are found in the f-row of the optimal tableau of the dual problem. The other elements of both tableaux are the same apart from a minus sign and a different arrangement.

Let us now consider the following general form of a linear programming problem. Maximize

$$
(3.19) \quad f = p_1 x_1 + p_2 x_2 + \dots + p_n x_n
$$

subject to

$$
(3.20) \quad
\begin{cases}
a_{11} x_1 + a_{12} x_2 + \dots + a_{1n} x_n \leq b_1 \,, \\
a_{21} x_1 + a_{22} x_2 + \dots + a_{2n} x_n \leq b_2 \,, \\
\dots \\
a_{m1} x_1 + a_{m2} x_2 + \dots + a_{mn} x_n \leq b_m \,;
\end{cases}
$$

$$
(3.21) \quad x_1, x_2, \dots, x_n = 0 \,.
$$

The dual problem of this problem can be set up as follows. Related with each constraint in (3.20) is a dual variable, so that there are m dual variables $u_1, u_2, \dots, u_m$. The dual objective function in these dual variables is *minimized* and has as its coefficients the corresponding constant terms of the constraints $b_1, b_2, ..., b_m$:

(3.22) $g = b_1 u_1 + b_2 u_2 + ... b_m u_m$.

Corresponding to each of the variables of the original problem $x_1, x_2, ...,$ x_n there is a constraint which has the coefficient of that variable in the objective function as its constant term; these constraints are:

(3.23)
$$\begin{cases} a_{11} u_1 + a_{21} u_2 + ... + a_{m1} u_m \geqq p_1 \,, \\ a_{12} u_1 + a_{22} u_2 + ... + a_{m2} u_m \geqq p_2 \,, \\ ... \\ a_1 u_1 + a_{1n} u_{2n} + ... + a_{mn} u_m \geqq p_n \,. \end{cases}$$

Note that these constraints can be read off vertically from (3.19) and (3.20). Finally, the dual variables are required to be nonnegative:

(3.24) $u_1, u_2, ..., u_m \geqq 0$.

3.4. The Dual Method

In the previous section it was observed that the minimum-cost cattlefeed problem could be solved indirectly by solving its dual problem by the simplex method; the solution to the original problem then appears in the row of the objective function. A method which closely corresponds with this, but which uses the original problem is the *dual method,* discovered by C.E. Lemke [13]. This method is just as fundamental as the simplex method but it is much less known and not so frequently used. The method will be explained by means of the minimum-cost cattlefeed problem.

In Section 1 it was shown that this problem can be put into a simplex tableau format as in Tableau 0 of Table 2, which is also Tableau 0 of Table 6. The solution of this tableau is not a feasible one, since there is a shortage of 20 units of protein ($y_1 = -20$) and a shortage of 5 units of fat ($y_2 = -5$). But this solution is optimal in a narrow sense, because all elements in the f-row are nonpositive; this means that if nonbasic variables are increased, total costs increase. The dual method eliminates the negative values of basic variables, while preserving the optimality of the solutions in the sense that the elements in the f-row are nonpositive. This contrasts with the simplex method, which eliminates the nonoptimality of a solution while preserving its feasibility. This

Table 6
Solution of the cattlefeed problem by dual method

Tableau	Basic Variables	Values Basic Variables	x_1	x_2	x_3	x_4
0	f	0	-24	-30	-40	-50
	y_1	-20	-12	-12	-40	$\underline{-60}$
	y_2	-5	-2	-6	-12	-2
			x_1	x_2	x_3	y_1
1	f	$16^2/_3$	-14	-20	$-6^2/_3$	$-^5/_6$
	x_4	$^1/_3$	$^1/_5$	$^1/_5$	$^2/_3$	$-^1/_{60}$
	y_2	$-4^1/_3$	$-1^3/_5$	$-5^3/_5$	$\underline{-10^2/_3}$	$-^1/_{30}$
			x_1	x_2	y_2	y_1
2	f	$19^3/_8$	-13	$-16^1/_2$	$-^5/_8$	$-^{12}/_{16}$
	x_4	$^1/_{16}$	$^1/_{10}$	$-^3/_{20}$	$^1/_{16}$	$-^3/_{160}$
	x_3	$1^3/_{32}$	$^3/_{20}$	$^{21}/_{40}$	$-^3/_{32}$	$^1/_{320}$

means that there is a certain symmetry relation between both methods.

In the dual method in each iteration an infeasibility is eliminated. Let us consider the equation of the row with the basic variable having the most negative value:

$$(4.1) \qquad -20 = -12x_1 - 12x_2 - 40x_3 - 60x_4 + y_1 .$$

The variable y_1 should be increased from -20 to 0 in order to eliminate the infeasibility. Let us consider an increase in the nonbasic variable x_1:

$$(4.2) \qquad -20 + 12x_1 = y_1 .$$

Hence an increase in x_1 increases y_1. But so does any other nonbasic variable with a negative coefficient in (4.1). Now we should look at the costs of eliminating the negative value of y_1 by increasing a nonbasic variable. If x_1 is increased, costs increase by $24x_1$, if x_2 is increased, costs increase by $30x_2$, and so on. Which nonbasic variable gives the cheapest increase in y_1, or in terms of the problem, which raw material supplies the cheapest protein? Barley costs \$24 per unit and yields 12 units of protein per unit, so that the costs of protein are $^{24}/_{12}$ = \$2. For oats, sesame flakes, and groundnut meal we find a similar way

$$^{30}/_{12} = 2^1/_2 , \qquad ^{40}/_{40} = 1 , \qquad ^{50}/_{60} = ^5/_6 .$$

The raw material with the least cost per unit of protein is groundnut meal, so that x_4 should be increased in order to get a nonnegative value of y_1. We have

(4.3) $-20 + 60x_4 = y_1 = 0$;

from this follows $x_4 = \frac{1}{3}$.

The same solution is obtained if x_4 replaces y_1 as basic variable, so that -60 is the pivot of the transformation. The result is Tableau 1 of Table 6. Note that the elements in the f-row are all nonpositive, so that the solution is still optimal in the narrow sense. Total costs have increased from 0 to $16\frac{2}{3}$, which can be interpreted as the quantity of groundnut meal times its price or the required amount of protein times the imputed price of protein:

(4.4) $\frac{1}{3} \cdot 50 = 16\frac{2}{3} = 20 \cdot \frac{5}{6}$.

The solution of Tableau 1 still contains a negative basic variable, $y_2 = -4\frac{1}{3}$, which means that there is a shortage of fat of $4\frac{1}{3}$ units. This can be eliminated by increasing any of the nonbasic variables since all coefficients in the equation of y_2 are negative:

(4.5) $-4\frac{1}{3} = -1\frac{3}{5}x_1 - 5\frac{3}{5}x_2 - 10\frac{2}{3}x_3 - \frac{1}{30}y_1 + y_2$.

Again we select the variable giving the cheapest increase in y_2, which is done by determining

(4.6) $\text{Min} \left(\dfrac{14}{1\frac{3}{5}}, \ \dfrac{20}{5\frac{3}{5}}, \ \dfrac{6\frac{2}{3}}{10\frac{2}{3}}, \ \dfrac{\frac{5}{6}}{\frac{1}{30}} \right) = \frac{5}{8}$.

Hence x_3 should replace y_2 as basic variable, so that $-10\frac{2}{3}$ is the pivot of the transformation.

In Tableau 2, all elements in the f-row are nonpositive, as they have to be. Moreover, the values of basic variables are nonnegative, so that the optimal solution is obtained. In the last iteration costs have increased from $16\frac{2}{3}$ to $19\frac{3}{8}$, due to the elimination of the negative value of y_2. Total costs can be interpreted in two ways:

(4.7) $\frac{1}{16} \cdot 50 + \frac{13}{32} \cdot 40 = 19\frac{3}{8} = 20 \cdot \frac{13}{16} + 5 \cdot \frac{5}{8}$.

In the two iterations the elements in the row of the negative basic variable and in the columns of nonbasic variables were all negative. This is not always the case; some or even all of these elements may be nonnegative. The nonbasic variables corresponding with the nonnegative elements should not be considered, since an increase in these variables does not increase the negative basic variable towards zero. If all elements concerned are nonnegative, there is no feasible solution to the problem. This can be shown as follows. Suppose all minus-signs of the elements in the row of y_1 and the columns of nonbasic variables in Tableau 0 are changed into plus-signs. Then the corresponding equation may be written as

$$(4.8) \qquad -20 - 12x_1 - 12x_2 - 40x_3 - 60x_4 = y_1 .$$

A solution of the problem should satisfy this equation. But the x-variables can only take nonnegative values, so that the left side always must be negative; hence y_1 cannot be nonnegative.

Formal rules for the dual method may be given as follows. Let the current tableau be given by the array

$$(4.9) \quad \left\{ \begin{array}{ccccc} a_{00} & a_{01} & a_{02} & \cdot & a_{0n} \\[2mm] a_{10} & a_{11} & a_{12} & \cdot & a_{1n} \\[2mm] a_{20} & a_{21} & a_{22} & \cdot & a_{2n} \\[2mm] \cdot & \cdot & \cdot & \cdot & \cdot \\[2mm] a_{m0} & a_{m1} & a_{m2} & \cdot & a_{mn} \end{array} \right. \cdot$$

It is assumed that the problem concerned is a minimization problem and that the elements $a_{01}, a_{02}, ..., a_{0n}$ are nonpositive, so that the solution is optimal in the narrow sense. On the other hand, a number of the elements $a_{10}, a_{20}, ..., a_{m0}$ may be negative; if not, the solution is optimal in the wide sense. The rules for one iteration are:

VARIABLE TO LEAVE THE BASIS: *Select the variable connected with*

$$(4.10) \qquad \text{Min } a_{i0} = a_{r0} ,$$

if $a_{r0} \geqq 0$, *the present solution is optimal in the wide sense.*

NEW BASIC VARIABLE: *Select the variable connected with*

$$(4.11) \qquad \underset{j}{\text{Min }} \left(\frac{a_{0j}}{a_{rj}} \mid a_{rj} < 0 \right) = \frac{a_{0k}}{a_{rk}} .$$

If all $a_{rj} \geqq 0$ *for all j, the problem has no feasible solution.*

It is not strictly necessary to select as the leaving basic variable the most negative basic variable; any negative basic variable may be chosen, but the choice of the most negative one will in larger problems generally lead to a smaller number of iterations than most other rules. Note that this corresponds to a similar observation for the choice of the new basic variable in the simplex method.

The transformation rules are identical to those given for the simplex method. It can easily be proved that the successive tableaux have nonpositive elements in the f-row. The transformed elements in the f-row, if the first element is deleted, are

$$(4.12) \qquad a_{01} - a_{0k}a_{rk}^{-1}a_{r1} \cdots - a_{0k}a_{rk}^{-1} \cdots a_{0m} - a_{0k}a_{rk}^{-1}a_{rm} \ ,$$

which may be written for $a_{rj} \neq 0$ as

$$(4.13) \qquad a_{r1}\left(\frac{a_{01}}{a_{r1}} - \frac{a_{0k}}{a_{rk}}\right) \cdots - \frac{a_{0k}}{a_{rk}} \cdots a_{rm}\left(\frac{a_{0m}}{a_{rm}} - \frac{a_{0k}}{a_{rk}}\right).$$

The expressions within brackets are, due to (4.11), nonnegative for columns with $a_{rj} < 0$, so that the elements in these columns are nonpositive. For $a_{rj} > 0$ the corresponding elements are negative, and for $a_{rj} = 0$, the corresponding elements have not changed. The element $-a_{0k}/a_{rk}$ is, of course, negative.

The value of the objective function has changed from a_{00} to $a_{00} - a_{0k}a_{rk}^{-1}a_{r0}$. If $a_{0k} = 0$, the value of f is unchanged; otherwise it is increased, since $a_{0k} < 0$ and $a_{r0}/a_{rk} > 0$. Let us call solutions with elements $a_{0j} = 0$ *dually degenerate solutions*. Then, if no dually degenerate solutions occur, the objective function increases in each iteration of the dual method. Hence no solution can recur and since there is only a finite number of combinations of basic and nonbasic variables, the dual method must find the optimal solution in a finite number of iterations. The same may be proved for cases in which dually degenerate solutions occur if (4.11) is slightly modified for a minimum which is not unique.

It can be shown that the dual method is equivalent to an application of the simplex method to the dual problem in the sense that the successive tableaux of both methods correspond to each other; values of basic variables in the dual method are equal, apart from sign, to the elements in the f-row in the simplex method, and *vice versa*.

Exercises

1. Solve the following problem, using x_1 and x_5 as basic variables for the initial solution. Minimize

$$f = x_1 + 6x_2 - 7x_3 + x_4 + 5x_5$$

subject to

$$5x_1 - 4x_2 + 13x_3 - 2x_4 + x_5 = 20 \,,$$
$$x_1 - x_2 + 5x_3 - x_4 + x_5 = 8 \,,$$
$$x_1, x_2, x_3, x_4, x_5 \geq 0 \,.$$

2. Solve the following problem using artificial variables. Minimize

$$f = 2x_1 + x_2$$

subject to

$$3x_1 + x_2 \geq 3 \,,$$
$$4x_1 + 3x_2 \geq 6 \,,$$
$$x_1 + 2x_2 \geq 2 \,,$$
$$x_1, x_2 \geq 0 \,.$$

3. Solve, using artificial variables: Maximize

$$f = 2x_1 + 3x_2$$

subject to

$$x_1 + 2x_2 \leq 18 \,,$$
$$x_1 + x_2 \geq 11\tfrac{1}{4} \,,$$
$$-3x_1 + 2x_2 \leq 1 \,,$$
$$5x_1 + 2x_2 \leq 35 \,,$$
$$x_1, x_2 \geq 0 \,.$$

Comment on the solution, using a graphical representation of the problem.

4. Consider the following diet problem. Three food products are available at costs of $1.00, $3.60 and $2.40 per unit, respectively. They contain 1,000, 4,000 and 2,000 calories per unit, respectively, and 200, 900 and 500 protein units per unit, respectively. Required is the minimum cost diet containing at least 20,000 calories and 3,000 units of protein.

   (a) Formulate this problem as a linear programming problem. Formulate and interpret its dual problem.

(b) Solve the problem by means of the simplex method, using artificial variables.

(c) Solve the problem by means of the dual method.

5. Solve the dual problem of the textile production planning problem by means of the dual method. Compare the successive solutions with those of the application of the simplex method to the primal (original) problem, and conclude that they correspond to each other. Trace these solutions in a geometrical representation of the dual problem and interpret the result.

6. A special kind of oil can be produced by mixing a number of available kinds of oil. The oil should satisfy some requirements: its viscosity should not exceed 30 and its sulphur content should not exceed 35% of its volume. The oils that can serve as components have the following properties and prices —

	Viscosity	Sulphur Content	Price
Oil A	20	0.30	0.25
Oil B	40	0.45	0.20
Oil C	40	0.25	0.30

It may be assumed that the viscosity of a mixture is varying linearly with that of the components (which is obviously true for its sulphur content).

(a) Determine the optimal mixture using the dual method.
   (Hint: Use $x_1 + x_2 + x_3 \geq 1$ instead of $x_1 + x_2 + x_3 = 1$)

(b) Interpret the dual variables of the optimal solution.

(c) Formulate the dual problem and give an interpretation of it.

7. (a) Solve Problem 2 by means of the dual method.

(b) Formulate the dual problem and solve it by the simplex method.

8. (a) Solve Problem 1 by means of the dual method. (Hint: introduce artificial variables without M-terms in the objective function and eliminate these while preserving optimality in the narrow sense).

(b) Formulate the dual problem and solve this by means of the simplex method. (Hint: dual variables corresponding to equalities have no non-negativity restrictions.)

4. SENSITIVITY ANALYSIS AND NEAR-OPTIMALITY ANALYSIS

4.1. Sensitivity Analysis of the Coefficients of the Objective Function

After the optimal solution of a linear programming problem has been computed for a given set of data, it frequently happens that these data change to some extent; it may also be that the data are not known with certainty. It is, of course, always possible to find the optimal solution for a slightly different set of data by solving the problem again, but a more fruitful approach is to ask for which changes in the data the present optimal solution remains optimal. This is called *sensitivity analysis.* Changes of all data may be considered, but here we shall only consider changes in the coefficients of the objective function, which are treated in this section, and changes in the constant terms of the constraints which are treated in the next.

A closely related subject, *parametric programming,* is treated in Chapter 6, where the optimal solutions are found for changes in data of coefficients of the objective function or constant terms which are described by a variation of one parameter over a given range. Parametric programming can be considered as an extension of sensitivity analysis.

Near-optimality analysis poses a different question: what are the feasible solutions giving a value of the objective function which is at least equal to a given value? The method to be used for this purpose is called the reverse simplex method, which is treated in Section 4 of this chapter.

First we shall consider the sensitivity analysis of coefficients in the objective function. As an example the textile company production planning problem is used again. Table 1 gives the set-up tableau and the tableau of the optimal solution both in extended form, that is with the columns of basic variables.

It will be shown that the row of f in Tableau I can be generated immediately from that of Tableau 0 by using the other rows of Tableau I. The coefficient in the f-row of x_3 can be made zero by adding 50 times the row of x_3 of Tableau I to the f-row of Tableau 0. The coefficient in the f-row of

Table 1
Set-up and optimal tableau

	Basic Variables	Values Basic Variables	x_1	x_2	x_3	x_4	f	y_1	y_2
	f	0	-9	-8	-50	-19	1	0	0
0	y_1	18,000	3	2	10	4	0	1	0
	y_2	3,000	0	0	2	$^1/_2$	0	0	1
	f	88,000	4	$^2/_3$	0	0	1	$4^1/_3$	$3^1/_3$
I	x_4	2,000	2	$1^1/_3$	0	1	0	$^2/_3$	$-3^1/_3$
	x_3	1,000	$-^1/_2$	$-^1/_3$	1	0	0	$-^1/_6$	$1^1/_3$

x_4 can be made zero by adding 19 times the row of x_4 of Tableau I to the
f-row of Tableau 0. Hence the f-row of Tableau I is found by adding 50
times the row of x_3 and 19 times the row of x_4 of Tableau I to the f-row of
Tableau 0. For the value of f we find

(1.1) $50 \cdot 1,000 + 19 \cdot 2,000 = 88,000$,

and for the coefficients of x_1, x_2, y_1, and y_2 in the f-row:

$$(1.2) \quad \begin{cases} -9 + 50 \cdot -^1/_2 + 19 \cdot 2 = 4 \ , \\ -8 + 50 \cdot -^1/_3 + 19 \cdot 1^1/_3 = ^2/_3 \ ; \\ 0 + 50 \cdot -^1/_6 + 19 \cdot ^2/_3 = 4^1/_3 \ , \\ 0 + 50 \cdot 1^1/_3 + 19 \cdot -3^1/_3 = 3^1/_3 \ . \end{cases}$$

If, instead of the numbers 9, 8, 50, and 19 the general notation p_1, p_2, p_3,
and p_4 is used, the following expressions are found for the coefficients in the
f-row.

$$(1.3) \quad \begin{cases} -p_1 + p_3 \cdot -^1/_2 + p_4 \cdot 2 \ , \\ -p_2 + p_3 \cdot -^1/_3 + p_4 \cdot 1^1/_3 \ , \\ 0 + p_3 \cdot -^1/_6 + p_4 \cdot ^2/_3 \ , \\ 0 + p_3 \cdot 1^1/_3 + p_4 \cdot 3^1/_3 \ . \end{cases}$$

In general, the coefficient in the f-row of the nonbasic variable x_j is found to be

$$(1.4) \qquad -p_j + \sum_i p_i \bar{a}_{ij},$$

where $\bar{a}_{ij}$ is the element in the current tableau in the i-row and the j-th column; p_i is the coefficient in the original objective function of the basic variable in the i-th row. For y-variables, the p's are zero. [1]

From (1.3) it can easily be determined for which values of the p's the optimal solution remains optimal; this is simply for all values of the p's for which the four expressions in (1.3) remain nonnegative.

Let us now consider separate variations of the p's, that is, one p is allowed to vary while all other p's take their given values. For p_1 we find

$$(1.5) \qquad -p_1 + 50 \cdot -\tfrac{1}{2} + 19 \cdot 2 \geqq 0,$$

or $p_1 \leqq 13$. It is somewhat easier to deal with the change in p_1; in this case we obtain

$$(1.6) \qquad -(9 + \Delta p_1) + 50 \cdot -\tfrac{1}{2} + 19 \cdot 2 \geqq 0,$$

or $\Delta p_1 \leqq 4$. This result can also be found immediately from Tableau I, where x_1 has a coefficient of 4. In the same way it is found that for an optimal solution we should have $\Delta p_2 \leqq \tfrac{2}{3}$.

For changes in coefficients of basic variables computations are more complicated. From (1.2) and (1.3) the following inequalities are obtained for Δp_3:

$$(1.7) \qquad \begin{cases} \Delta p_3 \cdot -\tfrac{1}{2} + 4 \geqq 0, \\ \Delta p_3 \cdot -\tfrac{1}{3} + \tfrac{2}{3} \geqq 0, \\ \Delta p_3 \cdot -\tfrac{1}{6} + 4\tfrac{1}{3} \geqq 0, \\ \Delta p_3 \cdot 1\tfrac{1}{3} + 3\tfrac{1}{3} \geqq 0, \end{cases}$$

or

$$(1.8) \qquad \begin{cases} \Delta p_3 \leqq 8, \\ \Delta p_3 \leqq 2, \\ \Delta p_3 \leqq 24, \\ \Delta p_3 \geqq -2\tfrac{1}{2}, \end{cases}$$

---

[1] In a number of textbooks, the elements in the f-row for an application of the simplex method are always computed according to (1.4); the usual notation then is $z_j - c_j$ where $z_j = \sum_i c_i \bar{a}_{ij}$ and c's are used instead of p's.

from which it is concluded that $-2^1/_2 \leqq \Delta p_3 \leqq 2$ or $6/7^1/_2 \leqq p_3 \leqq 52$ in order that the present optimal solution remains optimal.

In the same way we find for variations in p_4:

$$(1.9) \quad \begin{cases} \Delta p_4 \cdot 2 + 4 \geqq 0, \\ \Delta p_4 \cdot 1^1/_3 + {}^2/_3 \geqq 0, \\ \Delta p_4 \cdot {}^2/_3 + 4^1/_3 \geqq 0, \\ \Delta p_4 \cdot -3^1/_3 + 3^1/_3 \geqq 0, \end{cases}$$

or

$$(1.10) \quad \begin{cases} \Delta p_4 \geqq -2, \\ \Delta p_4 \geqq -{}^1/_2, \\ \Delta p_4 \geqq -6^1/_2, \\ \Delta p_4 \leqq 1. \end{cases}$$

From this is it concluded that the present solution is optimal for $-{}^1/_2 \leqq \Delta p_4 \leqq 1$ or $18^1/_2 \leqq p_4 \leqq 20$.

We shall now derive general expressions for the changes in the p's for which the solutions remain optimal. First consider changes in the coefficient of a nonbasic variable which affect only the reduced revenue in that column. We have

$$(1.11) \quad -(p_j + \Delta p_j) + \sum_i p_i \bar{a}_{ij} = -\Delta p_j - p_j + \sum_i p_i \bar{a}_{ij}$$

$$= -\Delta p_j + \bar{a}_{0j} \geqq 0.$$

or

$$(1.12) \quad \Delta p_j \leqq \bar{a}_{0j},$$

where $\bar{a}_{0j}$ is the element in the f-row in the column of the nonbasic variable concerned.

For changes in the coefficients of a basic variable x_ϱ we have

$$(1.13) \quad -p_j + \sum_i p_i \bar{a}_{ij} + \Delta p_\varrho \bar{a}_{\varrho j} \geqq 0.$$

where j runs over all nonbasic variables. This can be written as

(1.14) $\bar{a}_{0j} + \Delta p_\varrho \bar{a}_{\varrho j} \geqq 0$.

for all nonbasic variables. These inequalities can be split into two groups:

(1.15) $\Delta p_\varrho \geqq -\bar{a}_{0j}/\bar{a}_{\varrho j}$ for $a_{\varrho j} > 0$,

(1.16) $\Delta p_\varrho \leqq -\bar{a}_{0j}/\bar{a}_{\varrho j}$ for $a_{\varrho j} < 0$.

For $a_{0j} = 0$ no constraint for Δp results. Since all inequalities in (1.15) have to be satisfied in order to have optimality, (1.15) results in

$$\Delta p_\varrho \geqq \max_j \left(-\bar{a}_{0j}/\bar{a}_{\varrho j} \mid \bar{a}_{\varrho j} > 0\right) ;$$

Similarly we find from (1.16):

$$\Delta p_\varrho \leqq \min_j \left(-\bar{a}_{0j}/\bar{a}_{\varrho j} \mid \bar{a}_{\varrho j} < 0\right) .$$

- These can be combined as foilows:

(1.17) $\max_j \left(-\bar{a}_{0j}/\bar{a}_{\varrho j} \mid \bar{a}_{\varrho j} > 0\right) \leqq \Delta p_\varrho \leqq \min_j \left(-\bar{a}_{0j}/\bar{a}_{\varrho j} \mid \bar{a}_{\varrho j} < 0\right)$.

For example, in Tableau I of Table 1 we have for the coefficient of x_3:

$$\frac{-3\frac{1}{3}}{1\frac{1}{3}} \leqq \Delta p_3 \leqq \min \left(\frac{-4}{\frac{1}{2}}, \frac{-\frac{2}{3}}{-\frac{1}{3}}, \frac{-4\frac{1}{3}}{-\frac{1}{6}}\right) = 2 ,$$

or

$$-2\frac{1}{2} \leqq \Delta p_3 \leqq 2 .$$

4.2. Sensitivity Analysis of the Constant Terms

If the constant terms of the constraints of a problem change, the values of basic variables of the optimal solution change. The change of the constant terms may affect the optimal solution in two ways. Firstly, the change may give different values of basic variables, but the set of basic variables remains the same; this means that only the values of basic variables are changed, but all other elements of the tableau remain the same. In this case the elements in the f-row are unchanged, so that the shadow prices of the constraints and the reduced costs are the same as for the previous optimal solution.

Secondly, the change in the constant terms may be so large that other basic variables enter the basis to prevent negative values of basic variables. This implies a change of the set of basic variables and of the shadow prices and reduced costs. In sensitivity analysis of constant terms it is found out for which changes in the constant terms the same variables remain basic, which implies that the shadow prices and reduced costs also remain the same.

First we shall determine an expression of the values of basic variables of the optimal solution in terms of the changes of constant terms if the set of basic variables remains the same. If in Table 1, the set-up tableau 0, and the optimal tableau, Tableau I, are compared, it is easily noticed that the last three columns of Tableau 0 each contain one unit, each in a different row, and zero's elsewhere; for Tableau I this is not true anymore. Now Tableau I was found from Tableau 0 by means of a number of transformations which involved division of rows by a constant or addition of a multiple of a row to another row. Hence each row of Tableau I consists of a linear combination of the rows of Tableau 0. If it is known exactly which linear combination, it is easy to find the values of the basic variables of Tableau I, f, x_4, and x_3, as a function of the constant terms given in Tableau 0.

The f-column of Tableau 0 has a unit in the f-row and zero's elsewhere. The f-column of Tableau I registers what has been done with this f-row, that is, by which constant the first row has been divided and which multiples of this row have been added to other rows. According to the f-column of Tableau I, the f-row has not been divided, while no multiple of this row has been added to other rows. Looking at the y_1-column of Tableau 0 which has a unit in the second row, it is found from the y_1-column of Tableau I that this row has been divided by $1\frac{1}{2}$ (or multiplied by $\frac{2}{3}$), that $4\frac{1}{3}$ times the y_1-row of Tableau 0 has been added to the first row and $-\frac{1}{6}$ times this row has been added to the third row. According to the y_2-column of both tableaux, the third row of Tableau 0 has been multiplied by $1\frac{1}{3}$, while further $3\frac{1}{3}$ times this row has been added to the first row and $-3\frac{1}{3}$ times this row has been added to the second row. Hence we now know what has happened to all rows of Tableau 0 in the transformations leading to Tableau I, so that we can easily find the effects of changes in the constant terms which are the values of basic variables of Tableau 0 on the values of basic variables of Tableau I.

To put this into practice, the first constant term of Tableau 0 is changed to $18{,}000 + \Delta b_1$ and the second one to $3{,}000 + \Delta b_2$; for the sake of completeness the value of f which was 0 is changed into Δb_0. The value of f in Tableau I is found as follows:

$$(2.1) \qquad 1 \cdot \Delta b_0 + 4\tfrac{1}{3}(18{,}000 + \Delta b_1) + 3\tfrac{1}{3}(3{,}000 + \Delta b_2)$$

$$= 88{,}000 + \Delta b_0 + 4\tfrac{1}{3}\Delta b_1 + 3\tfrac{1}{3}\Delta b_2 \, .$$

Interpretation: to the unchanged first row, $4^1/_3$ times the second row of Tableau 0 and $3^1/_3$ times the third row of this tableau has been added. Note that the coefficients of Δb_1 and Δb_2 are the shadow prices of the constraints.

In the same way we obtain for the value of x_4 in Tableau I:

$$(2.2) \qquad 0 \cdot \Delta b_0 + {}^2/_3(18,000 + \Delta b_1) - 3^1/_3(3,000 + \Delta b_2)$$
$$= 2,000 + {}^2/_3 \Delta b_1 - 3^1/_3 \Delta b_2 \ .$$

Interpretation: the second row of Tableau I can be found by adding 0 times the first row, $^2/_3$ times the second row and $-3^1/_3$ times the third row of Tableau 0. For the value of x_3 in Tableau I we find

$$(2.3) \qquad 0 \cdot \Delta b_0 - {}^1/_6(18,000 + \Delta b_1) + 1^1/_3(3,000 + \Delta b_2)$$
$$= 1,000 - {}^1/_6 \Delta b_1 + 1^1/_3 \Delta b_2 \ .$$

Since basic variables should remain nonnegative, it can easily be determined for which values of Δb_1 and Δb_2 the solution of Tableau I remains feasible (and hence optimal in the wide sense). If only changes Δb_1 are considered, we find from (2.2) and (2.3)

$$(2.4) \qquad \begin{cases} 2,000 + {}^2/_3 \Delta b_1 \geqq 0 \ , \\ 1,000 - {}^1/_6 \Delta b_1 \geqq 0 \ , \end{cases}$$

which results in

$$(2.5) \qquad -3,000 \leqq \Delta b_1 \leqq 6,000 \ .$$

Hence a solution with the same basic variables and shadow prices is found for spinning capacity varying from 15,000 to 24,000 units (provided weaving capacity remains the same). The values of the basic variables, however, change; they are for a capacity of 15,000;

$$(2.6) \qquad \begin{cases} x_4 = 2,000 + {}^2/_3 \cdot -3,000 = 0 \ , \\ x_3 = 1,000 - {}^1/_6 \cdot -3,000 = 1,500 \ , \end{cases}$$

and for a capacity of 24,000:

$$(2.7) \qquad \begin{cases} x_4 = 2,000 + {}^2/_3 \cdot 6,000 = 6,000 \ , \\ x_3 = 1,000 - {}^1/_6 \cdot 6,000 = 0 \ . \end{cases}$$

For values of Δb_1 lying outside the bounds of (2.5) optimal solutions with different basic variables and shadow prices are found.

If changes in the weaving capacity Δb_2 are considered, the nonnegativity requirement for basic variables leads to

$$(2.8) \quad \begin{cases} 2,000 - 3^1/_3 \Delta b_2 \geq 0 \, , \\ 1,000 + 1^1/_3 \Delta b_2 \geq 0 \, , \end{cases}$$

from which the following bounds are found

$$(2.9) \quad -750 \leq \Delta b_2 \leq 600 \, .$$

Hence a solution with the same basic variables and shadow prices is found for weaving capacity varying from 2,250 to 3,600 units (provided spinning capacity remains at 18,000).

A special case occurs if the slack variable whose constant term is varied is still in the basis of the optimal solution; this does not occur in Tableau I since no slack variables are basic. Let us consider Tableau 1 of Table 2 in Chapter 2 and let us for a moment assume that this is the optimal solution, all elements in the f-row being nonnegative. The values of basic variables of this solution depend in the following manner on Δb_1:

$$(2.10) \quad \begin{cases} y_1 = 1 \cdot (18,000 + \Delta b_1) - 5(3,000) + 0 \times 0 = 3,000 + \Delta b_1 \, , \\ x_3 = 0 \cdot (18,000 + \Delta b_1) + ^1/_2 (3,000) + 0 \times 0 = 1,500 \, , \\ f = 0 \cdot (18,000 + \Delta b_1) + 25(3,000) + 1 \times 0 = 75,000 \, . \end{cases}$$

Hence a change Δb_1 only affects the related basic variable y_1; this is because the column y_1 has not changed since it is a basic variable in both tableaux. The bound for Δb_1 turns out to be

$$(2.11) \quad -3,000 \leq \Delta b_1 \, .$$

In general, it can be said that for changes in constant terms related to slack variables which are basic in the optimal solution only one lower bound is found equal to minus the value of the slack variable in the optimal solution. In more practical terms: an optimal solution remains unchanged if capacity on a machine with unused capacity in the optimal solution is reduced by at most the amount of the unused capacity. This is obvious without using tableaux anyway.

We can summarise our results as follows. For constant terms which have a corresponding basic slack variable with a value a_{0i} in the basis, the constraint is simply

$$(2.12) \quad \Delta b_i \geq - \bar{a}_{i0} \, .$$

For constant terms having nonbasic corresponding slack variables the following inequalities should be satisfied for $i = 1$ to m:

$$(2.13) \qquad \sum_{j=1}^{m} (b_j + \Delta b_j) b_{ij} \geq 0 \, ,$$

where b_{ij} is the element in the i-th row and in the column of the j-th slack variable. If a change Δb_ϱ is considered in the constant terms of the ϱ-th constraint, we have for $i = 1$ to m:

$$(2.14) \qquad \sum_{j=1}^{m} b_j b_{ij} + \Delta b_\varrho b_{i\varrho} \geq 0 \, ,$$

or

$$(2.15) \qquad \bar{a}_{i0} + \Delta b_\varrho b_{i\varrho} \geq 0 \, .$$

This results in

$$(2.16) \qquad \max_i \left(\frac{-\bar{a}_{i0}}{b_{i\varrho}} \,\middle|\, b_{i\varrho} > 0 \right) \leq \Delta b_\varrho \leq \min_i \left(\frac{-\bar{a}_{i0}}{b_{i\varrho}} \,\middle|\, b_{i\varrho} < 0 \right).$$

For instance, we find for Δb_1 in the problem of Table 1:

$$\frac{-2000}{{}^2/_3} \leq \Delta b_1 \leq \frac{-1000}{-{}^1/_6}$$

or

$$-3000 \leqq \Delta b_1 \leqq 6000 \, .$$

4.3. Alternative Optimal Solutions

Let us again consider the example given in Table 6 of Chapter 2. Tableau 3 of this table, which can also be found in Tableau 0 of Table 2 of this chapter, contains an optimal solution, since all elements in the f-row are non-negative. Two of these elements are zero, namely those in the columns of x_3 and y_3. What would happen if, say, x_3 would be increased? The basic variables can be written in terms of x_3 as follows:

$$(3.1) \qquad \begin{cases} 90 - 0x_3 = f, \\[4pt] 20 - 0x_3 = x_1 \, , \\[4pt] 10 - {}^1/_2 x_3 = x_4 \, , \\[4pt] 5 + {}^1/_4 = x_5 \, . \end{cases}$$

Table 2
Alternative optimal solutions for the production planning example

Tableau	Basic Variables	Values Basic Variables	Ratio	y_1	x_2	x_3	y_2	y_3
0	f	90		$1/2$	$1/2$	0	1	0
	x_1	20		0	4	0	-1	1
	x_4	10	20	$1/2$	$-6 1/2$	$1/2$	2	-2
	x_5	5		$-1/4$	$1 1/4$	$-1/4$	0	$1/2$

				y_1	x_2	x_4	y_2	y_3
1	f	90		$1/2$	$1/2$	0	1	0
	x_1	20	20	0	4	0	-1	1
	x_3	20		1	-13	2	4	-4
	x_5	10		0	-2	$1/2$	1	$-1/2$

				y_1	x_2	x_4	y_2	x_1
2	f	90		$1/2$	$1/2$	0	1	0
	y_3	20		0	4	0	-1	1
	x_3	100	50	1	3	2	0	4
	x_5	20	40	0	0	$1/2$	$1/2$	$1/2$

				y_1	x_2	x_5	y_2	x_1
3	f	90		$1/2$	$1/2$	0	1	0
	y_3	20	20	0	4	0	-1	1
	x_3	20	10	1	3	-4	-2	2
	x_4	40	40	0	0	2	1	1

				y_1	x_2	x_5	y_2	x_3
4	f	90		$1/2$	$1/2$	0	1	0
	y_3	10		$-1/2$	$2 1/2$	2	0	$-1/2$
	x_1	10		$1/2$	$1 1/2$	-2	-1	$1/2$
	x_4	30		$-1/2$	$-1 1/2$	4	2	$-1/2$

Hence f does not change for increasing values of x_3, but x_4 and x_5 do. For $x_3 = 20$, x_4 becomes equal to zero. The same solution can be obtained by pivoting on the element $1/2$ in Tableau 0; the result is Tableau I. This tableau also contains an optimal solution with, of course, the same value of the objective function. Not only the solution of (3.1) for $x_3 = 0$ and that for $x_3 = 20$ are optimal, but all solutions following from (3.1) for $0 \leqq x_3 \leqq 20$.

Other optimal solutions are obtained if y_3 is increased in the solution of Tableau 0:

$$(3.2) \quad \begin{cases} 90 = f, \\ 20 - y_3 = x_1, \\ 10 + 2y_3 = x_4, \\ 5 - \tfrac{1}{2}y_3 = x_5. \end{cases}$$

From this it is obvious that for $0 \leqq y_5 \leqq 10$, the solutions given by (3.2) are optimal. For $y_5 = 10$, $x_5 = 0$. The corresponding solution can also be obtained by pivoting on the element $\tfrac{1}{2}$ in the column of y_3; the result is Tableau 4.

In Tableau 1, other optimal solutions may be generated by introducing into the basis nonbasic variables with a zero in the f-row. If x_4 is introduced into the basis in the manner described before, Tableau 0 is found again. However, if y_3 is made a basic variable, x_4 leaves the basis and Tableau 2 is found. In the f-row of this tableau, zero's occur in the columns of x_4 and x_1. If x_4 is made a basic variable, x_5 leaves the basis and Tableau 3 is found. If x_1 is made basic, y_3 leaves the basis and Tableau 2 is found back. In Tableau 3, x_5 and x_1 have zero's in the f-row. If x_5 is made basic, Tableau 2 is found back, but if x_1 is introduced into the basis, x_3 leaves the basis and Tableau 4 results. This tableau has zero's in the f-row in the columns of x_5 and x_3. If x_5 is introduced into the basis, we find Tableau 0 and if x_3 is introduced into the basis, we find Tableau 3. All possibilities for introducing nonbasic variables with a zero in the f-row have been exhausted.

The solutions of Tableaux 0–4 are summarized in Table 3. Not only these solutions are of importance, but also combinations of these solutions, that is we may take as alternative optimal solutions a weighted sum of the solutions 0–4, provided these weights are nonnegative and add to 1; it can be proved that this gives the same results as increasing nonbasic variables with zero coefficients in the f-row.

Alternative optima may play a role in practice when it is desirable to leave some space for decisionmaking because it has not been possible to formulate the problem in an exact manner as a linear programming problem. For instance, it may be that apart from monetary considerations it is less desirable to produce Product 5. Ideally it should be possible to express this undesirability in terms of money, but this is not always very easy. From Tableau 3 it is obvious that in this case Solutions 3 or 4 should be used. There may be other conditions which cannot be expressed in a linear programming frame-

Table 3
Summary of alternative optimal solutions

Solution	f	x_1	x_2	x_3	x_4	x_5	y_1	y_2	y_3
0	90	20	–	–	10	5	–	–	–
1	90	20	–	20	–	10	–	–	–
2	90	–	–	100	–	20	–	–	20
3	90	–	–	20	40	–	–	–	20
4	90	10	–	–	30	–	–	–	10

work; among all alternative optimal solutions the solution which satisfies these other conditions may be found.

4.4. Near-Optimality Analysis Via the Reverse Simplex Method

Similar considerations may be valid for solutions having a value of the objective function not much lower than that of the optimal solution. Such solutions are called *near-optimal solutions*. It is therefore desirable to develop a method which generates all near-optimal solutions if a lower limit for the value of the objective function is given. Such a method is the *reverse simplex method* which will be explained by means of the textile production example. Suppose that all solutions having at least a value of the objective function of 80 are required.

Tableau 0 of Table 4 gives the tableau of the optimal solution found in Tableau 4 of Table 3 in Chapter 2. The value of the objective function is 88. None of the elements in the f-row are zero, so that there are no alternative optimal solutions. The reverse simplex method generates basic solutions according to decreasing values of the objective function.

If in Tableau 0, y_1 is increased, the decrease in the value of f is $4^1/_3$ per unit increase of y_1. The maximum increase of y_1 is determined as in the simplex method; this is 3. Hence the objective function decreases by $3 \cdot 4^1/_3$ = 13 if y_1 becomes a basic variable. The objective function then becomes $88 - 13 = 75$. This is of course the value of the objective function in a tableau resulting from pivoting on the underlined element $^2/_3$. This value of the objective function is entered in an additional row labelled f_{0j} in the column of y_1. For the other nonbasic variables of Tableau 0 the same is done. If x_1 is to become a basic variable, it will replace x_4 and the value of f will be

$$88 - 4 \cdot {}^2/_2 = 84 ,$$

Sensitivity analysis and near-optimality analysis

Table 4
Near-optimality analysis via the reverse simplex method

Tableau	Basic Variables	Values Basic Variables	y_1	x_1	y_2	x_2
0	x_4	2	$2/3$	2	$-3\,1/3$	$1\,1/3$
	x_3	1	$-1/6$	$-1/2$	$1\,1/3$	$-1/3$
	f	88	$4\,1/3$	4	$3\,1/3$	$2/3$
	f_{0j}		75	84	$85\,1/2$	87
			y_1	x_1	y_2	x_4
1	x_2	$1\,1/2$	$1/2$	$1\,1/2$	$-2\,1/2$	$3/4$
	x_3	$1\,1/2$	0	0	$1/2$	$1/4$
	f	87	4	3	5	$-1\,1/2$
	f_{1j}		75	84	72	—
			y_1	x_1	x_3	x_2
2	x_4	$4\,1/2$	$1/4$	$3/4$	$2\,1/2$	$1/2$
	y_2	$3/4$	$-1/8$	$-3/8$	$3/4$	$-1/4$
	f	$85\,1/2$	$4\,3/4$	$5\,1/4$	$-2\,1/2$	$1\,1/2$
	f_{2j}		0	54	—	72
			y_1	x_4	y_2	x_2
3	x_1	1	$1/3$	$1/2$	$-1\,2/3$	$2/3$
	x_3	$1\,1/2$	0	$1/4$	$1/2$	0
	f	84	3	-2	10	-2
	f_{3j}		75	—	54	—

which is entered in the new row f_{0j}. For y_2 and x_2 we find in the same way $85\,1/2$ and 87, which are written in the row f_{0j}. All solutions resulting from introduction of a nonbasic variable in Tableau 0 can easily be generated, but we shall first generate the solution with the highest value of the objective function. The largest number in the f_{0j}-row is 87, which occurs in the x_2-column, so that x_2 becomes a basic variable replacing x_4. The result is Tableau 1, which, as computed before, has an f-value of 87.

In this tableau the effects of introducing nonbasic variables are investigated as in Tableau 0. We find that if y_1, x_1, and y_2 are made basic variables, the corresponding values of the objective function are 75, 84, and 72, respectively. If x_4 is made basic in Tableau 1, the objective function increases, so that a new solution must be found with a higher value of the objective function if at least the value of the leaving basic varaible was positive. But it can be shown that such a solution should have been found before; it is easily seen that if x_4 is made basic in Tableau 1, Tableau 0 is found back. Hence it is not necessary to go into the possibility of the introduction into the basis of nonbasic variables with a negative element in the f-row; for this reason nothing is entered in the f_{0j}-element of x_4.

Apart from the optimal solution one near-optimal solution was generated. The next near-optimal solution is found by taking the maximum element in the f_{0j}-row in Tableau 0 and the f_{1j}-row in Tableau 1, excluding the values whose corresponding solutions have already been generated, such as in this case 87 in the x_2-column in Tableau 0; this maximum should be above the lower limit on f of 80. The maximum we find is $85^1/_2$, in the y_2-row of Tableau 2. The corresponding solution is generated by making y_2 basic, replacing x_3; using $1^1/_3$ as a pivot, Tableau 2 is found, for which the f_{2j}-row is generated as described before.

The solution to be generated next is determined by taking the maximum of the elements in the additional rows of Tableaux 0, 1, and 2, excluding the elements corresponding to solutions which have been generated. This maximum is 84 which occurs both in the x_1-column of Tableau 0 and in the x_1-row of Tableau 1. On closer inspection it is found that the same solution is generated if x_1 enters the basis in Tableau 0 or if it enters the basis in Tableau 1. Hence the next tableau may be generated by pivoting on the element 2 in Tableau 0 or the element $1^1/_2$ in Tableau 1. The result is in any case Tableau 3, for which the additional row with values of f for solutions to be generated from this tableau are found as described before.

In order to find the next solution we compare all elements in the last row of all tableaux generated so far, excluding elements corresponding to other solutions generated before. The maximum element found in this manner is 75, which occurs in the y_1-column in Tableaux 0, 1, and 3. Since 75 is less than the minimum required value of the objective function, 80, this solution, and solutions with lower values of f, should not be considered.

But it is not necessary to increase nonbasic variables so much that one of the basic variables becomes zero; of interest to us are solutions with an f-value of at least 80. If an increase of y_1 in Tableau 0 is considered, we have

Table 5
Summary of near-optimal solutions with $f \geq 80$

Solution	f	x_1	x_2	x_3	x_4	y_1	y_2
0	88	–	–	1	2	–	–
1	87	–	$1\frac{1}{2}$	$1\frac{1}{2}$	–	–	–
2	$85\frac{1}{2}$	–	–	–	$4\frac{1}{2}$	–	$\frac{3}{4}$
3	84	1	–	$1\frac{1}{2}$	–	–	–
4	80	–	–	$1\frac{4}{13}$	$1\frac{0}{13}$	$1\frac{11}{13}$	–
5	80	–	$\frac{7}{8}$	$1\frac{1}{2}$	–	$1\frac{3}{4}$	–
6	80	$\frac{5}{9}$	–	$1\frac{1}{2}$	–	$1\frac{1}{3}$	–
7	80	–	5	$\frac{4}{5}$	–	–	$1\frac{2}{5}$
8	80	–	–	–	$4\frac{4}{19}$	$1\frac{3}{19}$	$1\frac{7}{19}$
9	80	$1\frac{1}{21}$	–	–	$3\frac{5}{7}$	–	$1\frac{1}{7}$
10	80	–	$3\frac{2}{3}$	–	$2\frac{2}{3}$	–	$1\frac{2}{3}$
11	80	$1\frac{2}{3}$	–	$1\frac{3}{10}$	–	–	$\frac{2}{5}$

(4.1)
$$\begin{cases} 2 - \frac{2}{3}y_1 = x_4 \,, \\ 1 + \frac{1}{6}y_1 = x_3 \,, \\ 88 - 4\frac{1}{3}y_1 = f \,. \end{cases}$$

From the last equation it is found that $f = 80$ for $y_1 = 4/4\frac{1}{3} = \frac{12}{13}$. Hence another solution is found by substituting $y_1 = \frac{12}{13}$ in (4.1):

(4.2)
$$\begin{cases} \frac{10}{13} = x_4 \,, \\ 1\frac{4}{13} = x_3 \,, \\ 80 = f \,, \\ 1\frac{11}{13} = y_1 \,. \end{cases}$$

It is obvious that also the solutions obtained by substituting any value of y_1 between 0 and $\frac{12}{13}$ are near-optimal.

In the same manner near-optimal solutions may be generated from all elements in the last row of the tableaux which are less than 80. If y_1 were to replace x_2 as basic variable in Tableau 1, the same solution would be obtained as that resulting from a replacement of x_4 by y_1. But in this case y_1 can at most obtain a value for which $f = 80$; in this case another solution is obtained.

Similarly, solutions are found for an introduction of y_2 in Tableau 1, for an introduction of y_1, x_1, and x_2 in Tableau 2 and for an introduction of y_2 into the basis in Tableau 3. Table 5 gives a summary of all near-optimal solutions having at least an f-value of 80. As with alternative optimal solutions any weighted sum of the solutions with nonnegative weights adding to one is also a near-optimal solution.

Even in this extremely simple problem a large number of near-optimal solutions are found. In more realistic problems which are usually much larger, the number of near-optimal solutions will be very much larger, even if the deviation from the optimal value of the objective function is smaller. In most cases it will not be advisable to present management with such a large number of solutions, since it will require too much time to go through all of them. In order that the benefits of the analysis are not quite lost, it may be advisable in some cases to make a preselection according to some criteria of the solutions.

Exercises

1. Consider the minimum-cost cattlefeed problem.
   (a) By how much should the price of barley decrease in order that it should be included in the optimal feed? Answer the same question for oats.
   (b) For what price of the sesame flakes will it be no longer optimal to include it in the field? Answer the same question for groundnut meal.
   (c) For which required quantities of fat is a feed containing sesame flakes and groundnut meal optimal? Answer the same question for protein.
   (d) Find all near-optimal solutions of the minimum-cost cattlefeed problem with costs not exceeding 21.

2. A company can produce five products, using three production factors. Further data are as follows:

Production Factor	Available Quantity	Quantity Used per Product				
		A	B	C	D	E
R	10	1	2	1	0	1
S	24	1	0	1	3	2
T	20	1	2	2	2	2
Net Revenue per Unit		8	20	10	20	21

   (a) Determine the optimal production program.
   (b) Apply sensitivity analysis to the coefficients of the objective function.
   (c) Apply sensitivity analysis to the quantities available of the production factors.

(d) Assume that only production programs with at most two products are possible. Determine the optimal production program in this case by means of the reverse simplex metod.

3. Among all near-optimal solutions of Table 5 and their combinations, what are the best ones in terms of spare spinning capacity and spare weaving capacity? Are there near-optimal solutions with $f = 80$ such that the spare capacity of both spinning and weaving is at least 1000 units?

4. Answer the following questions for Problem 7 of Chapter 2.
   (a) Perform sensitivity analysis for the net revenues of wheat and cattle and indicate the nature of the solutions obtained when the revenues exceed the limits indicated.
   (b) Determine all solutions with a revenue greater than $36,000 and indicate the solution with the least labor involved.
   (c) Solve the second part of question (b) by means of direct minimization of labor with the constraint that profit should be at least $36,000.

5. In the textile production example, assume that the spinning capacity per unit of Yarn A and B is variable to some extent. For which values of spinning capacity required per unit of yarns A and B will production become profitable?

6. Perform a sensitivity analysis on the optimal solutions of Table 2 for the net revenues.

5. ANTI-CYCLING AND UPPER-BOUND METHODS

5.1. Degeneracy and the Anti-Cycling Method

In Chapter 2 it was shown that the value of the objective function increases in each iteration of the simplex method if no *degenerate solutions,* that is, solutions with basic variables having one or more zero values, occur. However, if degenerate solutions do occur, then if the leaving basic variable has a value zero, also the new basic variable has a value zero, so that the value of f remains unchanged. If the value of f stays the same in an iteration of the simplex method, there is the possibility that after a number of iterations of the simplex method without any change in the objective function, the same solution is found back again. Further application of the simplex method would then lead to another cycle of iterations, and so on. In this way the optimal solution of the problem is not found. In this case it is said that the simplex method *cycles.*

This would mean that the simplex method is not a completely dependable method for solving linear programming problems in which degeneracy occurs. Since linear programming problems arising in practice often have degenerate solutions, this could be a serious drawback for the simplex method. However, no case of cycling in practical applications of the simplex method is known. On the other hand, problems have been *constructed* in which an application of the simplex method leads to cycling.

However, a slight modification of the simplex method, which is in fact only an additional rule in case the choice of the leaving basic variable is not unique, can be shown to lead to the optimal solution of the problem at all times. It turns out that cycling can only occur if there are at least two basic variables with a value zero which correspond to the minimum ratio computed for the choice of the leaving basic variable.

Cycling and an example of its prevention by means of an anti-cycling method will be demonstrated using an example devised by Beale. Tableau 0 of Table 1 gives the setup tableau for the problem. x_1 is taken as the new basic variable. For the leaving basic variable, the following ratios are

Anti-cycling and upper-bound methods

Table 1
Example of cycling in the simplex method

Tableau	Basic Variables	Values Basic Variables	x_1	x_2	x_3	x_4
0	f	0	$-\frac{3}{4}$	20	$-\frac{1}{2}$	6
	y_1	0	$\frac{1}{4}$	-8	-1	9
	y_2	0	$\frac{1}{2}$	-12	$-\frac{1}{2}$	3
	y_3	1	0	0	1	0

Tableau	Basic Variables	Values Basic Variables	y_1	x_2	x_3	x_4
1	f	0	3	-4	$-3\frac{1}{2}$	33
	x_1	0	4	-32	-4	36
	y_2	0	-2	4	$1\frac{1}{2}$	-15
	y_3	1	0	0	1	0

Tableau	Basic Variables	Values Basic Variables	y_1	y_2	x_3	x_4
2	f	0	1	1	-2	18
	x_1	0	-12	8	8	-84
	x_2	0	$-\frac{1}{2}$	$\frac{1}{4}$	$\frac{3}{8}$	$-3\frac{3}{4}$
	y_3	1	0	0	1	0

Tableau	Basic Variables	Values Basic Variables	y_1	y_2	x_1	x_4
3	f	0	-2	3	$\frac{1}{4}$	-3
	x_3	0	$-1\frac{1}{2}$	1	$\frac{1}{8}$	$-10\frac{1}{2}$
	x_2	0	$\frac{1}{16}$	$-\frac{1}{8}$	$-\frac{3}{64}$	$\frac{3}{16}$
	y_3	1	$1\frac{1}{2}$	-1	$-\frac{1}{8}$	$10\frac{1}{2}$

Tableau	Basic Variables	Values Basic Variables	y_1	y_2	x_1	x_2
4	f	0	-1	1	$-\frac{1}{2}$	16
	x_3	0	2	-6	$-2\frac{1}{2}$	56
	x_4	0	$\frac{1}{3}$	$-\frac{2}{3}$	$-\frac{1}{4}$	$5\frac{1}{3}$
	y_3	1	-2	6	$2\frac{1}{2}$	-56

Tableau	Basic Variables	Values Basic Variables	x_3	y_2	x_1	x_2
5	f	0	$\frac{1}{2}$	-2	$-1\frac{3}{4}$	44
	y_1	0	$\frac{1}{2}$	-3	$-1\frac{1}{4}$	28
	x_4	0	$-\frac{1}{6}$	$\frac{1}{3}$	$\frac{1}{6}$	-4
	y_3	1	1	0	0	0

Table 1 (continued)

			y_2	x_1	x_3	x_4
	f	0	$1\frac{1}{2}$	2	$-1\frac{1}{4}$	$10\frac{1}{2}$
	y_1	0	$-\frac{1}{2}$	-2	$-\frac{3}{4}$	$7\frac{1}{2}$
1a	x_1	0	2	-24	-1	6
	y_3	1	0	0	$\underline{1}$	0

			y_2	x_2	y_3	x_4
	f	$1\frac{1}{4}$	$1\frac{1}{2}$	2	$1\frac{1}{4}$	$10\frac{1}{2}$
	y_1	$\frac{3}{4}$	$-\frac{1}{2}$	-2	$\frac{3}{4}$	$7\frac{1}{2}$
2a	x_1	1	2	-24	1	6
	x_3	1	0	0	1	0

compared:

$$\frac{0}{\frac{1}{4}}, \quad \frac{0}{\frac{1}{2}},$$

which belong to y_1 and y_2, respectively. Since there is no unique choice, the first variable, y_1, is taken as the leaving basic variable. This results in Tableau 1, which has the same value of f as Tableau 0. In Tableau 1, x_2 is taken as the new basic variable and y_2 is the unique choice for the leaving basic variable; since this variable has a zero value, the value of f remains the same. In Tableau 2, x_3 is the new basic variable; the leaving basic variable is determined using the ratios

$$\frac{0}{8}, \quad \frac{0}{\frac{3}{8}},$$

which belong to x_1 and x_2. Again the first variable, x_1, is chosen. In Tableau 3, x_4 is taken as the new basic variable and x_2 is the unique choice for the leaving basic variable. In Tableau 4, y_2 should enter the basis and x_4 is the unique choice for the leaving basic variable. Then the solution of Tableau 0 is found back, completing the cycle.

Such cycling can be avoided by what is called a *perturbation* procedure. In the initial tableau of the general linear programming problem, the values of basic variables are slightly changed in the following manner:

$$(1.1) \quad \begin{cases} b_1 + \epsilon, \\ b_2 + \epsilon^2, \\ b_3 + \epsilon^3, \\ \vdots \\ b_m + \epsilon^m, \end{cases}$$

where ϵ is a small number. If ϵ is small, ϵ^2 is smaller by a factor ϵ, and ϵ^3 again smaller by a factor ϵ, and so on. In the example we would have for the values of basic variables in Tableau 0:

$$(1.2) \quad \begin{cases} f = 0, \\ y_1 = 0 + \epsilon, \\ y_2 = 0 + \epsilon^2, \\ y_3 = 1 + \epsilon^3. \end{cases}$$

Let us now find the leaving basic variable in Tableau 0, x_1 again being the new basic variable. Then the following ratios are compared:

$$\frac{\epsilon}{^1/_4}, \quad \frac{\epsilon^2}{^1/_2}.$$

Now the minimum ratio is unique, being $2\epsilon^2$, which belongs to y_2; hence y_2 leaves the basis. The objective function now increases in terms of ϵ; it is $1^1/_2 \epsilon^2$ in the next tableau.

All ϵ-terms may be written in separate columns in the simplex tableau; the values of basic variables then consist of $m + 1$ columns. In the case of (1.2), these columns of values of basic variables can be indicated in the simplex tableau as follows:

Basic Variables	Values Basic Variables			
	1	ϵ	ϵ^2	ϵ^3
f	0	0	0	0
y_1	0	1	0	0
y_2	0	0	1	0
y_3	1	0	0	1

It will be noted that the ϵ-columns are identical to the columns of the y-variables of Tableau 0, which were deleted there because they were basic variables. If the ϵ-columns are identical to the columns of the y-variables in

Tableau 0, they will remain so in subsequent tableaux. Hence the ϵ-columns do not have to be written down explicitly since the corresponding elements of the columns of the y-variables can be used.

If x_1 replaces y_2 in Tableau 0, Tableau 1a results. The values of basic variables in this tableau may be written as

$$(1.3) \quad \begin{cases} f = 0 + 1 + 1\frac{1}{2}\epsilon^2 \,, \\ y_1 = 0 + \epsilon - \frac{1}{2}\epsilon^2 \,, \\ x_1 = 0 + 2\epsilon^2 \,, \\ y_3 = 1 + \epsilon^3 \,. \end{cases}$$

In Tableau 1a, the new basic variable is x_3. Since only one positive element appears in the x_3-column, the choice of the leaving basic variable is unique. If y_3 leaves the basic Tableau 2a is found, which contains the optimal solution, having a higher value of f than any of the solutions involved in the cycling. The ϵ-terms can, of course, now be ignored.

The perturbation procedure can be summarized as follows. If there is any tie when determining the leaving basic variable, then replace the values of basic variables in tied rows by the corresponding elements in the columns of y_1. If there are still ties, replace the elements in tied rows by the corresponding elements of the column of y_2, and so on.

It can be proved that, if this procedure is followed, the objective function increases in each iteration at least in terms of ϵ, so that the same solution cannot reappear in the course of an application of the simplex method. The perturbation procedure, which was originally developed by Charnes [2] in a slightly different way, is sometimes called *lexicographic ordering* which is due to a different interpretation of the same procedure.

5.2. The Simplex Method for Problems with Upper-Bound Constraints

In linear programming problems, constraints of the following type frequently occur:

$$(2.1) \quad x_j \leqq d_j \,,$$

d_j is called the *upper bound* of x_j. These constraints may be treated as ordinary constraints; however, the corresponding row of the set-up tableau has a very simple structure since it consists of zero elements apart from the elements in the constant-term column, the columns of x_j and the slack variable.

Due to the simplicity of such constraints, it is possible to deal with them without having rows in the tableaux for any of the *upper-bound constraints* which reduces the size of the tableau considerably; furthermore, as we shall see, it reduces the number of tableaux.

Suppose we have the following system with a basic feasible solution.

$$(2.2) \quad \begin{cases} f_1 = p_1 x_1 + p_2 x_2 & + f, \\ b_1 = a_{11} x_1 + a_{12} x_2 + x_3, \\ b_2 = a_{21} x_1 + a_{22} x_2 & + x_4. \end{cases}$$

We assume that the variables x_1, x_2, x_3, and x_4 have upper bounds of d_1, d_2, d_3, and d_4, but that the values of x_3 and x_4 in (2.2), b_1 and b_2 are not exceeding the upper bounds d_3 and d_4, so that the basic solution of (2.2) is also feasible for the upper-bound constraints.

According to the rules of the ordinary simplex method for a maximization problem, the nonbasic variable with the most negative element in the objective function row is introduced into the basis; let this be x_1. Hence x_1 should be increased from zero to a positive value. The system (2.2) may therefore be written as

$$(2.3) \quad \begin{cases} f_0 - p_1 x_1 = f, \\ b_1 - a_{11} x_1 = x_3, \\ b_2 - a_{21} x_1 = x_4. \end{cases}$$

The maximum value which x_1 can take is in the ordinary simplex method determined by

$$(2.4) \qquad x_1 = \min_i \left(\frac{b_i}{a_{i1}} \mid a_{i1} > 0 \right),$$

but now we should also take into account the upper bound of x_1 which is d_1; for the moment we disregard the other upper bounds. Hence the maximum value of x_1 is determined by

$$(2.5) \qquad x_1 = \min_i \left(\frac{b_i}{a_{i1}} \mid a_{i1} > 0, d_1 \right).$$

If the minimum is not connected with d_1, the system is transformed as usual with either a_{11} or a_{21} as a pivot.

In case the minimum is equal to d_1, x_1 should in the next iteration become equal to d_1. This can be done by keeping x_1 as a nonbasic variable, but putting it at a constant value d_1. Let us measure x_1 as a deviation from d_1.

This amounts to replacing x_1 by x_1^* which is defined as

(2.6) $\qquad x_1^* = x_1 - d_1 .$

Note that $x_1^* = 0$ for $x_1 = d_1$. We may substitute for x_1 in (2.2) according to (2.6). The result is

(2.7) $\qquad \begin{cases} f_0 - p_1 d_1 = p_1 x_1^* + p_2 x_2 & + f, \\ b_1 - a_{11} d_1 = a_{11} x_1^* + a_{12} x_2 + x_3 , \\ b_2 - a_{21} d_1 = a_{21} x_1^* + a_{22} x_2 \quad + x_4 , \end{cases}$

The only difference with (2.2), apart from having x_1^* instead of x_1, is that d_1 times the coefficient of x_1 is subtracted from the values of the basic variables. The values of basic variables are still nonnegative since they may be written as

(2.8) $\qquad a_{i1} \left(\dfrac{b_i}{a_{i1}} - d_1 \right) ,$

which is nonnegative for $a_{i1} > 0$ since d_1 was the minimum in (2.5) and which is also nonnegative for $a_{i1} < 0$.

The variable x_1^* differs from other nonbasic variables since it can be *decreased* but not increased; any increase would mean that x_1 would exceed its upper bound. The lower bound for a decrease of x_1^* is of course $-d_1$. The relation between x_1 and x_1^* may conveniently be indicated by the following figure:

the full line indicates the feasible range of both variables.

Starred variables like x_1^* are eligible as new basic variables. Let us consider a general system as (2.2) with x_1^* instead of x_1:

(2.9) $\qquad \begin{cases} f_0 = p_1 x_1^* + p_2 x_2 & + f , \\ b_1 = a_{11} x_1^* + a_{12} x_2 + x_3 , \\ b_2 = a_{21} x_1^* + a_{22} x_2 \quad + x_4 . \end{cases}$

If x_1^* is considered as a new basic variable we write

(2.10)
$$\begin{cases} f_0 - p_1 x_1^* = f, \\ b_1 - a_{11} x_1^* = x_3, \\ b_2 - a_{21} x_1^* = x_4. \end{cases}$$

Since x_1^* is decreased, the objective function increases for $p_1 > 0$. Hence starred nonbasic variables should have positive elements in the last row to be eligible as the new basic variable. Let us assume that $p_1 > 0$ and that x_1^* is selected as the new basic variable. Since x_1^* is decreased, x_3 increases if $a_{11} > 0$, but it decreases if $a_{11} < 0$. Only in the latter case it becomes zero and may become negative. Hence we should in this case determine the leaving basic variable as follows:

(2.11)
$$\min_i \left(\frac{b_i}{-a_{i1}} \mid a_{i1} < 0, d_1 \right).$$

If d_1 is the minimum, x_1^* reaches its lower bound, which means that $x_1 = 0$; hence x_1^* may be replaced by x_1 as nonbasic variable by substituting in (2.9), according to (2.6):

(2.12)
$$\begin{cases} f_0 + p_1 d_1 = p_1 x_1 + p_2 x_2 \qquad\quad + f, \\ b_1 + a_{11} d_1 = a_{11} x_1 + a_{12} x_2 + x_3, \\ b_2 + a_{21} d_1 = a_{21} x_1 + a_{22} x_2 \qquad + x_4. \end{cases}$$

This means that apart from deleting the star from x_1, we should add the coefficients of the column of x_1^* multiplied by d_1 to the values of basic variables.

If the minimum in (2.11) is not d_1, but, say, $b_1/-a_{11}$, the system is transformed with a_{11} as a pivot. The values of basic variables are after this transformation:

(2.13)
$$\begin{cases} f_0 - p_1 a_{11}^{-1} b_1 = (p_2 - p_1 a_{11}^{-1} a_{12}) x_2 - p_1 a_{11}^{-1} x_3, \\ a_{11}^{-1} b_1 = x_1^* + a_{11}^{-1} a_{12} x_2 + a_{11}^{-1} x_3, \\ b_2 - a_{21} a_{11}^{-1} b_1 = (a_{22} - a_{21} a_{11}^{-1} a_{12}) x_2 - a_{21} a_{11}^{-1} x_3 + x_4. \end{cases}$$

Since $a_{11} < 0$, x_1^* is negative, but it exceeds its lower bound $-d_1$ since $b_1/-a_{11} \leqq d_1$. It is now convenient to replace in (2.13) x_1^* by x_1 which is done by substituting for x_1^* according to (2.6); the second equation of (2.13)

if $k \in S$, select the row connected with

$$(2.24) \qquad \min_{i} \begin{cases} \text{(iv)} & \dfrac{b_i}{-a_{ik}} \mid a_{ik} < 0 , \\[3mm] \text{(v)} & \dfrac{d_i - b_i}{a_{ik}} \mid a_{ik} > 0 , \; i \in U , \\[3mm] \text{(vi)} & d_k \mid k \in U . \end{cases}$$

Let the row connected with the minimum in other cases than (iii) and (vi) be the r-th row.

TRANSFORMATION OF THE TABLEAU.

Case (i): Transform the tableau with a_{rk} as a pivot.

Case (ii): Subtract d_r from b_r, transform with a_{rk} as a pivot and include the column of the leaving basic variable in S.

Case (iii): Subtract $a_{ik}d_k$ from b_i for all rows; include k in S.

Case (iv): Transform with a_{rk} as a pivot and add d_k to the value of the new basic variable. Include the row of the new basic variable in N.

Case (v): Subtract d_r from b_r; transform with a_{ik} as a pivot and add d_k to the value of the new basic variable. Include the row of the new basic variable in N and the column of the leaving basic variable in S.

Case (vi): Add $a_{ik}d_k$ to b_i for all rows. Include k in N.

As an example of application of the upper-bound technique, the following problem, which can be interpreted as a variant of the production planning problem of Chapter 2, page 40, is used. Maximize

$$(2.25) \qquad f = 2\tfrac{1}{2} x_1 + \tfrac{1}{2} x_2 + 2x_3 + 2x_4$$

subject to

$$(2.26) \qquad \begin{cases} 4x_1 + x_2 + 2x_3 & \leqq 100 , \\ x_1 \quad\;\; + x_3 + 2x_4 \leqq 40 , \\ \tfrac{1}{2}x_1 \quad\;\; + x_3 + 2x_4 \leqq 60 , \end{cases}$$

$$(2.27) \qquad 0 \leqq x_j \leqq 15 , \quad j = 1, 2, 3, 4 .$$

The set-up tableau is Tableau 0 of Table 2, in which the second and third columns of the values of basic variables and the stars attached to x_1 and x_3 should for a moment be disregarded. The solution of this tableau is feasible,

Table 2
An application of the upper-bound technique

Tableau	Basic Variables	Values Basic Variables			x_1^*	x_2	x_3^*	x_4
0	f	0	$37\frac{1}{2}$	$67\frac{1}{2}$	$-2\frac{1}{2}$	$-\frac{1}{2}$	-2	-2
	y_1	100	40	10	4	1	2	0
	y_2	40	25	10	1	0	1	$\underline{\frac{2}{2}}$
	y_3	60	$52\frac{1}{2}$	$37\frac{1}{2}$	$\frac{1}{2}$	0	1	2
					x_1^*	x_2	x_3^*	y_2
1	f	$77\frac{1}{2}$			$-1\frac{1}{2}$	$-\frac{1}{2}$	-1	1
	y_1	10			4	$\underline{1}$	2	0
	x_4	5			$\frac{1}{2}$	0	$\frac{1}{2}$	$\frac{1}{2}$
	y_3	$27\frac{1}{2}$			$-\frac{1}{2}$	0	0	-1
					x_1^*	y_1	x_3^*	y_2
2	f	$82\frac{1}{2}$			$\frac{1}{2}$	$\frac{1}{2}$	0	1
	x_2	10 (−5)			$\underline{4}$	1	2	0
	x_4	5			$\frac{1}{2}$	0	$\frac{1}{2}$	$\frac{1}{2}$
	y_3	$27\frac{1}{2}$			$-\frac{1}{2}$	0	0	-1
					x_2^*	y_1	x_3^*	y_2
3	f	$83\frac{1}{8}$			$-\frac{1}{8}$	$\frac{3}{8}$	$-\frac{1}{4}$	1
	x_1	$(-1\frac{1}{4})$ $13\frac{3}{4}$			$\frac{1}{4}$	$\frac{1}{4}$	$\frac{1}{2}$	0
	x_5	$5\frac{5}{8}$			$-\frac{1}{8}$	$-\frac{1}{8}$	$\frac{1}{4}$	$\frac{1}{2}$
	y_3	$26\frac{7}{8}$			$\frac{1}{8}$	$\frac{1}{8}$	$\frac{1}{4}$	-1

so that it can be used as an initial solution. Since initially there are no starred variables, we take for the new basic variable simply the variable with the most negative coefficient in the last row, which is x_1. For the selection of the leaving basic variable, we compare the ratios

$$\frac{100}{4}, \quad \frac{40}{1}, \quad \frac{60}{\frac{1}{2}},$$

with the upper bound of x_1, which is 15; this upper bound is the minimum so that x_1 should be put at its upper bound. This is done by subtracting from the values of basic variables 15 times the x_1-column; the result is the second column of values of basic variables of Tableau 0; the nonbasic variable x_1 is given a star to indicate that it has reached its upper bound.

The next new basic variable is selected by comparing in the last row negative elements for columns of nonstarred variables and positive elements for starred variables; x_3 is then selected as the new basic variable. Since none of the basic variables has an upper bound we compare

$$\frac{40}{2}, \quad \frac{25}{1}, \quad \frac{52\frac{1}{2}}{1}$$

with the upper bound of x_3, 15. Again the upper bound is the minimum and x_3 is put at its upper bound by subtracting from the values of basic variables 15 times the column of x_3; the result is the third column of values of basic variables; to x_3 a star is attached.

The next variable selected to come into the basis is x_4. The leaving basic variable is determined by comparing

$$\frac{10}{2}, \quad \frac{37\frac{1}{2}}{2}$$

with the upper bound of x_4, which is 15. It is found that y_2 leaves the basis. Since case (i) applies, Tableau 0 can be transformed into Tableau 1 without any adjustment.

In Tableau 1, x_2 is the only variable eligible for new basic variable and y_1 is the variable leaving the basis since $10 < 15$. Again Case (i) applies; transforming the tableau, Tableau 2 is generated. The variable to enter the basis is now x_1^*, a variable put at its upper bound. To find the leaving basic variable, we should compare according to (2.24)

(iv) $\quad \dfrac{27\frac{1}{2}}{-(-\frac{1}{2})},$

(v) $\quad \dfrac{15-10}{4}, \quad \dfrac{15-5}{\frac{1}{2}},$

(vi) $\quad 15$.

The minimum ratio $1\frac{1}{4}$, occurs in (v) and is connected with x_2. Hence x_2 is the leaving basic variable; this variable is put at its upper bound. Before transforming Tableau 2, we subtract 15 from the value of x_2; the result, -5, is indicated within brackets. After that, a simplex transformation follows, which results in Tableau 3. The value of x_1 in this tableau is indicated within brackets, since we should adjust it for the fact that x_1 is no longer at its upper bound, which is done by adding 15 to it. Tableau 3 is found to be the optimal tableau.

In some problems variables occur with lower bounds:

(2.28) $x_j \geq c_j$.

These lower bounds usually occur in combination with upper bounds:

(2.29) $c_j \leq x_j \leq d_j$,

so that x_j is restrained to the range of values between c_j and d_j. Lower bounds can be treated by simply measuring the variable concerned from its lower bound. We define a new variable $\bar{x}_j$

(2.30) $\bar{x}_j = x_j - c_j$

which should be nonnegative, (2.30) should be substituted into the equation system; the upper bound for $\bar{x}_j$ is now $d_j - c_j$. If x_1 in the system (2.2) would have lower and upper bounds as in (2.29), it would be reformulated as

(2.31) $\left\{ \begin{array}{l} f_0 - p_1 c_1 = p_1 \bar{x}_1 + p_2 y_2 + f \\ b_1 - a_{11} c_1 = a_{11} \bar{x}_1 + a_{12} x_1 \quad + x_3 , \\ b_2 - a_{21} c_1 = a_{21} \bar{x}_1 + a_{22} x_2 \quad\quad + x_4 . \end{array} \right.$

For $\bar{x}_1$ we now have

(2.32) $0 \leq \bar{x}_1 \leq d_j - c_j$.

In this manner problems with lower bounds on some variables may be reformulated as problems without these bounds.

5.3. An Application: Upper Bounds for Sales

In Chapter 2 the production planning example was kept as simple as possible in order to focus on the technique of the simplex method. In this section this example will be somewhat generalized, which will allow us to apply the upper-bound technique.

The assumption that any quantity produced of a certain commodity can be sold at a given price is not realistic in many cases. Usually, there will be a maximum quantity which can be sold at a given price. We shall consider a variant of the production planning example used previously, in which these maximum quantities are given for the same prices as used before.

Let the maximum quantity to be sold of Yarn A be 1,000 units, that of Yarn B 800 units, that of Fabric A 1,000 units and that of Fabric B 1,500 units. Since in static one-period models without inventory it will never be

Table 3
The textile production example with sales constraints

Tableau	Basic Variables	Upper Bounds	Values Basic Variables			Nonbasic Variables			
						x_1	x_2	x_3^*	x_4^*
			(1)	(2)	(3)	1,000	800	1,000	1,500
0	f	–	0	50,000	78,500	−9	−8	−50	−19
	y_1	–	18,000	8,000	2,000	<u>3</u>	2	10	4
	y_2	–	3,000	1,000	250	0	0	2	$\frac{1}{2}$
						y_1	x_2^*	x_3^*	x_4^*
			(1)	(2)		–	800	1,000	1,500
1	f	–	84,500	86,100		3	−2	−20	−7
	x_1	1,000	$666^2/_3$	$133^1/_3$		$^1/_3$	$^2/_3$	$3^1/_3$	$1^1/_3$
	y_2	–	250	250		0	0	2	$\frac{1}{2}$

profitable to produce a quantity of any good without selling it, because direct costs never are negative, the following upper-bound constraints may be imposed on the quantities to be produced, x_1, x_2, x_3 and x_4:

$$x_1 \leqq 1{,}000 \,,$$

$$x_2 \leqq \ \ 800 \,,$$

$$x_3 \leqq 1{,}000 \,,$$

$$x_4 \leqq 1{,}500 \,.$$

This problem is solved in Table 3. In Tableau 0, first x_3 and then x_4 are put at their upper bounds, see solutions (2) and (3) of Tableau 0. Then x_1 enters the basis, replacing y_1. Tableau 1, x_2 is put at its upper bound, giving the optimal solutions to the problem indicated by (2).

The value of f is $86,100, against $88,000 in the case without upper bounds, which is easily explained by the presence of the additional constraints. The variables x_2, x_3, and x_4 are at their upper bounds. $y_2 = 250$, so that 250 hours of loom capacity are unused. It is interesting to look at the imputed costs. For spinning capacity, we find $3, which is less than before. The imputed costs of loom capacity are zero. For the imputed costs of the upper bounds on x_2, x_3, and x_4 we find 2, 20, and 7, respectively. This means that any sales of Yarn B, Fabric A or Fabric B will yield an additional revenue of $2, $20, or $7, respectively. This obviously has implications for the marketing of these products. If by means of extra sales promotion it is possible to increase the maximum sales of Fabric A by one additional unit, and the costs of the sales promotion are less than $20, it is advantageous to have the extra sales promotion.

The extra sales promotion could consist of price discounts or extra advertising. Price discounts should of course be limited to the marginal buyers because if they were applied to all sales, profits could drop considerably. It is of course possible to use straight price cuts, but in many cases the reaction of total sales to price changes is difficult to forecast. If the relation between prices and total sales for the different products is known, linear programming may be used for each combination of prices and sales. Alternatively, depending on the form of the demand curve, quadratic or nonlinear programming may be used, subjects which are not treated here.

Also, in case additional sales are generated by extra advertising, it will not be possible to forecast accurately what the results will be, nor will it be possible to generate exactly the desired amount of additional sales. Probably the best approach is to apply linear programming for each alternative advertising campaign and to select the one with the highest profit. The values of the shadow prices provide at least a valuable indication in which direction higher profits are likely to be found.

Exercises

1. Consider Tableau 1 of Table 1 as the set-up tableau of a problem with basic variables $y_1^* = x_1$, $y_2^* = y_2$, $y_3^* = y_3$ and nonbasic variables $x_1^* = y_1$, $x_2^* = x_2$, $x_3^* = x_3$, $x_4^* = x_4$. Solve the problem using the anti-cycling technique.

2. Formulate the dual problem of the problem given by Tableau 0 of Table 1 and perturb the coefficients of the objective function in the same way as the constant terms were perturbed for the primal problem. Then apply the dual method using these perturbed coefficients. Develop general rules for an anti-cycling procedure in the dual method.

3. Solve the cattlefeed problem with the additional constraints that at most $1/4$ unit of sesame flakes and $1/4$ unit of groundnut meal may be given to the animal in one day.

4. A company produces the products A, B, and C, using production factors I

and II of which the quantities available per period are 6750 and 4000 units respectively. A, B and C use 3, 6, and 2 units of production factor I, respectively, and 1, 2 and 2 units of production factor II, respectively. Maximum sales per period of A, B and C are 1000, 500 and 1500 units per period. Net revenues for A, B and C are \$4, \$12, and \$3 per unit.

(a) Find the optimal production program using upper-bound methods.

(b) Interpret the elements in the f-row.

(c) Find the optimal solution in the case that in addition to the above it is required that the minimum sales of A, B, and C have to be 500, 250, and 500 units.

5. Solve the following problem using upper-bound methods. Maximize

$$2\tfrac{1}{2}x_1 + 7x_2 + 12x_3 + 10x_4$$

subject to

$$x_1 + 6x_2 + 12x_3 + 8x_4 \leqq 21\tfrac{1}{2},$$
$$2x_1 + 2x_2 + 12x_3 + 4x_4 \leqq 14,$$
$$\tfrac{1}{2} \leqq x_1, x_2, x_3, x_4 \leqq 1\tfrac{1}{2}.$$

If there is a choice between a full iteration and an upper-bounding, then prefer the latter. If in other respects the choice of the leaving basic variable is not unique, then follow the anti-cycling rule, explaining your choice and indicating how the objective function has increased.

6. PARAMETRIC PROGRAMMING

6.1. Programming with a Parametric Objective Function

Frequently a number of linear programming problems have to be solved which are the same apart from one or a few coefficients. For instance, it may be that the production planning problem should be solved for different prices of some basic raw material or for different labour costs. Let us assume in the example for which data are given in Table 1 of Chapter 2, that labour costs for Yarn A and B are both $1 per unit, for Fabric A, $15 per unit, and for Fabric B, $8 per unit. But the general wage level may rise to a smaller or larger extent. If the general labour costs index is given by λ, labour costs for the four products are λ, λ, 15λ, and 8λ, respectively. If it is assumed that other direct costs and selling prices remain the same and that $\lambda = 1$ in Table 1, net revenue per unit is for Yarn A: $12 - (3 - 1) - \lambda = 10 - \lambda$; for Yarn B: $10 - (2 - 1) - \lambda = 9 - \lambda$; for Fabric A: $75 - (25 - 15) - 15\lambda = 65 - 15\lambda$; and for Fabric B: $29 - (10 - 8) - 8\lambda = 27 - 8\lambda$. The objective function can therefore be formulated as

$$(1.1) \qquad f = (10 - \lambda)x_1 + (9 - \lambda)x_2 + (65 - 15\lambda)x_3 + (27 - 8\lambda)x_4 .$$

The constraints of the problem have remained the same. In this case all optimal solutions will be found for $0 \leqq \lambda \leqq \infty$; in most cases the range of values of λ for which the solutions are required will be much narrower.

The function (1.1) is a linear function in the unknowns x_1, x_2, x_3, and x_4. The coefficients of these unknowns are not fixed but are dependent on a variable parameter λ. In parametric programming, the coefficients which are fixed in ordinary linear programming are dependent on a parameter for which a range of values is considered; then optimal solutions should be found for these values of the parameter.

The objective function (1.1) will be used to explain programming with a *parametric objective function*. It is also possible that one or more of the constant terms of the constraints vary parametrically; for instance, in the production planning problem the available capacity of a certain kind may vary and in the feed-mixing problem it may be that solutions are required for a range of values of protein or fat requirements. For this, a procedure for programming with *parametric constant terms* is developed which is explained in the next section.

The procedure given in the first two sections deal with cases in which only one parameter occurs in the coefficients of the objective function or the constant terms of the constraints. Cases in which more parameters occur in these coefficients, for instance a case in which both costs of a raw material and labour costs are varied parametrically, are much more complicated, though it is always possible to solve such problems by finding solutions for specific values of the parameters. It is also possible to vary parametrically the coefficients of the variables in the constraints, but again this procedure is rather complicated, so that we shall nto deal with it here.

In the last section of this chapter the *primal-dual method* is treated in which parametric programming is used as a means for solving ordinary linear programming problems; it is in fact an alternative for the dual method. The primal-dual method turns out to be especially useful for transportation problems which are linear programming problems of a certain type and which will be treated in Chapter 12.

Let us put (1.1), together with the constraints of the production planning problem, in a simplex tableau format; for (1.1), two rows are used, the first of which is indicated by f_c, and contains only the coefficients without λ, and the second of which, indicated by f_λ, indicates the coefficients of λ times the x-variables. The result is Tableau 00 of Table 1.

We start by generating a solution which is optimal for $\lambda = 0$; this is done by using the f_c-row as the objective function row and ignoring the f_λ-row since λ is zero. The simplex method is applied as usual and after three iterations Tableau 0 is obtained which contains the optimal solution for $\lambda = 0$. In these iterations the f_λ-row is transformed just as the other rows.

The coefficient of x_1 in the equation of the objective function for Tableau 0 may be written as

$$10\tfrac{1}{4} - 5\lambda .$$

This coefficient is positive for $\lambda < 2\tfrac{1}{20}$, it is zero for $\lambda = 2\tfrac{1}{20}$, and it is negative for $\lambda > 2\tfrac{1}{20}$. This means that for $\lambda > 2\tfrac{1}{20}$, the solution of Tableau 0 will not be optimal in any case. Similarly, the coefficient of x_2 in the equation of the objective function for Tableau 0 may be written as

$$4\tfrac{1}{2} - 3\lambda ,$$

Parametric programming

Table 1
Example of programming with a parametric objective function

Tableau	Basic Variable	Values Basic Variables	x_1	x_2	x_3	x_4
00	f_c	0	-10	-9	-65	-27
	f_λ	0	1	1	15	8
	y_1	18	3	2	10	4
	y_2	3	0	0	$\underline{2}$	$\frac{1}{2}$
			x_1	x_2	y_2	x_4
01	f_c	$99\frac{1}{2}$	-10	-9	$32\frac{1}{2}$	$-10\frac{3}{4}$
	f_λ	$-22\frac{1}{2}$	1	1	$-7\frac{1}{2}$	$4\frac{1}{4}$
	y_1	3	3	2	-5	$1\frac{1}{2}$
	x_3	$1\frac{1}{2}$	0	0	$\frac{1}{2}$	$\underline{\frac{1}{4}}$
			x_1	x_2	y_2	y_1
02	f_c	119	$11\frac{1}{2}$	$5\frac{1}{3}$	$-3\frac{1}{3}$	$7\frac{1}{6}$
	f_λ	-31	$-7\frac{1}{2}$	$-4\frac{2}{3}$	$6\frac{2}{3}$	$-2\frac{5}{6}$
	x_4	2	2	$1\frac{1}{3}$	$-3\frac{1}{3}$	$\frac{2}{3}$
	x_3	1	$-\frac{1}{2}$	$-\frac{1}{3}$	$\underline{1\frac{1}{3}}$	$-\frac{1}{6}$
			x_1	x_2	x_3	y_1
0	f_c	$121\frac{1}{2}$	$10\frac{1}{4}$	$4\frac{1}{2}$	$2\frac{1}{2}$	$6\frac{3}{4}$
	f_λ	-36	-5	-3	-5	-2
	x_4	$4\frac{1}{2}$	$\frac{3}{4}$	$\frac{1}{2}$	$2\frac{1}{2}$	$\frac{1}{4}$
	y_2	$\frac{3}{4}$	$-\frac{3}{8}$	$-\frac{1}{4}$	$\underline{\frac{3}{4}}$	$-\frac{1}{8}$
			x_1	x_2	y_2	y_1
1	f_c	119	$11\frac{1}{2}$	$5\frac{1}{3}$	$-3\frac{1}{3}$	$7\frac{1}{6}$
	f_λ	-31	$-7\frac{1}{2}$	$-4\frac{2}{3}$	$6\frac{2}{3}$	$-2\frac{5}{6}$
	x_4	2	2	$1\frac{1}{3}$	$-3\frac{1}{3}$	$\frac{2}{3}$
	x_3	1	$-\frac{1}{2}$	$\underline{-\frac{1}{3}}$	$\underline{1\frac{1}{3}}$	$-\frac{1}{6}$

Table 1 (continued)

Tableau	Basic Variables	Values Basic Variables	x_1	x_4	y_2	y_1
2	f_c	111	$3\frac{1}{2}$	-4	10	$4\frac{1}{2}$
	f_λ	-24	$-\frac{1}{2}$	$3\frac{1}{2}$	-5	$-\frac{1}{2}$
	x_2	$1\frac{1}{2}$	$1\frac{1}{2}$	$\frac{3}{4}$	$-2\frac{1}{2}$	$\frac{1}{2}$
	x_3	$1\frac{1}{2}$	0	$\frac{7}{4}$	$\frac{1}{2}$	0

			x_1	x_4	x_3	y_1
3	f_c	81	$3\frac{1}{2}$	-9	-20	$4\frac{1}{2}$
	f_λ	-9	$-\frac{1}{2}$	6	10	$-\frac{1}{2}$
	x_2	9	$1\frac{1}{2}$	2	5	$\frac{1}{2}$
	y_2	3	0	$\frac{1}{2}$	2	0

			x_2	x_4	x_3	y_1
4	f_c	60	$-2\frac{1}{3}$	$-13\frac{2}{3}$	$-31\frac{2}{3}$	$3\frac{1}{3}$
	f_λ	-6	$\frac{1}{3}$	$6\frac{2}{3}$	$11\frac{2}{3}$	$-\frac{1}{3}$
	x_1	6	$\frac{2}{3}$	$1\frac{1}{3}$	$3\frac{1}{3}$	$\frac{1}{3}$
	y_2	3	0	$\frac{1}{2}$	2	0

			x_2	x_4	x_3	x_1
5	f_c	0	-9	-27	-65	-10
	f_λ	0	1	8	15	1
	y_1	18	2	4	10	3
	y_2	3	0	$\frac{1}{2}$	2	0

which means that the solution cannot be optimal for $\lambda > 1\frac{1}{2}$. In the same way we find from the coefficients of x_3 and y_1 in the equation of the objective function for Tableau 0 that the solution cannot be optimal for $\lambda > \frac{1}{2}$ and $\lambda > 3\frac{3}{8}$. From this it is concluded that the tableau is optimal for $0 \leqq \lambda \leqq \frac{1}{2}$ and not optimal for $\lambda > \frac{1}{2}$, because for this value of λ at least one coefficient in the objective function, that of x_3, is negative.

Having found the optimal solution for $0 \leqq \lambda \leqq \frac{1}{2}$, we should find optimal solutions for a higher range of values of λ. This is done by introducing into the basis the variable whose coefficient in the objective function becomes negative first if λ is increased. This is x_3. The leaving basic variable is determined as in the simplex method because the solution should remain feasible. It is found that y_2 leaves the basis. The tableau is transformed with $\frac{3}{4}$ as the pivot, which results in Tableau 1. This new tableau is optimal for $\lambda = \frac{1}{2}$ since for this value of λ the coefficient of x_3 in the objective function row in Tableau 0 is zero. Since this is an element of the pivot column, the elements in its row do not change in the transformation. Because these elements were nonnegative for $\lambda = \frac{1}{2}$ in Tableau 0, they should be nonnegative for $\lambda = \frac{1}{2}$ in Tableau 1.

In Tableau 1, the objective function equation can be written as

$$(1.2) \qquad 119 - 31\lambda = (11\tfrac{1}{2} - 7\tfrac{1}{2}\lambda)x_1 + (5\tfrac{1}{3} - 4\tfrac{2}{3}\lambda)x_2$$

$$+ (-3\tfrac{1}{3} + 6\tfrac{2}{3}\lambda)y_2 + (7\tfrac{1}{6} - 2\tfrac{5}{6}\lambda)y_1 + f.$$

The maximum value of λ for which the coefficients of nonbasic variables are nonnegative is determined by

$$(1.3) \qquad \min\left(\frac{11\tfrac{1}{2}}{7\tfrac{1}{2}}, \frac{5\tfrac{1}{3}}{4\tfrac{2}{3}}, \frac{7\tfrac{1}{6}}{2\tfrac{5}{6}}\right) = 1\tfrac{1}{7}.$$

Hence the solution of Tableau 1 is optimal for $\frac{1}{2} \leq \lambda \leq 1\tfrac{1}{7}$. For $\lambda \geq 1\tfrac{1}{7}$, the coefficient of x_2 in the objective function equation becomes negative, so that x_2 should become a basic variable. The leaving basic variable is determined as usual and turns out to be x_4, so that the element $1\tfrac{1}{3}$ is the pivot of the transformation. This results in Tableau 2.

For the same reasons as given before the solution of Tableau 2 is optimal for $\lambda = 1\tfrac{1}{7}$. The maximum value of λ for which it is optimal is found from

$$(1.4) \qquad \min\left(\frac{3\tfrac{1}{2}}{\tfrac{1}{2}}, \frac{10}{5}, \frac{4\tfrac{1}{2}}{\tfrac{1}{2}}\right) = 2;$$

this maximum value of λ is connected with y_2, so that this is the new basic variable. The leaving basic variable turns out to be x_3. After a transformation with the element $\frac{1}{2}$ as a pivot Tableau 3 results, which is optimal for $\lambda = 2$. The maximum value of λ for which it is optimal is found from

$$(1.5) \qquad \min\left(\frac{3\tfrac{1}{2}}{\tfrac{1}{2}}, \frac{4\tfrac{1}{2}}{\tfrac{1}{2}}\right) = 7,$$

so that the solution of Tableau 3 is optimal for $2 \leq \lambda \leq 7$. x_1 is the new basic variable and x_2 turns out to be the leaving basic variable. In Tableau 4, the maximum value of λ for which its solution is optimal is $3\tfrac{1}{3}/\tfrac{1}{3} = 10$, so that

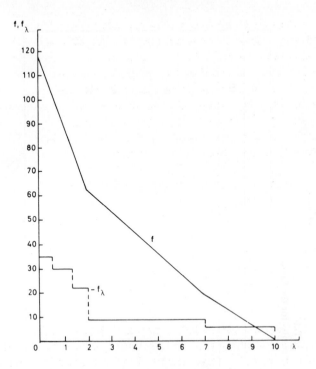

Fig. 1.

this solution is optimal for $7 \leqq \lambda \leqq 10$. The new basic variable is y_1, the leaving basic variable is x_1, Tableau 5 results in which the y-variables only are basic because the wage level has become so high that none of the products is profitable. No upper bound of λ for which the solution is optimal is found, so that the solution is optimal for $10 \leqq \lambda \leqq \infty$.

Table 2 gives a summary of the results. The second row gives the minimum and maximum values of λ for which the tableaux indicated in the first row are optimal; note that the minimum values of any tableau coincide with the maximum values of the previous tableau. The third row gives the values of the objective function for the optimal solutions corresponding with the indicated values of λ. f decreases for increasing λ, which is obvious since an increase of the costs of labour or raw materials can only lead to lower profits. Figure 1 gives a graphic representation of the relation between λ and f. The element in the column of value of basic variables and the row of f_λ can be interpreted as minus the number of units of labour used. This amount is 36 units for the

Table 2
Summary of results for the first example

Tableau	0	1	2	3	4	5
λ	0	$\tfrac{1}{2}$	$1\tfrac{1}{7}$	2	7	10
f	$121\tfrac{1}{2}$	$103\tfrac{1}{2}$	$83\tfrac{4}{7}$	63	18	0
$-f_\lambda$	36	31	24	9	6	—
x_1	$10\tfrac{1}{4}$	$7\tfrac{3}{4}$	$2\tfrac{13}{14}$	$2\tfrac{1}{2}$	6	—
v_1	—	—	$1\tfrac{1}{2}$	$1\tfrac{1}{4}$	6	—
x_2	$4\tfrac{1}{2}$	3	0	—	0	—
v_2	—	—	$1\tfrac{1}{2}$	—	—	—
x_3	$2\tfrac{1}{2}$	0	—	0	1	—
v_3	—	1	—	—	—	—
x_4	—	2	0	50	85	18
v_4	$4\tfrac{1}{2}$	—	—	$1\tfrac{1}{4}$	—	—
y_1	$6\tfrac{3}{4}$	$5\tfrac{3}{4}$	$3\tfrac{13}{14}$	33	53	—
u_1	$\tfrac{3}{4}$	0	—	1	0	—
y_2	—	0	$4\tfrac{2}{7}$	$3\tfrac{1}{2}$	—	3
u_2	—	—	—	0	3	3

solution of Tableau 0; it then decreases in the successive tableaux until it is zero for $\lambda > 10$. Figure 1 again gives a graphic representation. It can easily be proved that this amount is nonincreasing for increasing λ. (See Exercise 5.) Note that this amount varies discretely, having a different level for each tableau, but remaining the same for variations of λ within the range for that tableau.

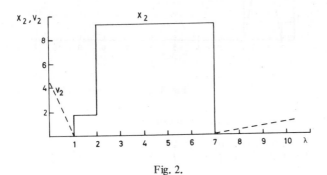

Fig. 2.

The other rows give the values of the x- and y-variables for the successive optimal solutions and also the values of minus the reduced revenues and imputed costs for the minimum and maximum value of λ for each tableau; as indicated in Chapter 3, these are the variables of the dual problem which are denoted as u- and v-variables. Figure 2 gives a representation of the relation between λ and x_2 and v_2; v_2 is minus the reduced revenue of x_2, and is, of course, always nonnegative for an optimal tableau. v_2 decreases continuously for increasing λ until it becomes zero for $\lambda = 1\frac{1}{7}$; x_2 then becomes basic, but at $\lambda = 7$ it becomes nonbasic again, after which v_2 increases from zero. Figure 3 gives the same relation for the slack variable for loom capacity, y_2, and its dual variable u_2 which is interpreted as imputed costs of loom capacity. For $0 \leqq \lambda \leqq \frac{1}{2}$, y_2 is positive and $u_2 = 0$; then y_2 becomes a nonbasic variable and the imputed costs of loomtime become positive, varying continuously with λ. At $\lambda = 2$, the imputed costs become zero and y_2 again becomes a nonbasic variable. Note that the u- and v-variables and also f vary continuously with λ; they are connected with prices and costs and so is λ. The x- and y-variables and f_λ, on the other hand, stand for quantities of products and capacities; they vary discontinuously with λ.

It is also possible to vary λ in a downward direction. For instance, it may be observed that Tableau 00, which is the same as Tableau 5, is optimal for $\lambda \to \infty$. Now the minimum value of λ for which this tableau is optimal should

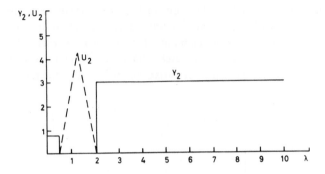

Fig. 3.

be found. This is found from (see Tableau 5)

$$(1.6) \qquad \max\left(\frac{9}{1}, \frac{27}{8}, \frac{65}{15}, \frac{10}{1}\right) = 10.$$

Now x_1 should become basic and y_1 leaves the basis; then Tableau 4 is found. It turns out that the same sequence of the tableaux is generated as before, but in the reverse direction.

It is easy to develop formal rules for this kind of parametric programming. Let the parametric objective function of a problem be

$$(1.7) \qquad f = (p_1 + q_1\lambda)x_1 + (p_2 + q_2\lambda)x_2 + \ldots + (p_n + q_n\lambda)x_n$$

subject to a number of linear constraints; optimal solutions should be found for $\underline{\lambda} \leq \lambda \leq \bar{\lambda}$. First an optimal solution for $\lambda = \bar{\lambda}$ should be found, which is done by an application of the simplex method with $p_j + q_j\lambda$ as coefficient of x_j in the objective function; the rows f_c and f_λ should be transformed in each iteration. The resulting tableau is called Tableau 0. Let the elements of this or any subsequent tableau be indicated as

$$
\begin{array}{ccccc}
a'_{00} & a'_{01} & a'_{02} & \cdot & a'_{0n} \\
a''_{00} & a''_{01} & a''_{02} & \cdot & a''_{0n} \\
a_{10} & a_{11} & a_{12} & \cdot & a_{1n} \\
a_{20} & a_{21} & a_{22} & \cdot & a_{2n} \\
\cdot & \cdot & \cdot & \cdot & \\
a_{m0} & a_{m1} & a_{m2} & \cdot & a_{mn}
\end{array}
$$

The first row is the f_c-row, the second the f_λ-row.

The maximum value of λ for which the solution of the tableau, say Tableau t, is optimal is found from

$$(1.8) \qquad \min_j \left(\frac{a'_{0j}}{-a''_{0j}} \,\middle|\, a''_{0j} < 0 \right) = \frac{a'_{0k}}{-a''_{0k}} = \bar\lambda_t \,.$$

If $a''_{0j} \geq 0$ for all j, there is no such maximum value of λ. The minimum value of λ for which the solution of the tableau is optimal is found from

$$(1.9) \qquad \max_j \left(\frac{-a'_{0j}}{a''_{0j}} \,\middle|\, a''_{0j} > 0 \right) = \frac{-a'_{0k}}{a''_{0k}} = \underline\lambda_t \,.$$

If $a'_{0j} \leq 0$ for all j, there is no such minimum value of λ. If optimal solutions for increasing values of λ are to be found, the variable corresponding with $\bar\lambda_t$ should become basic; for decreasing values of λ the variable connected with $\underline\lambda_t$ should become basic. The leaving basic variable in both cases is found as in the simplex method by determining

$$(1.10) \qquad \min_i \left(\frac{a_{i0}}{a_{ik}} \,\middle|\, a_{ik} > 0 \right).$$

If $a_{ik} \leq 0$ for all i, there is an infinite solution for $\lambda > \bar\lambda_t$ or $\lambda < \underline\lambda_t$.

6.2. Programming with Parametric Constant Terms

We shall now consider problems in which the constant terms of the constraints contain a variable parameter λ. This means that the problem has the following general form: Maximize

$$(2.1) \qquad f = p_1 x_1 + \ldots + p_n x_n$$

subject to

$$(2.2) \qquad \begin{cases} a_{11} x_1 + \ldots + a_{1n} x_n \leq b_1 + a_1 \lambda \,, \\ \ldots \\ a_{m1} x_1 + \ldots + a_{mn} x_n \leq b_m + a_m \lambda \,, \end{cases}$$

$$(2.3) \qquad x_1, \ldots, x_n \geq 0 \,.$$

All optimal solutions should be found for a given range of λ,

(2.4) $\underline{\lambda} \leq \lambda \leq \bar{\lambda}$,

where $\underline{\lambda}$ and $\bar{\lambda}$ are given lower and upper bounds. The general idea for a solution of this problem is the same as for the problem of the previous section. First a solution is found for $\lambda = \underline{\lambda}$; then optimal solutions are traced for higher values of λ until a solution is found which is optimal for $\lambda = \bar{\lambda}$.

Again the production planning problem involving yarn and fabric production will be used, but now the loom capacity is parametrically varied from 0 to ∞. The problem is therefore as follows. Maximize

(2.5) $f = 9x_1 + 8x_2 + 50x_3 + 19x_4$

subject to

(2.6) $\begin{cases} 3x_1 + 2x_2 + 10x_3 + 4x_4 \leq 18 , \\ \qquad\qquad 2x_3 + \tfrac{1}{2}x_4 \leq \lambda , \end{cases}$

(2.7) $x_1, x_2, x_3, x_4 \geq 0 .$

This problem is put into a simplex tableau format, see Tableau 00 of Table 3. The values of basic variables are split into two columns, one containing the terms without λ, which is called constant term, and one containing the coefficients of λ, which is called λ-term.

First an optimal solution should be found for $\lambda = 0$, which is done by using the simplex method for the problem with only the elements of the c-term column as values of basic variables. After four iterations the optimal solution for $\lambda = 0$ is found, see Tableau 0. Now the parametric variation of λ can be started. An increase of λ can affect the feasibility of the solution, since if an element in the λ-term column is negative, the value of the basic variable decreases. For x_2 in Tableau 0 we have

(2.8) $9 - 4\lambda = x_2 .$

From this, it is clear that $x_2 \geq 0$ for $\lambda \leq 2\tfrac{1}{4}$ and $x_2 < 0$ for $\lambda > 2\tfrac{1}{4}$. No other basic variables decrease for an increasing value of λ. Hence the present solution is optimal for $0 \leq \lambda \leq 2\tfrac{1}{4}$.

For $\lambda > 2\tfrac{1}{4}$, $x_2 < 0$, so that the solution is infeasible. The solution should therefore be changed in such a way that x_2 is increased towards zero and is replaced by a nonbasic variable in such a way that the solution remains opti-

Table 3
Parametric variation of loom capacity

Tableau	Basic Variables	Values Basic Variables		x_1	x_2	x_3	x_4
		$c-t$	$\lambda-t$				
00	f	0	0	-9	-8	-50	-19
	y_1	18	0	3	2	10	4
	y_2	0	1	0	0	$\underline{2}$	$\tfrac{1}{2}$
				y_1	x_1	y_2	x_3
0	f	72	6	4	'3	6	2
	x_2	9	-4	$\tfrac{1}{2}$	$1\tfrac{1}{2}$	-4	$\underline{-3}$
	x_4	0	2	0	0	2	4
				y_1	x_1	y_2	x_2
1	f	78	$3\tfrac{1}{3}$	$4\tfrac{1}{3}$	4	$3\tfrac{1}{3}$	$\tfrac{2}{3}$
	x_3	-3	$1\tfrac{1}{3}$	$-\tfrac{1}{6}$	$-\tfrac{1}{2}$	$1\tfrac{1}{3}$	$-\tfrac{1}{3}$
	x_4	12	$-3\tfrac{1}{3}$	$\tfrac{2}{3}$	2	$\underline{-3\tfrac{1}{3}}$	$1\tfrac{1}{3}$
				y_1	x_1	x_4	x_2
2	f	90	0	5	6	1	2
	x_3	$1\tfrac{4}{5}$	0	$\tfrac{1}{10}$	$\tfrac{3}{10}$	$\tfrac{2}{5}$	$\tfrac{1}{5}$
	y_2	$-3\tfrac{3}{5}$	1	$-\tfrac{1}{5}$	$-\tfrac{3}{5}$	$-\tfrac{3}{10}$	$-\tfrac{2}{5}$

mal in the narrow sense. Hence the leaving basic variable and the new basic variable are chosen as in the dual method. x_2 leaves the basis and the new basic variable is chosen by taking the minimum of the ratios

$$\frac{6}{4}, \quad \frac{2}{3},$$

so that x_3 is the new basic variable. The element -3 is the pivot of the iteration which results in Tableau 1. This tableau has the same values of basic variables for $\lambda = 2\tfrac{1}{4}$ as Tableau 0, which can be shown by indicating that the element in the old pivot row $9 - 4\lambda$ is 0 for this value of λ, so that for this value the values of basic variables do not change.

Since in Tableau 1 the element in the λ-term column in the row of x_4 is negative, x_4 decreases for increasing values of λ. x_4 becomes zero for

$$12 - 3\tfrac{1}{3}\lambda = 0$$

or $\lambda = 3\tfrac{3}{5}$. Hence Tableau 1 is optimal for $2\tfrac{1}{4} \leqq \lambda \leqq 3\tfrac{3}{5}$. For optimal solutions for higher values of λ, x_4 should leave the basis; the new basic variable is selected as in the dual method and turns out to be y_2. Taking $-3\tfrac{1}{3}$ as a pivot, Tableau 2 is found. None of the basic variables of this tableau decreases for increasing λ, so that the solution of this tableau is optimal for $3\tfrac{3}{5} \leqq \lambda \leqq$ $\leqq \infty$. In fact, we easily see from this tableau that any increase of loom capacity above 3,600 is not used at all.

Several interesting points of this example may be mentioned. First, since the λ-term column is always equal to the y_2-column, it is never necessary to write it down. Secondly, the opportunity costs of loom capacity can be found in the f-row and in the λ-term column in the various tableaux; this interpretation follows not only from the fact that this element is equal to the corresponding element of the y_2-column, but also from the observation that the value of the objective function for, for instance, Tableau 1 can be written as

$$78 + 3\tfrac{1}{3}\lambda .$$

The opportunity costs decrease or remain the same for increasing λ, which follows from the fact that the corresponding element in the old pivot column is positive or zero and the corresponding element in the new pivot row is positive. Thirdly, it should be observed that, in contrast with programming with a parametric objective function, here the values of basic variables vary continuously with λ, while the values of dual variables vary discontinuously; f varies continuously as before.

It is not difficult to give general rules for programming with parametric constant terms. Let the current optimal tableau be represented in the following manner:

Basic Variables	Values Basic Variables				
	c-term	λ-term	x_1	x_2 $\quad \cdot \quad$ x_n
f	a'_{00}	a''_{00}	a_{01}	a_{02} $\quad \cdot \quad$ a_{0n}
y_1	a'_{10}	a''_{10}	a_{11}	a_{12} $\quad \cdot \quad$ a_{1n}
y_2	a'_{20}	a''_{20}	a_{21}	a_{22} $\quad \cdot \quad$ a_{2n}
$\cdot$	$\cdot$	$\cdot$	$\cdot$	$\cdot$ $\quad \cdot \quad$ $\cdot$
y_m	a'_{m0}	a''_{m0}	a_{m1}	a_{m2} $\quad \cdot \quad$ a_{mn}

The nonbasic variables are indicated as x-variables and the basic ones as y-variables. The lower bound of λ for which this solution is optimal in say, Tableau t, is found from

$$(2.9) \qquad \underline{\lambda}_t = \max_i \left(\frac{-a'_{i0}}{a''_{i0}} \,\middle|\, a''_{i0} > 0 \right).$$

The upper bound of λ for which the solution is optimal is found from

$$(2.10) \qquad \bar{\lambda}_t = \min_i \left(\frac{a'_{i0}}{-a''_{i0}} \,\middle|\, a''_{i0} < 0 \right).$$

If the solution is optimal, the value found in (2.10) should be higher than that in (2.9). If λ is varied in a downwards direction, the leaving basic variable is the one corresponding with (2.9), if λ is varied upwards, then the leaving basic variable is connected with (2.10). If there is no positive a''_{i0}, there is no lower bound for λ, if there is no negative a''_{i0}, there is no upper bound for λ. The new basic variable is found as in the dual method by determining, if r is the index of the row of the leaving basic variable:

$$(2.11) \qquad \min_j \left(\frac{a_{0j}}{-a_{rj}} \,\middle|\, a_{rj} < 0 \right).$$

It is assumed that the problem is a maximization problem, so that all a_{0j} are nonnegative. If there is no negative element in the r-th row, there is no feasible solution for the values of λ lower than the lower bound if (2.9) was used or higher than the upper bound if (2.10) was used (see Exercise 6).

In the previous section an example was used in which the costs of labour (or any other resource) were varied; it was assumed that at the given price an unlimited quantity of the resource was available. Here we shall study the same example, but it is now the quantity of the resource that is varied, its costs being kept at zero. The problem may then be formulated as follows. Maximize

$$(2.12) \qquad f = 10x_1 + 9x_2 + 65x_3 + 27x_4$$

subject to

$$(2.13) \qquad \left\{ \begin{array}{l} x_1 + x_2 + 15x_3 + 8x_4 \leqq \mu, \\ 3x_1 + 2x_2 + 10x_3 + 4x_4 \leqq 18, \\ 2x_3 + \tfrac{1}{2}x_4 \leqq 3, \end{array} \right.$$

$$(2.14) \qquad x_1, x_2, x_3, x_4 \geqq 0.$$

Table 4
Parametric variation of quantity of labour

Tableau	Basic Variables	Values Basic Variables	x_1	x_2	x_3	x_4
00	f	0	-10	-9	-65	-27
	y_μ	0	$\underline{1}$	1	15	8
	y_1	18	3	2	10	4
	y_2	3	0	0	2	$\frac{1}{2}$
			y_μ	x_2	x_3	x_4
0	f	0	10	1	85	53
	x_1	0	1	1	15	8
	y_1	18	-3	$\underline{-1}$	-35	-20
	y_2	3	0	0	2	$\frac{1}{2}$
			y_μ	y_1	x_3	x_4
1	f	18	7	1	50	33
	x_1	18	-2	1	$\underline{-20}$	-12
	x_2	-18	3	-1	35	20
	y_2	3	0	0	2	$\frac{1}{2}$
			y_μ	y_1	x_1	x_4
2	f	63	2	$3\frac{1}{2}$	$2\frac{1}{2}$	3
	x_3	$-\frac{9}{10}$	$\frac{1}{10}$	$-\frac{1}{20}$	$-\frac{1}{20}$	$\frac{3}{5}$
	x_2	$13\frac{1}{2}$	$-\frac{1}{2}$	$\frac{3}{4}$	$-1\frac{3}{4}$	-1
	y_2	$4\frac{4}{5}$	$-\frac{1}{5}$	$\frac{1}{10}$	$\frac{1}{10}$	$\underline{-\frac{7}{10}}$
			y_μ	y_1	x_1	y_2
3	f	$83\frac{4}{7}$	$1\frac{1}{7}$	$3\frac{13}{14}$	$2\frac{13}{14}$	$4\frac{2}{7}$
	x_3	$3\frac{3}{14}$	$-\frac{1}{14}$	$\frac{1}{28}$	$\frac{1}{28}$	$\frac{6}{7}$
	x_2	$6\frac{9}{14}$	$-\frac{3}{14}$	$\frac{17}{28}$	$1\frac{17}{28}$	$-1\frac{3}{7}$
	x_4	$-6\frac{6}{7}$	$\frac{2}{7}$	$-\frac{1}{7}$	$-\frac{1}{7}$	$\underline{-1\frac{3}{7}}$
			y_μ	y_1	x_1	x_2
4	f	$103\frac{1}{2}$	$\frac{1}{2}$	$5\frac{3}{4}$	$7\frac{3}{4}$	3
	x_3	$7\frac{1}{5}$	$\underline{-\frac{1}{5}}$	$\frac{2}{5}$	1	$\frac{3}{5}$
	y_2	$-4\frac{13}{20}$	$\underline{\frac{3}{20}}$	$-\frac{17}{40}$	$-1\frac{1}{8}$	$-\frac{7}{10}$
	x_4	$-13\frac{1}{2}$	$\frac{1}{2}$	$-\frac{3}{4}$	$-1\frac{3}{4}$	-1

Table 4 (continued)

			x_3	y_1	x_1	x_2
5	f	$121\tfrac{1}{2}$	$2\tfrac{1}{2}$	$6\tfrac{3}{4}$	$10\tfrac{1}{4}$	$4\tfrac{1}{2}$
	y_μ	-36	-5	-2	-5	-3
	y_2	$\tfrac{3}{4}$	$2\tfrac{1}{2}$	$\tfrac{1}{4}$	$\tfrac{3}{4}$	$\tfrac{1}{2}$
	x_4	$4\tfrac{1}{2}$	$\tfrac{3}{4}$	$-\tfrac{1}{8}$	$-\tfrac{3}{8}$	$-\tfrac{1}{4}$

The parameter μ is used in order to distinguish it from the parameter λ in the variation of costs; μ stands for the quantity of labour available.

This problem may, after the introduction of the slack variables y_μ, y_1, and y_2, be put into a simplex tableau format, see Tableau 00 of Table 4. The μ-term column is deleted since it is always identical to the y_μ-column. After one iteration of the simplex method the optimal solution is obtained for $\mu = 0$, see Tableau 0. This tableau contains an optimal solution for $0 \leqq \mu \leqq 6$. In the manner described before, optimal solutions are generated for $6 \leqq \mu \leqq 9, 9 \leqq \mu \leqq 24$, $24 \leqq \mu \leqq 31$, $31 \leqq \mu \leqq 36$, and $\mu \geqq 36$, which are found in Tableaux 1–5.

This problem can be given in the following interpretation. In the problem of the previous section it was assumed that the resource was bought from outside at a varying price λ. Here it is assumed that a varying quantity μ of the resource is available. It is interesting to compare the results for both problems.

The values of basic variables of Tableau 0 in Table 4 are for $\mu = 0$ equal to the values of basic variables of Tableau 5 in Table 1; the dual variables (or opportunity costs) of the first tableau are equal to those of the last tableau for $\lambda = 10$. Such correspondences can be observed between Tableaux 0–5 of Table 4 and Tableaux 5–0 of Table 1, respectively. It may be observed that, whereas in Table 1 the dual variables change continuously and the primal variables change discontinuously, in Table 4 it is the other way around. Further it must be noted that for critical values of μ and λ, the solutions are entirely equal, except for the value of the objective function. Hence the use of prices of a resource as in the previous section leads to the same use of the resources as the direct optimization for a given quantity of the resource, if discontinuities are disregarded.

In Figure 1 of the previous section, the relation between λ, the price of resource, and $-f_\lambda$, the quantity used of the resource was given. If now $-f_\lambda$ is replaced by μ, the available quantity of the resource, and λ by u_μ, the opportunity cost of the resource, the same relation is valid for the present problem if μ is interpreted as the independent variable and u_μ as the dependent variable; hence the dashed pieces of the curve have relevance instead of the solid pieces.

  The values of the objective function for corresponding solutions are not quite the same. For instance, in Tableau 2 of Table 4, the value of the objective function for $\mu = 9$ is $63 + 2 \cdot 9 = 81$. For Tableau 3 of Table 1 which has the same solution for $\lambda = 2$ we find $81 - 2 \cdot 9 = 63$. But if in the quantity variation problem we subtract the quantity of the production factor times the opportunity costs, we obtain $81 - 9 \cdot 2 = 63$, which is the same as in the price variation problem. Alternatively, we could have added to the objective

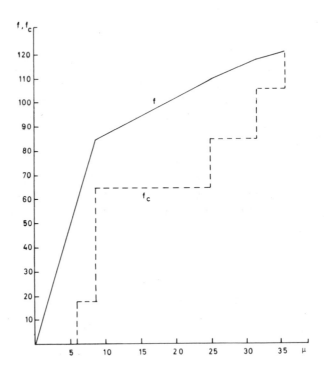

Fig. 4.

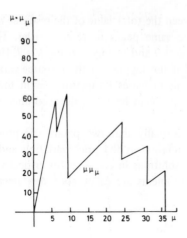

Fig. 5

function in the price variation problem the quantity of the resource used times its price. This can be explained in an intuitive manner by saying that in the quantity variation problem the quantity of the production factor is owned, whereas in the price variation problem it must be paid; if we adjust for this, equivalence is found.

Figure 4 gives f, the value of the objective function and f_c, the same value, adjusted for the quantity of the resource times its opportunity costs as a function of μ. Figure 5 gives the total value of the resource as a function of the quantity of labour μ; this is the difference between f and f_c in Figure 4. It is interesting to observe that this value has no unique local optimum. Figure 6

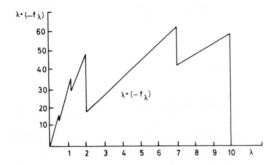

Fig. 6.

gives the relation between the total value of the resource in the price variation problem; it shows the same peaks in reverse order. The maximum 63 in Figure 5 is found for $\mu = 9$ and in Figure 6 for $\lambda = 7$. Hence the same maximum would be found if the supplier of the resource varies his price as in the price variation problems or varies its quantity as in the quantity variation problem if in the last problem he was paid according to the opportunity costs.

It may be proved formally that two parametric programming problems which have the same relation as the price variation and quantity variation problems always have solutions in common for critical values of the parameters; a pair of such problems are called *equivalent parametric problems*.

6.3. The Primal-Dual Method

In Section 3.2 an example was given of the use of artificial variables in case no initial feasible solution to the problem was available. The particular example used was the cattlefeed problem which was a minimization problem. After artificial variables had been inserted in the constraints and a "penalty term" consisting of M times the sum of the artificial variables was added to the objective function, the artificial variables were made basic for the entire equation system, which then had the following form:

$$
\text{(3.1)} \quad
\begin{cases}
25M = -(24 - 14M)x_1 - (30 - 18M)x_2 - (40 - 52M)x_3 \\
\qquad\quad - (50 - 62M)x_4 - My_1 - My_2 + f, \\[2mm]
20 = 12x_1 + 12x_2 + 40x_3 + 60x_4 - y_1 \quad + z_1, \\[2mm]
5 = \ 2x_1 + \ 6x_2 + 12x_3 + \ 2x_4 \ - y_2 \quad + z_2.
\end{cases}
$$

In Section 3.2, M was considered to be a large number. Then the simplex method was used, which should result in the elimination of the artificial variables from the basis. After this, the optimization of the proper objective function took place.

The primal-dual method uses the same equation system (3.1), but proceeds in a different way. Consider the first equation of (3.1). If M is put equal to zero, only the coefficients without M have to be considered. Since these coefficients all are nonpositive, the present basic solution is optimal in the narrow sense for $M=0$, because it is a minimization problem. However, the solution is not feasible because there are artificial variables in the basis. But

Table 5
An application of the primal-dual method to the cattlefeed problem

Tableau	Basic Variables	Values Basic Variables	x_1	x_2	x_3	x_4	y_1	y_2
0	f_c	0	-24	-30	-40	-50	0	0
	f_λ	25	14	18	52	62	-1	-1
	z_1	20	12	12	40	60	-1	0
	z_2	5	2	6	<u>12</u>	2	0	-1
			x_1	x_2		x_4	y_1	y_2
1	f_c	$16\frac{2}{3}$	$-17\frac{1}{3}$	-10		$-43\frac{1}{3}$	0	$-3\frac{1}{3}$
	f_λ	$3\frac{1}{3}$	$5\frac{1}{3}$	-8		$53\frac{1}{3}$	-1	$3\frac{1}{3}$
	z_1	$3\frac{1}{3}$	$5\frac{1}{3}$	-8		$\underline{53\frac{1}{3}}$	-1	$3\frac{1}{3}$
	x_3	$\frac{5}{12}$	$\frac{1}{6}$	$\frac{1}{2}$		$\frac{1}{6}$	0	$-\frac{1}{12}$
			x_1	x_2			y_1	y_2
2	f_c	$19\frac{3}{8}$	-13	$-16\frac{1}{2}$			$-\frac{13}{16}$	$-\frac{5}{8}$
	f_λ	0	0	0			0	0
	x_4	$\frac{1}{16}$	$\frac{1}{10}$	$-\frac{3}{20}$			$\frac{3}{160}$	$\frac{1}{16}$
	x_3	$\frac{13}{32}$	$\frac{3}{20}$	$\frac{21}{40}$			$\frac{1}{320}$	$-\frac{3}{32}$

if M is increased parametrically in such a way that the optimality in the narrow sense is preserved, then for $M \to \infty$ an optimal solution must be found which does not contain any artificial variables if a feasible solution to the problem exists. This is how the primal-dual method works.

In Table 5, the primal-dual method is applied to the equation system (3.1). Instead of M, the more usual notation λ for the parameter is adopted. Tableau 0 contains an optimal solution for $\lambda = 0$. The upper bound for λ for which this solution is optimal is found as described in Section 1 of this chapter, if the fact that this is a minimization problem instead of a maximization problem is taken into account. Hence we find

$$(3.2) \qquad \bar{\lambda}_0 = \min\left(\frac{24}{14}, \frac{30}{18}, \frac{40}{52}, \frac{50}{62}\right) = \frac{10}{13}.$$

Hence x_3 should enter the basis. The leaving basic variable is determined as in the simplex method and turns out to be z_2. The tableau is transformed, but the column of z_2 is deleted since we do not intend to take this variable into the basis again.

The upper bound of λ and the new basic variable for Tableau 1 are determined as follows:

$$(3.3) \qquad \bar{\lambda}_1 = \min \left(\frac{17\frac{1}{3}}{5\frac{1}{3}}, \frac{43\frac{1}{3}}{53\frac{1}{3}}, \frac{3\frac{1}{5}}{3\frac{1}{3}} \right) = \frac{13}{16}.$$

Hence x_4 enters the basis. It is found that z_1 leaves the basis. The solution of Tableau 2 is optimal for $\lambda \to \infty$. This solution does not contain any artificial variables, so that it must be the solution of the original problem.

The primal-dual method can be applied only if the initial solution is optimal in the narrow sense for $\lambda = 0$. It can therefore be used under the same circumstances as the dual method. In fact, both methods can be viewed as alternatives. If both methods are compared, the dual method seems preferable since the primal-dual method uses one more row (the λ-row) and a number of additional columns (since the slack variables are not used as basic variables, but instead of these, artificial variables are introduced). The main advantage of the primal-dual method lies in its application to transportation and network problems which will be treated in Chapters 12 and 13; it was in connection with these problems that the method has been developed.

It should be noted that the original formulation of the primal-dual method by Dantzig [5], Ford and Fulkerson [6] which can also be found in various textbooks is different from that given above. However, it has been proved that both formulations are equivalent in the sense that the same sequence of solutions is found for both. The formulation given above has the advantage that it is simpler than the original one.

Exercises

1. Assume that in the case of Problem 1 of Chapter 4, 10 additional units of production factor T are available at $30 per 10 units; either all or none of these 10 units should be bought. Determine using parametric programming, whether it is profitable to buy these units; if not, what is the maximum price for which these units should be bought.

2. Assume that in Problem 4 of Chapter 3 the cost of the three food products increase by $0.02, $0.10 and $0.06 per percentage point increase in the wage index. Determine by means of parametric programming the optimal diet for any increase in the wage index.

3. A company can produce four products with net revenues of $10, $12, $15 and $20 per unit. There are two bottlenecks in the production process, a facility used for all products and further labour. The average time required on the production facility is 6, 6, 9, and 6 respectively, for the four products, while further 200, 300, 350, and 450 minutes of labour are required per unit. The production facility can be used for 40 hours per week. 50 workers are available, each working 40 hours per week.
   (a) Determine the optimal production program.
   (b) Find the optimal production program for the number of workers varying from 0 to ∞.
   (c) Find optimal solutions for labour costs varying from 0 to ∞.
   (d) Compare the results of (b) and (c).

4. Solve the following parametric programming problem using the upper-bound method. Maximize

$$15x_1 + 10x_2$$

   subject to

$$0 \leqq x_1 \leqq 3,$$
$$0 \leqq x_2 \leqq 5,$$
$$2x_1 + x_2 \leqq 6(1+\lambda).$$

5. Prove that in a maximization problem with a parametric objective function the element in the row of f_λ and in the column of values of basic variables never decreases for increasing values of λ. (Hint: analyse the transformation formula for this element.) Explain in words why in Tableaux 0 and 1 of Table 1 the quantity of labour used for $\lambda = 2.05$ suddenly decreases from 36 to 31.

6. Prove that if in a linear programming problem with parametric constant terms no leaving basic variable can be found for a certain range of values of λ, no feasible solution exists for these values of λ.

7. Solve Problem 4 of Chapter 3 by means of the primal-dual method.

8. Given is the following linear programming problem. Minimize

$$f = 4x_1 + 2x_2 + 3x_3$$

   subject to

$$x_1 + x_2 + x_3 \geqq 1,$$

$$2x_1 + x_2 \qquad \geqq 3 \, ,$$
$$x_1 \qquad + 2x_3 \geqq 2 \, ,$$
$$x_1, x_2, x_3 \geqq 0 \, .$$

Apply the primal-dual method to the problem. Explain your result.

PART 2

APPLICATIONS OF LINEAR PROGRAMMING

7. LINEAR PROGRAMMING COMPUTATIONS WITH THE MPS-SYSTEM

7.1. Data Input

If calculations are done by hand or using a desk calculator, linear programming methods are only useful for small problems, since for bigger problems the amount of calculations soon becomes so large that it is too costly to execute them or they may simply not be feasible. In many cases the cost of calculations would then exceed the benefits of having the optimal solution instead of one which is not necessarily optimal. The computer makes the solution of linear programming problems of almost any size feasible at costs which are usually small in comparison with the benefits which can be gained.

To perform computations on computers, computer programs are needed which instruct the computer in a computer language what to do. For many kinds of computations computer programs have been written, so that these may be used. This is the case with linear programming, for which quite a number of programs have been written. One of these is the IBM *Mathematical Programming System,* the use of which will be explained in this chapter.

The advantage of so-called "package" programs as the MPS-system is that they are very flexible in the sense that many options which can be used for various purposes are available. Another advantage is that these carefully constructed programs usually are more efficient in the sense that they have a better allocation of memory space and a greater speed of computation due to a number of refinements which are incorporated in these programs. We have already mentioned that a modified form of the simplex method, called the product form of the inverse is more efficient for large problems; this feature is usually incorporated in commercially available computer programs such as the MPS-system. Apart from this, it is fairly time-consuming to write and test a computer program, so that for this reason alone it is preferable in many cases to use such package programs.

The chapter deals with the use of the MPS-system. No attempt will be made to indicate the numerous options which are available; only a few will be mentioned. Only the essentials necessary for the implementation of ordinary linear programming problems and of parametric programming problems will be treated.

Let us again consider the original textile production problem. Since the computer does the handling and printing, it is not necessary to use such very short names for the variables as $x_1, ..., x_n, y_1, ..., y_m$; names may be used which are more recognizable. Let us use YARNA for Yarn A, YARNB for Yarn B, FABRA for Fabric A and FABRB for Fabric B. These names are assumed to be associated with the columns of the set-up tableau. For the rows of the set-up tableau similar names can be used. Let us use for the F-row REV, for the row of spinning capacity SPCAP, and for the row of loom capacity, LOCAP. The data to be inserted can then be thought to be arranged as in Table 1.

Table 1
Data arrangement for MPS-input

Row ＼ Column	YARNA	YARNB	FABRA	FABRB	(type)	RHS
REV	9	8	50	19	N	
SPCAP	3	2	10	4	L	18000
LOCAP	0	0	2	0.5	L	3000

Note that the y-variables are not explicitly mentioned; they are thought to be associated with the various rows and will be automatically inserted once it is known whether the constraint concerned is an equality, or has a $\leq$- or $\geq$-sign. Hence we need for each row an indication for the type of row. The following code letters will be used. For a row with an $\leq$-sign, L is used (L for less), for a row with an $\geq$-sign, G is used (G for greater), for a row with an $=$-sign, E is used (E for equality), and for the row of the objective function, N is used.

Table 1 contains all the data we need; these should now be put on punched cards. A punched card can be considered as one line on which 80 symbols can be printed, including spaces. The data for the problem should be put on these cards according to a format which should be strictly followed and which is explained by means of the example.

It turns out that the data for our problem can be put on 15 cards, the contents of which is reproduced in Table 2. Two types of cards may be distinguished:

1. *Indicator cards,* which specify the type of data which follows,
2. *Data cards,* which contain the actual data values.

Table 2
Punched card input of data for MPS-system of textile production problem

field	f 1	field 2	field 3	field 4		field 5	field 6	
columns			11111 12345 67890	1111122222 1234567890	22222333333 1234567890123456	33334444444444 78901234567890	5555555555 1234567890	6666666666 1234567890 7777777778 1234567890
cards	NAME ROWS N L L COLUMNS	NAME REV SPCAP LOCAP	TEXPROD					
		YARNA	REV	9		SPCAP	3	
		YARNB	REV	8		SPCAP	2	
		FABRA	REV	50		SPCAP	10	
		FABRA	LOCAP	2				
		FABRB	REV	19		SPCAP	4	
		FABRB	LOCAP					
	RHS							
		CAP	SPCAP	18000		LOCAP	3000	
	RNDATA							

The indicator cards in Table 2 are NAME, ROWS, COLUMNS, RHS, ENDATA: indicator cards should always have the first character in card column 1. The other cards are data cards.

The 20 columns of a data card are divided into 6 fields as indicated in the first row of Table 2. Field 1 is used for codes, Fields 2, 3, and 5 for names and Fields 4 and 6 for values. The names in Fields 2, 3, and 5 should start in the first column of their field (it is then said that these names are *left-justified*), they may consist of letters, numbers and other characters (but should not begin with the symbol $ in Fields 3 and 5) and should contain no spaces (blanks).

The first card contains apart from NAME also the name of the data; for this name TEXPROD has been chosen. Then follows an indicator card with ROWS printed on it. Below that follow cards for each of the three rows. In Field 1 the type of that row is punched either in column 2 or 3, and in Field 2 the name of the row is punched; the remaining fields are left blank.

Then follows an indicator card with COLUMNS. The data card following this have in Field 2 the column name, in the first card YARNA. The coefficients of that column are indicated by first giving the name of the row in which they occur and then the value of the coefficient. The row-name is entered in Field 3 (in this case REV) and the value in Field 4 (in this case 9). Another coefficient of the same column may be entered on the same card in Fields 5 and 6; hence we find SPCAP in Field 5 and 3 in Field 6. Only coefficients with nonzero values should be entered; the other coefficients are put at zero automatically. The value of the coefficients may be entered with or without a decimal point; it is advisable to put the decimal point always in the same column.

The other coefficients are entered in the same manner. Note that two coefficients can be entered on one card if they occur in the same column; if they belong to a different column, separate cards should be used.

Next, the constant terms of the constraints are entered. First an indicator card with RHS is punched. Then follow the coefficients in the same manner as in the columns section, but first the column RHS should be given a name; in this case, CAP is chosen for this name. This separate name may be useful if we wish to solve the problem for different right-hand sides of constraints. This ends the data input for our problem which is indicated by an indicator card with ENDATA punched on it.

7.2. Control Program

So far, only the data input has been discussed. Because the MPS-program allows for a large number of possibilities, it should be indicated what should be done with these data. This is done in a *control program* which precedes the data input.

Table 3 gives the control program for the example. It consists of 13 cards. Each card contains one word which may or may not be followed by one or more words in brackets. In Table 3, these words begin in column 10, though they may begin in any column provided that column 71 is the last one used.

Table 3
Control program for textile production problem

```
          11111111112222222222333333333334
 12345678901234567890123456789022345 67890
          PROGRAM
          INITIALZ
          MOVE(XDATA,'TEXPROD')
          MOVE(XPBNAME,'EXAMPLE')
          CONVERT
          BCDOUT
          SETUP('MAX')
          MOVE(XOBJ,'REV')
          MOVE(XRHS,'CAP')
          PRIMAL
          SOLUTION
          EXIT
          PEND
```

The first card of the control program contains the word PROGRAM, which indicates to the computer that the control program is to follow. The second card contains INITIALZ. This statement is necessary for certain house-keeping needs of the computer; for instance, it sets all tolerances of computations at standard values. Next, the name of the data is entered for which TEXPROD was used; this is done by MOVE(XDATA, 'TEXPROD'). The problem is also given a name which may be used for storage of the solution of this problem; for this name EXAMPLE is chosen. This name is entered by MOVE (XPBNAME, 'EXAMPLE'). The next instruction is CONVERT which makes the computer check the input data and converts them into an internal representation. The statement BCDOUT is an instruction to print out the problem for which the data have been given. It prints these data in the same format except for the addition of a decimal point and zeros.

The instruction SETUP allocates memory space within the computer and adds slack variables where necessary. If just SETUP appears, it is assumed that the objective function should be minimized. For maximization we have to use SETUP('MAX'). Next we have to mention the objective function of the problem, since the data may contain a number of rows which may be used as such. In this case the data contains only one relevant row, REV, which is made the objective function row by the instruction MOVE(XOBJ, 'REV'). The data may also contain a number of right-hand sides, though in our example there is only one, namely CAP. CAP is made the right-hand side of the problem by the instruction MOVE(XRHS, 'CAP'). Then the instruction PRIMAL instructs the computer to apply a variant of the simplex method to the problem. The solution obtained in this manner is printed out in a certain form by giving the instruction SOLUTION. The instruction EXIT and PEND both terminate the program. The description of the program given here is not complete but is sufficient for our purposes.[1]

The control program and the data input are taken into different parts of the computer. The control program is compiled which means that it is translated into machine instructions for manipulation of the data.

We shall now describe the complete card deck which is represented by Table 4. The first card is the job card which is generally different for each computer center. It contains the name of the user and of the job and further accounting information. Then a card follows which instructs the computer to find and use the MPS-program which is usually stored on a disk or a tape.

---

[1] A complete description of the MPS-system can be found in Mathematical Programming System 360(360A-CO-14X) Linear and Separable Programming – User's Manual, IBM Application Program H20-0476-1.

Table 4
Card deck for MPS-system

```
                11111111
       12345678901234567
       (Job card)
       // EXEC MPS
       //MPS.SYSIN DD *
       (control program)
       //GO.SYSIN DD *
       (data input)
       /*
```

This card may be different for different systems. The third card instructs the computer where the data are, namely in a location called SYSIN which is the main systems input. Then the control program follows. The next statement instructs the computer to apply the control program to the data input. Data input follows. The card /* signifies the end of the data.

7.3. Computer Output

The computer output of MPS is copious, but only a few pages are of interest to us. The section PRIMAL on page 4 of the output which is reproduced in Table 5 reports what happens during the optimization.

The information on time, pricing and scale can be ignored. Instead of variables, the name vector is used; the vectors are given numbers, first the variables of the row and then those of the columns. Hence we have $f = 1$, $y_1 = 2$, $y_2 = 3$, $x_1 = 4$, $x_2 = 5$, $x_3 = 6$, $x_4 = 7$. In the first iteration x_4 enters the basis and y_1 leaves it; the resulting value of f is 85,500. In the second iteration x_3 enters the basis and y_2 leaves it; then the optimal solution is obtained with $f = 87,999$; the difference with 88,000 is due to rounding. It

Table 5
Output for 'PRIMAL' optimization

```
PRIMAL          OBJ = REV          RHS = CAP

TIME -      0.23  MINS.       PRICING     7
   SCALE =
   SCALE RESET TO    1.00000-
```

ITER NUMBER	NUMBER NONOPT	VECTOR OUT	VECTOR IN	REDUCED COST	FUNCTION VALUE
M 1	4	2	7	19.0000-	85500.0
2		3	6	2.5000-	98000.9
OPTIMAL SOLUTION					

should be noted that the choice of the new basic variable is different from the one proposed in Chapter 2. In fact, this program uses a somewhat more complicated rule for the choice of the new basic variable; with this different choice, the number of iterations is only 2 instead of 4 in Chapter 2. However, it should be noted that the numbers of the textile example have deliberately been chosen in such a way that the simplex method as described in Chapter 2 would need 4 iterations, which was done to make the example more interesting.

The output SOLUTION contains three pages, the content of which is reproduced in Table 6. The first page contains the time spent on this problem so far, the number of iterations used to find the optimal solution, the name and the value of the objective function and the name of the right-hand side used. The second page is called Section 1 and contains information about the rows and the associated slack variables. Let us first deal with row 2, which has the name SPCAP. The constraint for spinning capacity is

$$(3.1) \qquad 3x_1 + 2x_2 + 10x_3 + 4x_4 \leqq 18{,}000 \ .$$

The MPS-system has formulated this as follows, where SPCAP stands for spinning capacity used and y_1 for the corresponding slack variable:

$$(3.2) \qquad \left\{ \begin{array}{l} \text{SPCAP} = 3x_1 + 2x_2 + 10x_3 + 4x_4 \ , \\[2mm] 0 \leqq \text{SPCAP} \leqq 18{,}000 \ , \\[2mm] \text{SPCAP} + y_1 = 18{,}000 \ . \end{array} \right.$$

Using this, it is found that SPCAP is at its upper limit (UL) at 18,000, which means that all spinning capacity is fully used. Its slack activity is zero (.), it has no special lower limit apart from 0 and it has an upper limit of 18,000; its imputed cost (dual activity) is 4.33333 or $4\frac{1}{3}$. For loom capacity, the solution is given in a similar way. The objective function REV is reported in a similar way since it may be formulated as

$$(3.3) \qquad \left\{ \begin{array}{l} \text{REV} = 9x_1 + 8x_2 + 50x_3 + 19x_4 \ , \\[2mm] \text{REV} + y_0 = 0 \ , \end{array} \right.$$

where y_0 is a variable having no nonnegativity restriction. Hence if REV = 88,000 then $y_0 = -88{,}000$, which is found under slack activity in this row,

Table 6

Output for optimal solution

EXECUTOR.　MPS/360 V2-M8

SOLUTION (OPTIMAL)

TIME = 0.24 MINS. ITERATION NUMBER = 4

...NAME...	...ACTIVITY...	DEFINED AS
FUNCTIONAL	84925.00000	
RESTRAINTS		REV
BOUNDS....		CAP
RANGES....		SALES
		EMPL

SECTION 1 - ROWS

NUMBER	...ROW..	AT	...ACTIVITY...	SLACK ACTIVITY	..LOWER LIMIT.	..UPPER LIMIT.	.DUAL ACTIVITY
1	REV	BS	84925.00000	84925.00000-	NONE	NONE	1.00000
2	SPCAP	UL	18000.00000		15000.00000	18000.00000	4.75000-
3	LOCAP	BS	2737.50000	262.50000	2500.00000	3000.00000	.

SECTION 2 - COLUMNS

NUMBER	.COLUMN.	AT	...ACTIVITY...	..INPUT COST..	..LOWER LIMIT.	..UPPER LIMIT.	.REDUCED COST.
4	YARNA	LL	500.00000	9.00000	500.00000	1000.00000	5.25000-
5	YARNB	LL	300.00000	8.00000	300.00000	800.00000	1.50000-
6	FABRA	UL	1000.00000	50.00000	600.00000	1000.00000	2.50000
7	FABRB	BS	1475.00000	19.00000	500.00000	1500.00000	.

the minus-sign being written behind it. The imputed cost (dual activity) of the objective function is always 1.

On the next page in Section 2 follow the values of the variables associated with the columns of the set-up tableau. Apart from the values of the variables which are given in the column ACTIVITY and the reduced revenues which are given (with a minus-sign) in the last column, the coefficients in the original objective function are given (input cost) and lower and upper bounds (if any) for these variables are given. The column headed by AT indicates whether these variables are in the optimal solution at their lower limits (LL) or are basic variables (BS) or are at their upper limits (UL).

7.4. Bounds and Ranges

Let us now consider a more general case in which there are upper bounds in the problem as well as a "range" for the constraints. The last concept can be explained as follows. The maximum spinning capacity is 18,000. There may also be a constraint on the minimum spinning capacity used, say 15,000; this may for example, result from the wish to keep employment stable. In this situation the constraint on the maximum spinning capacity to be used is entered as usual, but the constraint on the minimum spinning capacity is entered by putting the *range* of SPCAP at 3000.

Let us again consider the textile production problem but now have the additional requirements that the spinning capacity used should be at least 15,000, that the loom capacity used should be at least 2500 and that there are the following upper and lower bounds on the production and rules of the production:

$$(4.1) \quad \begin{cases} 500 \leqq x_1 \leqq 1000 \,, \\ 300 \leqq x_1 \leqq 800 \,, \\ 600 \leqq x_3 \leqq 1000 \,, \\ 500 \leqq x_3 \leqq 1500 \,. \end{cases}$$

First, a name has to be given to each set of ranges and also to each set of upper and lower bounds. Let us use for the ranges EMPL and for the upper and lower bounds SALES. Only one card of the control program changes; in SETUP, the ranges and the bounds are to be mentioned in the following manner:

SETUP('MAX', 'RANGE', 'EMPL', 'BOUNDS', 'SALES') .

Table 7

Data cards for ranges and bounds

field	f 1	field 2	field 3	field 4	field 5	field 6
columns		1111111111222222222233333333334444444444455555555556				
	1234567890	1234567890	1234567890	1234567890	1234567890	1234567890
cards	RHS					
		CAP	SPCAP	18000	LOCAP	3000
	RANGES					
				3000		
		EMPL	SPCAP	3000	LOCAP	500
	BOUNDS					
	LO	SALES	YARNA	500		
	UP	SALES	YARNA	1000		
	LO	SALES	YARNB	300		
	LP	SALES	YARNB	800		
	LO	SALES	FABRA	600		
	UP	SALES	FABRA	1000		
	LO	SALES	FABRB	500		
	UP	SALES	FABRB	1500		
	ENDATA					

Hence in SETUP it is indicated that the ranges with the name of EMPL should be used and the bounds with the name SALES should be used.

The data for ranges and bounds appear between the RHS section and ENDATA. The contents of the punched cards is reproduced in Table 7. Both for ranges and bounds there is an indicator card. The format of the data cards for ranges is the same as that for columns. Data cards for bounds have LO or UP in Field 1 of it concerns a lower or an upper bound. Field 2 contains the name of the bounds, Field 3 the name of the variable concerned and Field 4 the value of the bound. Fields 5 and 6 are unused. Table 8 contains the three pages output of SOLUTION. It is interesting to compare the solution with that of Table 3 in Chapter 5, where the same upper bounds but not the lower bounds and the ranges were imposed. It should be noted that the dual variables connected with the constraints are quite different in both cases.

7.5. Parametric Programming

Next and last, the implementation of parametric programming will be described. First, parametric programming with a parametric objective function is explained for a numerical example the first example of Section 6.1 is used. The problem, was the same as the original textile production problem, but the objective function was

$$(5.1) \qquad f = 10x_1 + 9x_2 + 65x_3 + 27x_4 - \lambda(x_1 + x_2 + 15x_3 + 8x_4).$$

Table 8

Optimal solution for problem with ranges and bounds

SOLUTION (OPTIMAL)   EXECUTOR. MPS/360 V2-M8

TIME = 0.24 MINS. ITERATION NUMBER = 2

...NAME...	...ACTIVITY...	DEFINED AS
FUNCTIONAL	88000.00000	REV
RESTRAINTS		CAP

EXECUTOR. MPS/360 V2-M8

SECTION 1 - ROWS

NUMBER	...ROW..	AT	...ACTIVITY...	SLACK ACTIVITY	..LOWER LIMIT.	..UPPER LIMIT.	.DUAL ACTIVITY
1	REV	BS	88000.00000	88000.00000-	NONE	NONE	1.00000
2	SPCAP	UL	18000.00000	.	NONE	18000.00000	4.33333-
3	LOCAP	UL	3000.00000	.	NONE	3000.00000	3.33333-

EXECUTOR. MPS/360 V2-M8

SECTION 2 - COLUMNS

NUMBER	.COLUMN.	AT	...ACTIVITY...	..INPUT COST..	..LOWER LIMIT.	..UPPER LIMIT.	.REDUCED COST.
4	YARNA	LL	.	9.00000	.	NONE	4.00000-
5	YARNB	LL	.	8.00000	.	NONE	.66667-
6	FABRA	BS	1000.00000	50.00000	.	NONE	.
7	FABRB	BS	2000.00000	19.00000	.	NONE	.

In the data input, there are two rows, the first of which we again call REV and which contains the coefficients with λ and the second of which contains the coefficients which should be multiplied by λ; since this last row is associated with labour costs we call it LABOR. Both rows and their coefficients are entered in the usual fashion; the type of row which should be entered in the rows section in Field 1 is for both rows N. The coefficients are entered in the columns section as usual; for instance for YARNA we have the following two cards:

```
YARNA   REV     10      LABOR    -1
YARNA   SPCAP    3
```

The program operates by first finding the optimal solution for $\lambda = 0$; then optimal solutions are computed and printed, for values of λ increasing by fixed steps until a specified maximum value of λ is reached. Hence instead of finding solutions at critical values of λ, the program provides solutions at specified intervals of λ. For λ, the variable XPARAM is used which should first be put at 0. The maximum value of λ is called XPARMAX while the size of the steps by which λ has to be increased is indicated by XPARDELT. In this case we shall consider an increase of λ from 0 to 2 with steps of 0.5.

The control program is the same as that given in Table 3 apart from the addition of the following cards between MOVE(XRHS, 'CAP') and PRIMAL:

```
MOVE(XCHROW,'LABOR')
XPARAM = 0.
XPARMAX = 2.
XPARDELT = 0.15
```

Both XPARAM and XPARDELT should contain a decimal point. Then after SOLUTION follows the instruction

```
PARAOBJ('CONT')
```

In the output, first the optimal solution for the instruction SOLUTION is printed; here λ = XPARAM = 0. After this, optimal solutions for XPARAM = 0.5, 1.0, and 1.5 are printed. The optimal solution for XPARAM = 2.0 is not printed because the program stops as soon as XPARAM = XPARMAX. For reasons of space, the output is not reproduced here. The addition ('CONT') makes the program continue printing optimal solutions for the indicated values of λ in cases in which the solution has no upper bound for λ. If this addition is deleted, the program stops as soon as a solution is found with no upper bound for λ.

Parametric programming with parametric constant terms is very similar.

Two RHS columns are required, one of which is to serve as constant-term column and another as λ-term column. We use the example of Section 6.2. Let the constant-term column be indicated as CAP and the λ-term column as LOOM. The coefficients are arranged as follows:

	CAP	LOOM
REV	0	0
SPCAP	18000	0
LOCAP	0	3000

This is entered as follows in the data-input

```
RHS
        CAP       SPCAP      18000
        LOOM      LOCAP      3000
```

Suppose we wish to vary loom capacity from 0 to 5000 by steps of 1000. After change of 3000 into 1000, the relevant part of the control program is given by:

```
MOVE(XCHCOL,  'LOOM')
XPARAM = 0
XPARMAX = 6.
XPARDELT = 1.
PRIMAL
SOLUTION
PARARHS('CONT')
```

The output for PARARHS contains the optimal solutions for XPARAM = 0.0, 1.0, 2.0, 3.0, 4.0, and 5.0. It did not print out the solutions for λ = 6.0 and 5.0 because the program stops when XPARAM = XPARMAX. If the addition 'CONT' would have been deleted, the solutions for XPARAM = 4.0 and 5.0 would not have been printed because for the corresponding basic solution λ has no upper bound; note that solution of Tableau 2 of Table 4 of Chapter 6 is optimal in $3\frac{3}{5} \leq \lambda \leq \infty$.

The MPS-system contains a large number of options, a few of which will just be mentioned. One is RANGE which involves a postoptimality procedure similar to the near-optimality analysis given in Section 4.4. It is also possible to instruct the printing of columns or of rows of the optimal tableau, using the instructions TRANCOL and TRANROW. Furthermore, any row or column of the set-up tableau may be varied parametrically just as the objective function and the right-hand side were varied in ordinary parametric programming; the instructions for this are PARAROW and PARACOL. It is also possible to vary simultaneously the objective function and the right-hand side parametrically which is done by the instruction PARARIM. Nonlinear programming problems of a certain structure (called separable problems) can also be handled.

However, one of the most important advantages of the MPS-system has not yet been mentioned. This is that it gives the opportunity to experiment with large problems. Once the data of the problem are in the computer system, we may take various objective functions and constant terms of the constraints, exclude certain variables and apply parametric programming of various kinds without touching the data again. A person dealing with the application of linear programming to large problems will enhance his usefulness considerably by mastering all features of the MPS-system.

Exercises

1. Solve the problem of Table 6 of Chapter 2 using MPS.

2. Solve Problem 7 of Chapter 2 using MPS.

3. Solve Problem 9 of Chapter 3 using MPS.

4. Solve Problem 4 of Chapter 5 using MPS.

5. Solve Problem 3 of Chapter 6 using MPS.

8. FORMULATION AND STRUCTURE OF LINEAR PROGRAMMING PROBLEMS

8.1. Intermediate Products in Production Planning

Linear programming can handle very large and complicated problems. While the computations for these problems do not cause difficulties unless the problems are very large, the formulation is not always simple, so that it is useful to consider the formulation of problems more systematically.

In this section an example is given of a problem with intermediate products which occur frequently in more complicated problems. In the next section the formulation of a linear programming problem using the concept of *activities* is explained. Many realistic programming problems are of a dynamic nature. It is therefore useful to give a treatment of dynamic problems which is done in the last section, where the textile production planning problem is extended to cover a number of periods.

Let us return to the textile production planning example of Chapter 2. For the weaving of fabrics, yarns are used. In the example the quantities of yarn required for Fabrics A and B did not appear explicitly; instead the spinning capacity needed for the production of the yarn used for one unit of fabric was given. This capacity could have been found in the following manner. Let us assume that Fabric A requires per unit 2 units of Yarn A and 2 units of Yarn B. Since Yarn A uses 3 units of spinning capacity per unit and Yarn B 2 units of spinning capacity per unit, the total spinning capacity required for one unit of Fabric A amounts to

$$2 \cdot 3 + 2 \cdot 2 = 10 .$$

If Fabric B requires per unit 1 unit of Yarn A and $\frac{1}{2}$ unit of Yarn B, the total spinning capacity required per unit of Fabric B is

$$1 \cdot 3 + \frac{1}{2} \cdot 2 = 4 .$$

This agrees with the data given in Table 1 of Chapter 2.

143

Instead of giving the spinning capacity requirement for the fabrics, we may give their requirements in terms of Yarns A and B. This means that two additional constraints should be formulated, one in terms of Yarn A and one in terms of Yarn B. This also has an impact on direct costs, since the direct costs for the yarns used for the production of the fabrics are now taken into account by the yarn requirement and should therefore not be contained in the direct costs of the fabrics. Table 1 below gives the data for the textile problem modified as indicated above. Yarn A and B are now not only final products but also intermediate products.

Table 1
Modified data for textile production planning

	Yarn A	Yarn B	Fabric A	Fabric B
Selling Price $/unit	12	10	75	29
Direct Costs $/unit	3	2	15	6
Spinning Time h/unit	3	2	–	–
Loom Time h/unit	–	–	2	$^1/_2$
Units Yarn A/unit	–	–	2	1
Units Yarn B/unit	–	–	2	$^1/_2$

Let x_1 be the quantity produced of Yarn A both for internal use and for sale and x_2 be the similar quantity of Yarn B. x_5 stands for the quantity sold of Yarn A and x_6 for the quantity sold of Yarn B. Since no fabrics are used internally, production and sales of Fabrics A and B are identical; let therefore x_3 stand for the quantity produced and sold of Fabric A and x_4 for the quantity produced and sold of Fabric B.

The objective function which is to be maximized is then as follows:

$$(1.1) \qquad f = -3x_1 - 2x_2 + 60x_3 + 23x_4 + 12x_5 + 10x_6 .$$

Since x_1 stands for the *production* of Yarn A, only the direct costs of production should be entered in the objective function; the same is true for Yarn B. x_3 stands for the quantity produced and sold of Fabric A. The selling price is 75, the direct cost of production (excluding the direct costs of the intermediate products, Yarns A and B, which are $2 \cdot 3 + 2 \cdot 2 = 10$) are assumed to be 15, so that the net revenue per unit is 60. In the same way it is found that the net revenue for Fabric B is $29 - 6 = 23$. x_5 is the quantity sold of Yarn A and has therefore a net revenue of 12 per unit; the direct costs of production, which for Yarn A are 3, are accounted for by the term in x_1. Similarly, the net revenue of Yarn B is equal to its selling price, 10 per unit.

In this reformulation there are, apart from the nonnegativity conditions, four constraints. The first one is concerned with spinning capacity, which is used exclusively for the production of Yarns A and B. Hence we have

$$(1.2) \qquad 3x_1 + 2x_2 \leqq 18,000 \,.$$

x_3, x_4, x_5, and x_6 do not occur in this constraint, since production and sales of fabrics and sales of yarns do not directly use any spinning capacity. However, the production and sales of fabrics and sales of yarns do use quantities of yarns produced. The quantity of Yarn A used for the production of Fabric A and B and the sales of Yarn A is $2x_3 + x_4 + x_5$ and this should not exceed the quantity produced of Yarn A, which is x_1. Hence we have the following constraint:

$$2x_3 + x_4 + x_5 \leqq x_1 \,,$$

or

$$(1.3) \qquad -x_1 + 2x_3 + x_4 + x_5 \leqq 0 \,.$$

Similarly, there is the following constraint on the quantity produced of Yarn B:

$$2x_3 + \tfrac{1}{2}x_4 + x_6 \leqq x_2 \,,$$

or

$$(1.4) \qquad -x_2 + 2x_3 + \tfrac{1}{2}x_4 + x_6 \leqq 0 \,.$$

Finally, there is a constraint on loom capacity which is the same as in the original formulation:

$$(1.5) \qquad 2x_3 + \tfrac{1}{2}x_4 \leqq 3000 \,.$$

The equations (1.1)–(1.5) can easily be put into a simplex tableau format, which provides the set-up tableau given in Tableau 0 of Table 2; the constant terms have been divided by 1000. Since the solution of the set-up tableau is feasible, the simplex method can be applied immediately. After five iterations the optimal solution is obtained.

Tableau 5 of Table 2 contains this optimal solution. It is essentially the

Table 2
Set-up and final tableau for the reformulated textile production planning problem

Tableau	Basic Variables	Values Basic Variables	x_1	x_2	x_3	x_4	x_5	x_6
	f	0	3	2	-60	-23	-12	-10
	y_1	18	3	2	0	0	0	0
0	y_2	0	-1	0	2	1	1	0
	y_3	0	0	-1	2	$^1/_2$	0	1
	y_4	3	0	0	2	$^1/_2$	0	0
			y_3	y_4	y_2	x_5	y_1	x_6
	f	88	$10^2/_3$	$3^1/_3$	16	4	$4^1/_3$	$^2/_3$
	x_4	2	$1^1/_3$	$-3^1/_3$	2	2	$^2/_3$	$1^2/_3$
5	x_3	1	$-^1/_3$	$1^1/_3$	$-^1/_2$	$-^1/_2$	$-^1/_6$	$-^1/_3$
	x_1	4	$^2/_3$	$-^2/_3$	0	0	$^1/_3$	$^2/_3$
	x_2	3	-1	1	0	0	0	-1

same as the solution found in Chapter 2. Since the constant terms have been divided by 1000, all values of basic variables are expressed in thousands. 1000 units of Fabric A should be produced and sold and 2000 units of Fabric B should be produced and sold. Furthermore, 4000 units of Yarn A and 3,000 units of Yarn B should be produced, which evidently are used for the production of fabrics. The value of f stands at $88,000.

As before, the imputed costs of the constraints are of considerable importance. The imputed costs of spinning capacity and loom capacity are, as in Chapter 2, $4^1/_3$ and $3^1/_3$, see the elements in the f-row and in the columns of y_1 and y_4. The constraint (1.3) is stated in terms of available units of Yarn A and the imputed costs of the constraint can therefore be interpreted as the value of Yarn A, which is 16 in this case (the coefficient of y_2 in the f-row). Note that Yarn A is an intermediate product which is not actually sold at the market, so that its market price, 12, cannot be used. Hence this linear programming formulation assigns a value to an intermediate product.

The same value could be found after some computation in the formulation of Chapter 2: Yarn A requires 3 units of loom capacity, valued at $4^1/_3$ and its direct costs are 3, so that its value is $3 \cdot 4^1/_3 + 3 = 16$. The coefficients of y_3 in the f-row of Tableau 5 is the imputed cost of constraint (1.4), so that it gives the value of Yarn B, which is $10^2/_3$. Also this could have been found in the original formulation since Yarn B requires 2 units of spinning capacity valued at $4^1/_3$, to which the direct costs of 2 should be added.

Note that the imputed values of Yarns A and B, 16 and $10^2/_3$, exceed their selling prices 12 and 10. By formulating the dual problem it can in fact be shown that the selling prices give *lower bounds* for the imputed values of the yarns (see Exercise 1). This is plausible, since a lower value than the selling price cannot correspond with an optimal solution because it is then more advantageous to sell the product at the selling price. If it is possible to buy the intermediate products, the buying prices constitute *upper bounds* for the imputed values of the intermediate products.

8.2. Economic Activities in Linear Programming

The textile production planning problem will again be slightly extended in order to demonstrate an interpretation of the problem which facilitates its formulation as a linear programming problem. Let the data for the textile problem be as indicated in Table 3. The difference with the data given before is that a labour requirement has been added for each product; direct costs have been adjusted for this. It is assumed that for the period under consideration 2500 hours are available which are worked by the permanent staff. Additional hours of labour can be obtained by having the permanent staff work overtime or by hiring temporary help; in both cases the costs are $4 per hour. The cost of the permanent staff is considered fixed and is therefore not considered.

Table 3
Data for extended textile production planning problem

	Yarn A	Yarn B	Fabric A	Fabric B
Selling Price $/unit	12	10	75	29
Direct Costs $/unit	2	1	9	3
Labour h/unit	$^1/_4$	$^1/_4$	$1^1/_2$	$^3/_4$
Spinning Time h/unit	3	2	–	–
Loom Time h/unit	–	–	2	$^1/_2$
Units Yarn A/unit	–	–	2	1
Units Yarn B/unit	–	–	2	$^1/_2$

As in the previous section, x_1 and x_2 may be denoted as the quantity produced of Yarns A and B, x_3 and x_4 as the quantities produced and sold of Fabrics A and B, x_5 and x_6 as the quantities sold of Yarns A and B. Furthermore, x_7 is used for the amount of overtime worked or hours of temporary help.

Now the production of Yarn A may be considered as an *economic activity* which may be at various nonnegative levels. Such an activity has *inputs* and *outputs*, which are proportional to the level of that activity. For the production of Yarn A the inputs are money (direct costs), labor, and spinning time and the output is Yarn A. As unit level of the activity the obvious choice of 1 unit of Yarn A is made; the level of the activity can then be indicated by x_1.

For inputs and outputs of activities the name *commodities* may be used. In the present case we have the following commodities: money, labour, spinning time, loom time, Yarn A, and Yarn B. The inputs and outputs of an activity may be put in a column with the inputs having a positive sign and the outputs a negative one. For activity 1, the production of Yarn A, with a level of x_1, the following column of inputs and outputs is found, the commodities being arranged in the order in which they were enumerated:

(money)	$2x_1$
(labour)	$\frac{1}{4}x_1$
(spinning time)	$3x_1$
(loom time)	$0x_1$
(Yarn A)	$-x_1$
(Yarn B)	$0x_1$.

The activities of production of Yarn B, the production and sales of Fabric A and the production and sales of Fabric B are, respectively,

(money)	x_2	$-66x_3$	$-26x_4$
(labour)	$\frac{1}{4}x_2$	$1\frac{1}{2}x_3$	$\frac{3}{4}x_4$
(spinning time)	$2x_2$	$0x_3$	$0x_4$
(loom time)	$0x_2$	$2x_3$	$\frac{1}{2}x_4$
(Yarn A)	$0x_2$	$2x_3$	x_4
(Yarn B)	$-x_2$	$2x_3$	$\frac{1}{2}x_4$

Note that the outputs of the third and fourth activity are not production of Fabrics A and B, because we do not consider these commodities: instead they have money as an output because we assume that any production is sold.

Finally, we have activities concerned with buying and selling: the fifth and sixth activity are the sales of Yarns A and B and the seventh the buying of additional hours of labour. Selling Yarn A has Yarn A as input and money as output, selling Yarn B has Yarn B as input and money as output and buying labor hours has money as input and labor as output. The three activities concerned are therefore:

(money)	$-12x_5$	$-10x_6$	$4x_7$
(labour)	$0x_5$	$0x_6$	$-x_7$
(spinning time)	$0x_5$	$0x_6$	$0x_7$
(loom time)	$0x_5$	$0x_6$	$0x_7$
(Yarn A)	x_5	$0x_6$	$0x_7$
(Yarn B)	$0x_5$	x_6	$0x_7$.

The inputs and outputs of all commodities can be combined by adding them; then for each commodity except money the inputs minus the outputs should not exceed the initially available quantity of that commodity:

(labour)	$\frac{1}{4}x_1 + \frac{1}{4}x_2 + 1\frac{1}{2}x_3 + \frac{3}{4}x_4 + 0x_5 + 0x_6 - x_7 \leqq 2500$,
(spinning time)	$3x_1 + 2x_2 + 0x_3 + 0x_4 + 0x_5 + 0x_6 + 0x_7 \leqq 18{,}000$,
(loom time)	$0x_1 + 0x_2 + 2x_3 + \frac{1}{2}x_4 + 0x_5 + 0x_6 + 0x_7 \leqq 3000$,
(Yarn A)	$-x_1 + 0x_2 + 2x_3 + x_4 + x_5 + 0x_6 + 0x_7 \leqq 0$,
(Yarn B)	$0x_1 - x_2 + 2x_3 + \frac{1}{2}x_4 + 0x_5 + x_6 + 0x_7 \leqq 0$.

If for money the same combination of activities is made, we find

$$2x_1 + x_2 - 66x_3 - 26x_4 - 12x_5 - 10x_6 + 4x_7 .$$

This is inputs of money minus outputs of money; since f is the net output of money which is to be maximized, the combination of activities in terms of money stands for $-f$. We have now obtained a complete formulation of the problem in terms of economic activities.

The solution of this linear programming problem is as follows. For the basic variables we have (in thousands): $x_1 = 4, x_2 = 3, x_2 = 1, x_4 = 2, x_7 = 2\frac{1}{4}$, $f = 98$. For the elements in the f-row in the columns of nonbasic variables we find: for x_5: 4, for x_6: $\frac{2}{3}$, for y_1: 4, for y_2: $4\frac{1}{3}$, for y_3: $3\frac{1}{3}$, for y_4: 16, for y_5: $10\frac{2}{3}$. Hence the solution of this problem is essentially the same as that of the previous problem. The value of the objective function is now $10,000 higher, which is explained by the fact that the costs of permanent staff is now considered fixed and is therefore not included in the objective function.

The dual problem of this problem is as follows. Minimize

(2.1) $g = 2500u_1 + 18,000u_2 + 3000u_3$

subject to

(2.2) $\frac{1}{4}u_1 + 3u_2 - u_4 \geq -2$,

(2.3) $\frac{1}{4}u_1 + 2u_2 - u_5 \geq -1$,

(2.4) $1\frac{1}{2}u_1 + u_3 + 2u_4 + 2u_5 \geq 66$,

(2.5) $\frac{3}{4}u_1 + \frac{1}{2}u_3 + u_4 + \frac{1}{2}u_5 \geq 26$,

(2.6) $u_4 \geq 12$,

(2.7) $u_5 \geq 10$,

(2.8) $-u_1 \geq -4$,

(2.9) $u_1, u_2, u_3, u_4, u_5 \geq 0$.

Let us consider the constraints of the dual problem in some more detail. (2.2) can be written as follows:

$$2 + \frac{1}{4}u_1 + 3u_2 \geq u_4.$$

The u's can be interpreted as the imputed values of the various commodities, so that according to (2.2) the value of the inputs for the production of Yarn A should be at least as high as the value of its outputs. This condition for an optimal solution makes sense, because if it was not satisfied, it would be advantageous to increase the level of production, so that the present solution could not have been optimal. Furthermore, we know that the value of inputs and outputs are equal if the activity concerned is basic; this is true for production of Yarn A. Similar observations are valid for the other activities.

8.3. A Dynamic Production, Sales, and Inventory Model

The model used so far was a static one; it only refers to one period. In many cases it is possible to produce not only for the sales of the present period but also for those of future periods; sales for the present period may also be taken from inventory accumulated out of past production. In this way it is possible to smooth demand fluctuations which may be seasonal or caused in some other way. Let us assume that the planning period is four weeks and that we plan ahead for a year, that is 13 four-week periods. We assume that demand is known for these 13 periods. Let us indicate maximum sales for product i in period t by $\bar{r}_{it}$ and inventory of product i at the end of period t by z_{it}. The production of product i in period t is indicated by x_{it}. Inventory costs per period are 2 per cent of direct costs which, as in Table 1 of Chapter 2, are 3, 2, 25, and 10 for the four products.

In this dynamic model there are 13 sets of production constraints which are identical, apart from the indication of the period, to the production constraints in the static model:

$$(3.1) \qquad \begin{cases} 3x_{1t} + 2x_{2t} + 10x_{3t} + \ 4x_{4t} \leq 18{,}000 \, , \\[2mm] \phantom{3x_{1t} + 2x_{2t} + 10} 2x_{3t} + \tfrac{1}{2}x_{4t} \leq \ 3000 \, , \end{cases} \qquad t = 1, ..., 13 \, .$$

Since production is not necessarily equal to sales, a distinction must be made between the two. Let r_{it} stand for the sales of product i in period t. Since the sales of any produce in any period cannot exceed maximum sales, the following upper-bound constraints should be satisfied:

$$(3.2) \qquad r_{it} \leq \bar{r}_{it} \, , \qquad i = 1, ..., 4 \, , \qquad t = 1, ..., 13 \, .$$

The $\bar{r}_{it}$ are given constants and the r_{it} are variables. For inventories the following equations are valid:

$$(3.3) \qquad z_{it} = z_{i,t-1} + x_{it} - r_{it} \, , \qquad i = 1, ..., 4 \, , \qquad t = 1, ..., 13 \, .$$

In the static model, direct costs were subtracted from selling prices in order to obtain net revenue per unit produced. In the dynamic case, production and sales do not necessarily coincide, so that production costs should be allocated to the production variable and sales revenues to the sales variables. Using the data of Table 1 of Chapter 2, we find for sales revenue

$$f_s = \sum_{t=1}^{13} \left(12r_{1t} + 10r_{2t} + 75r_{3t} + 29r_{4t} \right) \, ;$$

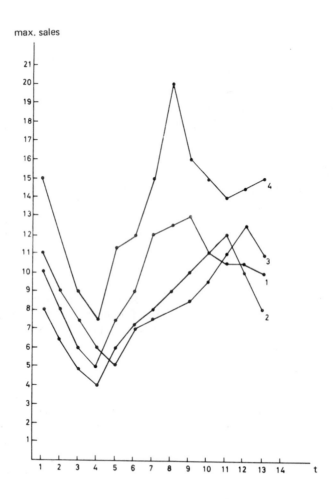

Fig. 1. Maximal sales for four products.

production costs are

$$f_p = \sum_{t=1}^{13} (3x_{1t} + 2x_{2t} + 25x_{3t} + 10x_{4t})$$

and inventory costs are

$$f_i = 0.02 \sum_{t=1}^{13} (3z_{1t} + 2z_{2t} + 25z_{3t} + 10z_{4t}) .$$

The objective function which is to be maximized is

(3.4) $f = f_s - f_p - f_i$;

the constraints are (3.1), (3.2), and (3.3); all variables should be nonnegative.

If the upper bounds $\bar{r}_{it}$ in (3.2) are given, the optimal solution to the problem may be found. Since this problem is fairly sizeable, use of computer computation is indispensable. If the pattern of maximum sales for the products 1–4 over the 13 periods given in Figure 1 is used, the solution displayed in the following figures is obtained.

In Figure 2.1 the solid line indicates production of product 1 in hundreds. The broken lines indicate sales and maximum sales; wherever they do not coincide, the lower indicates sales and the upper maximum sales. Note that the production and sales patterns are quite different. In the first period and in the last two periods sales differ from maximum sales. Figure 2.2 gives similar results for product 2. Production is here even more erratic, the production periods 1–4, 6–9, and 12–13 being interrupted twice. Only in period 1 sales are below maximum sales. Figure 2.3 gives the results for products 3 and 4. For product 3, sales are always equal to maximum sales and production follows sales, apart from the periods 10–12, where there is a small difference. For product 4, sales, maximum sales and production coincide entirely.

Figure 3 gives a representation of inventories. As can be expected from Figures 2.1 and 2.2, there is an inventory build-up for product 1 in early periods and for product 2 in later periods. There is a very small inventory of product 3 in the periods 10 and 11.

The following figures indicate the course of the corresponding imputed values. According to Figure 4, the imputed value of spinning capacity is 4 in period 1, decreases to 2.8 in period 2 and then increases slowly to 3.02 in period 13. Weaving capacity has some small positive imputed values in periods 12 and 13. The imputed values corresponding to the inventory balance equa-

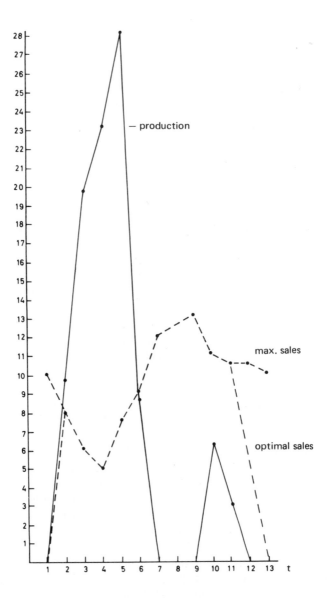

Fig. 2.1. Optimal production and sales for product 1.

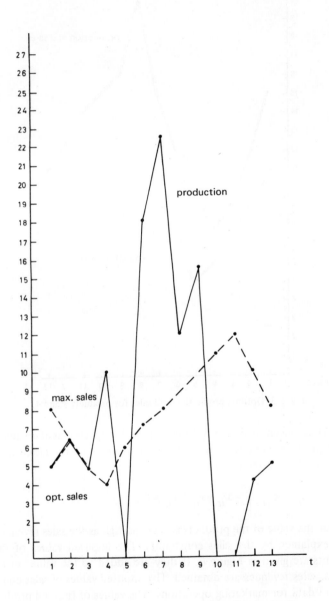

Formulation and structure of linear programming problems   155

Fig. 2.2. Optimal production and sales for product 2.

Fig. 2.3. Optimal production and sales for products 3 and 4.

tion (3.3) are given in Figure 5. They can be interpreted as the value of the finished product, because they correspond to an artificial slack variable y_{it} which could be inserted into (3.3):

$$(3.5) \qquad z_{it} - z_{i,t-1} - x_{it} + r_{it} + y_{it} = 0.$$

Note that the value of the products is never as high as the sales revenue which can be explained by the sales constraints. The imputed values of the sales constraints are given in Figure 6. If they are added to the values of finished products, sales revenues are obtained. The imputed values of sales constraints are useful data for marketing operations. The values of finished products can be used as accounting prices within the company.

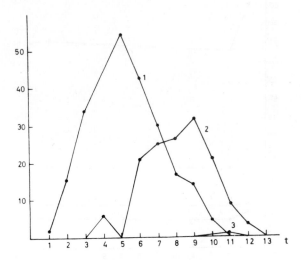

Fig. 3. Optimal inventories.

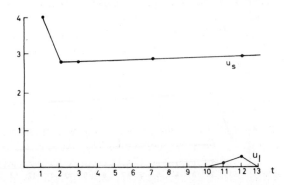

Fig. 4. Imputed values of spinning and loom capacity.

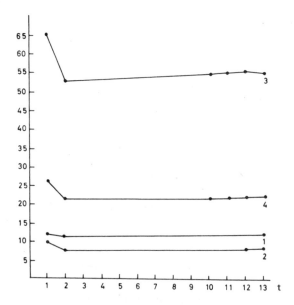

Fig. 5. Imputed values of the four products.

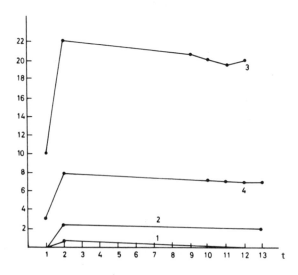

Fig. 6. Imputed values of sales constraints.

Since there is such a huge build-up in inventory of product 1 and a somewhat smaller one in product 2 it can be imagined that management considers such a large inventory too risky in view of possible obsolescence. In this case, upper limits to the inventory of a single product may be set, for example 3000 units for both products 1 and 2. The lower revenue found from the solution in which these constraints are imposed should be compared with the desirability of the smaller risk.

When the solution as a whole is considered, it is clear that spinning capacity is the production factor which is relatively scarce. The profitability of the products in terms of this production factor is 3, 4, 5, and $4\frac{1}{4}$ for products 1, 2, 3, and 4. Hence we may expect that the order of products of which maximum demand is not satisfied is 1, 2, 4, and 3. Looking at period 1, in which maximum demand is fairly high, it is found that demand for product 1 is not satisfied at all and that demand for product 2 is partly satisfied. Since product 2 is the marginal product, the imputed value of spinning capacity in period 1 is 4.

The remaining periods can be considered as a whole since it is possible by using inventories to produce in periods where maximum demand is low for periods in which maximum demand is higher. In this way, maximum demand for all products except product 1 can be satisfied in all periods. The maximum demand for product 1 in the last two periods cannot be satisfied. Since product 1 is the marginal product and spinning capacity the scarce factor, the imputed value of spinning capacity should be around 3, which is borne out by the results which are slightly different because of the interference of inventory costs. The imputed values of weaving capacity in periods 11 and 12 are quite small.

In fact, the solution for periods 2–13 can be compared with that of Table 3 of Chapter 5 where also product 1 was the marginal product. The imputed values of the sales constraints confirm this. Hence approximately the same solution could have been obtained by considering the periods 1–13 as a whole, so that it has one spinning capacity and one weaving capacity constraint and one maximum sales constraint for each product. However, this can be done only because inventory costs are relatively small. If they are more substantial, a different solution will emerge. Furthermore, it must be stressed that it is easy to reach these conclusions once the computer calculations have been made. A very careful analysis of the problem might have found the same solution, but would not be able to give the exact solution and would be more costly both in terms of time and money in most cases.

This model may be generalized in various ways. The possibility of overtime affects both production capacity and costs. Overtime may be included in the model by adding the terms v_{st} and v_{lt} to the right-hand sides of (3.1); v_{st} stands for the number of hours of spinning capacity in period t, which are added as overtime and v_{lt} as the number of hours of loom capacity in period t, which are added as overtime. The number of hours of overtime is usually limited, so that upper bounds have to be imposed:

$$(3.6) \qquad v_{st} \leqq \bar{v}_{st} , \quad v_{lt} \leqq \bar{v}_{lt} , \qquad t = 1, ..., 13 ;$$

$\bar{v}_{st}$ and $\bar{v}_{\varrho t}$ are the given upper bounds for v_{st} and v_{lt}. The marginal costs of this additional capacity should be included in the objective function by addition of the terms

$$(3.7) \qquad -\sum_{t=1}^{13} m_s v_{st} - \sum_{t=1}^{13} m_l v_{lt} ,$$

where m_s and m_l are the marginal costs of one hour of overtime spinning and loom capacity.

In some cases a restriction on inventories exists. This may be a space limitation valid separately for one or more products or it may be valid for two or more products simultaneously. In the first case, there are upper bounds on the z_{it}: in the second there are constraints of the following type:

$$(3.8) \qquad a_1 z_{1t} + a_2 z_{2t} + a_3 z_{3t} + a_4 z_{4t} \leqq a_0 , \qquad t = 1, ..., 13 ,$$

where a_0 is the total space available for inventories, and $a_1, ..., a_4$ the space required for one unit of the respective products.

It is also possible that management does not want the capital tied up in inventories to rise over a certain level. Such a constraint may be formulated analogously to (3.8). However, it is in this case useful to ask why such an upper bound of inventories is desired. If such an upper bound has been imposed because management wants to keep its return on capital high, this is not the best way to do it; if the capital cost component of inventory costs has been based on marginal revenue of capital, such extra constraints lead to lower profits. It may also be that liquidity plays a role, but in this case it is better to introduce explicit liquidity constraints which specify that the liquidities for each period should not be lower than given levels.

How many periods should be taken into account? This depends in the first place on the data available for future periods, especially those concerning future demand. If there is a strong seasonal fluctuation, it is advisable to have at least one full cycle, even if the data for future periods are rather uncertain.

In such cases we may compute the optimal solution for the pattern of demand which seems most likely at that instant; only the decision for the next period is implemented. After this period is over, the decision for the next period is taken in the same manner, but with demand data which are more up-to-date; further, the model now includes, instead of the period which just elapsed, a new future period. This may be called a *moving horizon* procedure.

Exercises

1. Consider the general form of the typical maximization problem with n products and m constraints: Maximize

$$f = p_1 x_1 + ... + p_n x_n$$

subject to

$$a_{11} x_1 + ... + a_{1n} x_n \leq b_1 ,$$

$$...$$

$$a_{m1} x_1 + ... + a_{mn} x_n \leq b_m ,$$

$$x_1, ..., x_n \geq 0 .$$

(a) Assume now that it is possible to buy quantities of resource i ($i = 1, ...,$ m) at prices $\bar{c}_i$. Modify the problem accordingly and formulate the corresponding dual problem. Prove that the $\bar{c}_i$ are upper bounds for the u_i in the optimal solution.

(b) Assume now instead that it is possible to sell quantities of the resources i ($i = 1, ..., m$) at prices $\underline{c}_i$. Use the resulting dual problem to show that the $\underline{c}_i$ are lower bounds for the u_i in the optimal solution.

(c) Now combine the assumptions of (a) and (b) and conclude that the u_i now have upper and lower bounds. Suppose that for some resource i, we have $\underline{c}_i > \bar{c}_i$. What can be said in this case about the solutions of the primal and the dual problem?

2. A company produces four final products, each of which uses the same basic material which is also produced by the company. The basic material is produced in a process of variable duration; duration and yield are related in the following manner

Process and duration (Minutes)	Yield of basic material (Units of bas. mat.)
20	25
30	31
40	36
50	40
60	42

Costs per process are $10; time-related cost of running the process are $30 per hour. The process can be run at most 16 hours per day.

There are four products, called A, B, C, and D which use 5, 4, 6, and 4 units of the basic material respectively. Products A and B are both processed on machine I and require both 12 minutes per unit on this machine. Products C and D are both processed on machine II and need both 6 minutes per unit on this machine.

There are 8 machine hours per day available on machine I and 12 on machine II. Selling price minus variable costs (excluding cost of basic material) are $13, $11, $17, and $13 for products A, B, C, and D. It is assumed that an unlimited amount of the four products can be sold. Determine the optimal production program and the imputed costs of the constraints.

3. A plant uses of a certain material 20 tons per week. The material should contain exactly 50 per cent of a certain ingredient. It is possible to buy material with a given content at a given price; the data are:

Per cent content	Price, $ per ton
30	25
35	40
40	55
45	70
50	90

Any of these materials may be refined which increases its content in a manner given by a curve in Figure 7. The material may be refined more than once; for instance, it may first be refined from 30 per cent to 40 per cent, then from 40 per cent to 49.25 per cent and then from 49.25 per cent to 52 per cent. Refining costs are $20 per ton per time. Maximum

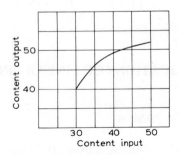

Fig. 7.

refining capacity is 25 tons per week. The exact content of 50 per cent may be achieved by mixing the material.

Find the minimum-cost purchasing and refining program using a computer. Hint: Use a discrete approximation of the curve.

9. SOME APPLICATIONS OF LINEAR PROGRAMMING

9.1. A Capital Budgeting Problem

Consider the following problem. Somebody wants to invest $100,000 for the time of five years in such a way that he ends up, after these five years, with the maximum amount of money. Each year he wants to take out $5,000. He can invest in five investment projects or he may buy a five-year bond or he may each year simply put his money into a bank and draw the interest on it. In order to keep the problem reasonably small no more possibilities are considered.

The usual procedure for handling problems of this type is to compute the internal rate of return for each project and select the project with the highest rate. However, this does not necessarily lead to the maximum revenue since it does not deal with all possibilities consisting of combinations of various projects, for which programming methods are admirably suited.

The investment projects may be described as follows. For one unit of participation in project 1, $1 should be invested in the beginning of year 1, another $1 in the beginning of year 2, and again $1 in the beginning of year 3. After this, the project starts to yield returns. $0.50 becomes available in the beginning of year 4 and the same amount in the beginning of year 5. The final return for one unit of participation which becomes available at the end of year 5 is given to be $3.50; this could be considered as the revenues over the remaining future periods discounted at the end of year 5. The same data can be found in Table 1, where returns apart from the final pay-off, are indicated with a minus-sign. The data for the other four projects can be found in the other columns of the same table.

It is assumed that there is no uncertainty as to the yield of the various projects which, admittedly, is in many cases not very realistic. It is possible to take uncertainty in capital budgeting problems into account by means of stochastic programming, which is not considered in this book. The linear programming approach can be used if the uncertainty is not very large or it may serve as a first approximation in other cases.

164

Furthermore, for the above problem it is assumed that any positive amount up to $100,000 can be invested in any of the projects. In some cases there is a maximum amount to be invested in any project which is smaller than the amount available; such cases can easily be located by using the upper-bound method of Section 5.2. More difficulties arise if there is a minimum amount to be invested in a project if any participation is made; it may even be that it is only possible to invest a fixed amount of money in any project or none at all. In these cases, an integer programming formulation is possible. Such a formulation is obvious if only integer multiples of given amounts can be invested, which may be the case for bonds. Here these difficulties will be disregarded.

Apart from the investment projects there is the possibility of buying five-year bonds paying 6 per cent annual interest, for which the principal (plus the last year's interest) is repaid at the end of the fifth year. Then the money may be put into a savings account for a year, in each year, which gives 5 per cent interest; this may be done in each of the five years. These possibilities are indicated by the next six columns of Table 1.

As pointed out before, the problem can best be formulated in terms of activities. Let activity 1 be one unit of participation in investment project 1. The commodities which are affected by this activity are the amount of money being available in years 1, 2, 3, 4, 5, and just after year 5. The inputs and outputs of this activity are then given by column 1 of projects in Table 1, except that the final pay-off which is an output is given by a plus-sign. The other activities are given in the same manner. Buying the bond is just one activity, but putting money in a savings account for a year should be expressed as five activities corresponding with the year during which the money is placed in the bank. The constant term is for year 1, 100,000 and for years 2–5, −5,000.

Let the levels of these activities be $x_1, ..., x_{11}$. The sum to be maximized, which is the sum available after five years is then

(1.1) $$f = 3.5x_1 + 11x_2 + 4x_3 + 6x_4 + 5x_5 + 1.06x_6 + 1.05x_{11}.$$

The constraint for the money available in year 1 is

(1.2) $$x_1 + x_2 + x_3 + x_4 + x_5 + x_6 + x_7 \leq 100,000.$$

The constraint for the available amount in the second year is

(1.3) $$x_1 + 2x_2 + 0.5x_5 + x_4 + 2.5x_5 + x_8 + 5,000 \leq 0.06x_6 + 1.05x_7.$$

Table 1
Data and solution for an example of a capital budgeting problem

	Capital input or output	Projects 1	2	3	4	5	5-year bond	Yearly interest 1	2	3	4	5	Optimal solution y-variables	Shadow costs
Year 1	100,000	1	1	1	1	1	1	1	0	0	0	0		1.60
Year 2	-5,000	1	2	0.5	1	2.5	-0.06	-1.05	1	0	0	0		1.52
Year 3	-5,000	1	3	0.5	1	2	-0.06	0	-1.05	1	0	0		1.45
Year 4	-5,000	-0.5	2	0.5	1	0	-0.06	0	0	-1.05	1	0		1.10
Year 5	-5,000	-0.5	1	0.5	1	-2	-0.06	0	0	0	-1.05	1		1.05
Final pay-off		3.5	11	4	6	5	1.06	0	0	0	0	1.05	134,400	
Optimal solution x-variables		31,721						68,279	34,972		10,860	22,264		
Reduced revenues			1.26	0.16	0.73	1.21	0.23			0.29				

For the amounts available in the third, fourth and fifth year, the constraints are

$$(1.4) \qquad x_1 + 3x_2 + 0.5x_3 + x_4 + 2x_5 + x_9 + 5000 \leqq 0.06x_6 + 1.05x_8 \,,$$

$$(1.5) \qquad 2x_2 + 0.5x_3 + x_4 + x_{10} + 5000 \leqq 0.5x_1 + 0.06x_6 + 1.05x_9 \,,$$

$$(1.6) \qquad x_2 + 0.5x_3 + x_4 + x_{11} + 5000 \leqq 0.5x_1 + 2x_5 + 0.06x_6 + 1.05x_{10} \,.$$

After addition of the usual nonnegativity constraints

$$(1.7) \qquad x_1, x_2, ..., x_{11} \geqq 0 \,,$$

the problem is completely formulated.

In this formulation the possibility of simply leaving the money unused for one or more years was not included because it is always better to put it in the savings account for one or more years. This possibility might have been included, however, by inserting the variable z_1, indicating the amount of unused money, into the left-hand side of (1.2) and the right-hand side of (1.3); z_2 is similarly invested into the left-hand side of (1.3) and the right-hand side of (1.4) and so on.

Since even this small problem is too large for convenient hand computation, it is solved on a computer. The solution is indicated in the last two rows and columns of Table 1. The outcome is that \$31,721 should be the participation in project 1. The remaining amount should be put into the savings account, in which \$68,279 is invested in the first year, \$34,972 in the second, nothing in the third, \$10,860 in the fourth year and \$22,264 in the fifth. None of the slack variables has a positive value, the reason for which is obvious. The total amount available after five years is \$134,400.

It is interesting to look at the shadow costs of the constraints which are given in the second column of the optimal solution, which are 1.60, 1.52, 1.45, 1.10, and 1.05 for the five constraints. They can be used for an alternative evaluation of the value of the objective function:

$$(1.8) \qquad 134,400 = 100,000 \cdot 1.60 - 5000 \, (1.52 + 1.45 + 1.10 + 1.05) \,.$$

From this, it may be concluded that the disbursements $4 \cdot \$5000 = \$20,000$ decreased the final pay-off by \$25,600.

It is also possible to deduce the effective interest rates from these shadow costs. The value of \$1 at the beginning of the first year is \$1.60 in terms of money at the end of five years. Hence the average annual interest r for the five years is computed from

$$(1.9) \qquad (1+r)^5 = 1.60 ,$$

where r is the interest rate. Hence $r = \sqrt[5]{1.60} - 1 = 0.10$. Hence the average interest rate is 10 per cent. The interest rates for each of the five years to be derived from the shadow costs are generally different. They are computed as follows: Let r_1 be the interest rate of year one to be derived from the shadow costs. Then the value of $1 + r_1$ dollars at the end of year 1 should be equal to the value of 1 dollar at the start of that year. The value of 1 dollar at the end of year 1 is 1.52 in terms of dollars at the end of the five years and the value of 1 dollar at the start of the first year is 1.60 in terms of dollars at the end of the five years. Hence we have

$$1.52 (1+r_1) = 1.60$$

or $r_1 = 0.05$. Hence the interest rate for year 1 derived from the shadow cost is 5 per cent. For the other four years, we find in the same manner

$$1.45 (1+r_2) = 1.52, \qquad r_2 = 0.05 ,$$
$$1.10 (1+r_3) = 1.45, \qquad r_3 = 0.32 ,$$
$$1.05 (1+r_4) = 1.10, \qquad r_4 = 0.05 ,$$
$$1.00 (1+r_5) = 1.05, \qquad r_5 = 0.05 .$$

This means that the effective interest rate in the third year is 32 per cent. This means that in this situation the investor could have paid up to 32 per cent interest for any money available for investment during the third year. This, of course, corresponds with the solution; the investor is prevented from investing more in project 1 than \$31,721 because he has no more money available in the third year.

9.2. Production Planning for a Dairy

In this section we shall consider the production planning of a dairy. The dairy concerned receives given quantities of whole milk from farmers; the final products are butter, buttermilk, powdered milk, Gouda cheese, Edam cheese and whey. The amount of whole milk delivered to the dairy varies with the seasons; in spring and summer the amounts are high, in fall and winter they are low. For the moment we shall assume that the amount of whole milk received is 5 million kg per week. The fat content is assumed to be 4 per cent.

Figure 1 illustrates the production process. Part of the whole milk is processed in the separator, which yields cream and skimmed milk; the remainder is used for cheesemaking. Cream is used in the creamery to produce butter and buttermilk. The farmers require a certain amount of buttermilk or skimmed milk as feed for their calves. It is assumed that the amount to be delivered in this manner is 150,000 kg per week, yielding 0.10 per kg (all monetary units are in Dutch guilders). Whole milk and skimmed milk are mixed in certain proportions giving cheesemilk for Gouda and Edam cheese, from which these cheeses are produced. Skimmed milk can be dried to produce powdered milk. All final products are sold at given prices. Variable costs are given either for a production process or for a final product. Total revenue should be maximized.

The problem seems relatively simple, because few alternatives are involved. We shall now discuss the production process in more detail and give the data at the same time. The whole milk delivered to the plant has a fat content (in terms of weight) of 4 per cent. The capacity of the separator is sufficient for the entire milk supply. The separator separates 1 kg milk of a 4 per cent fat content into 0.1016 cream with 39 per cent fat and 0.8984 kg skimmed milk with 0.04 per cent fat; the costs of running the separator are negligible. By mixing cream, wholemilk and skimmed milk a mixture of milk of any desired fat content between 0.04 and 39 per cent can be obtained. The cost of the creamery is 0.0025 per kg cream. From 1 kg cream, 0.5338 kg butter and 0.4662 kg buttermilk is obtained. Butter can be sold at 5.10 per kg and buttermilk at 0.04 per kg or it can be used as calves feed which is sold at 0.10 per kg. The amount of calves feed to be delivered is 150,000 kg per week.

The production of milk powder is quite simple. 1 kg of skimmed milk yields 0.092 kg powdered milk with variable cost of 0.0078 per kg skimmed milk. Powdered milk is sold at 1.25 per kg. There is sufficient capacity to dry any realistic amount of skimmed milk.

Next we describe cheese production. Both Gouda and Edam cheeses are produced in two steps. First unsalted cheese is produced which then is soaked in brine for a number of days; this results in the final product. The required fat content of milk for the production of Gouda cheese is 3.55 per cent. 1 kg cheesemilk for Gouda cheese yields 0.0997 kg unsalted Gouda cheese. For 1 kg Gouda cheese, ready for sale, 0.9785 kg unsalted cheese is required. 1 kg

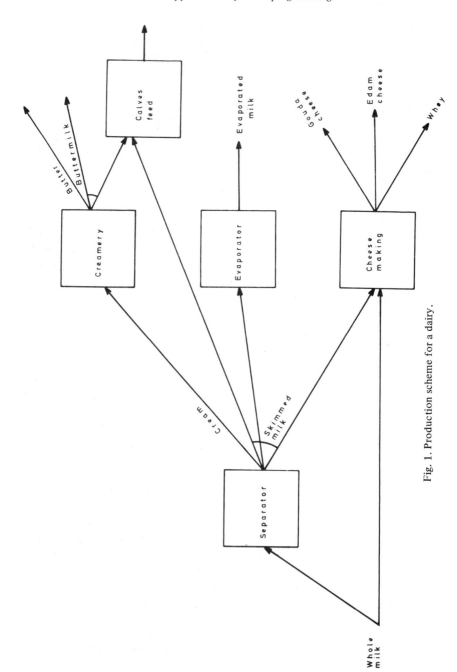

Fig. 1. Production scheme for a dairy.

Gouda cheese can be sold at 2.8245 per kg; variable production costs are 0.083 per kg. Per kg cheesemilk for Gouda cheese, 0.9003 kg whey results, which can be sold at 0.0147 per kg.

For Edam cheese, milk with 2.4 per cent fat is required. The yield of unsalted Edam cheese is 0.0946 per kg cheesemilk, leaving 0.9054 kg whey. Per kg Edam cheese, 0.975 kg unsalted Edam cheese is required. Edam cheese is sold at 2.6155 per kg; variable costs are 0.083 per kg.

The yields of unsalted cheese per kg cheesemilk vary with the seasons; in spring and summer the yields are higher and in autumn and winter the yields are lower. Since the fat content of cheese should be constant, the required fat percentage of cheesemilk for Gouda and Edam cheese also varies with the seasons. The data given above are therefore only valid for a certain part of the year.

The main capacity constraints for the dairy are in the production of cheese. For both Gouda and Edam cheese, the cheesemilk is put in tanks of 10,000 liters; after the cheese has settled, the whey is poured off and the cheese is put into forms. Per day 22 tanks of cheesemilk can be handled. It is given that 1 liter cheesemilk for Gouda cheese weighs 1.0295 kg and one liter of cheesemilk for Edam cheese weighs 1.0305 kg.

Unsalted Gouda cheese should be put in brine for 5 days and unsalted Edam cheese for 4 days. The brine tanks are shallow and the required capacity of brine tanks per unit of cheese can be expressed in terms of surface of brine tank. With the yields of unsalted Gouda and Edam cheese per kg cheesemilk as indicated above, it is given that 5 square meters of brining surface are needed per tank of cheesemilk for Gouda cheese and 4 square meters per tank of cheesemilk for Edam cheese. The total brining surface available is 390 square meters.

Since the production of unsalted cheese takes place only on workdays and the brining, which does not involve labor, can go on over the weekend, there is the problem of coordination between unsalted cheese production and brining. This could be easily solved by specifying variables for each day of the week, but this would lead to a 5- or 7-fold increase in the number of variables and constraints. As we shall see, the number of variables is already fairly large, so that such an increase should be avoided. Let us therefore first specify the constraints connected with cheesemaking. For the moment the units used will be tanks of cheesemilk. Let x_1 be the number of tanks of cheesemilk for Gouda cheese processed on Monday, x_2 those on Tuesday, x_3 those on Wednesday, x_4 those on Thursday and x_5 those on Friday; y_1, y_2, y_3, y_4, y_5 are the corresponding quantities of cheesemilk for Edam cheese. Since the maximum number of tanks of cheesemilk to be processed in any workday is

22, we have the following constraints for Monday up to Friday:

$$x_1 + y_1 \leqq 22,$$
$$x_2 + y_2 \leqq 22,$$
$$(2.1) \qquad x_3 + y_3 \leqq 22,$$
$$x_4 + y_4 \leqq 22,$$
$$x_5 + y_5 \leqq 22.$$

The maximum brining surface on Mondays is 390. At the end of the day on Monday the brining tanks will include, since Gouda cheese needs 5 days, the production of Gouda cheese for that day, x_1, the production of last Friday, x_5, and the production of last Thursday, x_4. Since Edam cheese needs 4 days in the brining tanks, the tanks will include at the end of the day on Monday the Edam cheese production of that day, y_1, and the production of the previous Friday, y_5. Since Gouda cheese needs 5 square meters per tank of cheesemilk and Edam cheese 4 square meters per tank of cheesemilk, and the available surface is 390 square meters, the following constraint is valid:

$$5(x_1 + x_4 + x_5) + 4(y_1 + y_5) \leqq 390.$$

For the other days of the week similar constraints can be constructed; all these constraints can be formulated as follows:

$$
\begin{aligned}
5x_1 \qquad\qquad + 5x_4 + 5x_5 + 4y_1 \qquad\qquad\qquad + 4y_5 &\leqq 390, \\
5x_1 + 5x_2 \qquad\qquad + 5x_5 + 4y_1 + 4y_2 \qquad\qquad\qquad &\leqq 390, \\
5x_1 + 5x_2 + 5x_3 \qquad\qquad + 4y_1 + 4y_2 + 4y_3 \qquad\qquad &\leqq 390, \\
(2.2) \quad 5x_1 + 5x_2 + 5x_3 + 5x_4 \qquad + 4y_1 + 4y_2 + 4y_3 + 4y_4 \qquad &\leqq 390, \\
5x_1 + 5x_2 + 5x_3 + 5x_4 + 5x_5 \qquad + 4y_2 + 4y_3 + 4y_4 + 4y_5 &\leqq 390, \\
5x_2 + 5x_3 + 5x_4 + 5x_5 \qquad\qquad + 4y_3 + 4y_4 + 4y_5 &\leqq 390, \\
5x_3 + 5x_4 + 5x_5 \qquad\qquad\qquad + 4y_4 + 4y_5 &\leqq 390.
\end{aligned}
$$

Since the constraints of the problem other than (2.1) can be considered to be in terms of the weekly production, it would be sufficient if the optimal weekly production pattern is known for different revenues of Gouda and Edam cheese.

Let us therefore consider the following objective function for the problem with constraints (2.2):

$$(2.3) \qquad f = r_g(x_1 + x_2 + x_3 + x_4 + x_5) + r_e(y_1 + y_2 + y_3 + y_4 + y_5) .$$

For $r_g > 0$, the solution which maximizes (2.3) also maximizes f/r_g:

$$(2.4) \qquad f^* = f/r_g = x_1 + x_2 + x_3 + x_4 + x_5 + \frac{r_e}{r_g}(y_1 + y_2 + y_3 + y_4 + y_5) ,$$

and *vice-versa* . (2.4) may be written as

$$(2.5) \qquad f^* = x_1 + x_2 + x_3 + x_4 + x_5 + \lambda(y_1 + y_2 + y_3 + y'_4 + y_5) ,$$

where $\lambda = r_e/r_g$. (2.5) is a parametric objective function and all solutions for which (2.5) is maximized subject to (2.2) may easily be found.

The solutions to this problem are summarized in Table 2. For each range of values of the ratio λ of the revenues of cheesemilk, Edam cheese to that for Gouda cheese the optimal weekly schedule is given and also the weekly totals. For instance, solution 2 is optimal for

$$0 \leqq \frac{r_e}{r_g} \leqq 0.8 ,$$

or

$$0 \leqq r_e \leqq 0.8 r_g .$$

This optimal schedule of processing 22 tanks for Edam cheese on Monday, the same number for Gouda cheese on Tuesday and Wednesday and 16.4 and 17.6 tanks for Gouda cheese on Thursday and Friday; altogether 78 tanks for Gouda cheese and 22 tanks for Edam cheese are processed per week.

Figure 2 gives all solutions in terms of weekly totals x and y of tanks of cheesemilk for Gouda and Edam cheese. It turns out that all these solutions are situated on three constraints which are

$$(2.6) \qquad\qquad x \leqq 78 ,$$

$$(2.7) \qquad 5x + 4y \leqq 478 ,$$

$$(2.8) \qquad\quad x + y \leqq 110 .$$

These constraints can be combined with the other constraints of the problem which are all stated in terms of weekly totals. However, x and y are given in

Table 2
Solutions for cheese production scheduling

Solution	1	2	3	4	5	6	7	8	9	10
$\bar{\lambda}$	0	0.8	0.8	0.8	0.8	0.92	0.95	1	1	∞
$x=\Sigma x_j$	78	78	60.4	55.6	42.8	38	38	38	88	110
$y=\Sigma y_j$	0	22	44	50	66	72	72	72	72	0
x_1	22	–	–	–	–	–	–	–	–	–
x_2	22	22	–	–	–	–	–	–	–	–
x_3	22	22	22	16	–	–	–	16	–	–
x_4	12	16.4	20.8	22	22	22	16	–	–	–
x_5	0	17.6	17.6	17.6	20.8	16	22	22	22	–
y_1	–	22	22	22	22	22	22	22	22	22
y_2	–	–	22	22	22	22	22	22	22	22
y_3	–	–	–	6	22	22	22	6	22	22
y_4	–	–	–	–	–	–	6	22	22	22
y_5	–	–	–	–	–	6	–	–	–	22

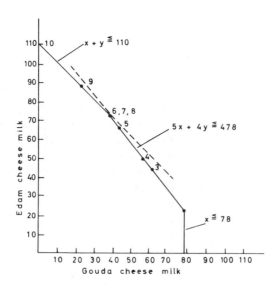

Fig. 2. Solution for weekly cheese production.

terms of tanks of cheesemilk of 10,000 liter whereas all other data are in terms of weight. If x and y are expressed in terms of units of 10,000 kg, we have to divide by the specific gravity of cheesemilk for Gouda cheese and Edam cheese which are 1.0295 and 1.0305. The following constraints are then obtained:

(2.9) $0.9713x + 0.9704y \leqq 110$,

(2.10) $0.9713x \leqq 78$,

(2.11) $4.8565x + 3.8816y \leqq 478$.

The complete model will now be described. It is given by Table 3. The names of rows and columns are abbreviations. All variables are expressed in units of 10,000 kg apart from monetary units which are 10,000 guilders and the cheese production constraints for which tanks of 10,000 liter and square meters of brining surface are used. The objective function which is to be maximized is the total revenue, the row of which is indicated by REV.

For whole milk there are two constraints, one for the entire quantity and one for the fat content. The first activity is cream production, which uses one unit of whole milk (WHMILK) 0.39 units of fat and yields 1 unit of cream (CREAM); all these coefficients can be found in the column CREM of Table 3.

The activity SKMK gives the production of skimmed milk, which has an input of one unit of whole milk and 0.0004 units of fat and an output of one unit of skimmed milk. In practice the production of cream and skimmed milk are simultaneous, but we may produce one product only by putting the other product back in the whole milk if this is desired. The activity creamery (CRMY) takes out one unit of CREAM and yields 0.5338 units of BUTTER and 0.4662 units of buttermilk (BUMILK) at a cost of 0.0025 per unit. The activity SBUT is the sale of butter which takes out 1 unit of butter and yields 5.10 per unit revenue.

The activity SKMF stands for putting skimmed milk into calvesfeed and hence takes 1 unit out of SKMILK and puts in one unit into calvesfeed (CALFEED). Similarly, the activity BUMF takes out one unit of buttermilk (BUMILK) and puts it into calvesfeed (CALFEED). The activity SCAL stands for the sale of calvesfeed; it takes out one unit of calvesfeed and has a revenue of 0.10 per unit. There is a bound which is an equality on this activity of 15, which means that it should be equal to 15. This activity could be deleted after making the appropriate changes in the constant terms but it

Table
Rows and columns for

Column / Row	CREM	SKMK	CRMY	SBUT	SKMF	BUMF	SCAF
REV			-0.0025	5.10			0.10
WHMILK	1	1					
FAT	0.39	0.0004					
CREAM	-1		1				
SKMILK		-1			1		
BUMILK			-0.5338			1	
BUTTER			-0.4662	1			
CALFEED					-1	-1	1
MIPOW							
UNSGC							
UNSEC							
WHEY							
CHPROD							
BRINE1							
BRINE2							
BOUNDS:EQ:							15

is easier to let the computer do this. The activity SBUM sells buttermilk, taking out one unit of BUMILK and yielding a revenue of 0.04 per unit. The activity PRMP stands for the production of milkpowder which converts one unit of skimmed milk into 0.092 units of milkpowder (MIPOW) at a cost of 0.0078. The activity SMP sells milkpowder at 1.25 per unit.

Then follows cheese production; first the production of Gouda cheese is treated. The activity PRGC stands for production of Gouda cheese; it takes one unit of whole milk and 0.0355 units of fat and yields 0.0997 units of unsalted Gouda cheese (UNSGC) and 0.9003 units of whey. It also takes 0.9713 units of cheese production capacity (CHPROD) (these are in fact tanks of 10,000 liters) and 0.9713 in brining capacity constraint 1 (BRINE1) and 4.8505 in brining capacity constraint 2 (BRINE2). The activity SGC stands for the sale of (salted) Gouda cheese. 1 unit of Gouda cheese requires 0.9785 units of unsalted Gouda cheese and gives a revenue (from which variable production cost have been subtracted) of 2.7415 per unit.

The activities PREC and SEC refer to the production and sale of Edam cheese and are similar to the corresponding activities for Gouda cheese. The activity SWH sells whey at a revenue of 0.0147 per unit. This completes all

3

dairy production problem

SBUM	PRMP	SMP	PRGC	SGC	PREC	SEC	SWH	TYPE	RHS
0.04	−0.0078	1.25		2.7415		2.5315	0.0147	N	500
			1		1			L	20
			0.0355		0.024			L	
								L	
	1							L	
1								L	
								L	
								L	
	−0.092	1						L	
			−0.0997	0.9785				L	
					−0.0946	0.975		L	
			−0.9003		−0.9054		1	L	
			0.9713		0.9704			L	110
			0.9713					L	78
			4.8565		3.8816			L	478

activities. The right-hand side is very simple. 5 million kg or 500 units of whole milk are coming in per week, they contain 4 per cent or 20 units of fat. The other three nonzero constant terms are the ones originating from the cheese production and brining constraints (2.9)–(2.11). The type of row constraints are all $\leq$ or L, apart from the constraints for cheesemilk and fat in cheesemilk which are equalities and the objective function row REV which has N.

Table 4 contains the output for the optimal solution which was obtained using the DUAL and PRIMAL procedures of MPS after 17 iterations. Total revenue for the week is 172.32401 or approximately 1.7 million Dutch guilders, which is approximately U.S. $470,000. The optimal production plan is as follows (all units are rounded). Of the 500 units of whole milk available, 44 are used for cream and 343 for skimmed milk; the remainder is used for the production of Edam cheese. The 44 units of cream are used in the creamery which yield $20\frac{1}{2}$ units of butter and $23\frac{1}{2}$ units of buttermilk of which 15 units are put in calvesfeed making up the required number of units, and $8\frac{1}{2}$ units are sold. 343 units of skimmed milk are dried yielding $31\frac{1}{2}$ units of milkpowder. The total quantity of cheesemilk for Edam cheese is

Table 4

MPS-output for dairy production problem

SECTION 1 - ROWS

NUMBER	...ROW..	AT	...ACTIVITY...	SLACK ACTIVITY	..LOWER LIMIT.	..UPPER LIMIT.	.DUAL ACTIVITY
1	REV	BS	172.32401	172.32401-	NONE	NONE	1.00000
2	WHMILK	UL	500.00000	.	NONE	500.00000	.10485-
3	FAT	UL	20.00000	.	NONE	20.00000	5.87595-
4	CREAM	UL	.	.	NONE	.	2.39647-
5	SKMILK	UL	.	.	NONE	.	.10720-
6	BUMILK	UL	.	.	NONE	.	.04000-
7	BUTTER	UL	.	.	NONE	.	5.10000-
8	CALFEED	UL	.	.	NONE	.	.04000-
9	MIPOW	UL	.	.	NONE	.	1.25000-
10	UNSGC	UL	.	.	NONE	.	3.14224-
11	UNSEC	UL	.	.	NONE	.	2.59641-
12	WHEY	UL	.	.	NONE	.	.01470-
13	CHPROD	UL	110.00000	.	NONE	110.00000	.01346-
14	BRINE1	BS	78.00000	78.00000	NONE	78.00000	.
15	BRINE2	BS	440.00000	38.00000	NONE	478.00000	.

SECTION 2 - COLUMNS

NUMBER	.COLUMN.	AT	...ACTIVITY...	..INPUT COST..	..LOWER LIMIT.	..UPPER LIMIT.	.REDUCED COST.
16	CREM	BS	43.95486	.	.	NONE	.
17	SKMK	BS	342.68982	.	.	NONE	.
18	CRMY	BS	43.95486	.	.	NONE	.
19	SBUT	BS	20.49176	.00250-	.	NONE	.
20	SKMF	LL	.	5.10000	.	NONE	.06720-
21	BUMF	BS	15.00000	.	.	NONE	.
22	SCAF	EQ	15.00000	.10000	15.00000	15.00000	.06000
23	SBUM	BS	8.46811	.04000-	.	NONE	.
24	PRMP	BS	342.68982	.00780-	.	NONE	.
25	SMP	BS	31.52746	1.25000	.	NONE	.
26	PRGC	BS	.	.	.	NONE	.
27	SGC	LL	.	2.74150	.	NONE	.
28	PREC	BS	113.35532	.	.	NONE	.
29	SEC	BS	10.99837	2.53150	.	NONE	.
30	SWH	BS	102.68190	.01470	.	NONE	.33318-

113, which yields a quantity for sale of Edam cheese of 11 units. 103 units of whey are sold. No Gouda cheese is made. This is the entire production plan.

The dual variables or shadow prices are of considerable interest. For the quantity of whole milk we find 0.10485 and for the fat content 5.876, so that the value of milk with 4 per cent fat is 0.105 + 0.04 ∘ 5.876 = 0.34. These figures can be used for decisions for paying out to members and for buying additional milk. The value of cream turns out to be 2.40 per kg and the value of skimmed milk 0.107 per kg. The value of buttermilk is, predictably, 0.04 per kg, and that of butter 5.10 per kg. The value of calvesfeed is 0.04, which at first seems strange because it is sold at 0.10, but it should be realized that only a fixed quantity can be sold; hence the value is equal to that of buttermilk. For milkpowder we find 1.25 which is equal to the selling price.

Next we come to cheese production. The value of unsalted Gouda cheese is 3.14 per kg. The activity SGC (selling Gouda cheese) uses 0.9785 unsalted Gouda cheese, the value of which is 3.14 · 0.9785 = 3.07, but the sales price is only 2.74, so that a loss of 0.33 per kg would be incurred. The value of unsalted Edam cheese is 2.60; for one kg of Edam cheese ready for sale (SEC), 0.975 kg of unsalted Edam cheese is required, the value of which is 0.975 ∘ 2.60 = 2.53, which is exactly the selling price.

One of the most interesting dual variables is the one for cheese production capacity, which turns out to be 0.1348. Since the cheese production capacity is expressed in tanks of 10,000 liter it is evident that an extra tank used for Edam cheese would yield 135 guilders additional revenue. The actual daily cheese production schedule is evidently solution 10 of Table 2, which involves 22 tanks per day for Edam cheese.

Finally, there is the question whether all this information could have been found without linear programming. The answer is affirmative, provided the optimal solution is known, but it is not very obvious how this should be done. The following is a description of how this could have been done. We proceed from the optimal solution as given in Table 4 and use Table 3 as a reference for the constraints. For activities which are basic, the values of the commodities in the column multiplied by their coefficients should be equal to the revenue (if primal variable is basic, then its corresponding dual variable should be zero). We start with the sale of milkpowder (SMP) which gives the value of milkpowder (MIPOW). If this last value is known, we can deduce from the production of milkpowder (PRMP) the value of skimmed milk. The values of butter and buttermilk follow immediately from their sales prices. This determines the value of cream via the activity CRMY. Then the activities CREM and SKMK simultaneously determine the values of WHMILK and FAT. Hence the values of whole milk and fat are determined by the prices for butter, buttermilk, and milkpowder.

Let us now turn to the production of Edam cheese. The activity SEC determines the value of unsalted Edam cheese. The values of whole milk and fat are known, and the value of whey is determined by SWH. Then from PREC the value of CHPROD, cheese production capacity, can be determined.

Since the model for this problem is relatively simple, it is possible to study its structure in detail, but even for a model of this size this is not easy, especially if the optimal solution is not known. In general, linear programming provides a means to perform all these calculations automatically.

We may also like to know for what values of the constant terms the basic solution remains unchanged. This information can be found using the MPS-system if the instruction RANGE is put in the control program behind SOLU-TION. Looking at cheese production, we find that the variables are basic for a cheese production capacity ranging from 0 to 119.5. At the latter point, the second brining constraint becomes binding. Since Edam cheese uses the least brining surface, it is not possible to produce more cheese than 119.5 units Edam cheese. Hence it makes no sense to expand the cheese production beyond 119.5 without increasing the brining surface at the same time.

Exercises

1. A company has to determine its capital budget for the coming three years. for which data (in thousands of dollars) are given in the following table.

Year	Avail. Inv. Cap.	Investment Projects					
		1	2	3	4	5	6
1	300	50	100	60	50	170	16
2	100	80	50	60	100	40	25
3	200	−20	20	60	150	−50	40
Disc. Fut. Revenues		−150	−210	220	−350	−200	−100

This means that the company has at the start of year 1 $300,000 available for investment; in year 2, another $100,000 becomes available and at the start of year 3, an additional $200,000 becomes available. Project 1 requires $50,000 at the start of year 1; another $80,000 is required at the start of year 2, while at the start of year 3, the project yield $20,000. The yield at the start of year 4 plus the discounted yields of later years amount to $150,000. The company can borrow at most $50,000 plus 20 per cent of the money invested so far in the various investment projects at an interest rate of 12 per cent per year. If the company deposits money at the bank, the interest rate is 8 per cent. The company has a bank debt of $10,000 on which it pays 11 per cent interest and which may be repaid at the start of any year. Find the optimal capital budget using the MPS-system (or a similar computer program). Assume that the company may undertake 100 per cent of each project or take a participation in it of less than 100 per cent. Explain parts of the computer output which are of importance.

2. In the dairy production problem assume that 200 million kg of whole milk with 3.9 per cent fat, 175 million kg with 4.0 per cent fat, and 125 million kg with 4.1 per cent fat. Solve the problem for this modification.

3. The whey resulting from cheesemaking contains 0.22 per cent fat. This whey may be put through the separator yielding whey with 0.04 per cent fat and whey cream with 39 per cent fat. The whey cream can be used for cheesemaking. Modify the model to take this into account and solve it. Compare the results with those of the text.

10. LINEAR PROGRAMMING MODELS AND ECONOMIC ANALYSIS

10.1. Activity Analysis and Economic Analysis

So far, linear programming has been used mainly as a problem-solving tool; maximum-profit or minimum-cost solutions to problems were found by means of a linear programming method. It was assumed that only one decisionmaker was taking decisions. However, linear programming and activity analysis may also be used for purposes of economic analysis.

In economic analysis the primary aim is *explanation* of the economic aspects of production and consumption, both of which are controlled by many decisionmakers. Activity analysis as it was presented in Section 8.2 gave a model for production controlled by a single decisionmaker. Here the same model will be used, but we shall drop the assumption that there is only one decisionmaker. After that we shall also consider the consumption of commodities and integrate this with the activity analysis model in such a way that a complete explanation of quantities to be produced and consumed and of prices of commodities and resources is obtained.

Let us assume that the production of the entire economy can be described by a large number of activities with given inputs and outputs in terms of a large number of commodities. The economy has at its disposal fixed quantities of resources, for instance labour, plants, equipment, raw materials, etc. For the moment we shall assume that the prices of final products are given, which means that for these prices any quantity can be sold that can be produced with the available resources. It may be imagined that the economy concerned is a small one which exports its final products to large markets abroad, so that their prices should be taken as given; later the assumption of given prices will be dropped.

Consider the situation in which decisions are entirely centralized. Then the central decisionmaker will maximize the profit to be gained by the entire economy and will determine the activity levels accordingly. This will amount to a huge linear programming problem which in principle can be solved without difficulty. The result will be, firstly, the activity levels corresponding with the optimal solution, but secondly, the shadow prices or imputed costs of the resources which were indicated as u-variables.

In reality no such central decisionmaker exists. Instead, there are a large number of decisionmakers, each of which controls one or more activities and smaller or larger amounts of some of the resources. Frequently, the individual decisionmakers do not own the resources which they need for their activities. But we assume that there is a market for these resources on which he can buy or sell any quantity of the resources at prices to be determined by demand and supply. This means that every input of an activity carries a cost and every output has a revenue. If a decisionmaker finds that for an activity total revenues exceed total costs at market prices of the resources and given prices for the final products, he will increase the level of that activity; if costs exceed revenue, this activity will be dropped. Expansion of an activity will require more resources which will increase the market price of these resources; dropping an activity will free resources, which will decrease their market price.

In this situation it is of importance to know the *equilibrium quantities and prices,* which are such that at these prices no decisionmaker will have reason for increasing or decreasing activity levels and such that at these activity levels no more resources are used than are available. The solution of the centralized decisionmaker turns out to have these properties. In the optimal solution of the linear programming problem of the central decisionmaker, an activity can only be positive if inputs and outputs, evaluated at given prices of final products and imputed costs of resources are equal. For no activity outputs exceed inputs and if the value of outputs is less than that of the inputs, the activity cannot be positive.

In the case of many decisionmakers and competitive adjusting markets there is an equilibrium for the same solution, which means that market prices should be equal to the imputed costs of resources because in that situation no individual decisionmaker would have reason to alter his activity level; furthermore, there is an equilibrium in the commodity market because at these prices the resources which have positive prices are exactly used up while the resources of which there is a surplus have a price of zero.

With this we have explained the market prices of resources in a situation with fixed resources and given prices of final products; we found that these market prices should be equal to the imputed costs of the resource constraints in the corresponding linear programming problem.

10.2. Equilibrium with Elastic Demand

Let us now consider a situation in which the prices of final goods are not given. Instead we assume that the quantity demanded of a commodity is a function of its price. To be concrete, let us again consider the original textile production example. This example is, of course, very tiny compared with an entire economy, but an example has to be small in order to be numerically manageable. For the moment we shall assume that the prices of yarns A and B and Fabric B are given but that the price for Fabric A is determined by supply and demand. The quantity demanded of Fabric A, to be indicated by d_3, is assumed to depend on its price p_3 in the following manner:

(2.1) $d_3 = 4750 - 50p_3$.

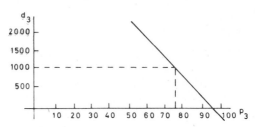

Fig. 1.

Figure 1 gives a graphical presentation of this function. For example, for a price of 75, the quantity demanded is

$$d_3 = 4750 - 50 \cdot 75 = 1000$$

For each dollar price increase, the quantity demanded decreases by 50 units and for each dollar price decrease, the quantity demanded increases by 50 units. The demand function (2.1) does not have to be valid everywhere, as obviously it is not, since demand can never be negative which this function is for $p_3 > 95$, but the real demand function may be approximated by this function in the relevant range of values of p_3.

Let us now consider the supply side of the economy. This is described by the optimal solutions to the linear programming problem of Chapter 2, in which the price of Fabric A, p_3, is not 75 but undetermined. These solutions may be found by parametric programming. It should be noted that in this case the net revenue is varied, which is equal to selling price minus variable costs of 25. It is then found that for a net revenue of less than $47\frac{1}{2}$, $x_3 = 0$, for a net revenue between $47\frac{1}{2}$ and 52, x_3 = 1000 and for a net revenue exceeding 52, x_3 = 1500. Hence for a selling price of less than $47\frac{1}{2}$ + 25 = $72\frac{1}{2}$, x_3 = 0, for a selling price between $72\frac{1}{2}$ and 77, x_3 = 1000 and for a selling price greater than 77, x_3 = 1500. In this way a supply function for Fabric A is created, see Figure 2.

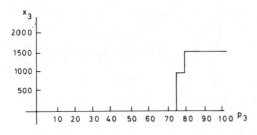

Fig. 2.

On the market for Fabric A there will be equilibrium if for some price supply and demand of Fabric A are equal. The supply and demand curves of Figures 1 and 2 can be put in one figure, Figure 3; and we find that demand and supply are equal for p_3 = 75, at which point they are equal to 1000. Hence the price of Fabric A has been explained.

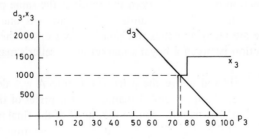

Fig. 3.

Because our textile example was artificially small the supply function had only two "steps". If there are a large number of activities, parametric programming problems, and therefore also supply functions, will usually have a large number of small steps, so that these functions are quite smooth. Nevertheless it is interesting to consider the effect of these steps. In Figure 3, the demand curve intersects the supply curve in a horizontal piece. Now let us assume that a shift in the demand curve occurs which amounts to an increase in demand of 50 units at all prices; the new demand curve is a line parallel to

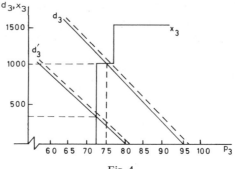

Fig. 4.

the previous one, but slightly above it. See Figure 4, which has a scaling different from the previous figures. The new demand curve intersects the supply curve to the right of the intersection with the old demand. 1000 units are sold at a price of 76 instead of 75. The increased demand has led only to a higher price. We may call this situation a seller's market.

Now consider the situation from the following demand function:

$$(2.2) \qquad d_3' = 4000 - 50p_3 .$$

This demand curve and the supply curve intersect at $72\frac{1}{2}$: the quantity demand and supply is then 375, see Figure 4. Again consider an upward shift of the demand function of 50 units. Then the result is the same price with demand and supply increased by 50 units. This situation is one of a buyer's market. If there are many activities and hence many steps in the supply function, the distinction between a buyer's market and a seller's market becomes meaningless.

In the case considered above the price for Fabric A was determined by means of interaction of supply and demand, but the prices of the other final products were given. Let us now assume that none of the final products have a given price but that they are all determined by the interaction of supply and demand. Since the production of all these products are interrelated it is not possible to deal with each product separately. Let us assume that we have the following demand functions:

$$(2.3) \qquad \begin{cases} d_1 = 1000 - 50p_1 , \\ d_2 = 1500 - 100p_2 , \\ d_3 = 4750 - 50p_3 , \\ d_4 = 4900 - 100p_4 . \end{cases}$$

These functions could have been made somewhat more general by making each demand dependent on the prices of the other products in addition to its own price, so that substitution and complementarity relations could have been included, but this is not done in order to keep the computations simple.

Firstly, again in order to keep computations simple, let us measure all products in 100 units. The relations (2.3) then become

$$(2.4) \quad \begin{cases} d_1 = 10 - \frac{1}{2}p_1 \,, \\ d_2 = 15 - p_2 \,, \\ d_3 = 47\frac{1}{2} - \frac{1}{2}p_3 \,, \\ d_4 = 49 - p_4 \,. \end{cases}$$

Secondly, let us express the p's in terms of the d's:

$$(2.5) \quad \begin{cases} p_1 = 20 - 2d_1 \,, \\ p_2 = 15 - d_2 \,, \\ p_3 = 95 - 2d_3 \,, \\ p_4 = 49 - d_4 \,. \end{cases}$$

On the production side, an equilibrium requires a feasible solution:

$$(2.6) \quad \begin{cases} 3x_1 + 2x_2 + 10x_3 + 4x_4 \leq 180 \,, \\ 2x_3 + \frac{1}{2}x_4 \leq 30 \,. \end{cases}$$

Note that the constant terms have been divided by 100 because the x-variables are expressed in 100 units. Furthermore, in each activity, the value of the outputs should not exceed the value of the inputs at the imputed costs of the resources, or in terms of linear programming, the constraints of the dual problem should be satisfied:

$$(2.7) \quad \begin{cases} 3u_1 \geq p_1 - 3 \,, \\ 2u_2 \geq p_2 - 2 \,, \\ 10u_1 + 2u_2 \geq p_3 - 25 \,, \\ 4u_1 + \frac{1}{2}u_2 \geq p_4 - 10 \,. \end{cases}$$

For equilibrium, demand should equal supply for all products, hence $d_1 = x_1, d_2 = x_2, d_3 = x_3, d_4 = x_4$. The d's in (2.5) may therefore be replaced by the corresponding x-variables, after which (2.5) is substituted in (2.7). We then obtain:

$$
(2.8) \quad
\begin{cases}
3u_1 \geq 17 - 2x_1 , \\
2u_1 \geq 13 - x_2 , \\
10u_1 + 2u_2 \geq 70 - 2x_3 , \\
4u_1 + \tfrac{1}{2}u \geq 39 - x_4 .
\end{cases}
$$

Slack variables v_1, v_2, v_3, and v_4 may be introduced into these equations; after rearranging terms we obtain:

$$
(2.9) \quad
\begin{cases}
-17 = -2x_1 \qquad\qquad -3u_1 \qquad +v_1 , \\
-13 = \qquad -x_2 \qquad -2u_1 \qquad +v_2 , \\
-70 = \qquad\qquad -2x_3 -10u_1 -2u_2 +v_3 , \\
-39 = \qquad\qquad\qquad -x_4 -4u_1 -\tfrac{1}{2}u_2 +v_4 .
\end{cases}
$$

After the introduction of the slack variables y_1 and y_2, the constraints of the primal problem may be written as:

$$
(2.10) \quad
\begin{aligned}
180 &= 3x_1 + 2x_2 + 10x_3 + 4x_4 + y_1 , \\
30 &= \qquad\qquad 2x_3 + \tfrac{1}{2}x_4 \quad + y_2 .
\end{aligned}
$$

For all variables we have nonnegativity constraints:

$$
(2.11) \quad x_1, x_2, x_3, x_4, y_1, y_2, u_1, u_2, v_1, v_2, v_3, v_4 \geq 0 .
$$

Furthermore, if a slack variable of a resource constraint is positive, then its market price must be zero, while if its market price is positive, the slack variable must be zero; hence the following equations must be satisfied.

$$
(2.12) \quad y_1 u_1 = 0 , \quad y_2 u_2 = 0 .
$$

Also, if an activity is positive, then the value of its inputs should be exactly equal to the value of the outputs (otherwise no equilibrium exists); hence if an x-variable is positive, the corresponding inequality in (2.7) is satisfied with an equality, which means that the corresponding v-variable should be zero. On the other hand, if a v-variable is positive, meaning that the activity leads to a loss, then the activity level should be zero. Hence we must have for an equilibrium solution:

$$(2.13) \qquad x_1 v_1 = 0, \quad x_2 v_2 = 0, \quad x_3 v_3 = 0, \quad x_4 v_4 = 0.$$

10.3. Numerical Solution with Quadratic Programming

The equilibrium solution should satisfy the conditions (2.9)–(2.13). The conditions (2.9), (2.10), and (2.11) are simply linear constraints for which we can easily solve. The conditions (2.12) and (2.13), however, are nonlinear. We are looking in fact for a basic nonnegative solution of (2.9) and (2.10) which is such that if an x-variable is basic then its corresponding v-variable is nonbasic and *vice versa* and if a y-variable is basic then its corresponding u-variable is nonbasic and *vice versa*; if this is so, the conditions (2.12) and (2.13) are automatically satisfied.

The conditions for an equilibrium solution (2.9)–(2.13) are the same as those for an optimal solution of a related quadratic programming problem. Hence a method for quadratic programming can be used. The best-known method for quadratic programming is the *Simplex Method for Quadratic Programming* which can be considered as a generalization of the simplex method for linear programming. We shall not go into a detailed explanation of this method but will simply state its rules.

We shall call a *standard solution* a basic solution of (2.9) and (2.10) in which no pair of corresponding primal and dual variables are both basic. Hence in a standard solution if x_1 is basic then v_1 is nonbasic and if u_1 is basic then y_1 is nonbasic. In this method there will be for nonstandard solutions only one pair of corresponding primal and dual variables which are both basic; which is called the *basic pair* and one pair which are both nonbasic which is called the *nonbasic pair*. For instance, the basic pair may be x_1 and v_1, the nonbasic pair y_1 and u_1.

As the simplex method for linear programming, the simplex method for quadratic programming requires an initial basic feasible solution, but the feasibility only refers to the primal variables. Hence the set-up tableau consisting of (2.9) and (2.10) gives an initial basic feasible solution which moreover is standard. We shall give here its asymmetric variant; for the symmetric variant see van de Panne and Whinston. [1]

---

[1] See Dantzig [5] and van de Panne and Whinston [16–18].

The rules for the selection of the new basic variable and the leaving basic variable are as follows:

SELECTION OF THE NEW BASIC VARIABLE. *For standard solutions take the primal variable corresponding to the most negative dual variable. For a nonstandard solution take the dual variable of the nonbasic pair. If in a standard solution all dual variables are positive, the optimal* (equilibrium) *solution has been found.*

SELECTION OF THE LEAVING BASIC VARIABLE. *Take the minimum ratio as in the simplex method for linear programming, but do this only for rows with primal basic variables and one other row. This latter row is for a standard solution the row of the dual variable of the new basic variable and for a nonstandard solution the dual variable of the basic pair.* The ratio in this row, if its denominator is nonzero is always positive, since both its numerator and denominator are negative.

It can be proved that this method leads to the optimal (in this case to the equilibrium) solution in a finite number of steps, provided certain conditions are met. One of these conditions require that the demand curves should not be backward sloping, which condition is usually satisfied.

Tableau 0 of Table 1 contains the set-up tableau for the problem; it is based on the equations (2.9) and (2.10). The solution of this tableau is feasible in the primal variables, so that the simplex method for quadratic programming may be applied. Since no pair of corresponding primal and dual variables are basic, the solution of Tableau 0 is a standard solution. The most negative dual variable is v_3, so that x_3 should enter the basis. The leaving basic variable is determined by taking ratios in the rows of v_3, y_1, and y_2.

$$\text{Min} \left(\frac{-70}{-2}, \frac{180}{10}, \frac{30}{2}, \right) = 15 \ .$$

This minimum is connected with y_2, which should therefore leave the basis. The element 2 is the pivot of the transformation which results in Tableau 1.

The solution of Tableau 1 is nonstandard because both v_3 and x_3 are basic; this is the basic pair. The nonbasic pair is u_2 and y_2. Hence u_2 is selected as the new basic variable. Ratios are now taken in the rows of v_3, y_1 and x_3, but since the relevant elements in the rows of y_1 and x_3 are nonpositive, v_3 is selected as the leaving basic variable and the element -2 is the pivot of a transformation which results in Tableau 2.

This is again a standard tableau. The most negative dual variable is v_4, so that x_4 enters the basis. The leaving basic variable is determined by taking the ratios in the rows of v_4, y_1 and x_3:

$$\text{Min} \left(\frac{-29}{-1.125}, \frac{30}{1.5}, \frac{15}{0.25} \right) = 20 .$$

The minimum is connected with y_1, so that x_4 replaces y_1 as a basic variable. Pivoting on the element -1.125, we find Tableau 3. The elements of this and the following tableaux have been rounded to three decimal figures, though they have been computed with a higher accuracy.

Tableau 3 has a nonstandard solution with x_4 and v_4 as the basic pair and u_1 and y_1 as the nonbasic pair. Hence the dual variable of the nonbasic pair, u_1, enters the basis. Ratios should be taken in the rows of v_4, x_4 and x_3, but only the ratio in row of v_4 turns out to be relevant, so that u_1 replaces v_4 as a basic variable. After transformation Tableau 4 results which has a standard solution. Note that its solution is the same as the optimal solution of the corresponding linear programming problem; however, the solution of the corresponding equilibrium problem is not optimal yet.

Since v_2 is the most negative dual variable, x_2 enters the basis. The leaving basic variable is determined according to

$$\text{Min} \left(\frac{-4.333}{3}, \frac{20}{1.333} \right) = 1.444 ,$$

so that v_2 leaves the basis. Tableau 5 again has a standard solution with v_1 nonnegative. However, now u_2, the computed cost of loom capacity, is negative, which means that it is better to leave some loom capacity unused y_1 enters the basis, the leaving basic variable is determined according to

$$\text{Min} \left(\frac{-4.370}{-5.185}, \frac{10.481}{0.741} \right) = 0.843 ,$$

u_2 leaves the basis and Tableau 6 results, which has a standard solution.

Now v_1 is the only negative dual variable, so that x_1 enters the basis. We determine the ratios:

$$\text{Min} \left(\frac{-1.914}{-2.129}, \frac{2.943}{0.086}, \frac{18.886}{0.171}, \frac{9.857}{0.214} \right) = 0.899 ,$$

so that v_1 leaves the basis.

Tableau 7 has a standard solution which, since it has no negative dual variables, contains the equilibrium values. The values of this solution, taking into account the change in units we made earlier:

Table 1
Tableaux for solution to equilibrium problem

Tab-leau	Basic Variables	Values Basic Variables	x_1	x_2	x_3	x_4	u_1	u_2
0	v_1	−17	−2	0	0	0	−3	0
	v_2	−13	0	−1	0	0	−2	0
	v_3	−70	0	0	−2	0	−10	−2
	v_4	−39	0	0	0	−1	−4	−0.5
	y_1	180	3	2	10	4	0	0
	y_2	30	0	0	2̲	0.5	0	0

			x_1	x_2	y_2	x_4	u_1	u_2
1	v_1	−17	−2	0	0	0	−3	0
	v_2	−13	0	−1	0	0	−2	0
	v_3	−40	0	0	1	0.5	−10	−2̲
	v_4	−39	0	0	0	−1	−4	−0̲.5
	y_1	30	3	2	−5	1.5	0	0
	x_2	15	0	0	0.5	0.25	0	0

			x_1	x_2	y_2	x_4	u_1	v_3
2	v_1	−17	−2	0	0	0	−3	0
	v_2	−13	0	−1	0	0	−2	0
	u_2	20	0	0	−0.5	−0.25	5	−0.5
	v_4	−29	0	0	−0.25	−1.125	−1.5	−0.25
	y_1	30	3	2	−5	1.5̲	0	0
	x_3	15	0	0	0.5	0̲.25	0	0

			x_1	x_2	y_2	y_1	u_1	v_1
3	v_1	−17	−2	0	0	0	−3	0
	v_2	−13	0	−1	0	0	−2	0
	u_2	25	0.5	0.333	1.333	0.167	5	−0.5
	v_4	−6.5	2.25	1.5	−4	0.75	−1̲.5	−0.25
	x_4	20	2	1.333	−3.333	0.667	0̲	0
	x_3	10	−0.5	−0.333	1.333	−0.167	0	0

			x_1	x_2	y_2	y_1	v_4	v_3
4	v_1	−4	−6.5	−3	8	−1.5	−2	0.5
	v_2	−4.333	−3.0	−3̲	5.333	−1.0	−1.333	0.333
	u_2	3.333	8	5̲.333	−14.667	2.667	3.333	−1.333
	u_1	4.333	−1.5	−1	2.667	−0.5	−0.667	0.167
	x_4	20	2	1.333	−3.333	0.667	0	0
	x_3	10	−0.5	−0.333	1.333	−0.167	0	0

Table 1 (continued)

Tableau	Basic Variables	Values Basic Variables	x_1	v_2	y_2	y_1	v_4	v_3
5	v_1	0.333	−3.5	−1	2.667	−0.5	−0.667	0.167
	x_2	1.444	1	−0.333	−1.778	0.333	0.444	−0.111
	u_2	−4.370	2.667	1.778	−5.185	0.889	0.963	−0.741
	u_1	5.778	−0.5	−0.333	0.889	−0.167	−0.222	0.056
	x_4	18.074	0.667	0.444	−0.963	0.222	−0.593	0.148
	x_3	10.481	−0.167	−0.111	0.741	−0.056	0.148	−0.037

			x_1	v_2	u_2	y_1	v_4	v_3
6	v_1	−1.914	−2.129	−0.086	0.514	−0.043	−0.171	−0.214
	x_2	2.943	0.086	−0.943	−0.343	0.029	0.114	0.143
	y_2	0.843	−0.514	−0.343	−0.193	−0.171	−0.186	0.143
	u_1	5.029	−0.043	0.029	0.171	−0.014	−0.057	−0.071
	x_4	18.886	0.171	0.114	−0.186	0.057	−0.771	0.286
	x_3	9.857	0.214	0.143	0.143	0.071	0.286	−0.143

			v_1	v_2	u_2	y_1	v_4	v_3
7	x_1	0.899	−0.470	0.040	−0.242	0.020	0.081	0.101
	x_2	2.866	0.040	−0.946	−0.322	0.027	0.107	0.134
	y_2	1.305	−0.242	−0.322	−0.317	−0.161	−0.144	0.195
	u_1	5.067	−0.020	−0.027	0.161	−0.013	−0.054	−0.067
	x_4	18.732	0.081	0.107	−0.144	0.054	−0.785	0.268
	x_3	9.664	0.101	0.134	0.195	0.067	0.268	−0.164

$$x_1 = 90, \quad x_2 = 287, \quad x_3 = 986, \quad x_4 = 1873,$$

$$y_1 = 0, \quad y_2 = 131.$$

For the imputed costs of spinning and loom capacity, we have

$$u_1 = 5.067, \quad u_2 = 0.$$

This can be compared with the solution of the linear programming problem with fixed prices

$$x_1 = 0, \quad x_2 = 0, \quad x_3 = 1000, \quad x_4 = 2000,$$

with imputed costs of spinning and loom capacity of

$$u_1 = 4\tfrac{1}{3}, \quad u_2 = 3\tfrac{1}{3}.$$

It is obvious that there is a substantial difference between the two solutions. In the equilibrium solutions all x-variables are basic, which means that all products are produced, whereas in the simple linear programming model only two products were produced. Intuitively this is explained by the fact that the net revenue for a product goes up as its supply decreases in the equilibrium case, so that it is likely that at least a small amount of each product is produced. In the simple linear programming model with fixed prices, the number of basic x-variables is equal to the number binding constraints for the optimal solution, which were 2 in the example. In the equilibrium model this is no longer true; the number of binding constraints for the optimal solution was one (spinning capacity), while the number of basic x-variables was 4.

If the imputed costs of spinning and loom capacity are compared for the two examples, it is found that the value of spinning capacity has gone up from $4\tfrac{1}{3}$ to 5.067 per unit, whereas the value of loom capacity has gone down from $3\tfrac{1}{3}$ to zero; 130 units of loom capacity go unused. The value of the existing capacities, evaluated at the imputed costs corresponding with the optimal solution is

$$5.067 \cdot 18{,}000 + 0 \cdot 3000 = 91{,}206.$$

The question can then be asked whether this is equal to the total profits in this situation. Total profits are

(3.1)
$$f = (p_1 - c_1)x_1 + (p_2 - c_2)x_2 + (p_3 - c_3)x_3 + (p_4 - c_4)x_4$$
$$= (17 - 2x_1)x_1 + (13 - x_2)x_2 + (70 - 2x_3)x_3 + (39 - x_4)x_4.$$

For the terms within brackets, we may substitute according to the equations in (2.9); this results in

(3.2)
$$f = (3u_1 - v_1)x_1 + (2u_2 - v_2)x_2 + (10u_1 + 2u_2 - v_3)x_3 +$$
$$+ (4u_1 + \tfrac{1}{2}u_2 - v_4)x_4.$$

For an optimal solution, we have according to (2.13):

$$v_1 x_1 = 0, \quad v_2 x_2 = 0, \quad v_3 x_3 = 0, \quad v_4 x_4 = 0,$$

so that (3.2) becomes

(3.3) $\qquad f = 3u_1 x_1 + 2u_1 x_2 + (10u_1 + 2u_2) x_3 + (4u_1 + \tfrac{1}{2}u_2) x_4$.

These terms can be rearranged according to the u-variables:

(3.4) $\qquad f = (3x_1 + 2x_2 + 10x_3 + 4x_4) u_1 + (0x_1 + 0x_2 + 2x_3 + \tfrac{1}{2}x_4) u_2$.

For the terms within brackets we may substitute according to (2.10) which results in

(3.5) $\qquad f = (18{,}000 - y_1) u_1 + (3000 - y_2) u_2$.

For an optimal solution we have according to (3.12): $u_1 y_1 = 0, u_2 y_2 = 0$, so that (3.5) becomes

(3.6) $\qquad f = 18{,}000\, u_1 + 3000 u_2$.

Hence also in the equilibrium model, total profits and resources evaluated at imputed costs are equal. The value for profits $91,206 can be compared with the value of profits in the fixed-price model, which was $88,000.

It should be noted the equilibrium model can be considered as a generalization of the simple linear programming model; if the coefficients of the d's in (2.5) are approaching zero, a linear programming model is obtained. This corresponds with an increase (in absolute value) of the coefficients of the p's in the demand functions (2.3).

10.4. The Case of a Monopolist

Let us now look back at what we have done. In the case of fixed prices for final products and given resources we have shown that the optimal solution in case of one decisionmaker is also an equilibrium solution in the case in which there are many decisionmakers operating in competitive markets. In the case in which the prices of final products are no longer fixed, but a demand function is given, we have been able to state conditions for equilibrium and to derive from these, using the rules of a method for quadratic programming, an equilibrium solution. Now the question may be asked whether this equilibrium solution is also the optimal solution in the case of óne decisionmaker maximizing his profits. The answer turns out to be negative.

Let us take up again the original textile production problem and let us assume that the demand for Fabric A depends on its price as indicated in (2.1):

$$d_3 = 4750 - 50p_3 .$$

For the other final products it is assumed that any quantity can be sold at the given price. The demand function (2.1) implies

$$p_3 = 95 - \frac{1}{50} d_3 .$$

If demand is equal to supply, we have $d_3 = x_3$ so that

(4.1) $$p_3 = 95 - \frac{1}{50} x_3 .$$

The objective function for the single decisionmaker who maximizes his profits is then:

$$f = (p_1 - c_1)x_1 + (p_2 - c_2)x_2 + (p_3 - c_3)x_3 + (p_4 - c_4)x_4$$

$$= (12 - 3)x_1 + (10 - 2)x_2 + (95 - \frac{1}{50}x_3 - 25)x_3 + (29 - 10)x_4$$

$$= 9x_1 + 8x_2 + 70x_3 - \frac{1}{50}x_3^2 + 19x_4 .$$

This means that we have an objective function which is quadratic in x_3. The problem is then a *quadratic programming problem* because it involves the maximization of a quadratic objective function subject to linear constraints. Because the objective function contains only one quadratic term, it can be solved graphically. The more general problem in which all prices are undetermined can be treated by means of the quadratic programming method which uses the same rules as the equilibrium problem treated before.

For an optimal solution to the quadratic programming problem essentially the same rules are valid as in the linear programming problem. In an optimal solution the increase in the objective function due to an increase in an activity which is positive should be equal to its costs, or in other words, activities which are in the production program should break even. If we have a quadratic objective function, the increase in the objective function due to an increase in the level of activity is not just equal to its net revenue as it was in linear programming. Let us compare for the objective function (4.2).

(4.3) $\dfrac{df}{dx_1} = 9$,

(4.4) $\dfrac{df}{dx_3} = 70 - \frac{1}{25}x_3$.

Note that (4.3) is constant while (4.4) varies with x_3. Since we assume that only x_3 has quadratic terms in f, and (4.4) plays the role of p_3, the optimal solution can be found by using the results for variable prices of x_3, which was given by the supply curve of Figure 2. The equivalent of the demand curve is then (4.4), which is indicated by d_3' in Figure 5. Since df/dx_3 is the marginal revenue of x_3 it is denoted by $mr(x_3)$.

This last curve intersects the supply curve in its first vertical piece, so that

(4.5) $95 - \frac{1}{2}x_3 = 72\frac{1}{2}$,

or

$x_3 = 562\frac{1}{2}$.

The price to be charged in order to get this net revenue is found where $x_3 = 562\frac{1}{2}$ intersects the real demand curve d_3:

(4.6) $p_3 = 95 - \frac{1}{50}\,562\frac{1}{2} = 83\frac{3}{4}$.

Hence the price is different from the marginal revenue which was $72\frac{1}{2}$. In most textbook expositions, the diagram has price and marginal revenue on

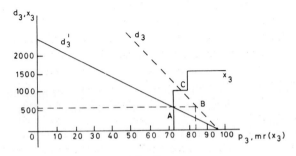

Fig. 5.

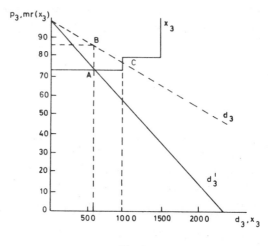

Fig. 6.

the vertical axis and quantities on the horizontal axis, see Figure 6, which has also a different scale.

Note that this solution which is given by B is different from the solution obtained under full competition which would be given by C. For the single decisionmaker the marginal revenue of Fabric A is different from its price, so that he uses his marginal revenue curve instead of the demand curve. The single decisionmaker acts as a monopolist.

Let us now consider the case in which a single decisionmaker faces a situation in which the demands for all products are dependent on their prices. Taking the same demand functions as in (2.3), we have

$$(4.7) \quad \begin{cases} d_1 = 1000 - 50p_1 , \\ d_2 = 1500 - 100p_2 , \\ d_3 = 4750 - 50p_3 , \\ d_4 = 4900 - 100p_4 . \end{cases}$$

The p's may be expressed in the d's; furthermore, since demand equals supply, the d's may be replaced by the corresponding x-variables. This results in the following relations:

$$(4.8) \quad \begin{cases} p_1 = 20 - 2x_1 \,, \\ p_2 = 15 - x_2 \,, \\ p_3 = 95 - 2x_3 \,, \\ p_4 = 4 - x_4 \,. \end{cases}$$

The net revenue which the decisionmaker wants to maximize is then

$$\begin{aligned} (4.9) \quad f &= (p_1 - c_1)x_1 + (p_2 - c_2)x_2 + (p_3 - c_3)x_3 + (p_4 - c_4)x_4 \\ &= (20 - 2x_1 - 3)x_1 + (15 - x_2 - 2)x_2 \\ &\quad + (95 - 2x_3 - 23)x_3 + (45 - 2x_4 - 10)x_4 \\ &= 17x_1 - 2x_1^2 + 13x_2 - x_2^2 + 70x_3 - 2x_3^2 + 39x_4 - x_4^2 \,. \end{aligned}$$

This is a quadratic function of the x-variables. If the demand relations (4.7) had contained other prices than that of the same product, (4.8) would have contained mixed terms as $x_1 x_2$, etc.

The conditions for an optimal solution to a quadratic programming problem with an objective function as given in (4.8) are a generalization of the similar conditions for linear programming. If the p's were fixed instead of variable we would have

$$(4.10) \quad \begin{cases} 3u_1 \geqq p_1 - c_1 \,, \\ 2u_1 \geqq p_2 - c_2 \,, \\ 10u_1 + 2u_2 \geqq p_3 - c_3 \,, \\ 4u_1 + \tfrac{1}{2}u_2 \geqq p_4 - c_4 \,. \end{cases}$$

In the linear programming problem, p_1 stands for the additional profit per unit of Yarn A and $p_1 - c_1$ for the additional net revenue of one unit of Yarn A. In the case of (4.9), the additional net revenue per unit of Yarn A is no longer fixed but depends on x_1. But in this case we can use the marginal net revenue of Yarn A which is defined as df/dx_1 which in this case is

$$(4.11) \quad \frac{df}{dx_1} = 17 - 4x_1 \,.$$

This is used in the first equation of (4.10) instead of $p_1 - c_1$. Also for the other products, the marginal revenue can be used instead of $p_i - c_i$. We then obtain the following inequalities.

$$(4.12) \quad \begin{cases} 3u_1 \geqq 17 - 4x_1 , \\ 2u_1 \geqq 13 - 2x_2 , \\ 10u_1 + 2u_2 \geqq 70 - 4x_3 , \\ 4u_1 + \tfrac{1}{2}u_2 \geqq 39 - 2x_4 . \end{cases}$$

Each of these inequalities can be interpreted as follows. The optimal solution and the corresponding imputed costs of the resources should be such that the marginal revenue should not exceed the inputs of resources evaluated at the imputed costs of the solution.

For basic variables (that is for variables which are normally positive) we should have an equality in (4.12). Furthermore, if the slack variables of the constraints of the original problem are basic (hence normally positive), then the corresponding u-variables should be nonbasic (i.e. zero).

The conditions (4.12) may after the introduction of nonnegative slack variables v_1, v_2, v_3, and v_4 be written as

$$(4.13) \quad \begin{cases} -17 = -4x_1 & -3u_1 & +v_1 , \\ -13 = & -2x_2 & -2u_1 & +v_2 , \\ -70 = & -4x_3 & -10u_1 & -2u_2 & +v_3 , \\ -39 = & -2x_4 & -4u_1 & -\tfrac{1}{2}u_2 & +v_4 . \end{cases}$$

The constraints of the original problem can be written as

$$(4.14) \quad \begin{cases} 18{,}000 = 2x_1 + 2x_2 + 10x_3 + 4x_4 + y_1 , \\ 3000 = \quad\quad\quad\quad\quad 2x_3 + \tfrac{1}{2}x_4 + y_2 . \end{cases}$$

All variables should be nonnegative:

$$(4.15) \quad x_1, x_2, x_3, x_4, y_1, y_2, u_1, u_2, v_1, v_2, v_3, v_4 \geqq 0 .$$

Furthermore, we have the condition that if an x-variable is basic (nonzero) its corresponding v-variable is zero, because then the corresponding equation in

(4.12) should be satisfied as an equality. If a v-variable is positive, this means that the marginal net revenue is less than the value of the resource used, so that the corresponding x-variable should be zero. Hence we have

(4.16) $x_1v_1 = 0$, $x_2v_2 = 0$, $x_3v_3 = 0$, $x_4v_4 = 0$.

Similarly, if a y-variable is positive, its corresponding u-variable (imputed costs) should be zero and *vice versa*, so that

(4.17) $y_1u_1 = 0$, $y_2u_2 = 0$.

The conditions (4.13)–(4.17) are necessary and sufficient conditions for the optimal solution of the quadratic programming concerned. These conditions are in fact a special form of the conditions for an optimal solution to general convex nonlinear programming problems which are called the *Kuhn-Tucker conditions*. In this book we shall not deal with quadratic or nonlinear programming problems because for a more complete exposition some more advanced mathematical concepts are needed.

The equations (4.13) and (4.14) are put in a set-up tableau, see Tableau 0 of Table 2. The solution of this tableau is feasible in terms of the primal variables, so that the simplex method for quadratic programming may be applied. After 7 iterations the optimal solution is obtained which is found in Tableau 7. The values of this solution and the corresponding values of the equilibrium solution are as follows:

	Monopolist	Equilibrium model
x_1	226	90
x_2	385	287
x_3	1087	966
x_4	1420	1873
u_1	2.651	5.067
y_2	116	131

Not much can be said about the values of the x-variables. The values for the monopolist tend to be more evenly distributed over all products than the equilibrium values. The imputed costs of spinning capacity is much lower than in the equilibrium model, which means that the monopolist would be much less likely to expand his spinning capacity than this would happen in the equilibrium model. A bit surprisingly, spare loom capacity is less than in the equi-

Table 2
Optimal solution for monopolist

Tableau	Basic Variables	Values Basic Variables	x_1	x_2	x_3	x_4	u_1	u_2
0	v_1	−17	−4	0	0	0	−3	0
	v_2	−13	0	−2	0	0	−2	0
	v_3	−70	0	0	−4	0	−10	−2
	v_4	−39	0	0	0	−2	−4	−0.5
	y_1	180	3	2	10	4	0	0
	y_2	30	0	0	2	0.5	0	0

Tableau	Basic Variables	Values Basic Variables	y_1	v_2	u_2	v_4	v_1	v_3
7	u_1	2.651	−0.027	−0.027	0.161	−0.054	−0.020	−0.067
	x_2	3.849	0.027	−0.473	−0.161	0.054	0.020	0.067
	y_2	1.156	−0.161	−0.161	−0.159	−0.072	−0.121	0.097
	x_4	14.198	0.054	0.054	−0.072	−0.393	0.040	0.134
	x_1	2.262	0.020	0.020	−0.121	0.040	−0.235	0.050
	x_3	10.872	0.067	0.067	0.097	0.134	0.050	−0.082

librium model, which is due to the fact that the monopolist has a slightly higher production of Fabric A which is the main user of loom capacity.

The value of spinning and loom capacity at imputed costs is for the monopolist

$$2.651 \cdot 180{,}000 + 0 \cdot 3000 = 57{,}718 \ .$$

We may then, as in the equilibrium model, ask the question whether this is equal to total profits of the monopolist. The answer should, of course, be negative, because, since the monopolist is maximizing profits, his profits should be at least as high as in the equilibrium model, where they were $91,206.

Total profits for the monopolist can be written as follows, see (4.9):

$$(4.18) \qquad f = 17x_1 - 2x_1^2 + 13x_2 - x_2^2 + 70x_3 - 2x_3^2 + 39x_4 - x_4^2 \ .$$

Using (4.13), this may be written as

$$f = 17x_1 + \tfrac{1}{2}x_1(-x_1) + 13x_2 + \tfrac{1}{2}x_2(-2x_2)$$

$$+ 70x_3 + \tfrac{1}{2}x_3(-4x_3) + 39x_4 + \tfrac{1}{2}x_4(-2x_4)$$

$$= 17x_1 + \tfrac{1}{2}x_1(-17 + 3u_1 - v_1) + 13x_2 + \tfrac{1}{2}x_2(-13 + 2u_1 - v_2)$$

$$+ 70x_3 + \tfrac{1}{2}x_3(-70 + 10u_1 + 4u_2 - v_3)$$

(4.19)

$$+ 39x_4 + \tfrac{1}{2}x_4(-39 + 4u_1 + \tfrac{1}{2}u_2 - v_4)$$

$$= \tfrac{1}{2}[17x_1 + 13x_2 + 70x_3 + 39x_4 + u_1(3x_1 + 2x_2 + 10x_3 + 4x_4)$$

$$+ u_2(2x_3 + \tfrac{1}{2}x_4) - v_1x_1 - v_2x_2 - v_3x_3 - v_4x_4] \; .$$

In this, we may substitute (4.14), which results in

$$f = \tfrac{1}{2}[17x_1 + 13x_2 + 70x_3 + 39x_4 + 18{,}000u_1 + 3000u_2]$$

(4.20)

$$+ \tfrac{1}{2}[v_1x_1 + v_2x_2 + v_3x_3 + v_4x_4 + u_1y_1 + u_2y_2] \; .$$

For an optimal solution, the second group of terms is zero, so that we may conclude that the objective function is equal to

(4.21) $$f = \tfrac{1}{2}(17x_1 + 13x_2 + 70x_3 + 39x_4) + \tfrac{1}{2}(18{,}000u_1 + 3000u_2) \; .$$

The value of the objective function for the optimal solution is therefore equal to the average of profits of products evaluated at the coefficients of the linear terms of the objective function and the value of the resources evaluated at imputed costs. Hence we find for total profits:

$$f = \tfrac{1}{2}(140{,}317 + 47{,}718) = \$94{,}017 \; .$$

This is higher than the profits in the equilibrium situation, as it of course should be.

Exercises

1. (a) Solve the parametric programming problem involving the parametric variation of the selling price of Fabric A which is indicated on page 5.
   (b) Prove that with increasing selling price of Fabric A the quantity produced of Fabric A increases or stays at least the same.

(c) Prove that in a maximization problem an increase in the coefficient of a variable in the objective function leads to an increase in that variable or the variable remains the same.

(d) Conclude that if in an economy with free competition production can be represented by a linear programming model supply curves consist of a number of increasing steps or a horizontal line.

2. Consider the textile production planning problem and assume that there are different decisionmakers for each product and markets for spinning and loom capacity. Construct a model in which the decisionmakers adjust their planned production according to the profit and loss to be made using the prices of capacities of the previous periods and in which the prices for capacities adjust to shortages or surpluses of capacities. Construct a computer program and simulate the model on the computer for given initial values for a number of periods.

3. Consider supply and demand functions as depicted in Figure 4 and assume that supply reacts with a lag of one period on prices. Trace out the adjustment paths for given initial prices and the demand curves d_3 and d_3'. (This adjustment path is known as the cobweb diagram.)

4. Solve the following quadratic programming problem. Maximize

$$f = 2x_1 + 2x_2 - 2x_1^2 + 2x_1 x_2 - 2x_2^2,$$

subject to

$$x_1 + x_2 \leq 1,$$

$$-x_1 + 6x_2 \leq 2,$$

$$x_1, x_2 \geq 0.$$

11. GAME THEORY

11.1. Introduction

In linear programming a solution is determined which maximizes *one* objective function subject to a number of constraints. This technique is applicable in situations in which there is only *one* decisionmaker or in which the interests of more than one decisionmaker coincide. In real-life situations, however, there are usually a number of decisionmakers with diverging interests. Quite often, the interests of decisionmakers are conflicting. *Game theory* deals with situations with at least two decisionmakers with diverging interests. The word game reflects the fact that most situations of this kind can be imagined in the harmless context of parlour games.

In view of the general prevalence of conflicts, it would seem that game theory applications should be numerous. The difficulty is that when most realistic cases of this nature are considered, the problems are so complicated that game theory can give few generally valid results. Only in very simple cases a general theory can be developed for situations with conflicting interests. With these cases, which are also the best known in game theory, we shall concern ourselves in this chapter.

The kind of games which are considered are the *two-person zero-sum* games. These games involve two decisionmakers with diametrically opposed interests. Each may select one alternative out of a finite number of alternatives; the outcome, which is also called *pay-off* (the value of the objective function for each player), depends on the decisions of both players. Because the game is zero-sum, the gain of one player is the loss of his opponent and *vice versa.*

Since in two-person zero-sum games the interests of the two sides are totally conflicting, these games should accurately reflect war situations. It is therefore not surprising that most well-known examples of application of game theory deal with armed conflict. A well-known example is the contest between British anti-submarine planes and German submarines in which both the planes and the submarines could have or not have radar equipment. Cold war situations lend themselves rather well to the application of game theory. Companies competing in the same market sometimes are in situations which may be approximated by two-person zero-sum games.

Game theory as a scientific field can be said to have its origin with the work of von Neumann and Morgenstern, *Theory of Games and Economic Behavior*. The authors hoped that the theory of games would play an important role in the explanation of economic behavior. So far this has not become true in any substantial way.

In the next section an explanation of the model of two-person zero-sum games will be given by means of an example. Then it will be shown that for both players decisions can be found which are optimal in a certain sense. The decision problem for both players is formulated as a linear programming problem, which is solved by the simplex method.

11.2. Example and Terminology

Consider the following situation. [1] A convoy of food trucks travels daily along a road where it is subject to occasional attacks by guerillas. The trucks are protected by an escort of four military vehicles equipped with machine guns and carrying a small force of infantry. The guerillas can pursue two courses of action:
1) they can stage a full-scale attack on the convoy,
2) they may develop sniping activity.
They have to decide which course of action should be followed before the convoy is seen and once they have decided they cannot change their decision.

To counter the guerilla attacks, the four military escort vehicles may be distributed in the convoy in various ways. In any case there should be at least one military vehicle in front and one in the rear, but the other two may be distributed as desired. This amounts to the following possibilities:
1) 1 vehicle in front and 3 in the rear,
2) 1 vehicle in front, 1 in the rear and 2 distributed in the convoy,
3) 2 vehicles in front and 2 in the rear,
4) 3 vehicles in front and 1 in the rear.

If the guerillas launch a full-scale attack on the convoy, the escort should preferably be concentrated and so placed that it tends to be carried towards the ambush position rather than away from it. If the guerillas are sniping, it is

---

[1] The example is based on a note by R.S. Beresford and M.H. Peston describing a situation in Malaya in which game theory was unconsciously applied.

desirable that the escort should be dispersed as much as possible, so that it can spot where the fire is coming from and return it quickly.

The various alternatives for both sides are called *strategies*; the escort has 4 strategies and the guerillas have 2. The total number of possible outcomes is therefore $4 \cdot 2 = 8$. We now assume that it is possible to evaluate the gains and losses of the escort for each of the outcomes in a single number, the pay-off. Suppose that these numbers are as in Table 1. Hence, if the escort has the 1,3 configuration and a full-scale attack is launched, the gain for the escort is 10, but if the guerillas have decided to snipe, the gain is −4, and so on.

Table 1
Pay-off matrix for example

Players			Guerillas	
	Strategy description		Full-scale attack	Sniping
		Strategy number	1	2
			Pay-off	
Escorts	1 front, 3 rear	1	10	−4
	Distributed	2	−6	3
	2 front, 2 rear	3	0	−4
	3 front, 1 rear	4	−2	−5

In this situation it can be assumed that any gain to the escort is a loss to the guerillas and *vice versa*; this means that it conforms to a two-person zero-sum game. The outcomes of the various strategies can be grouped into a rectangular array of numbers, which is called the *pay-off* matrix of the game. Since the escort wants to maximize the outcome of the game, it is called the *maximizing player*; its adversary, the guerilla group, is then the *minimizing player*. It is easy to reverse the role of both players, which is done by multiplication of the pay-off matrix by −1.

What is the best strategy for the escort? If it is known that the guerillas use their first strategy, a full-scale attack, the escort is advised to use its first strategy, thus gaining 10. If it is known that the guerillas use their second strategy, sniping, the escort should use its second strategy, thereby gaining 3. But the escort does not know the strategy of the guerillas, so that it cannot, in a straightforward manner, determine its best strategy. The guerillas are in entirely the same position. This is a typical situation in a game.

Let us compare the first and the third strategy of the escort. If the guerillas stage a full-scale attack, strategy 1 has a pay-off of 10 and strategy 3 a pay-off of 0. If the guerillas have decided to snipe, both strategy 1 and strategy 3 have the same pay-off of −4. Since strategy 1 has a higher outcome than strategy 3 if the guerillas use their first strategy and the same outcome if they use their second strategy, it is not rational for the escort to use their third strategy. It is said that the third strategy is dominated by the first strategy.

In general, a strategy *dominates* another strategy, if for all strategies of the opponent the first strategy has pay-offs which are at least as high as the other strategy, and at least one pay-off which is higher. For example, strategy 4 of the escort is dominated by strategy 1 and also by strategy 3. Since dominated strategies, if players are rational, will never be played, their rows or columns in the pay-off matrix may be deleted, which simplifies the game. In the example, the pay-off matrix is reduced to

$$
\begin{array}{cc}
10 & -4 \\
-6 & 3
\end{array}.
$$

The existence of dominated strategies for one player may lead to dominated strategies for the other player. Let us consider the game with the pay-off matrix given by Table 2. Player A is the maximizing player and player B the minimizing player. When inspecting the pay-off matrix, we find that for A strategy 1 is dominated by strategy 3. If B assumes that A will not play his strategy 1, he can delete the first row of his pay-off matrix. In the resulting matrix, the first strategy of B is dominated by the third one (note that B is

Table 2
Pay-off matrix for second example

		B			
		1	2	3	4
A	1	−2	2	−1	1
	2	1	4	−2	−3
	3	0	2	0	1
	4	−1	−2	−1	5

the minimizing player). Hence the first column can be deleted. The resulting pay-off matrix is

		B		
		2	3	4
	2	4	−2	−3
A	3	2	0	1
	4	−2	−1	5

There are various ways in which the players can select their strategy. One way is to determine the worst pay-off for each strategy, assuming that the opponent will select the strategy corresponding with this pay-off; then the strategy with the maximum of these minimum pay-offs is chosen. In the reduced pay-off matrix above, the worst pay-off in strategy 2 of A is −3, that in strategy 3 is 0 and that in strategy 4 is −2. The maximum of these three numbers is 0, which belongs to strategy 3. B can follow the same policy. Taking into account that B is the minimizing player, we find that the worst outcomes for his strategies 2, 3, and 4 are 4, 0, and 5. The minimum of these is 0 which corresponds to strategy 3.

Now suppose that both A and B play the strategies determined in this manner, hence both play their strategy 3. Then A will have no occasion to change his strategy, since if he plays his strategy 2 or 4, he will have a pay-off of −2 or −1. In the same way we find that B will have no occasion to play anything else than his strategy 3, because if he plays his strategy 2 or 4, the pay-off will be 2 and 1. Once A and B both play their strategy 3, they are not likely to deviate from these. This pair of strategies is called the *saddle-point* of the game. The saddle-point of a game is a pair of strategies such that there is no lower number in the row of the strategy of the maximizing player and no higher number in the column of the minimizing player. If a game has a saddle-point, it must be found by taking the maximum of the minima of the elements of each row for the maximizing player and the minimum of the maxima of each column for the minimizing player.

Not every game has a saddle-point. Let us return to the escort-guerilla game, for which the pay-off matrix is given in Table 1. The row-minima for the escorts are −4, −6, −4, and −5, the maximum of which is −4, which belongs to the strategies 1 and 3. The column maxima are 10 and 3; the minimum of these is 3, which belongs to strategy 2. Now the pairs of strategies (1,2) and (3,2) will not be saddle-points. Suppose that at one time the escorts use strategy 1 and the guerillas strategy 2. Then the escorts will next time, assuming that the guerillas will not change their strategy, change over to strategy 2. The next time, the guerillas will, assuming that the escorts will continue to use their strategy 2, change to strategy 1. Then next time the escorts are going to use their strategy 1, and so on. There is no single pair of strategies which both players continue to use because there is no saddle-point. We shall see that also for these games strategies can be found which guarantee each player a certain pay-off.

Instead of deciding to use one strategy, the escorts may decide to use more than one strategy. For instance, they may decide to play their strategy 1 with probability $\frac{1}{2}$ and their strategy 2 with probability $\frac{1}{2}$. This means that before each game is played, the escorts throw a coin; if heads come up, strategy 1 is used and if tails come up, strategy 2 is played. In this case it is said that a *mixed strategy* is used. As before it is assumed that at the start of the game the opponent does not know which specific strategy is going to be played by the first player. If the game is played a number of times and the first player is always using the same mixed strategy, the opponent may estimate the probabilities with which the different strategies are being played, but he does not know the strategy to be employed in any single game; until the player of the mixed strategy has thrown the coin or used a similar device, he does not know this himself.

If the escorts are using the mixed strategy of playing the first strategy with probability $\frac{1}{2}$ and the second strategy with probability $\frac{1}{2}$, the *average* pay-off will be if the guerillas are using their strategy 1:

$$\frac{1}{2} \cdot 10 + \frac{1}{2} \cdot (-6) = 2 \,,$$

and if the guerillas use their strategy 2,

$$\frac{1}{2}(-4) + \frac{1}{2} \cdot 3 = -\frac{1}{2} \,.$$

The summation of the pay-offs times the probabilities implies that the players do not have risk-preference or risk-aversion. If the outcome of a particular game is rather insignificant compared with the total interests of the player, such an approach is valid. This is the case in the cold war, where the pay-offs in local conflicts are relatively small and where a game may be repeated many times.

11.3. Game Theory and Linear Programming

If the escorts use the mixed strategy with probabilities of $\frac{1}{2}$, the worst average pay-off which the escorts may expect is $-\frac{1}{2}$, which is found when the guerillas are using their second strategy. This exceeds the minimum pay-off which is obtained by playing their pure strategies 1 or 2, where, if the guerillas accurately guessed the strategy to be played, the pay-offs would be -4 and -6. Now let us suppose that the escorts are using their first strategy with probability p_1 and their second strategy with probability p_2, where

(3.1) $\qquad p_1 + p_2 = 1$

and

(3.2) $\qquad p_1, p_2 \geqq 0$.

In selecting p_1 and p_2 the escorts may use the same objective as before, taking into account that for mixed strategies average pay-offs should be considered. Hence p_1 and p_2 should be determined in such a way that the average pay-off is maximized under the assumption that the opponent uses his best strategy. Let us call this maximum pay-off w. Then, if the guerillas use their first strategy, the average pay-off will be $10p_1 - 6p_2$ and since w is the pay-off obtained if the opponent uses his best strategy, this average pay-off should be at least equal to w:

(3.3) $\qquad 10p_1 - 6p_2 \geqq w$.

If the guerillas use their second strategy, the pay-off should be at least equal to w, so that the following relation should be valid:

(3.4) $\qquad -4p_1 + 3p_2 \geqq w$.

The escorts want to maximize w, so that the following objective function may be formulated:

(3.5) $\qquad f = w$.

The maximization of f as in (3.5) subject to the constraints (3.1) – (3.4) is a linear programming problem; it may be solved by the simplex method or any other linear programming method. Note that in this problem w has no non-negativity restriction.

Two remarks can be made. In the above, it was assumed that the guerillas used a pure strategy. Is the problem formulation (3.1) – (3.6) also valid if the guerillas use a mixed strategy too? Suppose that the guerillas use a mixed strategy with q_1 and q_2 as the probabilities for their first and second strategy. q_1 and q_2 should satisfy

$$(3.6) \qquad q_1 + q_2 = 1 ,$$

$$(3.7) \qquad q_1, q_2 \geqq 0 .$$

Then the average pay-off for the escorts will be $q_1(10p_1 - 6p_2) + q_2(-4p_1 + 3p_2)$ and this should be at least equal to w:

$$(3.8) \qquad q_1(10p_1 - 6p_2) + q_2(-4p_1 + 3p_2) \geqq w .$$

In view of (3.6) this inequality may be written as

$$(3.9) \qquad q_1(10p_1 - 6p_2) + q_2(-4p_1 + 3p_2) \geqq q_1 w + q_2 w .$$

If (3.3) and (3.4) are satisfied, then, since the q's are nonnegative, (3.9) is satisfied. Hence it is sufficient to consider only the pure strategies of the opponent.

What happens if the dominated strategies 3 and 4 of the escorts are also taken into account? Let us define p_1, p_2, p_3, and p_4 as the probabilities of the mixed strategy of the escorts. The constraints are now

$$(3.10) \qquad 10p_1 - 6p_2 + 0p_3 - 2p_4 \geqq w ,$$

$$(3.11) \qquad -4p_1 + 3p_2 - 4p_3 - 5p_4 \geqq w ,$$

$$(3.12) \qquad p_1 + p_2 + p_3 + p_4 = 1 ,$$

$$(3.13) \qquad p_1, p_2, p_3, p_4 \geqq 0 .$$

Now it may be proved that, if a mixed strategy is considered in which a dominated strategy occurs with a positive probability, then the probability of the dominating strategy may be increased at the expense of the dominated strategy, increasing the average pay-off or leaving it the same. For example, consider strategy 4 which is dominated by strategy 1. The terms in p_1 and p_4 in (10) – (12) may be written as

(3.14) $12p_1 - 2(p_1 + p_4)$,

(3.15) $p_1 - 5(p_1 + p_4)$,

(3.16) $(p_1 + p_4)$.

If p_1 is increased and p_4 is decreased by the same amount, $p_1 + p_4$ is unchanged, which means that both (3.14) and (3.15) increase; according to (3.10) and (3.11), w can be increased by the same amount. Hence no mixed strategy containing a positive value for p_4 can be optimal.

Now the optimal mixed strategy for the escrots will be determined by means of the simplex method. If slack variables are introduced, the problem can be formulated as follows: Maximize

(3.17) $f = w$

subject to

(3.18) $p_1 + p_2 = 1$,

(3.19) $10p_1 - 6p_2 - w - y_1 = 0$,

(3.20) $-4p_1 + 3p_2 - w - y_2 = 0$,

(3.21) $p_1, p_2, y_1, y_2 \geqq 0$.

Note that w is unrestricted. Artificial variables could be introduced into each of the equations (3.18), (3.19), and (3.20), but (3.19) and (3.20) may be multiplied by -1, after which y_1 and y_2 may be used as basic variables with a nonnegative value:

(3.22) $-10p_1 + 6p_2 + w + y_1 = 0$,

(3.23) $4p_1 - 3p_2 + w + y_2 = 0$.

In (3.18), the artificial variable z may be inserted:

(3.24) $1 = p_1 + p_2 + z$.

z is added to the objective function with the coefficient $-M$:

(3.25) $f = w - Mz$,

or

(3.26) $0 = -w + Mz + f$.

After subtraction of M times (3.24) from (3.26) we find

(3.27) $-M = -Mp_1 - Mp_2 - w + f$.

This can be used for the f_c- and f_M-row of the set-up tableau, see Tableau 0 of Table 3. The equations (3.22) – (3.24) furnish the remaining rows.

    After two iterations of the simplex method, the z-variable has disappeared from the basis; the optimal solution is found in one further iteration. Note that as long as z is a basic variable, the f_M-row is identical to minus the z-row; hence the f_M-row never needs to be written down. Furthermore, as long as w does not enter the basis, the f_c-row consists of zeroes except for the element in the w-column. After w has entered the basis, the f_c-row is identical to the w-row. Hence also the f_c-row can be deleted altogether.

    The optimal solution is

$$f = 6/23 ,$$

$$p_1 = 9/23 ,$$

$$p_2 = 14/23 .$$

This means that the escorts should, each time before the convoy starts, pick at random a number $1 - 23$; if it is $1 - 9$, the first strategy should be used, if it is $10 - 23$, the second strategy should be employed. The average pay-off is then at least $6/23$. Of course, if the guerillas are using their first strategy consistently, it is better for the escorts to use their first strategy; if the guerillas use their second strategy consistently, the escorts should use their second strategy. But if nothing is known about the strategies of the opponent, the solution outlined guarantees the escorts a minimum pay-off of $6/23$.

    The guerillas face a similar problem. They too can use a mixed strategy; let the probabilities associated with their first and second strategy be q_1 and q_2. The guerillas want to minimize the maximum pay-off as it is given by the pay-off matrix. Let the maximum pay-off be v. Then if the escorts use their first strategy, the pay-off would be $10q_1 - 4q_2$, and this should at most equal v:

Table 3
Application of the simplex method to the problem of the maximizing player

Tableau	Basic Variables	Values Basic Variables	Ratio	p_1	p_2	w
	f_c	0		0	0	−1
	f_M	−1		−1	−1	0
0	z	1	1	1	1	0
	y_1	0		−10	6	1
	y_2	0	0	<u>4</u>	−3	1
				y_2	p_2	w
	f_c	0		0	0	−1
1	f_M	−1		¼	−1¾	¼
	z	1	1¾	−¼	<u>1¾</u>	−¼
	y_1	0		2½	−1½	3½
	p_1	0		¼	−³4	¼
				y_2		w
	f_c	0		0		−1
2	f_M	0		0		0
	p_2	4/7		−⅟7		−⅟7
	y_1	6/7	6/23	2²/7		3²/7
	p_1	3/7	3	⅟7		<u>⅟7</u>
				y_2		y_1
	f	6/23		16/23		7/23
3	p_2	14/23		−⅟23		⅟23
	w	6/23		16/23		7/23
	p_1	9/23		⅟23		−⅟23

$$(3.28) \qquad 10q_1 - 4q_2 \leqq v.$$

If the escorts use their second strategy, the pay-off would be $-6q_1 + 3q_2$ and this should at most equal v:

$$(3.29) \qquad -6q_1 + 3q_2 \leqq v.$$

The probabilities q_1 and q_2 should be nonnegative and add to 1:

(3.30) $q_1 \geq 0, \quad q_2 \geq 0,$

(3.31) $q_1 + q_2 = 1.$

The maximum pay-off should be minimized, so that the objective function is: minimize $g = v$.

Hence the complete problem for the minimizing player is: Minimize

(3.32) $g = v$

subject to

$$
(3.33) \quad \left\{
\begin{array}{l}
10q_1 - 4q_2 - v \leq 0, \\[6pt]
-6q_1 + 3q_2 - v \leq 0, \\[6pt]
q_1 + q_2 = 1, \\[6pt]
q_1, q_2 \geq 0.
\end{array}
\right.
$$

The complete problem for the maximizing player was: Maximize

(3.34) $f = w$

subject to

$$
(3.35) \quad \left\{
\begin{array}{l}
10p_1 - 6p_2 - w \geq 0, \\[6pt]
-4p_1 + 3p_2 - w \geq 0, \\[6pt]
p_1 + p_2 = 1, \\[6pt]
p_1, p_2 \geq 0.
\end{array}
\right.
$$

It can be proved that the minimization problem is the dual problem of the maximization problem and *vice versa* (see Exercise 3). Hence the values of the basic variables of the dual problem should appear as the elements of the f-row in the primal problem. The optimal solution for the problem of the guerillas is therefore .

$$g \ = \ ^6\!/_{23} \ ,$$

$$q_1 = \ ^7\!/_{23} \ ,$$

$$q_2 = \ ^{16}\!/_{23} \ ,$$

The guerillas should, before they start out, take a random number $1 - 23$; if it is $1 - 7$, they should launch a full-scale attack, if it is $8 - 23$ they should display sniping activity. Neither party would in this situation be able to find a higher (for the escort) or lower (for the guerillas) average pay-off by changing their mixed strategy; in fact, if they did, the opponent could take advantage of it and have a better average pay-off.

Exercises

1. Two companies share a certain market. Each company can in any year follow two marketing strategies; it can advertise or give price discounts. In terms of market share for the first company the outcomes are as follows:

		B	
		Advertise	Price discount
A	Advertise	70	50
	Price discount	55	60

What are the optimal strategies for both companies if both companies maximize market shares? What is the corresponding average market share of company A?

2. Two superpowers, East and West, play a game for uncommitted nations. Suppose that 20 nations are at stake. Each can follow these strategies: 1. an aggression policy; 2. a neutral policy; 3. a defense-aid policy. The pay-off policy in terms of nations won or lost is for West as follows:

		East		
		1	2	3
West	1	12	8	6
	2	5	15	8
	3	15	8	10

If the (questionable) aim is to maximize the number of uncommitted nations committed to one's own side, what are the optimal strategies?

3. Given is a two-person zero-sum game in which the maximizing player A has n_A strategies and the minimizing player B has n_B strategies. The pay-off for A if he plays his ith strategy and B plays his jth strategy is a_{ij}. Formulate the problem of finding the optimal strategy for A as a linear programming problem. Do the same for B. Show that both problems are each other's dual problem.

4. Consider a situation in which there are two American presidential candidates who have to decide whether they will assume a hawkish or a dovish attitude; assume that the attitudes chosen will depend solely on the probability of winning the election. The pay-off matrix in terms of percentages of probability is taken to be as follows for candidate A:

		B	
		Hawkish	Dovish
A	Hawkish	55	35
	Dovish	40	45

What are the optimal strategies for both candidates?

5. Analyze the game with the following general pay-off matrix

		B	
		1	2
A	1	a	b
	2	c	d

for all values of a, b, c, and d.

PART 3

TRANSPORTATION AND NETWORK METHODS

12. TRANSPORTATION METHODS

12.1. A Production and Sales Allocation Problem

Let us consider the following allocation problem. An international company producing T.V. sets has two plants, one in Holland with a capacity of 100 units per week and one in Britain with a capacity of 200 units per week. The company has four countries as its markets for the sets, Holland, Britain, Germany, and Denmark; the maximum numbers of sets to be sold in these countries are 75, 100, 100, and 30 units per week respectively. The profit per unit differs according to the country of production and the country in which a set is sold due to differences in costs, customs duties, transportation charges, and selling prices; these profits are given by Table 1.

Table 1
Profits per unit

		Country of Sales			
		Holland	Britain	Germany	Denmark
Country of production	Holland	80	0	20	20
	Britain	116	144	76	148

It is assumed that only variable costs are calculated. The company may leave its productive capacity at both plants partly or wholly unused and it may leave demand in any country unsatisfied without any costs. How should it allocate the productive capacity of the two plants over the four markets in order to maximize total profits on T.V. sets?

A problem of such a small size can easily be solved by checking all possible allocations or just those that look promising. Even for problems that are only slightly larger this is not practical because of the number of different allocations that are possible. It is therefore necessary to develop a more systematic procedure.

The problem formulated above lacks reality in several respects. For instance, the possibilities of fluctuations in demand and production for inventory were not taken into account. However, the method which will be explained can easily be generalized for more complicated problems.

First the problem will be formulated in terms of equations. Let us indicate the number of sets produced by the Dutch plant for the Dutch market with x_{11}, the quantity produced by the same plant for the British market by x_{12}, the similar quantity for the German market by x_{13}, and that for the Danish market by x_{14}. In the same way the amounts produced by the British plant for the Dutch, British, German, and Danish market can be denoted by x_{21}, x_{22}, x_{23}, and x_{24}, respectively. Further, let the unused capacity of the Dutch plant be x_{10} and the unused capacity of the British plant x_{20}. Since total production of a plant plus its unused capacity must be equal to its capacity, the following equations are valid:

(1.1) $x_{10} + x_{11} + x_{12} + x_{13} + x_{14} = 100$,

(1.2) $x_{20} + x_{21} + x_{22} + x_{23} + x_{24} = 200$.

Let us denote the unsatisfied demands on the Dutch, British, German, and Danish markets by x_{01}, x_{02}, x_{03}, and x_{04}, respectively. Since in each country sales from both sources plus unsatisfied demand must equal maximum demand, the following equations are valid:

(1.3) $x_{01} + x_{11} + x_{21} = 75$,

(1.4) $x_{02} + x_{12} + x_{22} = 100$,

(1.5) $x_{03} + x_{13} + x_{23} = 100$,

(1.6) $x_{04} + x_{14} + x_{24} = 30$.

Let us add the equations (1.1) and (1.2). The result is

(1.7) $x_{00} + x_{10} + x_{20} = 300$,

where x_{00} is defined as

$$x_{00} = x_{11} + x_{12} + x_{13} + x_{14} + x_{21} + x_{22} + x_{23} + x_{24}.$$

In the same way, the equations (1.3) to (1.6) can be added, which results in

$$(1.8) \qquad x_{00} + x_{01} + x_{02} + x_{03} + x_{04} = 305 \ .$$

Since equation (1.8) can be obtained from the equations (1.1) to (1.7) [add (1.3) to (1.6), subtract (1.1) and (1.2), and add (1.7)], one of the equations of the equation system (1.1) to (1.8) is dependent on the other equations.

The equation system can be put into a particularly convenient form by arranging all x-variables in a rectangular array or tableau:

$$(1.9) \qquad \begin{array}{ccccc} x_{00} & x_{01} & x_{02} & x_{03} & x_{04} \\[2mm] x_{10} & x_{11} & x_{12} & x_{13} & x_{14} \\[2mm] x_{20} & x_{21} & x_{22} & x_{23} & x_{24} \end{array}$$

Equations (1.8), (1.1), and (1.2) state that the sum of the elements of the three rows should be constant and equal to 305, 100, and 200, respectively. Equations (1.7) and (1.3) to (1.6) state that the sum of the elements of the five columns should be constant and equal to 300, 75, 100, 100, and 30, respectively. This representation of the equations simplifies the solution of the problem to a great extent.

As a starting point of the method, we consider the particular solution in which the entire productive capacity is left unused and in which no sales are made in any market. This means:

$$(1.10) \qquad \begin{aligned} &x_{10} = 100 \ , \quad x_{20} = 200 \ , \\[2mm] &x_{01} = 75 \ , \quad x_{02} = 100 \ , \quad x_{03} = 100 \ , \quad x_{04} = 30 \ ; \end{aligned}$$

all other variables are equal to zero. This solution can be put into tableau-form as follows:

$$(1.11) \qquad \begin{array}{ccccc} 0 & 75 & 100 & 100 & 30 \\[2mm] 100 & 0 & 0 & 0 & 0 \\[2mm] 200 & 0 & 0 & 0 & 0 \ . \end{array}$$

In this solution as well as in the solutions we shall consider later on, we distinguish two kinds of variables, firstly *basic variables* which may have non-zero values and *nonbasic variables* which only have zero values. In (1.11) the basic variables are those with nonzero values given in (1.10) and x_{00} which happens to be zero; the nonbasic variables are all variables not in the first column and in the first row. In any basic solution, the number of basic variables is equal to the number of rows plus the number of columns minus one, which is equal to the number of independent equations on which the tableau was based.

Let us now consider total profits, which are equal to the sum of profits per unit times the number of units sold over the various countries and plants. Hence, if f is total profits, we have

$$
\begin{aligned}
f = \quad & 80x_{11} + \quad 0x_{12} + 20x_{13} + \quad 20x_{14} \\
& + 116x_{21} + 144x_{22} + 76x_{23} + 148x_{24} \,,
\end{aligned}
$$

(1.12)

which can be written as

$$
\begin{aligned}
f = \quad & 0x_{00} + \quad 0x_{01} + \quad 0x_{02} + 0x_{03} + \quad 0x_{04} \\
& + 0x_{10} + \quad 80x_{11} + \quad 0x_{12} + 20x_{13} + \quad 20x_{14} \\
& + 0x_{20} + 116x_{21} + 144x_{22} + 76x_{23} + 148x_{24} \,;
\end{aligned}
$$

(1.13)

note that the added terms have all zero coefficients. The function f will be called the objective function of the problem. This function may be indicated in a more convenient manner by only writing down the coefficients in a rectangular tableau, since the meaning of the coefficients will be clear from their position. This tableau is

0	0	0	0	0
0	80	0	20	20
0	116	144	76	148 .

(1.14)

If the solution given in (1.11) is substituted in (1.13), the value of f is zero, since all basic variables of (1.11) have zero coefficients in (1.13); the nonbasic variables are zero, so that terms in nonbasic variables cannot contribute anything to the objective function. Proceeding from (1.11), an improved solution will be sought which is done by increasing one of the non-basic variables. Let us take the nonbasic variable x_{24}.

If $x_{24} = \Delta$ there should be changes in the basic variables of solution (1.11) in order to keep the sums of the elements of rows and columns constant. Since the sum of the elements of the last column of (1.11) should remain constant, we should replace $x_{04} = 30$ by $x_{04} = 30 - \Delta$. Then, to keep the sum of the elements in the first row constant we should have instead of $x_{00} = 0$, $x_{00} = \Delta$. Since the sum in the first row should be kept constant, we change $x_{20} = 200$ into $x_{20} = 200 - \Delta$; by the last change the sum in the last row is also constant. The following solution is obtained:

Δ	75	100	100	$30 - \Delta$
100	0	0	0	0
$200 - \Delta$	0	0	0	Δ .

(1.15)

We have introduced a nonbasic variable at a nonzero value Δ and have determined the changes necessary in the basic variables in order that the equations (1.1) to (1.8) are still satisfied. The effect on the objective function of this change is only reflected in the coefficient of x_{24}, 148, since all basic variables have zero values in the objective function. For any nonbasic variable of (1.11), the same reasoning is valid. In general, introduction of a nonbasic variable at a nonzero value Δ causes changes in the basic variables; the effect on the objective function of the changing solution is given by the coefficient of the nonbasic variable only since the basic variables have zero coefficients. Let us therefore select as the variable to be increased the nonbasic variable with the largest positive coefficient in the objective function. According to tableau (1.14) this is x_{24}.

Tableau (1.15) gives the changed solution in terms of the value of x_{24}, Δ. The value of f is for this solution 148Δ and since profits should be maximized, Δ should be made as large as possible, without, however, making any variable of the solution negative. From (1.15) it is obvious that the maximum value of Δ is 30, for which value we find for the solution

30	75	100	100	0
100	0	0	0	0
170	0	0	0	30 .

(1.16)

We now have obtained another basic solution in which x_{24} is a basic variable having replaced x_{04} which now is a nonbasic variable.

This solution should be improved in the same way as the previous solution (1.11) was improved. To find an improved solution for (1.11), the objective function (1.13) was used which had zero coefficients for the basic variables of (1.11). For the new solution in (1.16), however, the objective function in (1.13) has a coefficient 148 for the basic variable x_{24}. It is therefore desirable to change the objective function in such a way that is has a zero ceofficient for x_{24}; the coefficient for x_{04} may become nonzero since x_{04} is not a basic variable in the new solution. This change in the objective function may be achieved by subtracting 148 times equation (1.6) from equation (1.13). The result is

$$f - 148 \cdot 30 = \quad 0x_{00} + \quad 0x_{01} + \quad 0x_{02} + \quad 0x_{03} - 148x_{04}$$

(1.17)
$$+ 0x_{10} + 80x_{11} + \quad 0x_{12} + 20x_{13} - 128x_{14}$$

$$+ 0x_{20} + 116x_{21} + 144x_{22} + 76x_{23} + \quad 0x_{24} \ .$$

It is obvious that this amounts to subtracting 148 from the elements of the last column of (1.14), so that we have in tableau-form

0	0	0	0	-148
0	80	0	20	-128
0	116	144	76	0 .

(1.18)

This form of the objective function has the property that it has zeros for the basic variables of the solution in (1.16), so that it can be used for improving this solution.

The transformation of the objective function can be interpreted as follows. The increase in x_{24}, which is British production for the Danish market, had to be halted because the market was satisfied. In this situation a unit of demand in Denmark is worth 148, since this is the profit made for x_{24}. When evaluating the profit of x_{14}, which is Dutch production on the Danish market and of x_{04} which denotes unsatisfied demand, this amount should be subtracted, so that we have -148 for the coefficient of x_{04} and $20 - 148 = -128$ for the coefficient of x_{14}. This means that if the solution (1.16) was changed by having $x_{04} = \Delta$ and corresponding changes in the basic variables, the decrease in profits would be 148Δ and if the solution (1.16) was changed by having $x_{14} = \Delta$ and corresponding changes in the basic variables, the decrease in profits would be 128Δ.

Since we wish to improve the solution, we select the nonbasic variable with the largest positive coefficient in (1.18), which is x_{22} with a coefficient of 144. Putting $x_{22} = \Delta$ and adjusting the other basic variables to keep the sums of elements of rows and columns constant, we find from (1.16):

$$
\begin{array}{ccccc}
30 + \Delta & 75 & 100 - \Delta & 100 & 0 \\
(1.19) \quad 100 & 0 & 0 & 0 & 0 \\
170 - \Delta & 0 & \Delta & 0 & 30 \; .
\end{array}
$$

The maximum value which Δ can take without making any basic variable negative is 100, so that the next solution is:

$$
\begin{array}{ccccc}
130 & 75 & 0 & 100 & 0 \\
(1.20) \quad 100 & 0 & 0 & 0 & 0 \\
70 & 0 & 100 & 0 & 30 \; .
\end{array}
$$

In this solution x_{22} is a basic variable, having replaced x_{02} which now is a nonbasic variable.

The adjustment in the objective function necessary to make the coefficient of x_{22} zero is obtained by subtracting 144 times equation (1.4) from the objective function implied by (1.18). The result is

$$
\begin{array}{ccccc}
0 & 0 & -144 & 0 & -148 \\
(1.21) \quad 0 & 80 & -144 & 20 & -128 \\
0 & 116 & 0 & 76 & 0 \; .
\end{array}
$$

The left side of the equation of the objective function is now

$$
(1.22) \qquad f - 148 \cdot 30 - 144 \cdot 100 = f - 18{,}840 \; ,
$$

which implies that, since, as before, the right-hand side is zero for the basic solution of (1.20) that $f = 18{,}840$.

Next, the solution (1.20) should be improved by selecting the nonbasic variable with the largest positive coefficient in the corresponding form of the objective function given by (1.21). Hence we put $x_{21} = \Delta$; after adjusting the basic variables for this we find

$$
\begin{array}{ccccc}
130 + \Delta & 75 - \Delta & 0 & 100 & 0 \\
100 & 0 & 0 & 0 & 0 \\
70 - \Delta & \Delta & 100 & 0 & 30 \, .
\end{array}
$$

(1.23)

The maximum value of Δ is found to be 70; for this value the solution is

$$
\begin{array}{ccccc}
200 & 5 & 0 & 100 & 0 \\
100 & 0 & 0 & 0 & 0 \\
0 & 70 & 100 & 0 & 30 \, .
\end{array}
$$

(1.24)

In this solution x_{21} has replaced x_{20} as a basic variable.

Now the objective function should be adjusted. In order to reduce the coefficient of x_{21} to zero, 116 times equation (1.2) is subtracted from the objective function having the coefficients given in (1.21). The resulting coefficients are

$$
\begin{array}{ccccc}
0 & 0 & -144 & 0 & -148 \\
0 & 80 & -144 & 20 & -128 \\
-116 & 0 & -116 & -40 & -116 \, .
\end{array}
$$

(1.25)

In this tableau x_{21} has a zero coefficient, but now the coefficients of the basic variables x_{22} and x_{24} are nonzero. Hence 116 times the equations (1.3) and (1.5) are added to the objective function equation which results in an equation having as coefficients

$$
\begin{array}{ccccc}
0 \, 0 & 0 & -28 & 0 & -32 \\
0 & 80 & -28 & 20 & -12 \\
116 & 0 & 0 & -40 & 0 \, .
\end{array}
$$

(1.26)

It is somewhat more convenient to perform the adjustment of the coefficients of the objective function in the following manner. Tableau (1.21) is the tableau to be transformed. Let us underline the coefficients of its basic variables, which are x_{00}, x_{01}, x_{03}, x_{10}, x_{21}, x_{22}, and x_{24}. The subtraction of 116 from the last row is provisionally indicated by a minus sign within brackets in front of the elements in the last row. It is then observed that the underlined coefficients of the basic variables x_{22} and x_{24} are nonzero. Hence 116 is added to the third and fifth columns which is provisionally indicated by a plus within brackets in front of the elements concerned. The following tableau is obtained:

$$
\begin{array}{cccccc}
& \underline{0} & \underline{0} & (+)-144 & \underline{0} & (+)-148 \\[2mm]
(1.27) & \underline{0} & 80 & (+)-144 & 20 & (+)-128 \\[2mm]
& (-)0 & (-)\underline{116} & (\pm)\underline{0} & (-)76 & (\pm)\underline{0}.
\end{array}
$$

It is observed that now all basic variables have zero coefficients, so that the indicated subtractions and additions may be performed, which results in (1.26).

The problem can be solved in this manner, but before any further steps are taken a more convenient organization of the tableaux will be indicated. It was pointed out before that the basic variables of a solution always have zero coefficients in the corresponding formulation of the objective function. On the other hand, nonbasic variables which may have nonzero coefficients have zero values in any basic solution. It is therefore possible to combine in one tableau values of basic variables and coefficients of nonbasic variables; an element of such a tableau is the value of a variable if this variable is basic and is a coefficient of the objective function if the variable is nonbasic. In order to distinguish between the two possibilities, the values of basic variables are underlined. [1] Tableau 0 of Table 2 combines in this way the tableaux (1.11) and (1.14), Tableau 1 combines the tableaux (1.16) and (1.18). Tableau 2 combines the tableaux (1.20) and (1.21) and Tableau 3 combines the tableaux (1.24) and (1.26). The Δ's within brackets behind an element refer to the new basic variable and the corresponding changes in the basic variables of the current solution; the plus- and minus-signs within brackets in front of an element have been used for the adjustment of the coefficients of the objective function as described before.

---

[1] In manual work, different colours may be used.

Table 2
Tableaux for TV production and sales example

Tableau		Unused Cap.	H	B	G	D
0	Uns. Dem.	0(△)	75	100	100	(−) 30(−△)
	H	100	80	0	20	(−) 20
	B	200(−△)	116	144	76	(−)148(△)
1	Uns. Dem.	30(△)	75	(−)100(−△)	100	−148
	H	100	80	(−) 0	20	−128
	B	170(−△)	116	(−)144(△)	76	30
2	Uns. Dem.	130(△)	75(−△)	(+)−144	100	(+)−148
	H	100	80	(+)−144	20	(+)−128
	B	(−) 70(−△)	(−)116(△)	(∓) 100	(−) 76	(∓) 30
3	Uns. Dem.	200(△)	(−) 5(−△)	(−)−28	100	(−)−32
	H	100(−△)	(−) 80(△)	(−)−28	20	(−)−12
	B	(+)−116	(∓) 70	(±) 100	(+)− 40	(±) 30
4	Uns. Dem.	205(△)	− 80	(+)−108	100(−△)	(+)−112
	H	95(−△)	5(△)	(+)−108	20	(+)− 92
	B	(−)−36	(−) 70(−△)	(∓) 100	(−) 40(△)	(∓) 30
5	Uns. Dem.	275(△)	(+)− 80	− 68	30(−△)	− 72
	H	(−) 25(−△)	(∓) 75	(−)−68	20(△)	(−)−52
	B	− 76	(+)− 40	100	(−) 70	30
6	Uns. Dem.	300	− 60	− 68	5	− 72
	H	− 20	75	− 88	25	− 72
	B	− 76	− 20	100	70	30

We shall proceed using these combined tableaux. In Tableau 3, the largest positive element which is not underlined is 80, corresponding with x_{11}, Dutch production for the home market. Hence x_{11} is the new basic variable; after the adjustments in the basic variables of the current solution it is found that x_{01} leaves the basis and that $\Delta = 5$. The values of the basic variables of Tableau 4 may be written down accordingly. The coefficients of the objective function are transformed by subtractions and additions of the coefficient of the new basic variable, 80. First a minus is put in front of the elements of the second column. The first element, 5, of this column is underlined, but the basic variable concerned, x_{01}, is becoming nonbasic. The third element of this column, 70, is underlined, so that it refers to a value of a basic variable. Hence a plus is put in front of the elements in the third row. Now two underlined elements, 100 and 30, have a sign which should be neutralized; this is done by putting minus-signs in front of the elements in the third and fifth columns. No underlined element has an uncompensated sign, so the actual adjustment can be performed by addition or subtraction of 80.

In Tableau 4 the largest positive element which is not underlined is 40, so that x_{23} should become basic. The changes in the basic variables are now somewhat more complicated but they are found in the manner indicated before. The leaving basic variable turns out to be x_{22} and $\Delta = 70$. Tableau 5 is found as described before. In Tableau 5, x_{13} is the new basic variable and x_{10} is the leaving basic variable; Tableau 6 is then found without difficulty.

In Tableau 6, there is no nonbasic variable with a positive coefficient so that it does not pay to increase any nonbasic variable; in fact, since the coefficients of nonbasic variables are all negative, any increase in value of these variables, each one separately or any number of them in linear combinations would decrease the objective function. Since they cannot become negative, all nonbasic variables should be zero. Hence the values of basic variables given by the basic solution of Tableau 6 constitute the optimal solution. This solution is

$$
\begin{aligned}
&x_{00} = 300, \quad x_{03} = 5, \quad x_{11} = 75, \quad x_{13} = 25, \\
&x_{22} = 100, \quad x_{23} = 75, \quad x_{24} = 30.
\end{aligned}
$$

(1.28)

The production of the Dutch plant should therefore be assigned to the home market and the German market, and the production of the British plant should be assigned to the home market, the German market, and the Danish market; there is an unsatisfied demand on the German market of 5.

Not only the values of basic variables of the optimal tableau are of importance, but also the coefficients of the objective function. The coefficient of x_{21}, for example, which is -20, can be interpreted as the loss that would be incurred per unit if British-made sets were sold in Holland. The coefficients of x_{10} and x_{20} can be interpreted in the same manner; they are equal to the loss of leaving a unit of productive capacity unused in Holland and Britain. But they can also be interpreted as minus the value of additional capacity in the two plants. This is obvious since any additional unit produced in Holland would give in Germany a profit of 20 guilders per unit; for a set produced in Britain this profit would be 76 guilders. In a similar way, the coefficients of x_{01}, x_{02}, x_{03}, and x_{04} can be interpreted as the loss incurred if a unit of Dutch, British, German, or Danish demand is left unsatisfied or as the profit to be made on additional units of demand. Hence the profits to be ascribed to the Danish market are 72 guilders per unit, that for the British and Dutch market 68 and 60 guilders per unit, and that for the German market is zero.

Since the coefficients of the objective function in the first column and the first row are the amounts that have been subtracted from the rows and columns, respectively, it is easy to check whether any errors have been made in adjusting the objective function. For instance, according to Tableau 6, 60 is subtracted from the elements of the first column and 20 and 76 from the elements of the second and third rows. Hence the coefficients of x_{11} and x_{21}, which are 80 and 116 in Tableau 0, should be in Tableau 6: $80 - 60 -20 = 0$ and $116 - 60 - 76 = -20$, which agrees with the concerned elements of Tableau 6.

The value of the objective function may either be computed at each step of the method by adding the increase or it may be computed for the optimal solution. The last computation can be performed in two ways. Firstly, the values of the basic variables may be multiplied with their coefficients and the resulting products added. The value of the objective function for the solution of Tableau 6 is then found as follows:

$$(1.29) \qquad f = 80 \cdot 75 + 20 \cdot 25 + 144 \cdot 100 + 76 \cdot 70 + 148 \cdot 30 = 30{,}660 \,.$$

Alternatively, we may multiply the available capacity of each plant and the maximum demand in each country by the values that can be ascribed to them which are given by the coefficients in the optimal tableau of the variables x_{10}, x_{20}, x_{01}, x_{02}, x_{03}, and x_{04}. For the example this is

$$(1.30) \qquad f = 20 \cdot 100 + 76 \cdot 200 + 60 \cdot 75 + 68 \cdot 100 + 0 \cdot 100 + 72 \cdot 30$$
$$= 30{,}660 \,.$$

Because the problem in the example was small and simple it was not diffi-cult to find the changes in the values of basic variables of the current basic solution due to the introduction of the new basic variables at a level Δ. In larger and more complicated problems, these changes may not be so obvious. For instance, a case like the following may occur

$$
\begin{array}{cccc}
\underline{1} & \underline{4} & 1 & 2 \\[4pt]
(1.31) \qquad 5 & \underline{2} & \underline{2} & \underline{1} \\[4pt]
-3 & -2 & -1 & \underline{5}
\end{array}
$$

x_{10} is chosen as the new basic variable and we put therefore $x_{10} = \Delta$. In order to keep the sum of the elements in the second row constant, one of the variables x_{11}, x_{12}, or x_{13} should be decreased by Δ, but which one? One rule that can be given is that a basic variable should be selected which has at least one other basic variable in its column, since otherwise it is impossible to get a chain of basic variables to be adjusted. This means that x_{12} should not be selected. Two other choices, x_{11} and x_{13}, remain among which it is im-possible to choose without any further exploration. Hence we should try first one variable; if it is not possible to complete a chain of terms with Δ and $-\Delta$ in this way, we should try the other variable. It can be proved that there is always one and only one chain of adjustments of basic variables for each nonbasic variable.

The adjustment of the coefficients of the objective function is an easier matter. The coefficient of the new basic variable may be subtracted either from the coefficients of its row or from the coefficients of its column. If by doing this, basic variables get nonzero coefficients, the same coefficient is added to the columns or rows of these basic variables. If then other basic variables have nonzero coefficients, the coefficient is subtracted from the rows and columns of these variables, and so on; if a basic variable has obtained a nonzero coefficient via a row, it should shed this coefficient via a column and *vice versa*. It can be proved that this always leads to a tableau having zero coefficients of basic variables.

The method which has been described is usually called the *transportation method of linear programming*. The name transportation method refers to a transportation problem for which the method has been devised and which will be treated in the next section.

The problem treated can be considered as a linear programming problem of a special structure. Because of this special structure it was not necessary to use the main method for solving linear programming problems, the simplex method, but the so-called transportation method could be used. This transportation method is equivalent to the simplex method in the sense that it generates the same successive solutions, but the computations are much simpler. Wherever it is necessary to distinguish this method from other methods of the same type, we shall call it the *simplex transportation method.*

12.2. The Classical Transportation Problem

A company has plants in A, B, and C and warehouses in D, E, and F. In A, B, and C it has 4, 4, and 2 units available of a certain commodity, while in D, E, and F, 1, 6, and 3 units of this commodity are required. The transport costs per unit from any plant to any warehouse are given in Table 3. Which transportation program minimizes total transportation costs?

Table 3
Available and required quantities and transport costs

			Warehouses		
			D	E	F
		Quantities	1	6	3
			Costs per unit		
	A	4	6	8	3
Plants	B	4	2	3	1
	C	2	2	5	6

In terms of equations, this problem may be formulated as follows. Let x_{11} be the quantity transported from A to D, x_{12} the quantity transported from A to E, and so on. The problem is then to minimize total transport costs

$$f = 6x_{11} + 8x_{12} + 3x_{13}$$

(2.1) $$+ 2x_{21} + 3x_{22} + x_{23}$$

$$+ 2x_{31} + 5x_{32} + 6x_{33}.$$

The solution should satisfy the constraints

(2.2) $x_{11} + x_{12} + x_{13} = 4$,

(2.3) $x_{21} + x_{22} + x_{23} = 4$,

(2.4) $x_{31} + x_{32} + x_{33} = 2$,

(2.5) $x_{11} + x_{21} + x_{31} = 1$,

(2.6) $x_{12} + x_{22} + x_{32} = 6$,

(2.7) $x_{13} + x_{23} + x_{33} = 3$,

and

(2.8) $x_{11}, x_{12}, ..., x_{33} \geqslant 0$.

In the problem of the previous section we maximized the objective function whereas it is minimized here. This is a difference which is easily changed, because instead of minimizing a function, we may maximize minus that function. A much more important difference is that the problem of the previous section contained the variables $x_{00}, x_{01}, ..., x_{30}$ which could be used as a starting solution of the problem because their coefficients in the objective function were zero. In the classical transportation problem no such obvious starting solution is available.

The variables $x_{00}, x_{01}, ..., x_{30}$ do not occur in the problem as formulated in (2.1) to (2.8) but we may include them in the formulation as artificial variables, except for x_{00} which is nonnegative. Hence the problem may be formulated as follows: Minimize

$$
\begin{aligned}
f = \ & 0x_{00} + 0x_{01} + 0x_{02} + 0x_{03} \\
& + 0x_{10} + 6x_{11} + 8x_{12} + 3x_{13} \\
& + 0x_{20} + 2x_{21} + 3x_{22} + \ x_{23} \\
& + 0x_{30} + 2x_{31} + 5x_{32} + 6x_{33},
\end{aligned}
$$

(2.9)

subject to the constraints

(2.10) $x_{00} + x_{01} + x_{02} + x_{03} = 10$,

(2.11) $x_{10} + x_{11} + x_{12} + x_{13} = 4$,

(2.12) $x_{20} + x_{21} + x_{22} + x_{23} = 4$,

(2.13) $x_{30} + x_{31} + x_{32} + x_{33} = 2$,

(2.14) $x_{00} + x_{10} + y_{20} + x_{30} = 10$,

(2.15) $x_{01} + x_{11} + x_{21} + x_{31} = 1$,

(2.16) $x_{02} + x_{12} + x_{22} + x_{32} = 6$,

(2.17) $x_{03} + x_{13} + x_{23} + x_{33} = 3$,

(2.18) $x_{01}, x_{02}, x_{03}, x_{10}, x_{20}, x_{30} = 0$.

All variables should be nonnegative. The constraints (2.10) and (2.14) are added as explained in Section 1.

Apart from the fact that the objective function is minimized instead of maximized and the conditions (2.10), the formulation of the problem is the same as in the previous section. Hence we may put the problem in a transportation tableau format, underlining basic variables. Tableau 0 of Table 4 gives this tableau in which the variables given in (2.18) are basic.

The solution of this tableau obviously does not satisfy (2.18). Since the simplex transportation method needs a feasible solution to start with, first a feasible solution must be generated. This may be done using the *north-west corner rule* which is explained as follows. The values of basic variables according to Tableau 0 of Table 4 are

(2.19)

$\underline{0}$	$\underline{1}$	$\underline{6}$	$\underline{3}$
$\underline{4}$	0	0	0
$\underline{4}$	0	0	0
$\underline{2}$	0	0	0

Now a solution should be generated in which no variable in row and column 0 apart from x_{00} has a nonzero value. Beginning in the north-west corner of that part of the tableau where basic variables are allowed, we

Table 4
Tableaux for transportation example

Tableau		0	D	E	F
0	0	$\underline{0}$	$\underline{1}$	$\underline{3}$	$\underline{3}$
	A	$\underline{4}$	6(1)	8(3)	3
	B	$\underline{4}$	2	3(3)	1(1)
	C	$\underline{2}$	2	5	6(2)
1	0	10	−6	−8	−6
	A	$\underline{0}$	$\underline{1}(-\Delta)$	$\underline{3}(\Delta)$	−3
	B	5	1	$\underline{3}(-\Delta)$	$\underline{1}(\Delta)$
	C	0	(+)−4(Δ)	−3	$\underline{2}(-\Delta)$
2	0	10	(+)−2	−8	(+)−6
	A	$\underline{0}$	(+)4	$\underline{4}(-\Delta)$	(+)−3(Δ)
	B	5	(+)5	$\underline{2}(\Delta)$	(+)$\underline{2}(-\Delta)$
	C	(−)0	(±)$\underline{1}$	(−)−3	(±)$\underline{1}$
3	0	10	(−)1	−8	−3
	A	$\underline{0}$	(−)7	$\underline{2}(-\Delta)$	$\underline{2}(\Delta)$
	B	5	(−)8	$\underline{4}$	3
	C	(+)−3	(+)$\underline{1}$	(+)−6(Δ)	(+)$\underline{1}(-\Delta)$
4	0	10	−5	−8	−3
	A	$\underline{0}$	1	$\underline{1}$	3
	B	5	2	$\underline{4}$	3
	C	3	1	$\underline{1}$	6

assign as many units as possible to x_{11}. The following solution results from this

	$\underline{1}$	0	$\underline{6}$	$\underline{3}$
(2.20)	$\underline{3}$	1	0	0
	$\underline{4}$	0	0	0
	$\underline{2}$	0	0	0

If the usual procedure is followed, now the coefficients of the objective function should be adjusted. However, it is in this case more efficient first to generate a feasible solution and then adjust the objective function accordingly in one step.

Since in (2.20) the quantity required in D is exhausted, but the available quantity in A is not, x_{12} should be made as large as possible. The result is

(2.21)

$\underline{4}$	0	$\underline{3}$	$\underline{3}$
0	$\underline{1}$	$\underline{3}$	0
$\underline{4}$	0	0	0
$\underline{2}$	0	0	0

Now the quantity available at A is exhausted. Since we started to reduce the required quantity in E, we go on with this by making x_{22} as large as possible. The result is

(2.22)

$\underline{7}$	0	0	$\underline{3}$
0	$\underline{1}$	$\underline{3}$	0
$\underline{1}$	0	$\underline{3}$	0
$\underline{2}$	0	0	0

The required quantity in E is exhausted but the quantity available in B is not, so that x_{23} is made as large as possible. The result is

(2.23)

$\underline{8}$	0	0	$\underline{2}$
0	$\underline{1}$	$\underline{3}$	0
0	0	$\underline{3}$	$\underline{1}$
$\underline{2}$	0	0	0

Since now the required quantity in F should be reduced, the value of x_{33} is made as large as possible. The result is

(2.24)

$\underline{10}$	0	0	0
0	$\underline{1}$	$\underline{3}$	0
0	0	$\underline{3}$	$\underline{1}$
$\underline{0}$	0	0	$\underline{2}$

In the last step the new basic variable was x_{33}. As the basic variable becoming nonbasic we may select either x_{03} or x_{30}. This means that x_{30} or x_{03} remains a basic variable but has a value zero. In fact, we may select any of the variables x_{01}, x_{02}, x_{03}, x_{10}, x_{20}, x_{30}, to be a basic variable with a value zero instead of x_{30} or x_{03}.

Having obtained a basic feasible solution to the problem, we now turn to the adjustment of the objective function. The coefficients we have initially are

$$(2.25) \quad
\begin{array}{c|ccc}
0 & 0 & 0 & 0 \\
\hline
\underline{0} & \underline{6} & \underline{8} & 3 \\
0 & 2 & \underline{3} & \underline{1} \\
0 & 2 & 5 & \underline{6}
\end{array}$$

Now the *coefficients* of basic variables are underlined. x_{10} is chosen as a basic variable with value zero instead of x_{30} or x_{03}. From each row or column a quantity should be subtracted in such a manner that the underlined elements are zero; the amount to be subtracted will be the coefficient of x_{20}, x_{30}, x_{01}, x_{02}, and x_{03} with a minus-sign. Disregarding the other tableau elements for a moment, we have, reducing the coefficient of x_{11} to zero

$$(2.26) \quad
\begin{array}{c|ccc}
 & -6 & 0 & 0 \\
\hline
0 & 0 & 8 & \\
0 & & 3 & 1 \\
0 & & & 6
\end{array}$$

Subtracting 8 from column 2, we find

$$(2.27) \quad
\begin{array}{c|ccc}
 & -6 & -8 & 0 \\
\hline
0 & 0 & 0 & \\
0 & & -5 & 1 \\
0 & & & 6
\end{array}$$

The coefficient of x_{22} is reduced to zero by adding 5 to the elements of row 2, which results in

(2.28)

	−6	−8	0
0	0	0	
5		0	6
0			6

In order to reduce the coefficient of x_{23} to zero, we subtract 6 from the elements in column 3. This results in

(2.29)

	−6	−8	−6
0	0	0	
5		0	0
0			0

All basic variables having zero coefficients, we now determine the other coefficients by adding the marginal number of each row or column of (2.29) to the elements of each row and column of (2.25). The result is

(2.30)

0	−6	−8	−6
0	6+0−6	8+0−8	3+0−6
5	2+5−6	3+5−8	1+5−6
0	2+0−6	5+0−8	6+0−6

=

0	−6	−8	−6
0	0	0	−3
5	1	0	0
0	−4	−3	0

These are the cost coefficients corresponding with the basic solution of (2.24) in which x_{10} is taken as a basic variable. (2.24) and (2.30) can be combined to give Tableau 1 of Table 4.

We can now proceed as indicated in the last section, keeping in mind not to take into the basis any of the variables x_{01}, x_{02}, x_{03}, x_{20}, and x_{30}; further it should be remembered that the objective function is minimized instead of maximized, so that the nonbasic variable with the most negative coefficient should be selected as the new basic variable. Hence x_{31}, which has a coefficient of -4, is selected. After the necessary adjustments are made for the variables of the current basic solution, x_{11} is found as the basic variable becoming nonbasic and Δ is put at 1. The coefficients of the objective function are adjusted by adding 4 to the coefficients of column 1.

The following two steps are similar and result in Tableau 3 and Tableau 4. The solution of Tableau 4 is optimal since none of the coefficients of nonbasic variables is negative, which means that no decrease in the objective function can take place.

Again we can interpret the coefficients of nonbasic variables as the loss that would be incurred if in deviation from the optimal solution the nonbasic variable would be given a unit value.

The coefficients of x_{10}, x_{20}, and x_{30} can be interpreted as minus the costs of any additional unit available in A, B, and C and the coefficients of x_{01}, x_{02}, and x_{03} as minus the costs of any additional unit required in D, E, and F. Since in this problem any additional unit available implies an additional unit required, these costs should be added for any of the plants and warehouses. Hence the costs of transporting an additional unit from A to D are $-0 - (-5)$ $= 5$. The change in the optimal solution due to such an additional unit can be found by adding Δ to one of the basic variables in the same row, subtracting Δ from one of the basic variables in the column in which Δ was added, and so on, until finally Δ is added in the column of the additional unit. For an additional quantity transported from A to D, we have the following changes

$$(2.31) \quad \begin{array}{c|ccc} 10(\Delta) & & & \\ \hline \underline{0} & & 1(\Delta) & 3 \\ & & 4 & \\ & 1(\Delta) & 1(-\Delta) & \end{array}$$

It may be checked that the increase in transport costs is really 5. Should an additional unit be transported from A to E, then the additional costs would be $-0 - (-8) = 8$. In this case the change in the optimal solution would simply be an addition of Δ to x_{12}. The transport costs of an additional unit may also be negative, which is the case for transport from C to E; the costs are in this case $-5 - (-3) = -2$. We may check this by finding the change in the optimal solution, which is given by

$$
\begin{array}{c|cc}
10(\Delta) & & \\
\hline
0 & 1(-\Delta) & 3(\Delta) \\
& 1 \quad 4\,(\Delta) &
\end{array}
$$

(2.32)

In fact, the coefficients in row 0 and column 0 imply an entire charge schedule for transport from A, B, and C to D, E, and F. This schedule is

(2.33)

	D	E	F
A	5	8	3
B	0	3	−2
C	2	5	0

It should be noted that all these costs are independent of the choice of x_{10} as a basic variable. For instance, if we would have chosen x_{02} as a basic variable with value zero instead, the coefficients of the objective function should be adjusted by adding 3 to the coefficients in row 0 and subtracting 3 from the elements in column 0. The costs of an additional unit available in A, B, and C would increase by 3 but the costs of any unit required in D, E, and F would decrease by the same amount.

A slight difficulty in the application of the north-west corner rule occurs if the choice of the leaving basic variable is not unique. Let us consider the problem with the following data:

(2.34)

0	1	2	2	3
1	0	0	0	0
4	0	0	0	0
3	0	0	0	0

Putting $x_{11} = 1$, we find that either x_{10} or x_{01} can leave the basis. In this case it does not matter which variable is chosen. Hence we have either

	$\underline{1}$	$\underline{0}$	$\underline{2}$	$\underline{2}$	$\underline{3}$
0	$\underline{1}$	$0.$	0	0
$\underline{4}$	0	0	0	0
$\underline{3}$	0	0	0	0

(2.35)

or

	$\underline{1}$	0	$\underline{2}$	$\underline{2}$	$\underline{3}$
$\underline{0}$	$\underline{1}$	0	0	0
$\underline{4}$	0	0	0	0
$\underline{3}$	0	0	0	0

(2.36)

If we proceed from (2.35), we have, continuing to decrease x_{01}, even though it has a value zero:

	1	0	$\underline{2}$	$\underline{2}$	$\underline{3}$
0	$\underline{1}$	0	0	0
$\underline{4}$	$\underline{0}$	0	0	0
$\underline{3}$	0	0	0	0

(2.37)

Continuing in the same fashion, we find after a number of basic changes:

	$\underline{8}$	0	0	0	$\underline{0}$
0	$\underline{1}$	0	0	0
0	$\underline{0}$	2	$\underline{2}$	0
0	0	0	0	$\underline{3}$

(2.38)

It should be noted that this solution is degenerate. As in the simplex method for linear programming, degeneracy may cause cycling in theory, but again as in the simplex method it never occurs in practice.

12.3. The Dual Transportation Method

In the previous sections of this chapter, the simplex transportation method was treated, which is equivalent to the simplex method for linear programming. It is then obvious to ask whether transportation methods exist which are equivalent to other methods of linear programming, such as the dual method and the primal-dual method. The answer is affirmative. In general it can be said that for problems of the transportation type, transportation methods (that is methods using transportation tableaux) can be devised which are equivalent to any given method for general linear programming. In this section, the dual transportation method which is equivalent to the dual method for linear programming is treated; the next section will give a treatment of the primal-dual transportation method which is equivalent to the primal-dual method for general linear programming given in Section 6.3.

Let us again consider the example of the transportation problem treated in Section 12.2. As an initial solution we take all variables in row 0 and column 0 as basic and the other variables as nonbasic. The corresponding transportation tableau is then as follows:

0	1	6	3
4	6	8	3
4	2	3	1
2	2	5	6

This solution is infeasible, since the artificial variables $x_{10}, x_{20}, x_{30}, x_{01}, x_{02}$, and x_{03} all have nonzero values. On the other hand, the solution is optimal in the narrow sense because all nonbasic variables have nonnegative coefficients given the fact that the objective function is minimized.

In general linear programming, this would be a situation to which the dual method would be applicable. Here we must find the transportation equivalent of the dual method.

The dual method works by eliminating the infeasibilities while preserving the optimality in the narrow sense. The largest infeasibility is the value of x_{02}, which is 6. Hence x_{02} should be the leaving basic variable. The new basic variable should be determined in such a way that the optimality in the narrow sense is preserved. This implies that any adjustment in the coefficients of the objective function due to a replacement of x_{02} as a basic variable should be done in such a way that the coefficients of nonbasic variables remain negative.

This adjustment will involve the subtraction of an amount which will be called θ from the coefficients of the column or the row containing the leaving basic variable and corresponding further adjustments if there are other basic variables in that column or row. In our example the leaving basic variable is x_{02}. Let us subtract θ from the coefficients of column 2. The result is:

0	1	6$(-\theta)$	3
4	6	$8-\theta$	3
4	2	$3-\theta$	1
2	2	$5-\theta$	6

Since no other basic variable occurs in column 2, no further adjustment is necessary. For $\theta = 3$, the coefficient of x_{22} equals 0 while the other coefficients of nonartificial nonbasic variables are still nonnegative:

0	1	6(-3)	3
4	6	5	3
4	2	0	1
2	2	2	6

Note that the coefficient of x_{02} has become negative, but x_{02} is an artificial variable.

Now x_{22} can be made a basic variable instead of x_{02}; the adjustment of values of basic variables is as follows:

$0 + \Delta$	1	$6 - \Delta$	3
$\underline{4}$			
$\underline{4 - \Delta}$		Δ	
$\underline{2}$			

Then Δ is given such a value that $x_{02} = 0$; hence $\Delta = 6$. The complete tableau of the new solution is therefore

$\underline{6}$	$\underline{1}$	-3	$\underline{3}$
$\underline{4}$	6	5	3
$\underline{-2}$	2	$\underline{6}$	1
$\underline{2}$	2	2	6

Note that in this solution x_{20} is negative. Since x_{20} is an artificial variable, any nonzero value indicates an infeasibility, so that this does not mean much. But even if some nonartificial basic variable would become negative, this would not matter, since the dual method only preserves optimality in the narrow sense; any new infeasibility is eliminated in later iterations.

Now the largest infeasibility is $x_{10} = 4$, so that x_{10} is the leaving basic variable. Subtracting θ from the coefficients in row 1, we obtain:

$\underline{6}$	$\underline{1}$	-3	$\underline{3}$
$\underline{4}(-\theta)$	$6 - \theta$	$5 - \theta$	$3 - \theta$
$\underline{-2}$	2	$\underline{6}$	1
$\underline{2}$	2	2	6

Since no other basic variable appears in row 1, no further adjustment is necessary. We put θ equal to the least coefficient appearing with a $(-\theta)$-term, which is 3, so that x_{13} becomes the new basic variable. Now the values of basic variables are adjusted in the following manner

$6 + \Delta$	1		$3 - \Delta$
$4 - \Delta$			Δ
-2		6	
2			

or, taking $\Delta = 4$, and writing down the coefficients for $\theta = 3$,

10	1	-3	-1
-3	3	2	4
-2	2	6	1
2	2	2	6

The largest infeasibility (in absolute value) is now -2, which is the value of x_{20}. Since we want to raise the value of x_{20} to zero, it should not cost anything to transport from origin 2, but since there are two units short in this origin, a positive value θ should be attached to it. This is done by *adding* θ to the coefficients of the row or column in which x_{20} appears. But if θ is added to the coefficients of row 2, the basic variable x_{22} obtains a nonzero coefficient. This is eliminated by subtracting θ from the coefficients of column 2. No basic variables appear in column 2, so that no further adjustment is necessary. The tableau is then as follows:

$10 - \Delta$	1	$-3 - \theta$	-1Δ
-3	3	$2 - \theta|\Delta$	$4 - \Delta$
$-2 + \Delta|\theta$	$2 + \theta$	$6 - \Delta$	1
2	2	$2 - \theta$	6

For $\theta = 2$, the coefficient of x_{12} becomes zero, while all other coefficients of nonartificial nonbasic variables are still nonnegative. Selecting x_{12} as the new basic variable, the following adjustment of values of basic variables should take place:

$10 - \Delta$	1		$-1 + \Delta$
		Δ	$4 - \Delta$
$-2 + \Delta$		$6 - \Delta$	
2			

Now Δ is given such a value that the leaving basic variable x_{20} becomes zero, hence $\Delta = 2$. Putting $\theta = 2$, we find for the complete new tableau

8	1	−5	1
−3	3	2	2
2	4	4	1
2	2	0	6

All these iterations can be found in the usual tableau-form, see Table 5, Tableaux 1–3. Instead of subtraction and addition of θ, minus- and plus-signs within brackets are used in front of the coefficients of nonbasic variables. In Tableau 3, three infeasibilities are remaining, since the artificial variables x_{01}, x_{03}, and x_{30} have nonzero values. First x_{30} is eliminated and x_{32} enters the basis, which results in Tableau 4. Then x_{01} is chosen as the leaving basic variable, x_{31} enters the basis and Tableau 5 is generated which, because it contains no infeasibilities, is the optimal solution.

The rules for the dual transportation method may more formally be stated as follows.

SELECTION OF THE LEAVING BASIC VARIABLE. *From the artificial basic variables with nonzero values and the nonartificial basic variables with negative values take the variable with the largest absolute value.*

SELECTION OF THE NEW BASIC VARIABLE. *Put a minus-sign (plus-sign) in front of the coefficients in the row or column of the leaving basic variable if this variable is positive (negative). If other basic variables occur in this row or column, make opposite adjustments in the columns and rows in which they occur. Reapply this until no basic variable has an uncompensated sign. The new basic variable is the nonartificial nonbasic variable with a minus-sign having the smallest coefficient.*

Table 5
An example of application of the dual transportation method

Tableau		0	1	2	3
0	0	0(Δ)	1	(−)6(−Δ)	3
	1	4	6	(−)8	3
	2	4(−Δ)	2	(−)3(Δ)	1
	3	2	2	(−)5	6
1	0	6(Δ)	1	−3	3(−Δ)
	1	(−)4(−Δ)	(−)6	(−)5	(−)3(Δ)
	2	−2	2	6	1
	3	2	2	2	6
2	0	10(−Δ)	1	(−)−3	−1(Δ)
	1	−3	3	(−)2(Δ)	4(−Δ)
	2	(+)−2(Δ)	(+)2	(∓)6(−Δ)	(+)1
	3	2	2	(−)2	6
3	0	8(Δ)	1	−5	1(−Δ)
	1	−3	3	2(−Δ)	2(Δ)
	2	2	4	4	3
	3	(−)2(−Δ)	(−)2	(−)0(Δ)	(−)6
4	0	10	(−)1(−Δ)	−5	−1(Δ)
	1	−3	(−)3	0(Δ)	4(−Δ)
	2	2	(−)4	4	3
	3	0	(−)2(Δ)	2(−Δ)	6
5	0	10	−2	−5	0
	1	−3	1	1	3
	2	2	2	4	3
	3	0	1	1	6

TRANSFORMATION OF TABLEAU. *Put the value of the new basic variable equal to Δ and find the adjustments of other basic variables. Put Δ equal to the absolute value of the leaving basic variable. Adjust the coefficients of nonbasic variables by adding or subtracting the coefficient of the new basic variable according to the plus- and minus-signs.*

It should be noted that the dual transportation method is only applicable if the starting solution is optimal in the narrow sense. However, it should be remembered that the simplex transportation method can only be used if an initial basic feasible solution is available; if not such a solution should first be generated, for instance by using the north-west corner rule. For classical transportation problems such as the one used as an example, the dual transporta-

tion method should be preferred to the simplex transportation method since
it is not necessary to generate an initial basic feasible solution.

12.4. The Primal-Dual Transportation Method

Apart from the simplex method and the dual method, the only other
method for general linear programming which was treated was the primal-dual
method, see Section 6.3. Also for this method there exists a corresponding
transportation method which generates the same sequence of solutions. As
stated in Section 6.3, this method requires, just as the dual method, an
initial basic solution which is optimal in the narrow sense. The same example
as used in the two previous sections may therefore be employed.

For this method the problem is formulated as in the equations (2.9) −
(2.17) but instead of imposing equation (2.18) which specifies that the
variables x_{01}, x_{02}, ..., x_{30} should be zero, the coefficients of these variables
in the objective function are changed from zero into the variable parameters
λ:

$$f = 0x_{00} + \lambda x_{01} + \lambda x_{02} + \lambda x_{03}$$

$$+ \lambda x_{10} + 6x_{11} + 8x_{12} + 3x_{13}$$

(4.1)

$$+ \lambda x_{20} + 2x_{21} + 3x_{22} + x_{23}$$

$$+ \lambda x_{30} + 2x_{31} + 5x_{32} + 6x_{33} .$$

For $\lambda = 0$ and for small positive values of λ, the basic solution

$$(4.2) \qquad x_{00} = 0, \quad x_{01} = 1, \quad x_{02} = 6, \quad x_{03} = 3,$$

$$x_{10} = 4, \quad x_{20} = 4, \quad x_{30} = 2$$

is optimal. But for higher values of λ this solution ceases to be optimal
and for $\lambda \to \infty$ no solution with a nonzero value of a variable with a coefficient λ in (4.1) can be optimal. On this the primal-dual method is based. We
start with the basic solution (4.2) and determine how the optimal solution
changes for increasing values of λ. The optimal solution for $\lambda \to \infty$ must be
the optimal solution of the problem. λ can be considered as a penalty factor
which drives the variables to which it is attached to zero.

The coefficients of the objective function in (4.1) can be written as follows:

$$\begin{array}{cccc} \underline{0} & \underline{\lambda} & \underline{\lambda} & \underline{\lambda} \\ \underline{\lambda} & 6 & 8 & 3 \\ \underline{\lambda} & 2 & 3 & 1 \\ \underline{\lambda} & 2 & 5 & 6 \end{array}$$

(4.3)

The underlined coefficients belong to basic variables and should therefore be made equal to zero. This is done by subtracting λ from all rows except the first and from all columns except the first. The result is

(4.4)

$$\begin{array}{cccc} \underline{0} & \underline{0} & \underline{0} & \underline{0} \\ \underline{0} & 6-2\lambda & 8-2\lambda & 3-2\lambda \\ \underline{0} & 2-2\lambda & 3-2\lambda & 1-2\lambda \\ \underline{0} & 2-2\lambda & 5-2\lambda & 6-2\lambda \end{array}$$

This is the tableau of coefficients corresponding to the basic solution in (4.2). This solution is optimal if all coefficients of nonbasic variables are nonnegative. The largest value of λ for which the coefficients are nonnegative is $1/2$, since for $\lambda > 1/2$ the coefficient of x_{23} is negative.

In order to find the optimal solution for values of λ greater than $1/2$, x_{23} is introduced into the basis. In the usual manner we find for the resulting basic solution

(4.5)

$$\begin{array}{cccc} \underline{3} & \underline{1} & \underline{6} & 0 \\ \underline{4} & 0 & 0 & 0 \\ \underline{1} & 0 & 0 & \underline{3} \\ \underline{2} & 0 & 0 & 0 \end{array}$$

The adjustment of the coefficients is performed by subtraction of $1-2\lambda$ from the element of the last column, which results in

$$
\begin{array}{cccc}
\underline{0} & \underline{0} & \underline{0} & -1 + 2\lambda \\[2mm]
\underline{0} & 6 - 2\lambda & 8 - 2\lambda & 2 \\[2mm]
\underline{0} & 2 - 2\lambda & 3 - 2\lambda & \underline{0} \\[2mm]
\underline{0} & 2 - 2\lambda & 5 - 2\lambda & 5 \; .
\end{array}
$$

(4.6)

   The solution of (4.5) is optimal for $\frac{1}{2} \leq \lambda \leq 1$, since for these values the coefficients in (4.6) are nonnegative. For $\lambda > 1$, the coefficient of x_{21} is negative, so that in order to have an optimal solution for $\lambda > 1$, x_{21} should become a basic variable. We then find for the basic solution, selecting x_{20} as the basic variable which becomes nonbasic,

$$
\begin{array}{cccc}
\underline{4} & \underline{0} & \underline{6} & 0 \\[2mm]
\underline{4} & 0 & 0 & 0 \\[2mm]
0 & \underline{1} & 0 & \underline{3} \\[2mm]
\underline{2} & 0 & 0 & 0 \; .
\end{array}
$$

(4.7)

   The coefficients of the objective function should be adjusted accordingly, which is done by subtracting $2 - 2\lambda$ from the elements of row 2 in (4.6). The result is

$$
\begin{array}{cccc}
\underline{0} & \underline{0} & \underline{0} & -1 + 2\lambda \\[2mm]
\underline{0} & 6 - 2\lambda & 8 - 2\lambda & 2 \\[2mm]
-2 + 2\lambda & \underline{0} & 3 - 2\lambda & \underline{-2 + 2\lambda} \\[2mm]
\underline{0} & 2 - 2\lambda & 5 - 2\lambda & 5 \; .
\end{array}
$$

(4.8)

Now the basic variable x_{23} has the nonzero coefficient $-2 + 2\lambda$. Subtracting this coefficient from the last column, we find

Table 6
Tableaux for an application of the primal-dual transportation method

Tableau		Sign	0	D	E	F
		Sign		−	−	−
0	0		0(Δ)	1	6	(−)3(−Δ)
	A	−	4	6	8	(−)3
	B	−	4(−Δ)	2	3	(1)1(Δ)
	C	−	2	2	5	(−)6
				−	−	+
1	0		3(Δ)	1(−Δ)	6	(+)−1
	A	−	4	6	8	(+)2
	B	−	(−)1(−Δ)	(−)2(Δ)	(−)3	(±)3
	C	−	2	2	5	(+)5
				−	−	−
2	0		4(Δ)	(−)0(−Δ)	6	(−)1
	A	−	4	(−)6	8	(−)4
	B	+	(+)−2	(±)1	(+)1	(±)3
	C	−	2(−Δ)	(−)2(Δ)	5	(−)7
			+	−	+	
3	0		4(Δ)	−2	6(−Δ)	(+)−1
	A	−	4	4	8	(+)2
	B	−	(−)0	(−)1(−Δ)	(−)3(Δ)	(±)3
	C	−	2(−Δ)	0(Δ)	5	(+)5
			+	−	−	
4	0		5(Δ)	−2	5(−Δ)	(−)2
	A	−	4(−Δ)	4	8	(−)5(Δ)
	B	+	−3	−3	1(Δ)	(−)3(−Δ)
	C	−	1	1	5	(−)8
			+	−	+	
5	0		8(Δ)	(+)−2	2(−Δ)	−7
	A	−	1	(+)4	8	3
	B	+	−3	(+)−3	4	−5
	C	−	(−)1(−Δ)	(±)1	(−)5(Δ)	(−)3
				−	−	+
6	0		9(Δ)	3	1(−Δ)	(+)−7
	A	−	(−)1(−Δ)	(−)9	(−)8(Δ)	(±)3
	B	+	−3	2	4	(+)−5
	C	+	−5	1	1	(+)−2
				−	−	−
7	0		10	3	0	1
	A	+	−8	1	1	3
	B	+	−3	2	4	3
	C	+	−5	1	1	6

$$\begin{array}{cccc}
\underline{0} & \underline{0} & \underline{0} & 1 \\[6pt]
\underline{0} & 6 - 2\lambda & 8 - 2\lambda & 4 - 2\lambda \\[6pt]
-2 + 2\lambda & \underline{0} & 3 - 2\lambda & \underline{0} \\[6pt]
\underline{0} & 2 - 2\lambda & 5 - 2\lambda & 7 - 2\lambda \, .
\end{array}$$

(4.9)

Hence the basic solution in (4.7) is optimal for $\lambda = 1$; for $\lambda > 1$, the coefficient of x_{31} becomes negative, so that x_{31} should enter the basis.

Also in this method it is convenient to use combined tableaux for the values of basic variables and the coefficients of nonbasic variables. It is also convenient to deal with the λ-term of the coefficients of nonbasic variables in a somewhat different manner. Instead of putting the term -2λ in (4.4) behind each coefficient, we may indicate this term by putting a minus in front of each row and each column except the first ones in the initial tableau, see Tableau 0 of Table 6. A coefficient in a row and a column which are both labelled in this manner with a minus are supposed to have the term -2λ. In adjusting the coefficients, subtracting the coefficients in a certain row or column by a coefficient containing the term -2λ, changes the sign of that row or column from a minus to a plus, addition changes the sign from a plus to a minus. A coefficient having a plus-sign in its row and a minus-sign in its column or *vice versa* does not have a λ-term; a coefficient having a plus-sign in its row and its column has the term $+2\lambda$.

This means that the rule for the selection of the new basic variable is as follows. *Select from the elements which are not underlined and which have a minus both in its row and in its column the smallest one.* The basic variable which becomes nonbasic is selected as in the simplex transportation method. The optimal solution to the problem has been obtained if there are no elements having a minus in its row and in its column. In Table 6, this solution is obtained in Tableau 7. This tableau is the same as Tableau 4 of Table 4, apart from the fact that the last tableau has x_{10} as a basic variable instead of x_{02}; as explained before this difference is trivial.

Exercises

1. A company producing one product has three plants, A, B, and C, and three wholesale outlets, D, E, and F. It has 7,000, 5,000, and 4,000 units available in A, B, and C. The maximum sales in D, E, and F are 2,000, 6,000, and 7,000. The product is such that transportation costs per unit are sig-

nificant; the net profit per unit of product produced in a given plant and sold in a certain outlet are given by the following table:

	D	E	F
A	1	4	2
B	3	1	2
C	4	5	2

(a) Determine the optimal supply program. Interpret each element of the optimal tableau.

(b) Determine, using transportation tableaux, all extreme-point feasible solutions with a loss not exceeding $2,000.

2. An oil company has refineries in Rotterdam, Southampton and Yokohama; the monthly input of crude oil of these refineries is 15, 10, and 10 units, respectively. The crude oil is supplied by three countries, Kuwait, Libya and Venezuela; the available quantities are 24, 6, and 11 units per month, respectively. Variable costs (inclusive transportation costs) per unit supplied by a given country to a given refinery are as follows:

	Rotterdam	Southampton	Yokohama
Kuwait	20	18	25
Libya	12	11	33
Venezuela	17	17	40

(a) What is the optimal supply schedule for the refineries?

(b) What are the costs of supplying an additional unit to the Rotterdam refinery and what are the resulting changes in the supply schedule? What are the revenues of an additional unit of crude oil in Libya and what are the resulting changes in the supply schedule? Use the optimal supply schedule found in (a) as a starting point.

(c) Libya is considering an extra tax on exported crude oil which would increase variable costs. What is the maximum tax level which does not decrease exports? What changes in the supply schedule would result from higher taxes than this maximum level? On the other hand, Kuwait is considering a decrease of its existing tax. How large should this decrease be to induce an increase in crude oil exports and what changes in the existing supply schedule would follow from such a decrease?

3. A company has plants in A, B, and C, and warehouses in D, E, F, and G. Of a certain product, 5, 10, and 12 units are available in A, B, and C, respectively, and 8, 7, 5, and 7 units are required in D, E, F, and G. Transport costs per unit are given by the following table:

	D	E	F	G
A	9	3	14	4
B	17	19	6	19
C	8	10	24	9

(a) Use the simplex transportation method to determine the supply program with minimum costs; if it is not unique, determine all alternative optimal programs.

(b) Answer the same question as in (a), using the primal-dual transportation method.

(c) Answer the same question as in (a), using the dual transportation method.

(d) Give an interpretation of all elements in the tableau of the optimal solution. How much do costs increase if an additional unit is available in A, while an additional unit is required in D? Answer the same question for all plants and all warehouses. Explain a case in which costs decrease. What is the most expensive warehouse to supply? What is the cheapest origin?

(e) Suppose now that each plant has sufficient stock to supply all warehouses. What is the optimal supply program?

4. A company specializing in a certain kind of automotive repair has three workshops indicated by I, II, and III, which are located in different areas. Per four-week period these shops can handle at most 500, 900, and 400 repair jobs, respectively, the demands for repair jobs in the three areas are 300, 600, and 500 repair jobs. It is possible to have repair jobs of one area done by a workshop in a different area, but then transportation costs are involved which are in dollars per repair job as follows:

	I	II	III
I	–	5	8
II	5	–	4
III	8	4	–

The gross profit (revenue minus variable cost) per repair job is $15. The company can also rebuild engines at each shop; this takes the same time as 10 repair jobs and yields $90 in net revenue. The maximum demand for rebuilding engines is 10 per four-week period.

(a) First the optimal production program.

(b) Interpret every element in the optimal tableau.

(c) What is the minimum net revenue the company would require to undertake an (additional) order to rebuild exactly 10 engines?

(d) What is the maximum amount the company would be prepared to spend on an advertising campaign which increases the demand for repair jobs by 10 per cent?

5. A Canadian company has plants in Vancouver, Calgary, London (Ontario) and Halifax. The plants in Vancouver and Calgary each have a normal capacity of 12,000 and 10,000 hours per year and the two other plants each have a normal capacity of 30,000 and 20,000 hours per year. If overtime is used, these capacities can be increased by 25%. Finished products are shipped to warehouses for further destination; each plant has a warehouse and in addition to this, Winnipeg and Quebec each have a warehouse. The quantities required per year are given below and also the variable cost (mainly labor) per hour capacity; overtime increases variable costs by $33\frac{1}{3}$ per cent, the product requires $\frac{1}{2}$ hour capacity per unit. Transportation costs for the finished product from the plant to the warehouse at the same location are zero but to a warehouse at another location $0.20 per unit shipped and $0.003 per mile per unit. A distance table for the relevant locations is given below.

	Vanc.	Calg.	London	Hal.	Win.	Quebec
Req. quant. 1000 units/year	25	15	52	11	17	28
Variable costs $/hour	6.00	4.60	5.20	4.00	–	–
Distances in 100 miles						
Vancouver	–	6	15	37	15	31
Calgary		–	23	32	8	25
London			–	14	14	6
Halifax				–	24	8

(a) Find the optimal production and warehouse supply program.

(b) Interpret all elements of the optimal tableau.

(c) Develop a criterion for shutting down the Vancouver or the Calgary plant.

13. VARIANTS OF TRANSPORTATION MODELS

13.1. The Assignment Problem

Let us consider a company with a number of jobs to be filled and the same number of people who should fill these jobs. For each person it is known how well he does on each job by means of a performance coefficient which may be the monetary gain for the company. For instance, let there be four jobs and four persons and let the coefficients of the gain of the various persons filling the jobs be given by Table 1. Hence if person 1 fills job 1, the gain is 4, if he fills job 2, the gain is 2, if he fills job 3, the gain is 0, and so on.

Table 1
Data for assignment problem

		Jobs			
		1	2	3	4
	1	4	2	0	3
	2	2	4	4	3
Persons	3	2	6	2	3
	4	4	5	3	4

Let us indicate person 1 filling job 1 as $x_{11} = 1$, and person 1 not filling job 1 as $x_{11} = 0$, person 1 filling job 2 as $x_{12} = 1$ and the same person not filling job 2 as $x_{12} = 0$. We assume that it is not possible that a person partly fills one job and partly another (though if it was, the solution method and the optimal solution would be the same). The problem may then be formulated as follows. Maximize

(1.1) $f = 4x_{11} + 2x_{12} + 0x_{13} + 4x_{14} + \ldots + 4x_{44}$

subject to

$$\text{(1.2)} \begin{cases} x_{11} + x_{12} + x_{13} + x_{14} = 1, \\[2mm] x_{21} + x_{22} + x_{23} + x_{24} = 1, \\[2mm] x_{31} + x_{32} + x_{33} + x_{34} = 1, \\[2mm] x_{41} + x_{42} + x_{43} + x_{44} = 1, \end{cases}$$

$$\text{(1.3)} \begin{cases} x_{11} + x_{21} + x_{31} + x_{41} = 1, \\[2mm] x_{12} + x_{22} + x_{32} + x_{42} = 1, \\[2mm] x_{13} + x_{23} + x_{33} + x_{43} = 1, \\[2mm] x_{14} + x_{24} + x_{34} + x_{44} = 1, \end{cases}$$

$$\text{(1.4)} \qquad x_{11} + x_{12}, ..., x_{44} \geq 0,$$

$$\text{(1.5)} \qquad x_{11}, x_{12}, ..., x_{44} = 0 \text{ or } 1.$$

The constraints (1.2) arise from the fact that each person can take only one job and those of (1.3) from the fact that the same job can be done only once. The constraints (1.4) and (1.5) reflect that no job can be performed at a negative level and that each person has to restrict himself to one job.

Apart from the constraints (1.5) which make the problem an integer programming problem and the fact that this is a maximization problem instead of a minimization problem this is a transportation problem of a somewhat special structure, since what may be interpreted as required and available quantities are all 1. However, the difference between a maximization problem and a minimization problem is a trivial one, since one may be transformed into the other by a multiplication by -1. Furthermore, it can be proved that the solution of a transportation problem with available and required quantities that are integers, has always integer values. This means that any solution of the problem (1.1) to (1.4) without (1.5) will always satisfy (1.5). Hence transportation methods are applicable to the assignment problem. Here the problem will be solved by the primal-dual transportation method.

Table 2 gives the successive tableaux. Tableau 0 is the initial tableau. The coefficients are left as they are in a maximization problem; the signs are kept as in minimization problems. Since we are now dealing with a maximiza-

Table 2
An application of the primal-dual transportation method to an assignment problem

Tableau			0	1	2	3	4
		Sign	−	−	−	−
0	0		0(Δ)	1	1(−Δ)	1	1
	1	−	1	4	2	0	3
	2	−	1	2	4	4	3
	3	−	(−)1(−Δ)	(−)2	(−)6(Δ)	(−)2	(−)3
	4	−	1	4	5	3	4
			−	−	−	−
1	0		1(Δ)	1	(−)0(−Δ)	1	1
	1	−	1	4	(−)2	0	3
	2	−	1	2	(−)4	4	3
	3	+	(+)−6	(+)−4	(±)1	(+)−4	(+)−3
	4	−	1(−Δ)	4	(−)5(Δ)	3	4
			−	+	−	−
2	0		1(Δ)	1(−Δ)	−5	1	1
	1	−	(−)1(−Δ)	(−)4(Δ)	(−)−3	(−)0	(−)3
	2	−	1	2	−1	4	3
	3	−	−1	1	1	1	2
	4	−	1	4	0	3	4
			−	−	−	−
3	0		4	0	−1	0	0
	1	+	−4	1	−3	−4	−1
	2	+	−4	−2	−1	1	−1
	3	+	−5	−3	1	−3	−2
	4	+	−4	0	0	−1	1

tion problem, we should look for the largest coefficient with a minus in both rows and columns. In Tableau 0 this is the coefficient of x_{32} which is 6. In fact, this coefficient should be interpreted as $6 + 2\lambda$. For $\lambda \leqq -3$, this and all other coefficients are non-positive so that for this value the solution of Tableau 0 is optimal. For $\lambda > -3$, this coefficient is positive, so that x_{32} should be introduced into the basis. The leaving basic variable is found as usual. In this case it can be x_{03} or x_{20}; let us take x_{03}. The values of basic variables, the signs of rows and columns and the new cost coefficients are found as before. In Tableau 1, the maximum coefficient in minus rows and columns is 5, so that x_{42} enters the basis, and so on.

After 3 iterations, the optimal solution is obtained. The outcome is that

Job 1 should be allocated to Person 1, Job 2 to Person 3, Job 3 to Person 2, and Job 4 to Person 4. The basic variables with value 0 have no obvious interpretation. The reduced revenues found in row 0 and column 0 can be interpreted as the values to be attached to the jobs and the persons. These values are not very meaningful in all cases because the "quantities available" and the "quantities required" are all 1. For instance, if x_{02} is made basic, it has a value zero, so that the objective function does not change. Note that in this case the equalities in (1.2) and (1.3) could have been $\leqq$-signs without changing the solution of the problem.

13.2. Dynamic Production Planning

Transportation methods can also be used for problems which at first sight have no connection with transportation. This is the case with dynamic production planning problems of the following type. For a number of periods required deliveries are given. Production takes place using an installation which can work during working hours or in overtime, but then at extra costs. It is possible to store part of the production of a period for deliveries in one of the future periods, but then inventory costs are involved. Late delivery may be allowed, which means that production of one period may be used for sales in a previous period, but at extra costs. Total costs should be minimized.

As an example let us take the following problem for which the data can be found in Table 3. Deliveries, normal capacity, overtime capacity, costs per unit for normal capacity and overtime capacity are given for four periods, say quarters of a year. Further it is given that inventory costs are $1 per unit per period; in this example it is not allowed to deliver after deliveries have been due. This problem can be formulated as a transportation problem by con-

Table 3
Data for dynamic production planning problem

Period	1	2	3	4
Sales	5	6	9	6
Normal capacity	9	6	7	9
Overtime capacity	3	1	2	3
Costs per unit, normal capacity	1	4	2	4
Costs per unit, overtime capacity	2	6	5	6

sidering the normal capacities and the overtime capacities in the four periods as the quantities available in the origins and the quantities to be delivered in the four periods as the required quantities in the destinations.

Let us denote the quantity produced in period i, using normal capacity and delivered in period j, by x_{iaj} and the quantity produced in period i using overtime capacity and delivered in period j by x_{ibj}. Since it is not possible to exceed delivery dates, we have $x_{iaj} = 0$ and $x_{ibj} = 0$ for $i > j$.

Table 4

Solution of dynamic production planning problem by successive minimum-cost allocation

Tableau	Period	0	1	2	3	4
	0		5, 0	6, 2, 0	9, 2, 1, 0	6, 0
I	1a	9, 4, 0	5 1	4 2	3	4
	1b	3, 1, 0	2	2 3	1 4	5
	2a	6, 5		4	1 5	6
	2b	1		6	7	8
	3a	7, 0			7 2	3
	3b	2			5	6
	4a	9, 3				6 4
	4b	3				6
	0	26	−3	−4	−5	−4
II	1a	2	5	4	0	2
	1b	1	0	2	1	2
	2a	5		0	1	2
	2b	1		2	2	4
	3a	3			7	2
	3b	2			0	2
	4a	3				6
	4b	3				2

The set-up tableau for the problem is then given by Tableau I of Table 4; of the multiple entries in row 0 and column 0 only the first ones should be considered, while in the remaining cases only entries which are not underlined have validity for the set-up tableau. These last elements are the coefficients of x_{iaj} and x_{ibj}. In the cases $i = j$ they are immediately taken from Tableau 3; in the cases $i < j$ these coefficients are found by adding \$1 inventory costs per period of storage. The variables x_{iao} and x_{ibo} can be considered as slack variables, whereas the variables x_{jo} should be interpreted as artificial variables.

This problem can be solved by any transportation method. For instance first a feasible solution could be found by means of the north-west corner rule, after which the simplex transportation method can be employed to find the optimal solution. Since the set-up tableau has an optimal solution which is infeasible because of the artificial variables, both the dual transportation method and the primal-dual transportation method can be applied immediately to the solution of the set-up tableau. However, it turns out that another method is simpler and more direct.

This method is in fact a kind of north-west corner rule in which costs are taken into account. The starting point is Tableau I of Table 4, in which initially in column 0 and row 0 only the first underlined number is given and in other entries of the tableau only the cost coefficients. We start by allocating the required 5 units for period 1 to the cheapest origin, which is normal capacity in period 1. Since the available capacity is 9 units, all 5 units can be produced, so that an underlined 5 is put in row 1a and column 1, and 0 is put behind the $\underline{5}$ in row 0 and column 1 indicating that x_{01} should become nonbasic and $9 - 5 = \underline{4}$ is put behind $\underline{9}$ in row 1a and column 0, indicating that the available normal capacity in period 1 has been reduced to 4. For convenience the basic variable x_{00} is not adjusted until the end of the procedure. Next, the 6 units of deliveries of the second period are allocated to the cheapest origin which is normal capacity in period 1, of which 4 units are still available. Hence $x_{1a2} = 4$, behind the $\underline{4}$ in row 1a and column 0 we put 0, indicating that no more capacity is left and that x_{1a0} is nonbasic. Behind the $\underline{6}$ in row 0 and column 2 we put $\underline{2}$ to indicate that 2 units of deliveries for period 2 should still be allocated. The next cheapest source of supply has costs 3; this is overtime capacity in period 1, of which 3 units are available. Hence $x_{1b2} = 2, x_{1b0} = 1$, and x_{02} becomes nonbasic, which is indicated by 0.

Next the 9 units to be delivered in period 3 should be allocated. The cheapest source of supply is in row 4a, with costs 2, of which 7 units are available. Hence $x_{3a3} = 7$, x_{3a0} becomes nonbasic and $x_{03} = 2$. The next cheapest source of supply is in row 1a, but no capacity is left there. The next cheapest source of supply is in row 1b, of which 1 unit is left. Hence $x_{1b3} = 1$, x_{1b0} becomes nonbasic and $x_{03} = 1$. The next cheapest source of supply for period 3 is in rows 2a and 3b, of which we take that of 2a, allocating 1 unit to it, so that $x_{2a3} = 1, x_{2a0} = 5$, and x_{03} becomes nonbasic. Now the 6 units required for period 4 have to be allocated. Since the capacities of rows 3a and 1a are exhausted, row 4a is taken as the source of cheapest supply. Its capacity is 9, so that all 6 units can be supplied from it. We put $x_{4a4} = 6$, $x_{4a0} = 3$ and x_{04} becomes nonbasic. Now all required deliveries are allocated.

It can be shown (which will not be done here) that the optimal solution is always obtained in this manner. To check that this is indeed true in this example, the complete tableau corresponding with the final solution will be generated. This is done as follows. First the reduced costs for nonbasic variables in row 0 and column 0 are found. Since x_{2a0} is basic, its reduced costs are 0; and this is also true for x_{2a3}. Hence 5 must have been subtracted from the cost coefficients in column 3, so that the reduced costs of x_{03} is -5. Since x_{1b3} is basic, its reduced costs is 0. It was 4, but 5 has been subtracted from it, so that 1 must be added to it in order to obtain a reduced cost of 0. Hence the reduced cost of x_{1b0} is 1. The other reduced costs in row and column 0 are obtained in a similar manner; after that, the reduced costs of other nonbasic variables are determined.

Tableau II of Table 4 contains the complete tableau of the solution generated in Tableau I. First of all, it should be observed that this is indeed an optimal solution, since all reduced costs of nonbasic variables, apart from the artificial variables, are nonnegative. Secondly, the optimal solution is not unique, since three reduced costs are zero, so that a number of alternative optimal solutions can be generated. Finally, we come to the interpretation of the reduced costs of variables in row 0 and column 0. Consider the coefficient -3 for x_{01}, which is related to the equation

$$ x_{01} + x_{1a1} + x_{1b1} = 5 . $$

If x_{01} takes a value 1 instead of 0, the equation becomes

$$ x_{1a1} + x_{1b1} = 4 . $$

This is equivalent to a decrease by 1 unit of the required deliveries in period 1. According to Tableau II this decreases total costs by 3. Hence, the coefficients of x_{01}, x_{02}, x_{03}, and x_{04} can be interpreted as minus the marginal costs of deliveries in periods 1, 2, 3, and 4. The coefficients for x_{1a0}, x_{1b0}, and x_{3a0}, 2, 1, and 3, indicate the values of 1 unit of normal capacity in period 1, 1 unit of overtime capacity in the same period, and one unit of normal capacity in period 3.

This method can be shown to be equivalent to a step wise primal-dual method which can be described as follows. First consider the sales in period 1 as the only infeasibility and apply the primal-dual method to eliminate it. Proceeding from the solution obtained, consider the sales in period 2 as the infeasibility which should be eliminated by the primal-dual method. The same is done for the remaining periods. After seven iterations, which are equivalent to what happened in Tableau I of Table 4, the optimal solution is obtained.

13.3. Upper Bounds in Transportation Methods

In the previous chapter it was shown that transportation-type problems can be solved efficiently by transportation versions of methods for general linear programming. One would expect that other topics in general linear programming, such as sensitivity analysis, parametric programming, the anti-cycling method and the upper-bound method have their equivalents for transportation-type problems. This is indeed the case, but for reasons of space we shall not deal with all of them; moreover, given the methods for general linear programming, it is not difficult to develop the corresponding transportation methods. Only one topic will be treated here, that of upper bounds, because it will be needed later in the next chapter. As before, it will be explained by means of an example.

The example to be used is a slight variation of the example of classical transportation problem treated in Section 12.2. Instead of the quantities to be transported from the origins which were 4, 4, and 2 units we have now 40, 40, and 28 units, and instead of the quantities to be delivered in the destinations which were 1, 6, and 3 units we have now 10, 60 and 31 units. The transportation costs are the same. These data are given in Tableau 0 of Table 5 in which the figures within brackets should for a moment be ignored. The additional upper-bound constraints are that none of the variables should exceed 25.

It is possible to use upper bounds with the dual and the primal-dual method, but since the treatment of the upper-bound technique for general linear programming was limited to the simplex method, we shall treat here the upper-bound technique for the simplex transportation method.

This means that for the classical transportation problem first an initial basic feasible solution should be found. The starting point is the basic solution given in Tableau 0. Applying the north-west corner rule we find first the solution

$$\underline{0} \qquad\qquad \underline{60} \qquad \underline{35}$$

$$\underline{30} \qquad \underline{10}$$

$$\underline{40}$$

$$\underline{10}$$

If there were no upper-bounds then next $x_{12} = 30$ would be chosen, but since

Table 5

An application of the simplex transportation method with upper bounds to a classical transportation problem

Tableau	Or/Dest.	0	1	2	3
0	0	<u>0</u>	10	60	<u>35</u>
	1	<u>40</u>	6(10)	8(25*)	3(5)
	2	<u>40</u>	2	3(25*)	1(15)
	3	<u>25</u>	2	5(10)	6(15)
1	0	<u>100</u>	(+)−9	−5	−6
	1	3	(+)<u>10</u>(−Δ)	6*	<u>5</u>(+Δ)
	2	5	(+)−2	3*	<u>15</u>
	3	<u>0</u>	(+)−7(Δ)	10	<u>15</u>(−Δ)
2	0	<u>100</u>	−2	−5	(+)−6
	1	(−)3	(−)7	(−)6*(−Δ)	(±)<u>15</u>(+Δ)
	2	(−)5	(−)5	(−)3*	(±)<u>15</u>
	3	<u>0</u>	10	<u>10</u>(+Δ)	(+)<u>5</u>(−Δ)
3	0	<u>100</u>	−2	−5	(−)0
	1	−3	1	<u>20</u>(−Δ)	(−)<u>20</u>(+Δ)
	2	(+)−1	(+)−1(Δ)	(+)−3*	(∓)15(−Δ)
	3	<u>0</u>	<u>10</u>(−Δ)	<u>15</u>(+Δ)	(−)6
4	0	<u>100</u>	−2	−5	−1
	1	−3	1	<u>15</u>	−1*
	2	0	<u>5</u>	−2*	<u>10</u>
	3	<u>0</u>	<u>5</u>	<u>20</u>	5

this exceeds 25, x_{12} is put at its upper bound 25 and remains nonbasic, which is indicated by a star. The basic solution is then

$$\underline{0} \qquad \underline{35} \quad \underline{35}$$

$$\underline{5} \qquad \underline{10} \qquad *$$

$$\underline{40}$$

$$\underline{10}$$

Continuing, we find

<u>0</u>		<u>35</u>	<u>30</u>
	<u>10</u>	*	<u>5</u>
<u>40</u>			
<u>10</u>			

Again, without the upper bound, x_{22} would get the value 35, but because of the upper bound, it is put at its upper bound which is indicated by a star

<u>0</u>		<u>10</u>	<u>30</u>
	<u>10</u>	*	<u>5</u>
<u>15</u>		*	
<u>10</u>			

After some further allocation, the following basic solution is obtained which is indicated within brackets in Tableau 0 and more explicitly in Tableau 1:

<u>0</u>			
	<u>10</u>	*	<u>5</u>
<u>15</u>		*	<u>15</u>
<u>10</u>		<u>10</u>	<u>15</u>

The reduced costs for this solution are found by adjusting the reduced costs in such a manner that the reduced costs of basic variables are zero.

Now the simplex method can be applied. Nonbasic variables are made basic if they have negative reduced costs, or in case they are at their upper bounds if they have positive reduced costs, because in the latter case costs can be reduced by decreasing the variable from its upper bound. This means that in Tableau 1, x_{21}, x_{31}, x_{12} and x_{22} are eligible as new basic variable. Since x_{31} has reduced costs with the largest absolute value, it is selected as the new basic variable. The Δ-loop is constructed as usual but when choosing the maximum value for Δ, we also should prevent basic variables exceeding their upper bound. Hence we find for Δ:

$\Delta = \text{Min}(10,25-5,15) = 10$.

Since the minimum is connected with an ordinary nonbasic variable, an ordinary iteration follows, which results in Tableau 2.

Now x_{12}, a variable at its upper bound, is the new basic variable. This variable is decreased from its upper bound, so that in the construction of the Δ-loop, we have $-\Delta$ there; the remainder of the Δ-loop is straightforward. Δ is determined by

$$\Delta = \text{Min}(25,25-15,25-10,5) = 5 ,$$

so that x_{33} leaves the basis, after which Tableau 3 is found. In this tableau, x_{21} is chosen as the new basic variable. The leaving basic variable is found from the Δ-loop as follows:

$$\Delta = \text{Min}(10,25-15,20,25-20,15) = 5 .$$

This means that x_{13} should be put at its upper bound. After this is done, Tableau 4 results which contains the optimal solution.

From this it will be clear that the upper-bound technique for transportation problems is even simpler than in general linear programming; for this reason no explicit rules will be given. We shall not go into upper-bound techniques for the dual and the primal-dual transportation methods; the reader is expected to be able to construct these when they are needed.

13.4. The Transshipment Problem

In the problems considered so far there was only one way to transport from an origin to a destination. This may be generalized by considering also the possibility of transport from a given origin first to another origin or destination and then from this point to the final destination. In this case it is said that a *transshipment* has taken place. Such a case may in principle be formulated as a transportation problem of the type treated before if between each origin and each destination the shortest distance or lowest costs is determined which may or may not use other origins or destinations as intermediate points. For larger problems it is not very convenient to determine the shortest distances from all possible paths arising between two locations; furthermore, for other problems an explicit solution of the transshipment problem is required in the sense that it should be known how much is

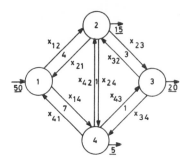

Fig. 1.

shipped between two adjacent locations even if these are not the origin or the final destination of the shipments.

In the transshipment problem it is convenient to use a network representation of the problem. We shall in particular consider the problem given by the network in Figure 1. In this network there are four nodes which are interconnected except for nodes 1 and 3. In node 1 there are 50 units available which can be used to satisfy the requirements of the other nodes, 2, 3, and 4, which are 15, 20, and 5, respectively; we assume that these requirements have to be met exactly. In order to formulate the problem, the following array of variables is used:

$$(4.1) \quad \begin{bmatrix} x_{00} & x_{01} & x_{02} & x_{03} & x_{04} \\ x_{10} & x_{11} & x_{12} & x_{13} & x_{14} \\ x_{20} & x_{21} & x_{22} & x_{23} & x_{24} \\ x_{30} & x_{31} & x_{32} & x_{33} & x_{34} \\ x_{40} & x_{41} & x_{42} & x_{43} & x_{44} \end{bmatrix} ;$$

x_{ij} denotes the number of units to be transported from node i to node j; the cases $i = j$ and i or $j = 0$ will become clear below.

The available amount in node 1 is 50; this means that the amounts shipped from node 1 to other nodes minus the amounts shipped from other nodes to node 1 should not exceed 50. This yields the following relation:

(4.2) $x_{12} + x_{13} + x_{14} - x_{21} - x_{31} - x_{41} \leqq 50$.

Let us define

(4.3) $x_{11} = -(x_{21} + x_{31} + x_{41})$,

and insert the slack variable x_{10} in (4.2) and the artificial variable x_{01} in (4.3). (4.2) and (4.3) then may be written as

(4.4) $x_{10} + x_{11} + x_{12} + x_{13} + x_{14} = 50$,

(4.5) $x_{01} + x_{11} + x_{21} + x_{31} + x_{41} = 0$.

x_{11} is equal to minus the amount shipped from other nodes to node 1. Note that according to (4.3), x_{11} always will be nonpositive for any nonnegative values of x_{21}, x_{31}, and x_{41}. Since node 1 itself serves as a source of supply for other nodes, $-x_{11}$ is said to be the amount transshipped through node 1. As in the transportation problems treated before, the equations (4.4) and (4.5) can also be found from the array of the transportation variables, see in this case (4.1). (4.4) states that the sum of the variables in the second row should be equal to 50 and that the sum of the variables in the second column should be zero, while x_{01} should be interpreted as an artificial variable.

If node 2 is considered, the requirement is found that it should have shipped to it an amount of exactly 15. This means that the amounts shipped to it from other nodes minus the amounts shipped from it to other nodes should equal 15:

(4.6) $x_{12} + x_{32} + x_{42} - x_{21} - x_{23} - x_{24} = 15$.

Let us define

(4.7) $x_{22} = -(x_{21} + x_{23} + x_{24})$.

x_{22} is minus the amount transshipped from node 2, which itself requires 15 units, to other nodes. For any nonnegative values of x_{21}, x_{23}, and x_{24}, x_{22} will always be nonpositive. (4.7) can be substituted into (4.6). Into (4.6), the artificial variable x_{02} can be inserted and into (4.7) the artificial variable x_{20}. The equations (4.6) and (4.7) may then be written as

(4.8) $x_{02} + x_{12} + x_{22} + x_{32} + x_{42} = 15$,

(4.9) $x_{20} + x_{21} + x_{22} + x_{23} + x_{24} = 0$.

These equations state that the sum of the variables in the third column of (4.1) should be equal to 15 and the sum of the variables in the third row should be equal to 0; x_{02} and x_{20} are taken to be artificial.

For nodes 3 and 4 similar equations can be found, implying that the sum of the variables in the fourth and fifth columns of (4.1) should equal 20 and 5 and that the sum of the variables in the fourth and fifth rows of (4.1) should both equal 0. The variables x_{30}, x_{40}, x_{03}, and x_{04} are artificial. Two additional equations involving the first row and column of (4.1) can be obtained by definition of x_{00} and summation as in Section 12.1. This means that the constraints of this problem have exactly the same structure as the transportation problem treated before, the difference being that the transshipment variables x_{ii} for $i = 1$, 2, 3, and 4 are nonpositive if the other variables are nonnegative, see (4.3) and (4.7).

It should be noted that in the present problem it is not possible to ship directly from node 1 to node 3 or *vice versa*, which means that x_{13} and x_{31} both should be kept zero; this is best done by never considering them as basic variables, and, since they are not basic in any initial solution, by not considering them at all.

The objective function for this transportation problem is as follows:

$$f = 0x_{11} + 3x_{12} + 7x_{14}$$

$$+ 4x_{24} + 0x_{22} + 3x_{23} + x_{24}$$

(4.10)

$$+ 3x_{32} + 0x_{33} + x_{34}$$

$$+ 7x_{41} + x_{42} + x_{43} + 0x_{44} ;$$

the coefficients of the variables x_{ii} are 0 since the costs of the transshipments are accounted for by other variables.

Tableau 0 of Table 6 gives the set-up tableau for the example. In such a tableau, all transshipment variables can be made basic by replacing the basic variable with a value of zero in their row or column; if the node supplies units, then it replaces the basic variable in its column (as for node 1), if the node requires units it replaces the basic variable in its row (as for the other nodes). All replaced basic variables are artificial variables. The result is the modified set-up tableau given in Tableau 1 of Table 6.

For the solution of the problem either the simplex transportation method,

Table 6
Set-up tableau and modified set-up tableau for the transshipment problem

Tableau	Nodes	0	1	2	3	4
0	0	<u>0</u>	<u>0</u>	15	20	<u>5</u>
	1	<u>50</u>	0	4	–	7
	2	<u>0</u>	4	0	3	1
	3	<u>0</u>	–	3	0.	1
	4	<u>0</u>	7	1	1	0
1	0	<u>0</u>	0	15	20	<u>5</u>
	1	50	<u>0</u>	4	–	7
	2	0	4	<u>0</u>	3	1
	3	0	–	3	<u>0</u>	1
	4	0	7	1	1	<u>0</u>

Table 7
Solution of a transshipment problem by the simplex transportation method

Tableau	Nodes	0	1	2	3	4
00	0	<u>0</u>	0	(-4)<u>15</u>	(-7)<u>20</u>	(-7)<u>5</u>
	1	<u>50</u>	<u>0</u>	$(-4)4$	–	$(-7)7$
	2	$(+4)0$	$(+4)4$	(±4)<u>0</u>	$\binom{-7}{+4}3$	$\binom{+4}{-7}1$
	3	$(+7)0$	–	$\binom{+7}{-4}3$	(±7)<u>0</u>	$(\pm7)1$
	4	$(+7)0$	$(+7)7$	$\binom{-4}{+7}1$	$(\mp7)1$	(±7)<u>0</u>
0	0	<u>40</u>	0	-4	-7	$(\div)-7$
	1	<u>10</u>	<u>0</u>	$35(\Delta)$	–	$(-)$<u>5</u>$(-\Delta)$
	2	4	8	$-$<u>20</u>$(-\Delta)$	<u>20</u>	$(-)-2(\Delta)$
	3	7	–	6	<u>0</u>	$(-)1$
	4	$(+)7$	$(+)14$	$(+)4$	$(+)1$	$(\pm)$<u>0</u>
1	0	<u>40</u>	0	-4	$(\div)-7$	-5
	1	<u>10</u>	<u>0</u>	<u>40</u>	–	2
	2	4	8	$-$<u>25</u>	$(-)$<u>20</u>$(-\Delta)$	$5(\Delta)$
	3	$(+)7$	–	$(+)6$	$(\pm)$<u>0</u>	$(+)$
	4	5	12	2	$(-)-1(\Delta)$	<u>0</u>$(-\Delta)$
2	0	<u>40</u>	0	-4	-6	-5
	1	<u>10</u>	<u>0</u>	<u>40</u>	–	2
	2	4	8	$-$<u>25</u>	1	<u>25</u>
	3	6	–	5	<u>0</u>	2
	4	5	12	2	<u>20</u>	$-$<u>20</u>

Variants of transportation models

Table 8
Solution of a transshipment problem by the primal-dual transportation method

Tableau	Nodes	Sign	0	1	2	3	4
		Sign	0	−	−	−	−
00	0	+	0	0	15	20	5
	1	0	50	0(Δ)	4	−	7
	2	0	0	4	0(Δ)	3	1
	3	0	0	−	3	0(Δ)	1
	4	0	0	7	1	1	0(Δ)
			0	0	−	−	−
0	0	+	0(Δ)	0	(−)15(−Δ)	20	5
	1	0	50(−Δ)	0	(−)4(Δ)	−	7
	2	+	0	(+)4	(+)0	(+)3	(+)1
	3	+	0	−	(−)3	0	1
	4	+	0	7	(−)1	1	0
			0	0	0	−	−
1	0	+	15(Δ)	0	−4	20	(−)5(−Δ)
	1	0	35(−Δ)	0	15(Δ)	−	(−)7
	2	0	4	8	0(−Δ)	7	(−)5(Δ)
	3	+	0	−	−1	0	(−)1
	4	+	(+)0	(+)7	(+)−3	(+)1	(±)0
			0	0	0	−	0
2	0	+	20(Δ)	0	−4	(−)20(−Δ)	−5
	1	0	30(−Δ)	0	20(Δ)	−	2
	2	0	4	8	−5(−Δ)	(−)7	5(Δ)
	3	+	(+)0	−	(+)−1	(±)0	(+)−4
	4	0	5	12	2	(−)6(Δ)	0(−Δ)
			0	0	0	0	0
3	0	+	40	4	−4	−6	−5
	1	0	10	0	40	−	2
	2	0	4	8	−25	1	25
	3	0	6	−	5	0	2
	4	0	5	12	2	20	−20

the dual transportation method, or the primal-dual transportation method may be employed. For the simplex transportation method first an initial basic feasible solution should be found. Let us take the initial solution with basic variables x_{12}, x_{14}, and x_{23}; this means that nodes 2 and 4 are supplied from 1 and node 3 is supplied via node 2. Tableau 00 of Table 7 gives the modified set-up tableau with the changes of coefficients of nonbasic variables in the objective function indicated. Tableau 0 gives the initial feasible solution. After two iterations of the simplex transportation method, the optimal solution is found in Tableau 2. The numbers 0, -4, -6, and -5 in row 0 can be interpreted as minus the costs of supplying a unit to the nodes 1, 2, 3, and 4.

More obvious methods for the solution of transportation problems of this type are the dual and the primal-dual transportation methods. For the primal-dual method the artificial variables corresponding with the requirement of nodes 1, 2, 3, and 4 are assigned a factor λ which initially has a value 0 and which then is increased parametrically. Since these variables are basic variables in the set-up tableau, λ must be subtracted from all coefficients of nonbasic variables in their columns, which is symbolically indicated by putting the minus-sign above their columns (see Tableau 00 of Table 8); since basic variables should have a coefficient of zero, λ is added to the coefficients in the first row, which is indicated by a plus-sign in this row. Then the transshipment variables are made basic in the same manner as in Table 6, a slight complication being the signs of the rows and columns. The result is Tableau 0, where the primal-dual method can be started by picking the smallest coefficient of a nonbasic variable which has as its sign a minus if the signs of its row and column are added as if we have $+\lambda$ for $+$ and $-\lambda$ for $-$. After three iterations the optimal solution is found, see Tableau 3.

Exercises

1. (a) Solve the assignment problem of Section 1 by means of the simplex transportation method.
   (b) Solve the same problem by means of the dual transportation method.

2. Apply the stepwise primal-dual method as described in Section 2 to the example.

3. In an application of "Operation Match" matching pairs should be formed out of 4 men and women. The data available are as follows:

Variants of transportation models

Women	Age	Index of music interest
A	18	1
B	20	3
C	26	2
D	33	4

Men	Age	Index of music interest
R	20	2
S	22	4
T	24	3
U	35	2

Pairs should be matched in such a way that the differences in age and music interest is minimized. The differences are weighted in the following manner. If a woman is 0–4 years younger than a man, this counts as 0 points; if she is 5–9 years younger, this counts as 1 point; if she is 10–14 years younger, this counts as 2 points, and if she is 15–19 years younger, this counts as 4 points. If a woman is 0–4 years older, this counts as 1 point; for 5–9 years older, 2 points, and for 10–14 years older, 4 points. As to music interests, the absolute value of the difference of the index is taken.

(a) Formulate this problem as an assignment problem.
(b) Solve it by the primal-dual method.
(c) Determine all alternative optimal solutions.

4. A company produces a certain pharmaceutical product. According to a contract the following amounts are to be delivered in the coming year:

1st 4 months	120 units
2nd 4 months	184 units
3rd 4 months	236 units

The available production capacity is:

1st 4 months	102 units
2nd 4 months	260 units
3rd 4 months	238 units

The remaining units can be purchased in the first 4 months as $35 per unit, in the second 4 months at $34.50 per unit and in the third 4 months at $34 per unit.

Production costs are $25 per unit and inventory costs are $0.50 per unit per 4 months. If the product is sold 8 months after production it should first be filtered and tested, which costs $5 per unit. Delayed delivery is possible, but this costs $2.50 per unit for 4 months delay and $4.50 per unit for 8 months delay. The optimal production-, inventory- and purchasing-program is required.

(a) Formulate this problem as a transportation problem.

(b) Solve it by the primal-dual transportation method.

(c) What is the minimum price for the company for an additional amount of one unit to be delivered in the third period and which changes in the optimal program are caused by this delivery?

(d) How do costs change if additional production capacity for one unit becomes available in the third period and what changes in the optimal program result from this? Both answers should refer to the optimal tableau found in (b).

5. A plant produces one product which is used within the company and is sold outside. Planning of production is considered for one year in 3 4-month periods. Maximum capacity for any 4-month period is 20 units. For each of the three periods 5 units have to be supplied for internal use of the company. The maximum quantities which may be sold in the three periods are 11, 24, and 10 units. The net revenues of the quantities sold are $10 per unit. Inventory holding is possible; inventory costs are $1 per unit per 4-month period. There should be no inventory after the planning year has elapsed. Late delivery of sales is not possible.

(a) Formulate this problem as a transportation problem and determine the solution with the highest revenue. Interpret all elements of the tableau of the optimal solution.

(b) If internal accounting prices of the company should be based on market prices, what should be the accounting prices for the three periods? Use an example to show that a decrease of the required delivery within the company leads to an increase in revenue equal to the accounting price.

14. TRANSPORTATION NETWORKS

14.1. Network Representation of Transportation Problems

In the previous chapter transportation-type problems were solved by a number of methods based on transportation tableaux. The same problems can be solved by the same methods but based on network representation of the problems. Especially for transshipment problems, a network representation may be more convenient than a transportation tableau representation.

A network consists of nodes, each pair of which may be linked in one or in both directions by arcs. Figure 1 gives an example of a network with four nodes. There are six arcs joining these four nodes; each arc is identified by its initial and its terminal node. Hence we have in Figure 1 the arcs (1,2), (2,3), (2,4), (3,1), (3,4), and (4,2). Note that some nodes have no direct connection, for instance nodes 1 and 3, but there may be indirect connections via other nodes. Furthermore, two nodes may be connected directly in one direction only, for example nodes 1 and 2, but there may be an indirect connection via other nodes, such as the connection of nodes 2 and 1 via 3.

In networks for transportation problems, each arc has a variable flow which is usually required to be nonnegative. In addition to proper arcs which have both an initial and a terminal node, we shall use pseudo arcs which have an

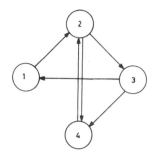

Fig. 1.

initial node or a terminal node but not both; the flow in these arcs is always fixed at a constant level.

In the networks we consider in this chapter, the following requirement should always be met: for any node, the sum of flows of incoming arcs should always be equal to the sum of flows of outgoing arcs. We shall find that in all transportation problems except transshipment problems, a node has either a number of variable outgoing flows and one fixed incoming flow or a number of variable incoming flows and one fixed outgoing flow.

All transportation-type problems may be formulated in a network representation. Let us first consider the example of T.V. – distribution considered in Section 12.1. Figure 2 gives a network representation of this problem. As nodes we have H_p, production in Holland, B_p, production in Britain, H_s, B_s, G, and D, which stand for sales in Holland, Britain, Germany and Denmark. For each of these nodes the sum of the incoming flows and outgoing flows should be equal, which corresponds to the constraints of the transportation problem. For instance, for production in Holland we have

$$(1.1) \qquad x_{10} + x_{11} + x_{12} + x_{13} + x_{14} = 100 .$$

The 100 is given as a constant flow entering H_p. The node B_p has an in-

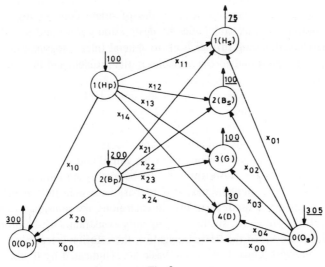

Fig. 2.

coming constant flow of 200, while the destinations H_s, B_s, G, and D have outgoing constant flows of 75, 100, 100, and 30, respectively. For these nodes, constraints similar to (1.1) are valid.

Corresponding with column 0 in transportation tableaux there is a node O_p for which the following equation is valid:

$$(1.2) \qquad x_{00} + x_{10} + x_{20} = 300 \, .$$

We know that x_{00} can be interpreted as the total number of units transported from origins to destinations. We may also draw a node O_s corresponding with row 0 in transportation tableaux. The equation valid for the flows at this node is

$$(1.3) \qquad x_{00} + x_{01} + x_{02} + x_{03} + x_{04} = 305 \, .$$

It was shown in Chapter 12 that the variable x_{00} in this equation is the same one as in (1.2) and has the same interpretation. Since it is the same variable, one arc may be drawn from O_s to O_p, but any flow along this arc should not be interpreted as a physical flow of units from O_s to O_p.

Note that in this problem the nodes of the network can be distinguished in node of origin, which are H_p, B_p and O_s, and nodes of destination, H_s, B_s, G, D, and O_p. Nodes of origin have outgoing arcs only (apart from the constant-term arc) and nodes of destination have incoming arcs only (again apart from the constant-term arc). Nodes of origin corresponds to rows in transportation tableaux and nodes of destination correspond to columns in these tableaux. Looking further back to general linear programming, we find that the arcs correspond to the variables in the problem and the nodes to the equations.

Consider now the basic solution of the set-up tableau of the T.V.-distribution problem, see Tableau 0 of Table 2 in Chapter 12. This solution is given in network representation in Figure 3.0, where the basic arcs are indicated by double lines. The names of the variables corresponding to the arcs are deleted, because they are obvious from the initial and terminal node of each arc. The values of the flows through the basic arcs are indicated by underlined numbers. The numbers near the nonbasic arcs indicate the net revenue per unit if the arc is used. Note that in each node the sums of incoming and outgoing flows are equal, so that the equality constraints of the problem are satisfied; since none of the flows is negative, the solution is feasible.

If the network consisting of the basic arcs (indicated by double lines) is considered, it is noted that this is a *tree. A tree is a connected network con-*

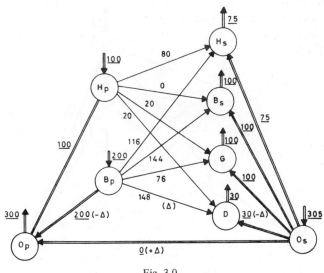

Fig. 3.0.

taining no loops. It can be shown that this is always true for any basic solution of the transportation problem. Furthermore, it should be noted that this tree contains all nodes of the entire network, which again is true for any basic solution.

14.2. The Simplex Network Method

Let us now consider increasing the flow through one of the nonbasic arcs; for the reason indicated before the nonbasic arc with maximum net revenue is selected, which is x_{24}. A flow of one unit will increase total revenue by 148. Let the flow through x_{24} be Δ. Since in D an additional Δ units arrive from B_p one of the incoming flows should be reduced by the same amount (or one of the outgoing flows should be increased by the same amount, but this is not relevant in this case). Hence x_{04} should decrease by Δ. Since in O_s the outgoing flow x_{04} decreases by Δ, one of the other outgoing flows should increase by Δ; we select for this x_{00}. Since in O_p, x_{00} increases by Δ, one of the other incoming flows should decrease by Δ; let this be x_{20}. This compensates the increase in outgoing flows in B_p caused by $x_{24} = \Delta$. We have now completed a loop with changes of Δ in the flows. The maximum value of

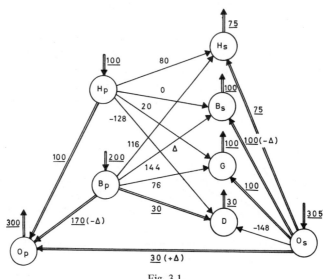

Fig. 3.1.

Δ which does not make any flow negative is 30, for which value $x_{04} = 0$. Hence x_{24} should replace x_{04} as a basic arc. Substituting $\Delta = 30$, we find the basic solution indicated in Figure 3.1. The basic arcs again form a tree passing through all nodes.

Note that what has been done is the same as what happens in transportation tableaux; in tableaux the sum of variables in rows and columns is kept constant and in networks the sum of outgoing or incoming flows at each node is kept constant.

Now the reduced revenues of nonbasic arcs have to be adjusted. Whereas before the change, incoming units in D (from x_{04}) yielded a revenue of 0, now they yield 148 (from x_{24}). In order to determine the increase in profits of alternative supplies in D, 148 should be subtracted from the net revenue of these arcs, since an increase in x_{14} or x_{04} of one unit would cause a decrease in x_{24} of one unit. Hence we find for x_{14}: $20 - 148 = -128$, and for x_{04}: $0 - 148 = -148$. This adjustment is again the same as in transportation tableaux, where 148 is subtracted from the coefficients of the objective function of variables in the column of D. x_{04} is a nonbasic arc having been replaced as a basic arc by x_{24}, so that its reduced revenue can be nonzero. If in D there had been more basic arcs, additional adjustments would have to follow in order to have a network with zero reduced revenues for basic arcs.

The network given in Figure 3.1 then results. Now the nonbasic arc with the largest reduced revenue (coefficient in the objective function) should be selected, which is x_{22}. Increasing the flow between B_p and B_s by Δ implies a decrease in an incoming basic flow in B_s; since x_{02} is the only incoming basic flow, it is decreased by Δ. Then x_{00} is increased by Δ and x_{20} is decreased by Δ, after which the loop is completed. The maximum value of Δ along this loop is 100, for which value x_{02} becomes zero. Hence x_{22} replaces x_{02} as a basic arc and $\Delta = 100$. The adjustment of reduced revenues is done by subtracting 144 from all incoming nodes in B_s. The result is the network given in Figure 3.2.

Now x_{21} has the largest positive net revenue, so that it is increased by Δ. Then one of the basic outgoing arcs in B_p has to be reduced by Δ; these are x_{22}, x_{24} and x_{20}. It is easily observed that going along x_{22} and x_{24} will not lead to a loop, so that x_{20} is reduced. Then x_{00} is increased by Δ, x_{01} is decreased by Δ and a loop is found. The same loop could be found somewhat more quickly by decreasing a basic arc in H_s, since in H_s there is only one such arc. The highest value which Δ can take without making the flow in any basic arc negative is 70 for x_{20}, so that x_{21} is replacing x_{20} as a basic arc.

The adjustment for reduced revenues of nonbasic arcs is slightly more complicated in this case. The adjustment can be started either in the initial or

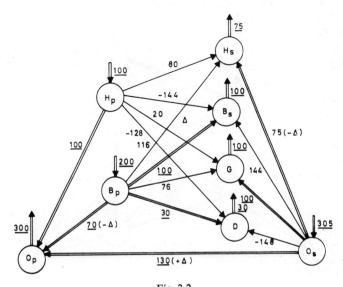

Fig. 3.2.

in terminal node of the new basic arc. It is usually more efficient to start the adjustment in the node which is closest to the arc which is replaced as a basic variable; in this case this is B_p. Hence we subtract 116 from the reduced revenues of all outgoing arcs at B_p. This means that the basic arcs x_{22} and x_{24} also get a reduced revenue of -116. The net revenue of x_{22} is removed by *adding* to the reduced revenue of incoming arcs at B_s 116 and the reduced revenue of x_{24} is removed by adding 116 to the reduced revenue of all incoming arcs at D. In the resulting network, no basic arcs have a nonzero revenue, so that another iteration can be started.

After three additional iterations a network is obtained with nonpositive reduced revenues for nonbasic arcs, so that the optimal solution is obtained, see Figure 3.3. Note that the network of basic arcs is a tree. Since all flows in basic arcs are nonnegative and all reduced revenues of nonbasic arcs are nonpositive, an optimal solution is obtained. The arcs x_{10} and x_{20} can be interpreted as the slack variables of production and their reduced revenue can be interpreted as minus the imputed value of production capacity in Holland and Britain. Similarly, x_{01}, x_{02}, x_{03}, and x_{04} can be interpreted as slack variables of sales and their reduced revenues can be interpreted as minus the imputed values of sales opportunities in the four markets.

The procedure we have applied is the network version of the simplex

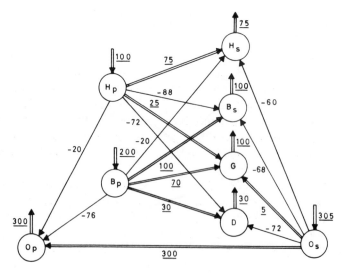

Fig. 3.3.

transportation method which may be called the simplex network method. It may be summarized as follows. As an initial condition a basic feasible solution should be available, which means that (1) the sum of incoming flows should equal the sum of outgoing flows in any arc, (2) each of the arcs should have a nonnegative flow, (3) the basic arcs should form a tree passing through all nodes.

In an iteration, the new basic arc is selected by taking the nonbasic arc with the largest positive reduced revenue; if all reduced revenues are nonpositive, an optimal solution has been obtained. This new basic variable is given a value Δ and a loop of changes of value Δ of flows in basic arcs is constructed in such a way that the sum of incoming and outgoing flows at any node remains equal. The basic arc which becomes zero first for increasing Δ is designated as the leaving basic arc.

Then the reduced revenues are adjusted. Since all basic arcs should have a reduced revenue of zero, the reduced revenue of the new basic arc should be made to vanish, which is done by subtracting its reduced revenue from all arcs either at its initial node or at its terminal node. If as a result of this, any basic arc obtains a nonzero reduced revenue, this is eliminated by subtracting this from the reduced revenues of all arcs at the node of this arc which was not used yet. This process goes on until there is no basic arc having a nonzero net revenue. Then another iteration may begin.

14.3. The Dual and the Primal-Dual Network Methods

Other transportation methods such as the dual and the primal-dual transportation methods may be applied to network problems. The dual and the primal-dual method are especially suitable in cases in which the set-up tableau and the corresponding network solution is opúimal but not feasible. Once the network formulation of transportation problems and the rules for adjusting values of basic variables and reduced revenues of nonbasic variables are known, the network formulation of the dual and of the primal-dual method is straightforward.

Consider an application of the dual method to the example of the classical transportation problem used in Sections 12.2 and 12.3, see Table 5. Figure 4.0 gives the network representation of the set-up tableau for this problem. The arcs coming from A, B, and C into O_d and those coming from O_o into D, E, and F are artificial; these are crossed. Since all nonbasic arcs have nonnegative reduced costs, the solution is optimal. In the dual method infeasibilities are reduced one by one while reduced costs are kept nonnegative.

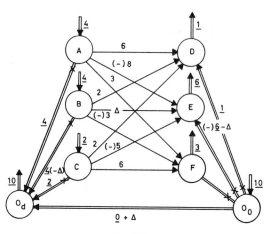

Fig. 4.0.

Let us first eliminate the largest infeasibility which is the flow of 6 units in the artificial arc (O_0,E). In order to determine the new basic arc, a minus-sign is put at each arc coming into E. Since no basic arc is involved other than the leaving basic arc (O_0,E), we do not have to adjust any further.

The same result would have been obtained if we started by putting a minus-sign at all arcs going out from O_0; there are (O_0,D), (O_0,E), (O_0,F) and (O_0,O_d). Since (O_0,D) is a basic arc, its minus-sign is compensated by putting a plus-sign at any arc leading into D. Other signs at basic arcs are compensated in the same manner, until there are no uncompensated signs at basic arcs, after which the only uncompensated minus-signs are found at the arcs (A,E), (B,E), and (C,E).

According to the dual transportation method, the new basic arc is the nonbasic arc having a minus-sign which has the smallest reduced cost; in this case this is (B,E). Then a Δ-loop is completed in the usual manner; this loop necessarily includes the leaving basic arc (O_0,E) with $-\Delta$. Δ is then given the value 6 and a new basic solution emerges, see Figure 4.1. The reduced costs for this solution are found by subtracting the reduced costs of the new basic arc from the reduced costs of arcs with a minus-sign and adding it to those with a plus-sign (in this case there are none).

In the network of Figure 4.1 we select as the leaving basic arc the artificial arc (A,O_d) with value 4. Putting a minus-sign at all arcs leading out of A, we find immediately the new basic arc AF. The Δ-loop is constructed, we take $\Delta = 4$ and adjust reduced revenues by subtracting 3 from the reduced costs of arcs with a minus-sign, after which the network of Figure 4.2 is found.

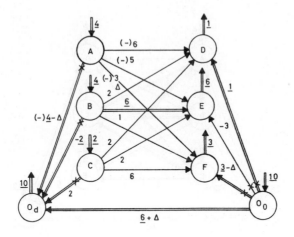

Fig. 4.1.

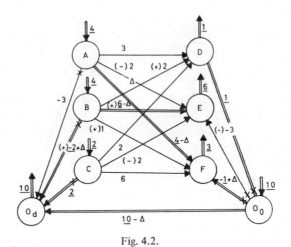

Fig. 4.2.

In this network, the artificial arc (B, O_d) with a flow -2 is selected as the leaving basic arc. Because the flow is negative, a plus is added to all arcs leading out of B. Since now the basic arc (B,E) has a plus-sign, a minus-sign is written at all arcs leading into E, after which there are no basic arcs left with uncompensated signs. The nonbasic arc with a minus-sign having the smallest reduced costs is found to be (A,E) (the minimum is not unique, we could

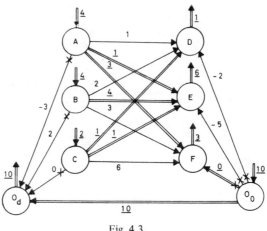

Fig. 4.3.

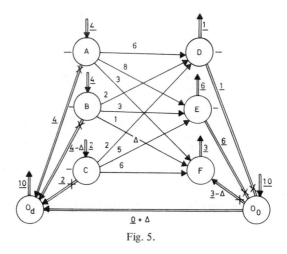

Fig. 5.

also have taken (C,E)). Then the Δ-loop can be completed and Δ is put equal to 2. After the adjustment of reduced costs as indicated by the signs, another solution is found.

After a few additional iterations, a solution is found which is both optimal and feasible, see Figure 4.3. The interpretation of this network is entirely the same as that of the corresponding optimal tableau in the transportation tableau representation.

If the primal-dual network method is applied to the same example, the network corresponding to the set-up tableau is the same, except that the nodes A, B, C, D, E, and F all have minus signs see Figure 5. In this method the new basic arc is selected as the nonbasic arc between two nodes with a minus-sign having the smallest reduced costs. The Δ-loop is constructed as usual. The leaving basic arc is found as in the simplex transportation method by selecting among basic arcs with $-\Delta$ the one with the smallest flow; then Δ is put equal to this flow. The reduced costs of nonbasic variables are adjusted as usual, but if the reduced costs of the new basic variable is subtracted from the reduced costs of arcs at any node, the "sign" of the node changes from a minus to a plus, or if it is added, from a plus to a minus. The method terminates when there are no nonbasic arcs left between two nodes with a minus-sign.

14.4. Networks with Transshipments

We shall now consider the most general and most useful transportation network problems, namely those in which transshipment may occur in any node. In Section 13.4 it was shown that these problems can be treated as transportation problems after introduction of transshipment variables x_{11}, x_{22}, ... which take nonpositive values. We shall show that in the network formulation of transportation methods, these transshipment variables, which are arcs in networks, are not necessary.

Let us consider the rather trivial network problem given by Figure 6. In node 1, 20 units are available, in nodes 2 and 3, 5 and 10 units are required. Transport costs in either direction between 1 and 2 are 2 and between 2 and 3 are 3. Transportation costs for putting the required units in nodes 2 and 3 should be minimized. Tableau 0 of Table 1 gives the set-up tableau for this problem. The modified set-up tableau in which the transshipment variables x_{11}, x_{22}, and x_{33} are made basic by replacing the basic variable in its row or

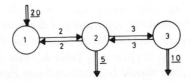

Fig. 6.

Table 1
Transportation tableaux for transshipment problem

Tableau	Nodes	0	1	2	3
0	0	0	0	5	10
	1	20	0	2	–
	2	0	2	0	3
	3	0	–	3	0
1	0	0	0	5+Δ	(–)10–Δ
	1	20	0	2	–
	2	0	2	0–Δ	(–)3Δ
	3	(+)0	–	(+)3	(±)0
3	0	0+Δ	0	(–)15–Δ	(–)–3
	1	20–Δ	0	(–)2Δ	–
	2	(+)0	(+)2	(±)–10	(∓)10
	3	+3	–	(±)6	(±)0
4	0	15	0	–2	–5
	1	5	0	15	–
	2	2	4	–10	10
	3	5	–	6	0

column with a zero value is given Tableau 1. Then an application of the dual method follows. After two iterations the optimal solution has been obtained.

Consider now a network representation of the transportation tableaux of Table 1. In previous sections we noted that each row and also each column has a corresponding node in the network. Hence in the network we should have a node 1_o which gives 1 as an origin and a node 1_d which gives 1 as a destination. In the tableau the origin 1 and the destination 1 are linked by the transshipment variable x_{11}. Hence in the network 1_o and 1_d should be linked by an arc; the flow through this arc is the value of x_{11}. In this manner Figure 7 is constructed, which gives the network corresponding to Tableau 1 of Table 1. Note that each node of origin $(0_o,1_o,2_o,3_o)$ has outgoing arcs only except the constant-term arcs, and that each node of destination $(0_d, 1_d,2_d,3_d)$ has incoming nodes only, apart from the constant-term arcs.

This network can be used for application of the dual network method as described in the previous section. What happens in the network is then entirely equivalent to what happened in Table 1. Since the arcs $(0_o,2_d)$ and $(0_o,3_d)$ are artificial, they should become nonbasic. First $(0_o,3_d)$ is chosen as the leaving basic variable. All arcs coming into node 3_d are given a minus-sign. Then since the transshipment arc $(3_d,3_o)$ is basic, all arcs going out of 3_o

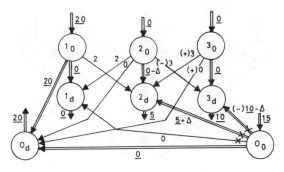

Fig. 7.

are given a plus-sign, after which there is no basic arc with an uncompensated sign. We select as the new basic variable the nonbasic arc with a minus-sign having the smallest reduced revenue; this is $(2_o, 3_d)$.

This arc is given a flow Δ and the Δ-loop is constructed. The basic arcs are adjusted by putting $\Delta = 10$ and the nonbasic arcs by adding or subtracting, according to the signs, the reduced revenue of the new basic are $(2_o, 3_d)$, which is 3. Then another iteration can start, and so on, until the optimal solution is obtained.

It should be noted that even for such a small problem, the network of Figure 7 is rather complicated. A considerable simplification is obtained when the nodes of origin and nodes of destination are combined into one node, deleting the transshipment arc. Since the transshipment arcs remain basic all the time, we do not need information about these; the value of its flow can, if necessary, be found from the flows of arcs entering and leaving this node.

In Figure 8.0 all separate nodes of origins and destinations have been combined, so that we have halved the number of nodes. Note that since also the O-nodes are combined, the constant-term flow of the resulting node O is the algebraic sum of the constant-term flows of the nodes O_o and O_d.

Because of the combination of nodes and the elimination of transshipment flows, the rules for adjustment of values of flow (Δ-loop) and adjustment of reduced revenues should be modified. For adjustment of the flows, the rule is still valid that the sum of incoming and outgoing flows should remain equal, so that any changes in flows should compensate each other. Hence if a flow in an arc entering a node is increased by Δ, then a flow in a basic arc entering this node should be decreased by Δ or a flow in a basic arc leaving the node should be increased by Δ. If the flow of an arc leaving the node increases by Δ, either the flow of a basic arc leaving the node should be decreased by Δ, or the flow of a basic arc entering the node should be increased by Δ.

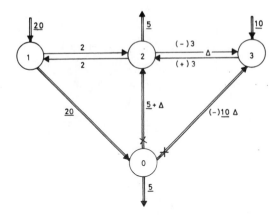

Fig. 8.0.

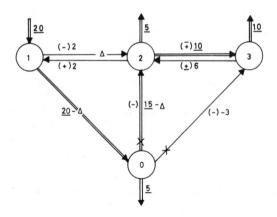

Fig. 8.1.

Reduced costs are adjusted by subtracting the same number from reduced costs of arcs entering the node and adding it to reduced costs of arcs leaving the node, or subtracting it from costs of arcs leaving the node and adding it to the costs of arcs entering the node.

The figures 8.0–8.2 indicate an application of the dual method to the example. In Figure 8.0 the artificial arc (O,3) is taken as the leaving basic arc. A minus-sign is indicated at all arcs entering node 3 and a plus-sign at all arcs leaving this node. Since no basic arc has an uncompensated sign, the arc having

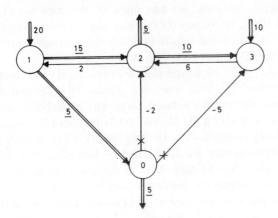

Fig. 8.2.

a minus-sign and the smallest reduced costs is taken as the new basic arc; this is arc (2,3). Then the Δ-loop is completed as indicated. Putting $\Delta = 10$ and adjusting the reduced costs as indicated by the signs, we obtain the network of Figure 8.1. Now the artificial arc (O,2) should be eliminated. All arcs entering node 2 are given a minus-sign and those leaving a plus-sign. Since now the basic arc (2,3) has a plus-sign, all arcs entering node 3 are given a minus-sign and those leaving node 3 a plus-sign. The non-basic arc with a minus-sign having the minimum reduced costs is (1,2) so that it becomes the new basic arc. Then the Δ-loop is constructed. We put $\Delta = 15$, and adjust reduced costs according to the signs. The result is the network of Figure 8.2 which contains no infeasibilities, so that the optimal solution is found.

It should be noted that in contrast with the transportation tableaux of Table 1 and their network representation such as in Figure 7, no superfluous information such as transshipment quantities and reduced costs of the slack variables of origin and destination for the same row and column are given. For instance, in Tableau 4 of Table 1 the reduced revenue of x_{20} and x_{02} are 2 and -2; it can be proved that these revenues are always the same, apart from sign, so that only one of them is needed.

Let us now consider an application of the network version of the dual transportation method to the example of Section 13.4. In this example 50 units are available in node 1, and 15, 5, and 20 units are required in nodes 2, 3, and 4, respectively. There are arcs in both directions between the following pairs of nodes (1,2), (1,3), (2,4), (2,3), (3,4) with costs of 4, 7, 3, 1, and 1 per unit. The requirements at nodes 2, 3, and 4 should be met with least transportation costs.

For the set-up network, we add node O, the slack arc (1,O) and the artificial arcs (O,2), (O,3), and (O,4); these arcs are taken as basic arcs. Then the network of Figure 9.0 results in which for a moment the signs within brackets and the Δ's should be disregarded.

In the dual method we should start with a solution which is optimal apart from infeasibilities. The basic solution in Figure 9.0 is optimal since all non-basic arcs have nonnegative reduced costs. The infeasibilities consist of the artificial basic arcs (O,2), (O,3), and (O,4) indicated by crosses. We start by making (O,4) nonbasic first. Hence a minus is put at each arc entering node 4′and a plus at each arc leaving node 4. Since there is no basic arc with an uncompensated sign, we may select as the new basic arc the nonbasic arc with a minus-sign having the smallest reduced costs. This is (3,4). Hence the flow in (3,4) is put at Δ. The flow in (O,4) then becomes 20 − Δ and the flow in (O,3), 5 + Δ. Δ is put at 20, the reduced costs are adjusted by subtracting 1 (the net revenue of (3,4)) from the reduced costs of arcs with a minus-sign and adding it where there is a plus-sign. Then Figure 9.1 results.

Here we decide to eliminate the flow in the arc (O,3). A minus is put at arcs coming into node 3 and a plus at arcs going out of node 3. Then the basic

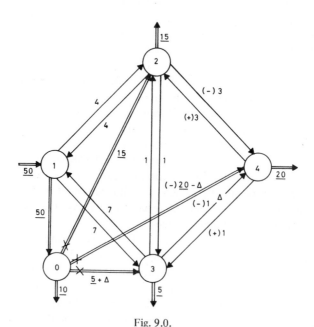

Fig. 9.0.

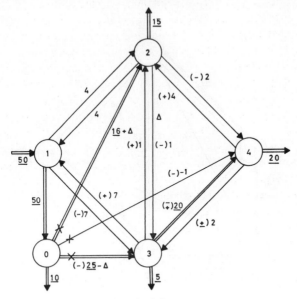

Fig. 9.1.

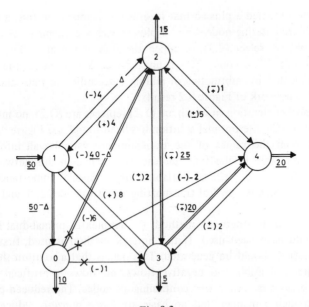

Fig. 9.2.

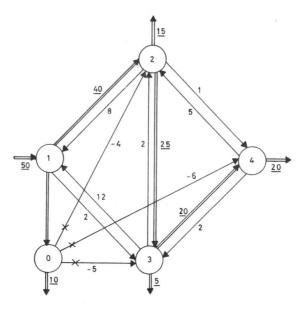

Fig. 9.3.

arc (3,4) has obtained a plus so that in order to compensate this, a minus is put at each arc entering node 4 and a plus at each arc leaving node 4. As the new basic arc we select (2,3), in which the flow is put at Δ. The flows in (0,4) and (0,2) then becomes $25 - \Delta$ and $15 + \Delta$. Δ is put at 25, the reduced costs are adjusted by subtracting or adding 1 according to plus- and minus-signs and the network of Figure 9.2 results.

After another iteration in which arc (1,2) replaces arc (0,2), no infeasibilities remain so that the optimal solution has been found, see Figure 9.3. Note that apart from the values of the transshipment variables all information which was available in the final tableau is available in this network. The reduced costs of the artificial variables are of special importance; from them we know that the cost of transporting a unit to nodes 2, 3, and 4 are 4, 5 and 6 respectively.

Instead of the dual network method, the simplex or primal-dual network method could have been used. If the simplex method is used, first a basic feasible solution should be generated. This means that a solution should be found which is feasible (no negative flows, no flows in artificial arcs) in which the basic arcs form a tree containing all nodes. The reduced costs are adjusted in such a manner that no basic arc has a nonzero reduced costs.

Then the iteration may start. As new basic arcs, a nonbasic arc with a negative reduced cost is taken. A Δ-loop is constructed and the leaving basic arc is the one with the smallest flow having $-\Delta$. Δ is put equal to this flow, reduced costs are adjusted in such a way that the new basic arc has zero reduced costs and if the resulting reduced costs are not all nonnegative, another iteration follows.

14.5. Example of Crude Oil Distribution

In this section we shall deal with a generalization of the problem of the previous section. Again we shall deal with a network having nodes with quantities available and required, but now it is assumed the quantities available in node i have a given cost c_i; furthermore, the same node may have a quantity available and a quantity required. Note that it is not possible to work with the difference of quantity available and required, because the quantities available may have such a high price that it is cheaper to supply the required quantities from elsewhere. Finally, there will be upper bounds on some flows. The main difficulty resides in the construction of the initial tableau- or network-solution. This construction is explained in Figure 11 and Table 2. Let us consider in detail a node having both a supply and a demand, such as node 1 in Figure 11.0, which is separated in the node of origin, 1_o, and the node of destination 1_d. Node 2 stands for a typical other node. Transportation cost per unit from node 1 to node 2 is c_{12}, and in the reverse direction c_{21}. Arc $(1_o,1_d)$ stands for the number of units taken from the quantity available and used for the quantity required in node 1. Arc $(1_d,1_o)$ is the quantity transshipped through node 1 (this quantity is nonnegative). Since

Table 2
Construction of initial solution for primal-dual method

Tableau	Nodes	0		1	2
0	0	$0(-\Delta)$		$\underline{5}(+\Delta)$	
	1	$(-)\underline{10}(+\Delta)$	10	$(-)c_1(-\Delta)$	$(-)c_{12}+c_1$
	2			c_{21}	
1	0	$\underline{0}$		$\underline{5}$	
	1	$-c_1^*$	10	$\underline{0}$	c_{12}
	2			c_{21}	

the units available in node 1 cost c_1, arc $(1_o,1_d)$ has a cost coefficient of c_1 and arc $(1_o,2)$ a cost coefficient of $c_{12} + c_1$. Arc $(1_d,1_o)$ supplies a unit in node 1 and has therefore a cost coefficient of $-c_1$. The same solution can be obtained if we start with arc $(1_o,0)$ having a cost coefficient $-c_1$, arcs $(1_o,1_d)$ and $(1_d,1_o)$ one of O and arc $(1_o,2)$ one of c_{12}; since arc $(1_o,0)$ is basic, c_1 should be added to arcs leaving node 1_o and subtracted from arcs entering this node.

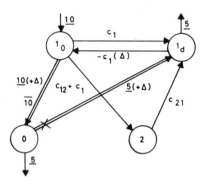

Fig. 10.0.

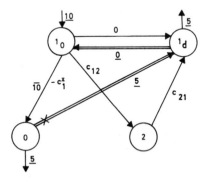

Fig. 10.1.

The solution of Figure 10.0 is neither feasible (because of the artificial arc $(O,1_d)$) nor optimal in the narrow sense (because of the arc $(1_d,1_o)$ having a negative cost coefficient). However, optimality in the narrow sense can easily be obtained by making arc $(1_d,1_o)$ basic. A Δ-loop is constructed.

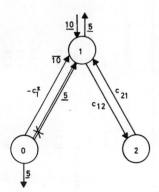

Fig. 10.2.

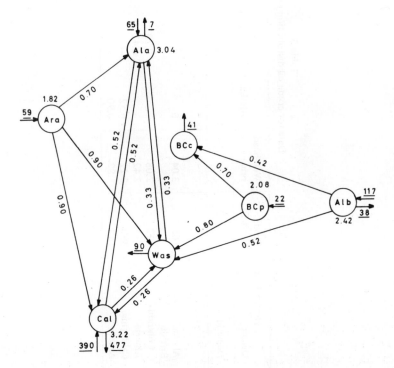

Fig. 11.

Table 3
Data for crude oil distribution problem

Destination / Origin	Prod. Capacity	Well-head price	Alaska	British Columbia	Alberta	California	Washington
Demand			7	41	38	477	90
			Transportation cost				
Alaska	65	3.04	0	—	—	0.52	0.33
British Columbia	22	2.08	—	0.70	—	—	0.80
Alberta	117	2.42	—	0.42	0	—	0.52
California	390	3.22	0.52	—	—	0	0.26
Arabia	59	1.82	0.90	—	—	0.90	0.90

Arc $(1_o,0)$ has an upper bound of 10 because only the 10 units available have the value c_1. Hence we find for the minimum value of Δ: $10 - 10 = 0$. Arc $(1_d,1_o)$ replaces arc $(1_o,0)$ which is put at its upper bound 10. Figure 10.1 is the resulting network after transformation. The solution of this network is optimal in the narrow sense, so that the primal-dual or the dual method may be applied to it. If the nodes 1_o and 1_d are combined, the initial network is as given in Figure 10.2.

The same manipulations may be performed in transportation tableaux. Tableau 0 of Table 2 corresponds with Figure 11.0. The variable x_{11} now corresponds to the algebraic sum of the flows in arcs $(1_o,1_d)$ and $(1_d,1_o)$ and may therefore be positive or negative. Because c_1 is positive and x_{11} unrestricted, the solution is not optimal in the narrow sense. x_{11} is introduced into the basis in a negative direction, the Δ-loop is completed. Since x_{10} has an upper bound of 10 for the reason given before, this variable is put at its upper bound. After the transformation Tableau 1 results.

As an application, crude oil distribution in the Pacific area of North America will be studied. [1] In this area there are a number of oil-producing fields which for simplicity are thought to be concentrated in oil-producing centers. The daily production capacity of these centers for 1968 is assumed to be as given in Table 3 and Figure 11. The cost of the oil is also assumed to be given as indicated in this table by the well-head price. Furthermore, the table gives the quantities required per day in each of the demand centers. Finally, the transportation cost per unit between each production center and each demand center are given in case a direct link exists and transportation is possible and legal. There are a number of limitations. For instance, it is not legal to import oil into Western Canada. Other oil transports which would be very expensive, and therefore certainly not optimal, such as transportation from British Columbia to Alaska, have been left out.

As data for production capacity and demand, average production in the production centers and consumption in the demand centers for 1968 have been taken. Production is not necessarily equal to production capacity, but the model, if applicable, will uncover where unused capacity should reside.

For the given data, costs for supplying the demands will be minimized. Such a minimization would be relevant if all refineries would be in one hand, but the solution would also be an equilibrium solution if each refinery tried to minimize cost by competing for the productive capacity.

Let us now proceed to the construction of the initial solution. Figure 12 gives the initial solution in network form and Tableau 0 of Table 4 does the

---

[1] This is based on an M.A. thesis by V.G. Taylor.

Table 4

An application of the primal-dual method to a crude oil distribution problem

Tableau	Node	Sign	0	u.b.	Ala	BCc	Alb	Cal	Was
		Sign	0		—	—	(−)—	—	—
0	0		$\underline{0}$(+Δ)		—	—	(—)—	—	—
	Ala	+	−3.04*	65	$\underline{7}$ / 0	$\underline{41}$	(−)$\underline{38}$(−Δ)	$\underline{447}$	$\underline{90}$
	BCp	+	$\underline{22}$		—	—	—	0.52	0.33
	Alb	0	(+)−2.42*(−Δ)	117	—	2.78	—	—	2.88
	Cal	(+)+	−3.22*		0.52	(+)0.42	(+)$\underline{0}$(+Δ)	—	(+)0.52
	Was	+	0		0.33	—	—	$\underline{0}$ / 0.26	0.26
	Ara	0	$\underline{59}$	390	2.72	—	—	2.72	$\underline{0}$ / 2.72
			0				0		
1	0		$\underline{38}$(+Δ)		—	—	0	—	—
	Ala	+	−3.04*	65	$\underline{7}$ / 0	$\underline{41}$	−2.42	$\underline{477}$(−Δ)	$\underline{90}$
	BCp	+	$\underline{22}$		—	—	—	0.52	0.33
	Alb	0	$\underline{79}$	117	—	2.78	$\underline{38}$	—	2.88
	Cal	0	−3.22*		0.52	2.84	—	—	2.94
	Was	+	0		0.33	—	—	$\underline{0}$ / 0.26	0.26
	Ara	(−)0	(−)$\underline{59}$(−Δ)	390	(−)2.72	—	—	(−)2.72(Δ)	$\underline{0}$ / (−)2.72
			0				0		
2	0		$\underline{97}$(Δ)		—	—	0	—	—
	Ala	+	−3.04*	65	$\underline{7}$ / 0	$\underline{41}$(−Δ)	−2.42	$\underline{418}$	$\underline{90}$
	BCp	+	(−)$\underline{22}$(−Δ)		—	—	—	0.52	0.33
	Alb	(−)0	$\underline{79}$	117	—	(−)2.78(Δ)	$\underline{38}$	—	(−)2.88
	Cal	0	−3.22*		0.52	2.84	—	—	2.94
	Was	+	0		0.33	—	—	$\underline{0}$ / 0.26	0.26
	Ara	+	−2.72	390	0	—	—	$\underline{59}$	$\underline{0}$ / 0

Table 4 (continued)

Tableau	Node	Sign	0	u.b.	Ala	BCc	Alb	Cal	Was
	0		0		–	(–)–	0	–	–
3	0	+	119(+Δ)		7	(–)19(–Δ)	–2.42	418	90
	Ala	+	–3.04*	65	0			0.52	0.33
	BCp	(+)+	(+)–2.78			(∓)22	38		(+)0.10
	Alb	0	79(–Δ)	117		(–)2.84(Δ)			2.94
	Cal	+	–3.22*		0.52			0	0.26
	Was	+	0		0.33			0.26	0
	Ara	+	–2.72	390	0			59	0
4	0	0	653		–3.04	–3.27	2.85	–3.56	–3.37
	Ala	0	0	65	2			0.28	30
	BCp	0	0.49			22(–Δ)			0(Δ)
	Alb	0	0.43	117		19(+Δ)	38		60(–Δ)
	Cal	0	0.34		1.04			390	0.45
	Was	0	0.37		0.66			0.07	0
	Ara	0	0.84	390	0.54			59	0.19

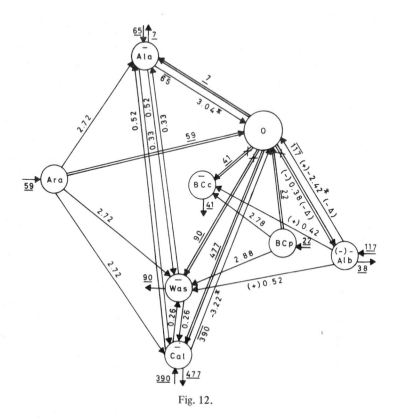

Fig. 12.

same in tableau form. As indicated before, the nodes which have both a supply and a demand are given an artificial basic arc from node 0 to that node and a nonbasic slack arc at its upper bound from that node to node 0; the cost coefficient of that node is equal to minus the well-head price. This explains the arcs between node 0 and Alaska, Alberta and California. Whereas the physical separation of supply and demand in Alaska, Alberta and California was neglected, this cannot be done for British Columbia, so that separate nodes for production and consumption are used. Arabia and British Columbia (production) are pure production nodes, so that their slack arc is taken as basic; to the transportation cost of all outgoing arcs, the well-head prices are added. Washington and British Columbia (consumption) are pure demand centers, which have an artificial basic arc from node 0.

The solution generated in this manner is optimal in the narrow sense none of the cost coefficients is negative for unstarred arcs or positive for starred arcs. The variables corresponding to the diagonal in Tableau 0 are unrestricted as to sign for Alaska, Alberta, and California since they stand for a combination of internal use and transshipment. The diagonal variable for Washington stands for transshipment only, so that it should be nonpositive, whereas the diagonal variable for British Columbia stands for internal use only and should therefore be nonnegative.

The solution is infeasible, since all demands are supplied by artificial arcs. Feasibility while retaining the optimality can be obtained by the dual or the primal-dual method; here the latter method is used. In the network all nodes with artificially supplied demand are given a minus-sign. In Tableau 0 of Table 4, the artificial variables in row 0 are initially given a cost of λ which is then eliminated by subtracting it from all columns and adding it to rows having a diagonal basic variable. This results in the signs as indicated in the rows and columns. Note that the sign is not valid for x_{00}, but this is not important.

Now the first iteration of the primal-dual method can be started; first the network will be considered. For the new basic arc, the following arcs should be compared. Nonbasic arcs not at their upper bound, going from a node without a minus-sign to one with a minus-sign, and nonbasic arcs at their upper bound, going from a node with a minus-sign to one without a minus sign should be considered; the former arcs all have positive cost coefficients and the latter negative ones. Of these arcs, the one with the smallest (in absolute value) cost coefficient is selected.

In Figure 12, the following arcs (with cost coefficients within brackets) are compared:

Ala-0(−3.04), Ara-Ala(2.72), Ara-Was(2.72), Ara-Cal(2.72), BCp-BCc(2.78). BCp-Was(2.88), Alb-0(−2.42), and Cal-0(−3.22).

The smallest coefficient is that of Alb-0, so that this is the new basic arc. Since it is at its upper bound, it should be decreased, so that we start with $-\Delta$. The Δ-loop contains only two arcs, the artificial arc 0-Alb becomes nonbasic. The flow in arc Alb-0 becomes $117 - \Delta = 117 - 38 = 39$. All cost coefficients of arcs entering and leaving the node Alb are adjusted and so is the minus-sign of that node.

Let us now consider the tableau form, see Tableau 0 of Table 4. As new basic arcs we consider nonstarred elements with a minus as combined row- and column-sign and starred elements with a plus as combined row- and column-sign. The same elements are found as in the network and the one with the smallest (in absolute value) cost coefficient is selected. Alb-0 is then taken as the new basic variable which is decreased by Δ. After construction of the Δ-loop, the arc 0-Alb is found as the leaving basic variable. Δ is put at 38, the cost coefficients and signs are adjusted and Tableau 1 results.

We can proceed with either the network or the tableau, but since it is rather cumbersome to draw all successive networks, only the tableaux will be reproduced. After 9 iterations, the optimal solution is obtained, see Tableau 4 of Table 4.

The interpretation of the basic variables in this tableau is rather straight-forward. The fact that the arc Ala-0 is basic means that if there is unused production capacity it should be in Alaska. Figure 13 gives the basic flows in network form. Alberta supplies British Columbia and Washington, the production of British Columbia goes to consumption of British Columbia, Washington is also supplied by Alaska, and California is supplied both by Alaska and Arabia. Since the cost coefficient of BCp-Was is zero, an alternative optimal solution exists, in which the entire supply of British Columbia goes to Washington and the demand of British Columbia is supplied by Alberta.

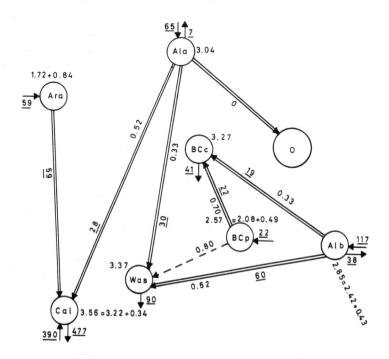

Fig. 13.

The interpretation of cost coefficients in rows and columns other than 0 is straightforward; they stand for the losses per unit if oil were transported along these routes. The cost coefficients in row 0 stand for minus the cost of one additional unit of demand in these nodes. Hence crude oil in Alberta costs $2.85 per barrel and is therefore the cheapest while oil in California costs $3.56 per barrel and is therefore the most expensive demand to satisfy. The elements in column 0 stand for the premium which crude oil in these supply centers should have over the well-head price if the model was correct and there was free competition; for Washington it gives merely the value of crude oil. The fact that the premiums are nonzero points out that the model differs from reality. Also the flows of the optimal solution differ from those observed in reality. In 1968 14 million barrels a day were shipped from Arabia to Washington, reducing the supply of Arabia to California and that of Alaska to Washington by the same amount and increasing the supply of Alaska to California by the same amount. According to our model this results in a loss of $14,000,000 \cdot \$19 = \$2.66$ million per day.

It should, of course, be realized that the model was not realistic in a number of respects. Firstly U.S. import restrictions have not been included properly. The amount of offshore crude available was taken to be 59 million barrels per day; in reality the regulations are much more complex. Furthermore there is no free competition within the area, since a number of companies have both production and refining in various centers and will usually prefer their own crude. However, the objective of this section has been to explain the application of transportation and network techniques and not the construction of a model which explains reality in all respects. A more complicated model which takes all complications into account will probably explain reality adequately or point out irrational allocations.

Figure 13 also illustrates the price structure of the optimal solutions. The basis of the price structure is the well-head price of Alaska, $3.04. This, plus the transportation costs 0.52 and 0.33 sets the prices in California and Washington at $3.56 and $3.37, so that the premium for California is $3.56 - 3.22 = 0.34$. The price in Washington, $3.37, determines the price in Alberta by subtraction of the transportation cost of 0.52 at $2.85, which gives a premium in Alberta of $2.85 - 2.42 = 0.43$. The price of Alberta $2.85, puts the price at the demand center of British Columbia at 2.85 plus 0.42 transportation costs at $3.27. This determines the price at the production center of British Columbia at $3.27 - 70 = 2.57$, so that the premium in this last center is $2.57 - 2.08 = 49$. The price of Arabian oil is determined from the price in California: $3.56 - 0.90 = 2.66$, so that the premium is $2.66 - 1.72 = 0.84$.

According to the model, the oil price in this area depends on the production center with spare capacity which is Alaska. Any price increase or decrease in Alaska would be followed by the same change in the entire area.

Exercises

1. Given is the following network:

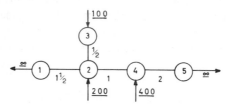

In the nodes 2, 3, and 4 there is a net supply as indicated. The numbers at the arcs indicate the transportation costs per unit between the two nodes concerned. In nodes 1 and 5 there is an unlimited (world) demand at a price $30 per unit in node 1 and $32 per unit in node 5. Find by means of the simplex transportation method or the simplex network method the optimal allocation and the effective price at each node. (Note that the answers can easily be obtained without applying this method; however, it is important to get the formulation of the initial tableau or network right.)

2. The network below indicates supply and demand for a product in 5 centers; the supply prices in centers 2 and 4 are $0.80 and $0.90 and the transportation costs between the centers are as indicated.

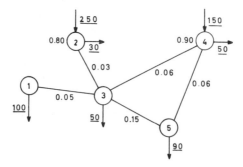

(a) Find the optimal (equilibrium) solution by means of the primal-dual method; indicate the effective prices in all centers.

(b) If center 4 wants to clear its entire supply, by how much should it decrease its price?

(c) Suppose that in center 1 a large source of supply becomes available at $0.74 per unit. What is the resulting solution? How should centers 2 and 4 change their prices in order not to loose any sales to the new supply source?

(d) Suppose that transportation costs increase parametrically but the supply prices remain the same. How does the optimal solution change?

(e) How much would center 2 be prepared to pay per period for a direct link between it and center 4 which would have a cost of 0.05 per unit?

3. Supply and demand in three centers over the next four periods are as follows:

		Period			
		1	2	3	4
	1 (supply)	180	100	40	150
Center	2 (demand)	45	30	70	55
	3 (demand)	35	50	80	45

Transportation costs from 1 to 2 are 0.75, from 1 to 3, 0.5 and from 2 to 3, 0.3. Inventory costs per unit are 0.1 per unit per period in center 1, and 0.3 and 0.4 in centers 2 and 3. The maximum amount of inventory in centers 2 and 3 is 50 and 40. Formulate this problem as a network problem and solve it by the primal-dual method. *Hint*: construct a network with a node for each center in each period. The arc between the node for center 1 in period 1 and the node for center 1 in period 2 is then the amount of inventory kept in center 1 between periods 1 and 2, and so on.

PART 4

DECISION TREE METHODS

15. BRANCH-AND-BOUND METHODS

15.1. Introduction

In the linear programming problems we have treated before, the variables were continuous or an approximation by continuous variables was valid. In some decision problems, a number of variables are not continuous. The most typical case is that in which a number of variables can only take the values 0 or 1. In that case the problem is called a *zero-one integer programming problem*. If some variables can take any integer value 0, 1, 2, 3, ..., the problem is called a *general integer programming problem*.

As an example, let us consider the following problem. Maximize

$$(1.1) \qquad f = x_1 + 3x_2$$

subject to

$$(1.2) \qquad 3x_1 + 4x_2 \leqq 6 ,$$

$$(1.3) \qquad x_1, x_2 = 0 \text{ or } 1 .$$

The condition (1.3) makes the problem an integer problem. If (1.3) is replaced by

$$(1.4) \qquad 0 \leqq x_1 , \ x_2 \leqq 1 ,$$

it is an ordinary linear programming problem with upper bounds on x_1 and x_2.

Figure 1 gives a geometric representation of both problems. The integer problem has as its feasible points B, C, and D, and this is all; the ordinary linear programming problem has the entire shaded region as feasible solution. This indicates that integer problems are basically different from ordinary linear programming problems. Whereas in the last type of problems the

313

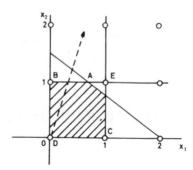

Fig. 1.

feasible solutions are all points in a certain area, the feasible solutions of integer problems are a number of isolated points. It can be shown that the feasible region of a linear programming problem is convex, which means that for any two feasible points, a point on a straight line in between those two points is also feasible. For integer problems this is obviously not true. The lack of this property makes integer problems much harder to solve. Methods to solve integer problems must therefore also be different.

   In general, the approach of solving an integer problem by solving first the problem without the integer requirements and rounding the solution obtained to integers, is not going to work. For instance, let us apply this to the problem (1.1) – (1.3). The problem without the integer requirement is obtained by replacing (1.3) by (1.4); the optimal solution is then point A in Figure 1, which is $x_1 = {}^2\!/_3$, $x_2 = 1$. If this is rounded, we find $x_1 = 1, x_2 = 1$, point E, which is infeasible. Of course, in such a very small problem, the optimal solution to the integer problem which is point B in this case, can easily be found, but if the number of integer variables is not quite small, the problem is difficult to solve without special methods for integer programming, and even then methods can only solve problems which are not too large.

   One approach to the solution of integer problems is to enumerate partly the feasible solutions of the problem in an efficient manner, leaving out the feasible solutions which can be demonstrated not to be optimal. Branch-and-bound methods, which are the subject of this chapter, can be considered as partial enumeration methods. Branch-and-bound methods for integer programming have been originally proposed by Land and Doig [12] and can be considered to be one of the most successful methods computationally.

   Another approach to the solution of integer problems is the cutting-plane technique which was developed by Gomory [7]. In this technique parts of the feasible region of the problem without the integer requirements, which do not contain integer solutions, are removed by imposing extra linear constraints; the feasible region is whittled down in this way until the optimal solution results. Though it has been proved that cutting plane methods can solve integer problems in a finite number of iterations, computational experience has not been encouraging.

Branch-and-bound methods can be applied to a number of problems which are not integer problems. These problems have in common that some discrete solution should be found. Integer problems are not the most simple problems to which branch-and-bound methods can be applied; in fact, they may be considered as the more complicated problems for which these methods can be used.

A large variety of problems can be formulated as integer programming problems. Formulation as integer problems does not guarantee that problems can be solved because resulting problems may be too large for application of some method for integer programming on the available computational equipment. In a number of cases it is not even useful to formulate the problem as an integer problem because it is more efficient to solve the problem as it is. This is the case with the traveling-salesman problem and the fixed-charge problem, which can both be formulated as integer problems, but which can be solved directly by branch-and-bound methods.

In this chapter first the concept of a decision tree, which underlies the branch-and-bound methods, will be explained by means of an example, after which the application of these methods is illustrated. The remaining sections deal with applications to more complicated problems. Section 4 is concerned with the traveling-salesman problem. In this chapter linear programming is not used. In the next chapter branch-and-bound methods and linear programming will be combined to deal with integer programming problems.

15.2. Decision Trees

Let us consider the following problem. A company has to decide whether to lease equipment in the four quarters of the coming year. Leasing equipment costs $5,000 per quarter if it is leased for the first time, $4,000 if it has been leased the previous quarter and $3,000 if it has been leased at least two previous quarters. If equipment has been leased in the same year, but not in the previous quarter, leasing costs are $4,500. It is this last piece of information which prevents us from solving the problem by network methods. The availability of equipment reduces direct costs per unit produced by $100 per unit. The production plan for the four quarters is 20, 80, 60, and 25 units. During which quarters, if at all, should equipment be leased?

Table 1
Leasing costs and direct cost reduction ($1,000)

Quarter	1	2	3	4
Production	20	80	60	25
Costs when not leasing	2	8	6	$2^1/_2$
Leasing costs with 0 previous quarters	5	5	5	5
$-1-$		4	4	4
$-2-$			3	3
$-3-$				3

The data for the problem, apart from the $4,500 lease, can conveniently be summarized in Table 1. At the beginning of each quarter a decision has to be taken, to lease or not to lease. This decision must be based on a comparison of costs in all following quarters, since if we lease this quarter, the leasing costs in following quarters are reduced. But in order to know the costs of the following quarters, we have to know whether we are going to lease in the future or not.

A problem like this can be represented by means of a decision tree. Let us first consider the decision for the first quarter and the costs of the two alternatives in that quarter, which are 2 for not leasing and 5 for leasing. If 1 stands for leasing and $\bar{1}$ for not leasing, this decision and its costs can be represented as follows:

For the second quarter we can again lease or not lease. These decisions and the total costs for the two quarters are indicated by branching out from the two end points, so that the following tree is obtained:

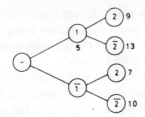

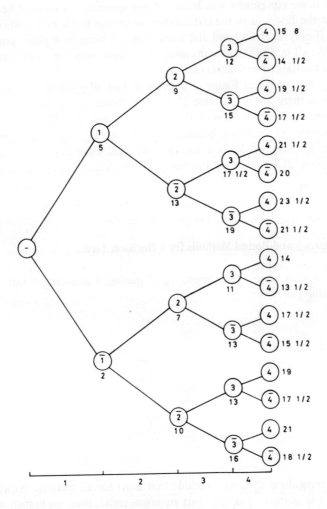

Fig. 2.

The accumulated costs are easily derived from Table 1. In the same manner we can branch out for the decisions in quarter 3 and indicate the accumulated costs and after that branch out for the decisions in quarter 4 and indicate the accumulated costs. Then Figure 2 results.

The figures next to the extreme nodes (tips of the tree) indicate the costs for the decisions made belonging to that branch of the tree. For example, if the equipment had been leased in all quarters, the accumulated costs would be 15; if no equipment was leased in any quarter, costs would be $18\frac{1}{2}$, if only in the first and in the last quarter equipment was leased, costs would be $23\frac{1}{2}$, if only in the second and third quarter leasing took place, costs would be $13\frac{1}{2}$, all in $1,000. The decisions with least costs are easily found to be the last-mentioned with costs of $13\frac{1}{2}$.

The final nodes in Figure 2 indicate in fact all possible combinations of decisions; there are in this case $2^4 = 16$ combinations of decisions. In larger and more realistic problems of this nature it is not possible to enumerate all combinations of decisions, because their number may be quite large, nor is it possible to draw the decision tree. But we shall show that it is not necessary to generate all branches of the tree when branch-and-bound procedures are used.

15.3. Branch-and-Bound Methods for a Decision Tree

Let us start again at the beginning of quarter 1 and branch out from the root of the tree:

After having done this, we conclude that costs for all quarters are at least 2, since for subsequent quarters costs are nonnegative. Now we branch out from the node with least costs, which is $\overline{1}$:

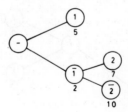

We now conclude that total costs are at least 5 and branch out from the corresponding node 1. The result is

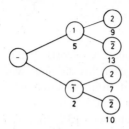

The node with the least costs is now 2 with costs 7; branching out from this node we find

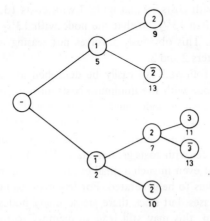

The node with least costs is now the upper node 2 with costs 9, so we branch out here.

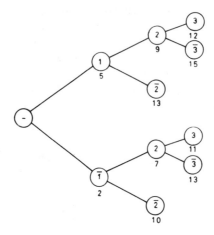

Then we branch out from node 2 with costs 10 and find node 3 with costs 13 and node $\bar{3}$ with costs 16. After this the node with the minimum costs is 3 with costs 11. Branching out from here we find node 4 with costs 14 and node $\bar{4}$ with costs $13\frac{1}{2}$. Since the last two nodes are final nodes, their costs are total costs for the four quarters. $13\frac{1}{2}$ may therefore be considered as an upper bound for minimal costs. This means that any node with a higher cost need not be considered for branching any more. In this case there are node $\bar{3}$ with costs 15 and node $\bar{3}$ with costs 16.

Next we branch out from node 3 with costs 12, then from node $\bar{2}$ with costs 13, node $\bar{3}$ with costs 13 and node 3 with costs 13. The end-nodes all have costs higher than $13\frac{1}{2}$, so that the node with $13\frac{1}{2}$ must be the minimum-cost solution. This obviously involves not leasing in quarters 1 and 4 and leasing in quarters 2 and 3.

The procedure followed can easily be described as follows: Branch out each time at the node with the minimum costs until the minimum-cost node is a final node. Then this node must correspond with the optimal solution. In this problem, $2 + 4 + 8 + 16 = 30$ nodes had to be generated for the entire tree; in our case 22 were generated so that the procedure saved us from generating the 8 nodes with costs greater than $13\frac{1}{2}$. This is not much, but we shall see below that even in such a small problem only a small fraction of the nodes of the tree has to be generated. For larger problems this fraction will be small in most cases, but since there are so many nodes in a decision tree for a large problem, this may still lead to memory requirements exceeding those of the available computational equipment.

The procedure described above we shall call Variant I. An alternative procedure, to be called Variant II, which has some advantages is as follows. We start by branching out the two nodes 1 and 1, then branch out at the least-cost node of these, which is $\overline{1}$ and generate nodes 2 (7) and $\overline{2}$ (10). Now we continue branching out from the least-cost node of the last two nodes only, which is 2 (7), thus generating 3 (11) and $\overline{3}$ (13). Then we branch out from 3 (11) and generate nodes 4 (14) and $\overline{4}$ ($13\frac{1}{2}$). We have now reached one of the many tops of the tree. The part of the tree generated so far is now:

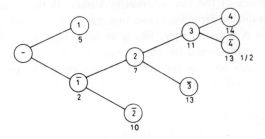

Since the complete decision sequence ($\overline{1}$,2,3,$\overline{4}$) has costs of $13\frac{1}{2}$, this cost figure gives an upper bound for costs. This means that any node having higher costs than $13\frac{1}{2}$ should not be considered, nor its branches. From node $\overline{4}$ go back, considering branching at each node we encounter. So from node $\overline{4}$ ($13\frac{1}{2}$) we go to node 3 (11). We found before that node 4 (14) has higher costs so that we do not consider it. We go up to node 2 (7). Then the alternative branch is taken which is $\overline{3}$ (13). Since this is less than $13\frac{1}{2}$, we branch out from it and find 4 ($17\frac{1}{2}$) and $\overline{4}$ ($15\frac{1}{2}$), (see Figure 2) which gives higher costs. Continuing going upwards, node $\overline{1}$ (2) is met, where the alternative branch leading to node $\overline{2}$ (10) is found. From here we branch out and find $\overline{3}$ (16) and 3 (13). The first node can be cut out, the second is used for branching out, after which 4 (19) and $\overline{4}$ ($17\frac{1}{2}$) are found.

No node with lower cost than $13\frac{1}{2}$ having been found for the alternative branch out of ($\overline{1}$), the alternative branch of the initial node is taken, so that node 1 (5) is considered. We branch out from here and find nodes 2 (9) and $\overline{2}$ (13). Branching out from the minimum-cost node, we find 3 (12) and $\overline{3}$ (15), and again branching out from the minimum-cost node we find 4 (15) and $\overline{4}$ ($14\frac{1}{2}$). No node with lower costs than $13\frac{1}{2}$ has been found so far. From 3 (12) we go back again and take the alternative node at 2 (9) which is $\overline{3}$ (15). Since this node has higher costs, it and its subsequent branches need not be considered. We now move backwards from 2 (9) and take the alternative node at 1 (5) which is $\overline{2}$ (13). By branching out here, nodes 3 ($17\frac{1}{2}$)

and $\overline{3}$ (19) are found which should not be considered because they have higher costs. Now we move back again, to 1 (5), where both alternatives have been considered and then to the initial node where both alternatives have been considered. We have considered all branches and all have ended up in 2 nodes with costs higher than $13\frac{1}{2}$. Hence the decision $\overline{1}$, 2, 3, $\overline{4}$ must be the least-cost solution.

This variant has some advantages over Variant I described earlier. Firstly, in the earlier procedure, the nodes considered successively may be on quite different branches of the tree whereas in Variant II the nodes which were successively evaluated are always close together. In cases in which the computation of costs is not so simple, this is an advantage. Secondly, in the last procedure, an upper bound for costs is reached after a treetop is evaluated, which is done very soon, in this case after four steps; this upper bound can be used to cut off branches beginning with nodes having higher costs.

In our example the reduction of nodes of the decision tree to be evaluated was not very large. A much larger reduction can be obtained if the following transformation of costs is used. From the costs in each quarter the costs of the alternative with minimum costs may be subtracted. Returning to Table 1, we see that for not leasing in quarter 1, the costs are 2 and for leasing, they are 5. Hence we subtract 2 from each number and have as the costs 0 and 3. For the second quarter, we have as costs 8, 5, and 4. After subtracting the minimum, 4, we find 4, 1, and 0. For quarters 3 and 4, the same can be done. The resulting costs are found in Table 2. The subtraction is justified because we subtracted a constant number from the costs in each period which leaves the effect of decisions on costs the same; only the minimum costs for each period are subtracted since otherwise costs would be negative,

Table 2
Reduced costs ($1000)

Quarter	1	2	3	4
Costs when not leasing	0	4	3	0
Leasing costs with 0 previous quarters	3	1	2	$2\frac{1}{2}$
– 1 –		0	1	$1\frac{1}{2}$
– 2 –			0	$\frac{1}{2}$
– 3 –				$\frac{1}{2}$

in which case the branch-and-bound procedure would not be applicable any more.

With the reduced costs, the following decision tree is found for the branch-and-bound procedure.

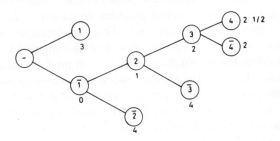

It is interesting to observe that the decision tree is the same for the first and second variant of the branch-and-bound method.

15.4. The Traveling Salesman Problem

Consider the following situation. Somebody (he may be a traveling salesman, a business man, a diplomat or even a tourist) wants to visit the following cities: London, Moscow, New York, Tokyo, Sydney, and Buenos Aires, and should come back to the city he started in; the problem then is to find the route which minimizes total traveling costs. Table 3 gives the airplane fares, tourist class, low season 1968/69, in U.S. dollars, between these cities.

Table 3
Airplane fares between six cities (tourist class, low season, 1968/69, U.S.$)

to / from	1 London	2 Moscow	3 New York	4 Tokyo	5 Sydney	6 B. Aires
1. London	–	185.40	210	677.70	694.50	463
2. Moscow	185.40	–	384.20	761.70	789.80	609
3. New York	210	384.20	–	479	649.50	340
4. Tokyo	677.70	761.70	479	–	476.10	756
5. Sydney	694.50	789.80	649.50	476.10	–	893
6. B. Aires	463	609	340	756	893	–

Problems of this type are called traveling-salesman problems. More generally, the traveling-salesman problem can be stated as that of a network with *n* nodes, connected by links having given lengths; a route should be found which passes each node once, and returns to its starting point, having minimal total length. The distance of node *i* to node *j* may be different from that of node *j* to node *i*. In actual problems the length of links may reflect distance, but also time traveled or, as in the six-city example, traveling costs.

The following industrial example also may be formulated as a traveling-salesman problem. On an installation a number of products are produced in a cycle of given duration, for instance two weeks. The set-up costs of each product vary according to the product which preceded it. For instance, it costs much more to clean up if white paint is produced after black paint than if black paint is produced after white paint. It is required to find the sequence of products which minimizes total set-up costs. It is obvious that the products can be interpreted as the nodes and the set-up costs for product *i* after product *j* has been produced as the distance between node *i* and node *j*. Note that in these cases the distances in opposite direction usually will be different. In some cases total set-up time or a linear combination of set-up costs and set-up time should be minimized.

A number of methods have been devised for the solution of the traveling salesman problem, the most effective of which is the method of Little, c.s. [14]. It is possible to formulate the traveling-salesman problem as an integer programming problem, but in most cases the resulting problems are too large to be solved. The problem also may be attacked using dynamic programming, but the resulting method is computationally less efficient than that of Little, c.s. which is explained in the following.

One way to solve the problem is to enumerate all possible combinations of nodes in a route and to compare the total distance of the resulting routes. Since the starting point of the route is fixed or irrelevant, because the minimal route is the same for all starting points, the first node of a route is given. The second node can be chosen in *n*-1 ways, the third one in *n*-2 ways, and so on, so that (*n*-1)! is the number of all possible routes. For the six-city example the number of possible routes is 120, which is rather large for hand computation. The method of Little, c.s. can be considered as a branch-and-bound method.

The first entry in each element of Tableau A0 of Table 4 gives the costs of traveling from any city to any other city, as in Table 3, but, for computational convenience, rounded and expressed in $10. Now if from all elements

Table 4
Successive reduced costs tableau

A0

City	1	2	3	4	5	6	Red.
1	—	19 0^{19}	21 2	68 49	69 50	46 27 14	19
2	19 0^{19}	—	38 19	76 57	79 60	61 42 29	19
3	21 0^{0}	38 17	—	89 68	90 69	34 13 0^{15}	21
4	68 20	76 28	89 41	—	48 0^{63}	76 28 15	48
5	69 21	79 31	90 42	48 0^{65}	—	89 41 28	48
6	46 12	61 27	34 0^{14}	76 42	89 55	—	34
Red.						13	202

A1

(4,5)

City	1	2	3	4	6	Red.
1	—	0^{12}	2	49 7	14	
2	0^{15}	—	19	57 15	29	
3	0^{0}	17	—	68 26	0	
5	21 0	31 10	42 21	—	28 7	21
6	12	27	0^{2}	42 0^{7}	—	
Red.				42		265

A2

(4,5)
(2,1)

City	2	3	4	6	Red.
1	—	2 0^{5}	7 5	14 12	2
3	17 14	—	26	0^{14}	
5	10 3 0^{0}	21 14	—	7 0	
6	27 21 0^{0}	0	0	—	
Red.	10				277

Table 4 (continued)

A3

City	3	4	6	Red.
1	0^{12}	—	12	
3	—	26	0^{38}	
6	0^0	0^{26}	—	
Red.				277

(4,5) (2,1) (5,2)

A4

City	3	4	Red.
1	0^0	—	
6	0	0^0	
Red.			277

(4,5) (2,1) (5,2) (3,6)

B0

City	1	2	3	4	5	6	Red.
1	—	0^{13}	2	49	50	14	
2	0^{10}	—	19	57	60	29	
3	0^0	17	—	68	69	0^0	
4	20	28	41	—	—	15	
5	21	31	42	0^{63}	—	28	
6	12	27	0^7	42	55	—	
Red.	5	13	26	5	50	0^5	267

$\overline{(4,5)}$

Inner reduced values: column 4: 0^5, 10, 19, —, 5 (Red. 5); column 5: 50, 60, 69, —, 55 (Red. 50); column 6: 14, 29, 0^0, 15, 28 (Red. 15)

B1

City	1	2	3	5	6	Red.
1	—	0^{13}	2	0^5	14	
2	0^{13}	—	19	10	29	
3	0^0	17	—	19	0^0	
4	5	13	26	—	0^5	
6	12	27	0^7	5	—	
Red.						267

$\overline{(4,5)}$ (5,4)

Table 4 (continued)

B2 $\overline{(4,5)}$, (5,4), (1,2)

City	1	3	5	6	Red.
Red.		9	0^{14}	19	10
2	—	19	10	29	
3	0^5	—	19	0^0	
4	5	26	—	0^5	
6	12	0^{14}	5	—	
Red.					277

B3 $\overline{(4,5)}$, (5,4), (1,2), (2,5)

City	1	3	6	Red.
3	0^{12}	—	0^0	
4	—	26	0^{26}	
6	12	0^{38}	—	
Red.				277

B4 $\overline{(4,5)}$, (5,4), (1,2), (2,5), (6,3)

City	1	6	Red.
3	0^0	0^0	
4	0^0	—	
Red.			277

in the same row the same amount is subtracted, this does not alter the solution of the problem, since each eligible route contains one link going from the city of that row to another city. Similarly, if from each element in the same column the same amount is subtracted, this does not alter the solution since each eligible route must contain one link going from some city to the city of that column. Hence the cost tableau may be reduced by subtracting the same amount from a row or a column. In Tableau A0 the smallest number of any row or column is subtracted from the elements of each row and column, then yielding the second and in case of column 6 the third entry in the element. First 19 is subtracted from all elements in row 1, then 19 from all elements in row 2, and so on. Turning to the columns, it is found that 13 can be subtracted from the elements of column 6. After this it is found that all rows and columns contain at least one zero element [1], so that no further reduction can take place. The amounts subtracted from each row are indicated in an additional column and the amounts subtracted from each column are indicated in an additional row. The total amount subtracted is 202; this can be interpreted as a lower bound for any route, since the amounts subtracted were the minimum costs of going from a given city to another or coming from a city to a given city.

In our new cost tableau some links may be considered for inclusion in the minimum cost tour. The most attractive links are those which have zero costs in the reduced cost tableaux. But since the tableau contains many zeroes we must choose among these. A criterion for choosing among the zero-cost links is how indispensible they are in terms of costs, that is, by how much costs would increase if that link would not be used in a tour. Take the element (1,2) which is zero. If the link (1,2) is not used, some other link in row 1 would have to be used; the element with least costs other than (1,2) is that of (1,3) which has 2 as costs; furthermore some other link in column 2 would have to be used; the element with least costs other than (1,2) is that of (3.2) with cost 17. This means that if (1,2) is not used, the lower bound on the costs of the tour would increase by at least $2 + 17 = 19$. This number is entered as a superscript to the zero. The other zero-elements in the Tableau A0 are treated in the same manner. Now the link with zero costs having the largest superindex, that is the most indispensable link is chosen for inclusion in the tour. In Tableau A0 this is link (4,5), where the zero-element has the superindex 65, meaning that if (4,5) is not included in the tour the lower

---

[1] The superscript of the zero-elements should for a moment be disregarded.

bound on costs would be at least 65 higher, so that the lower bound would be 202 + 65 = 267.

If link (4,5) is used in a tour, it should be decided which other links to use. If we go from 4 to 5, we do not have to go from 4 to any other city or from any other city to 5, so that the row 4 and column 5 of the cost tableau may be deleted. This results in the costs given in the first entries in Tableau A1. If the link (4,5) is used, the link (5,4) cannot be used because the sub-tour 4,5,4, would be created in this manner, which would not be connected with other nodes. Hence a dash is entered for the link (5,4).

Since in Tableau A1 some links have disappeared, a further reduction in costs may be possible. This is indeed the case; it turns out that 21 may be subtracted from row 5 and 42 from column 4; this means that if link (4,5) is used, costs are going to be at least 202 + 21 + 42 = 265. Hence we have the alternative of using links (4,5), giving a lower bound of costs of 265, or not using it, giving a lower bound of costs of 267. The alternative may be depicted as follows:

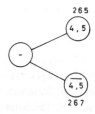

where $\overline{4,5}$ means not using link (4,5).

If link (4,5) is used, other links to be used in the tour must be found. One of the links with zero costs in Tableau A1 should be used, but there are a number of these. Again the increase in the lower bound of costs is deter-mined if each one of these links is not used. Hence if link (1,2) is not used, there would be at least a cost of 2 coming from city 1 and at least a cost of 10 going to city 2, so that 2 + 10 = 12 is entered as a superindex to the cost of link (1,2). The zero-element with the highest superindex belongs to link (2,1), so that the possibility of including or not including link (2,1) is con-sidered. If (2,1) is not included the lower bound on costs is 265 + 15 = 280. If (2,1) is included, a new tableau can be formed in which row 2 and column 1 is deleted, because no link is required from city 2 or to city 1. Further-more, the link (1,2) should be excluded, otherwise the subtour 2,1,2 could be created. In this way Tableau A2 is found from Tableau A1. Some further reduction in costs is possible; 5 may be subtracted from row 1 and 10 from column 2, which results in a lower bound for costs of $265 + 2 + 1 - = 277$. The alternatives considered so far can be indicated by the following decision tree.

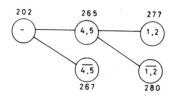

We go on to consider the alternative with link $(1,2)$. In Tableau A2 the zero-elements are given superindices as indicated before and the link with zero costs having the maximum superindex is chosen, which is link $(5,2)$ with a superindex of 14. This means that not taking link $(5,2)$ has costs of at least $277 + 14 = 291$. Row 5 and column 2 are deleted from Tableau A2, which results in Tableau A3. In order to avoid subtour $5,2,5$, link $(2,5)$ should be excluded, but it does not occur in the tableau anyway. Further the sub-tours $4,5,2,4$ should not be possible so that link $(2,4)$ should be excluded; also the subtour $5,2,1,5$ should not be possible, so that link $(1,5)$ should be excluded; finally the subtour $4,5,2,1,4$ should be impossible, so that link $(1,4)$ should be excluded. Only link $(1,4)$ has to be explicitly excluded. No further cost reduction is possible, so that the lower bound of costs for in-clusion of link $(5,2)$ remains at 277. The alternative of taking link $(5,2)$ or not can be found in the decision tree of Figure 1, which is the decision tree for the entire problem.

In Tableau A3 the superindices of the zeroes are determined in the usual manner. Then link $(3,6)$ is considered. Tableau A4 is generated which leads to the further links $(1,3)$ and $(6,4)$. The decision tree is expanded accordingly. Now we have found the tour $1,3,6,4,5,2,1$ at a total cost of 277. Is this the minimum-cost tour? Not necessarily, because if the alternatives are checked it is found that not choosing link $(4,5)$ at the start has a lower bound of 267, which is less than 277. All other alternatives with lower bounds higher than 277 need not be considered.

In order to develop the alternative in which $(4,5)$ is not chosen, Tableau A0 is taken (the last entries) but $(4,5)$ is excluded. This results in Tableau B0. After cost reduction, a lower bound of 267 is found, which is, of course, the same as found before. The zeroes are given superindices in the manner de-scribed before and the link with the highest superindex is selected which is $(5,4)$. The remaining links of the tour are found as described for the tour

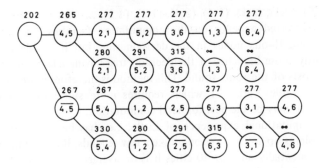

Fig. 3.

including (4,5). Successively Tableaux B1, B2, B3, and B4 are found and the decision tree is completed accordingly.

The resulting tour is 1,2,5,4,6,3,1, which is, as can be expected because fares are the same in the opposite direction, the tour found before in reverse order. This kind of duplication could have been avoided if in the decision tree the branch 5,4 was ignored because it is bound to lead to the tour of the branch 4,5 in reverse order.

Hence, the least-cost tour turns out to be London, New York, Buenos Aires, Tokyo, Sydney, Moscow, London or the same tour in reverse order. This is slightly different from what one would expect from a cursory inspection of the globe. Total costs of this tour are $2.770.

Now the method will be described in a more complete manner. The starting point of the method is the cost or distance tableau. This tableau is reduced so that at least one zero appears in each row and each column and the zeroes are given superindices. Then the link with a zero having the largest superindex is chosen. The row and column of this link are deleted and links leading to subtours are excluded. The resulting tableau is treated in the same manner. This results in a tour with given costs. If there is any alternative in the corresponding decision tree having a smaller lower bound than the costs of this chain, then this alternative is developed until a lower bound is reached which is higher than the costs of tour found before or until a new tour is found with lower costs than the first tour. If in the last case there are alternatives with smaller lower bounds the tour with the lowest costs, these alternatives are developed in the same fashion.

Instaed of always going down the decision tree at the upper branch, Variant II of the branch-and-bound method, it is also possible to use Variant I. In that case we would have chosen the following sequence of nodes: (0),

(4,5), ($\overline{4,5}$), (2,1), ($\overline{2,1}$), (5,4), ($\overline{5,4}$), (1,2), ($\overline{1,2}$), ... Which of both methods is to be preferred depends on the computation facilities. Variant II may compute superfluous nodes in the decision tree, but it is able to cut out permanently those branches of the decision tree having a larger lower bound than the costs of the route found. This method is therefore more suitable for computers, while Variant I which requires more storage places but less computations may be the best for hand computation.

The computational experience of Little, c.s., has been that on an IBM 7090 problems up to 20 cities only take a few seconds. But the time required grows exponentially and for 40 cities it is on average a little over 8 minutes. As a rule of thumb, adding 10 cities multiplies the time by a factor 10.

Exercises

1. In six successive weeks the following quantities should be produced

Week:	1	2	3	4	5	6
Quantity:	22	38	31	18	15	48

Production in any week requires a set-up with costs of $40; once a set-up has been made, an unlimited quantity can be produced. Inventory costs are $1 per unit per week. The objective is to minimize the sum of set-up and inventory costs. Solve this problem by means of branch-and-bound method. *Hint*: Consider the situation in which there are set-ups in every week without costs. Then for one week either pay the set-up cost or do not produce. Continuing from these alternatives, do the same for other weeks.

2. A company wants to set up productive facilities in Western Canada. Yearly demands for its products in the various centers as well as distances are given below. The investment in establsihing production in a center are estimated at $320,000, the interest rate is assumed to be $12\frac{1}{2}\%$. Transportation costs are assumed to be $0.10 per mile per unit. By means of a branch-and-bound method determine where the productive facilities should be set up to minimize the sum of interest and transportation cost.

	Quantities demanded	C	E	V	R
			distances in miles		
Calgary	370				
Edmonton	450	183			
Vancouver	650	648	835		
Regina	220	473	497	1121	
Winnipeg	550	827	850	1475	354

3. Solve the travelling salesman problem based on the following distance table in kilometres.

	Paris	Calais	Nantes	Limoges	Lyon	Reims
Paris	—	293	392	375	459	165
Calais		—	661	668	752	304
Nantes			—	296	649	557
Limoges				—	363	540
Lyon					—	477
Reims						—

4. Suppose a tourist wants to visit all cities of problem 3, beginning in Calais and ending up in Lyon. Develop a method for finding the route which minimizes the total distance travelled.

5. A soft drink company is considered setting up production in various parts of Canada, namely the Maritimes, Quebec, Ontario, the Prairies and British Columbia. The fixed costs per year are given below. The company can produce four products A, B, C, and D; if any product is produced at all Product A should always be in the production program if production is set up. It is impossible to sell any product anywhere without national advertising; yearly costs of marketing are for A $350,000 and for the other products $200,000. Sales estimates for each product in each region are given below. Profit on product A is $500 per unit, on B $400 per unit, on C $300 per unit and on D $200 per unit.
(a) Try to reduce the possibilities to be considered.
(b) Use Variant II of the branch-and-bound method to determine the optimal plant location and product selection program.

		Mar.	Que.	Ont.	Prair.	B.C.
Fixed costs (000$)		100	110	140	120	130
Expected sales (000)	A	80	500	800	150	100
	B	90	150	200	150	150
	C	90	300	250	50	40
	D	160	200	100	150	300

16. BRANCH-AND-BOUND METHODS FOR INTEGER PROGRAMMING

16.1. The Fixed-Charge Problem

The methods treated in Chapter 15 were unrelated to linear programming. In the present chapter linear programming and branch-and-bound methods will be combined to yield methods for integer programming. It should be emphasized that the integer programming method treated here is only one of the many existing methods. However, for an understanding of the structure of a problem, a detailed treatment of one method of solution will be of considerable use. Once a method is fully understood, it is not too difficult to comprehend an alternative method quickly.

Three problems will be treated of increasing complexity. The fixed-charge problem is a relatively simple problem which can be formulated as a zero-one integer programming problem but which can be better solved as it is. The zero-one integer programming problem is the most common integer problem; the general integer problem seems to be less prevalent.

In some problems, the assumption that the revenues and the capacity requirements of a product vary proportionally with the amount produced, an assumption necessary for the application of linear programming, is not valid. Frequently the start of production causes a fixed amount of costs, after which the increase in costs is proportional to the increase in production. For instance, the cost of a product j of which x_j is produced may be

(1.1)
$$C_j = \bar{c}_j + c_j x_j \quad \text{for} \quad x_j > 0,$$
$$C_j = 0 \quad \quad \text{for} \quad x_j = 0;$$

see Figure 1. $\bar{c}_j$ may be called the fixed charge for product j. If the selling price for product j is p_j the revenue for product j is given by f_j:

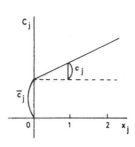

Fig. 1.   Fig. 2.

$$(1.2) \qquad \begin{array}{ll} f_j = -\bar{c}_j + (p_j - c_j)x_j & \text{for} \quad x_j > 0 , \\[2mm] f_j = 0 & \text{for} \quad x_j = 0 ; \end{array}$$

see Figure 2.

It is obvious that cost functions of this sort change the nature of the problem. In addition to the problem of how much should be produced, there is the problem whether to produce or not to produce. Suppose that there is only the product j so that (1.2) is the objective function. If the only constraint is $0 \leq x_j \leq \bar{x}_j$, where $\bar{x}_j$ is a given upper bound of x_j, then from Figure 2 it is obvious that $x_j = 0$ is the optimal solution for any given $\bar{x}_j$ between 0 and the break-even point B and $x_j = \bar{x}_j$ for any $\bar{x}_j$ at least equal to the break-even point. The optimal solution jumps for increasing upper bounds $\bar{x}_j$ from 0 to B at the break-even point without any intermediate values being optimal. If in (1.2), $-\bar{c}_j > 0$, the problem would not arise; in that case the solution $x_j = 0$ would never be optimal unless $\bar{x}_j = 0$.

Apart from direct cost, set-ups may also require production capacity. The production capacity of the i-th production factor used for the j-th product, to be denoted by r_{ij} can be formulated as follows:

$$(1.3) \qquad \begin{array}{ll} r_{ij} = b_{ij} + a_{ij}x_j & \text{for} \quad x_j > 0 , \\[2mm] r_{ij} = 0 & \text{for} \quad x_j = 0 . \end{array}$$

b_{ij} is the fixed charge of product j in terms of capacity of production factor i. Expressions like (1.2) and (1.3) can be written as

$$f_j = q_j + p_j x_j \quad \text{for} \quad x_j > 0 \, ,$$

(1.4)

$$f_j = 0 \qquad\quad \text{for} \quad x_j = 0 \, .$$

An equivalent formulation is

(1.5) $\quad f_j = q_j \delta_j + p_j x_j, \; \delta_j = 0 \text{ or } 1 \, ,$

$$x_j \geq 0 \quad \text{if} \quad \delta_j = 1 \, ,$$

$$x_j = 0 \quad \text{if} \quad \delta_j = 0 \, .$$

This is the formulation which will be used in the following.

For completeness' sake we note that the fixed-charge problem can also be given in the following integer programming formulation:

$$f_j = q_j \delta_j + p_j x_j \, ,$$

(1.6) $\quad x_j \leq k_j \delta_j \, ,$

$$\delta_j = 0 \text{ or } 1 \, .$$

k_j is some upper bound for x_j; if the problem does not contain such an upper bound, we may take for it some large number which x_j is not likely to exceed anyway. For $\delta_j = 0$, $x_j = 0$ according to the second relation. For $\delta_j = 1$, this constraint is not effective since x_j cannot exceed k_j according to the upper-bound constraint. Hence (1.6) is equivalent to (1.5). (1.6) is a part of a general integer programming problem because the condition $\delta_j = 0$ or 1 may be written as

$$0 \leq \delta_j \leq 1 \, ,$$

(1.7)

$$\delta_j = \text{integer} \, .$$

Let us return to our textile company example and assume that the fixed charges (set-up costs) of Yarn A, Yarn B, Fabric A, and Fabric B are 2, 2, 12, and 5, respectively. The set-up times for spinning are $\frac{1}{2}$, $\frac{1}{2}$, 2, and 1 and the set-up times for looms are 0, 0, $\frac{1}{4}$, and $\frac{1}{10}$. This problem can be formulated as follows. Maximize

(1.8) $\qquad f = -2\delta_1 + 9x_1 - 2\delta_2 + 8x_2 - 12\delta_3 + 50x_3 - 5\delta_4 + 19x_4$

Table 1

Tableaux and solutions for an example of the fixed-charge problem

Tableau	Basic variables	Values Basic Variables (−)	(1)	(2)	(3)	(4)	x_1	x_2	x_3	x_4	δ_1	δ_2	δ_3	δ_4
0	f	0					-9	-8	-50	-19	2	2	12	5
	y_1	18					3	2	10	4	$\frac{1}{2}$	$\frac{1}{2}$	2	4
	y_2	3					0	0	$\underline{2}$	$\frac{1}{2}$	0	0	$\frac{1}{4}$	$\frac{1}{2}$

Tableau	Basic variables	Value					x_1	x_2	y_2	x_4	δ_1	δ_2	δ_3	δ_4
1	f	75					-9	-8	25	$-6\frac{1}{2}$	2	2	$18\frac{1}{4}$	$17\frac{1}{2}$
	y_1	3					3	2	-5	$1\frac{1}{2}$	$\frac{1}{2}$	$\frac{1}{2}$	$\frac{3}{4}$	$1\frac{1}{2}$
	x_3	$1\frac{1}{2}$					0	0	$\frac{1}{2}$	$\overline{\frac{1}{4}}$	0	0	$\frac{1}{8}$	$\frac{1}{4}$

Tableau	Basic variables	(−)	(1)	(2)	(3)	(4)	x_1	x_2	y_2	y_1	δ_1	δ_2	δ_3	δ_4
2	f	88	$83\frac{5}{6}$	$83\frac{5}{6}$	$66\frac{1}{2}$	64	4	$\frac{2}{3}$	$3\frac{1}{3}$	$4\frac{1}{3}$	$4\frac{1}{6}$	$4\frac{1}{6}$	$21\frac{1}{2}$	24
	x_4	2	$1\frac{2}{3}$	$1\frac{2}{3}$	$1\frac{1}{2}$	1	2	$1\frac{1}{3}$	$-3\frac{1}{3}$	$\frac{2}{3}$	$\frac{1}{3}$	$\frac{1}{3}$	$\frac{1}{2}$	1
	x_3	1	$1\frac{1}{12}$	$1\frac{1}{12}$	1	1	$-\frac{1}{2}$	$\underline{-\frac{1}{3}}$	$\underline{1\frac{1}{3}}$	$-\frac{1}{6}$	$-\frac{1}{12}$	$-\frac{1}{12}$	0	0

Tableau	Basic variables	$(\bar{3})$					x_1	x_2	x_3	y_1	δ_1	δ_2	δ_3	δ_4
3	f	$85\frac{1}{2}$					$5\frac{1}{4}$	$1\frac{1}{2}$	$-2\frac{1}{2}$	$4\frac{3}{4}$	$4\frac{3}{8}$	$4\frac{3}{8}$	$21\frac{1}{2}$	24
	x_4	$4\frac{1}{2}$					$\frac{3}{4}$	$\frac{1}{2}$	$2\frac{1}{2}$	$\frac{1}{4}$	$\frac{1}{8}$	$\frac{1}{8}$	$\frac{1}{2}$	1
	y_3	$\frac{3}{4}$					$-\frac{3}{8}$	$-\frac{1}{4}$	$\frac{3}{4}$	$-\frac{1}{8}$	$-\frac{1}{16}$	$-\frac{1}{16}$	0	0

Table 1 (continued)

Tableau 4 — Basic variables: $f,\ x_2,\ x_3$

Basic variables	$(\bar 4)$	$(4,3,1)$	$(\bar 4,2)$	$(4,3)$	x_1	x_4	y_2	y_1	δ_1	δ_2	δ_3	δ_4
f	87	83	83	$65\frac{3}{4}$	3	$-\frac{1}{2}$	5	4	4	4	$21\frac{1}{4}$	$23\frac{1}{2}$
x_2	$1\frac{1}{2}$	$1\frac{1}{4}$	$1\frac{1}{4}$	$1\frac{1}{8}$	$1\frac{1}{2}$	$\frac{3}{4}$	$-2\frac{1}{2}$	$\frac{1}{2}$	$\frac{1}{4}$	$\frac{1}{4}$	$\frac{3}{8}$	$\frac{3}{4}$
x_3	$1\frac{1}{2}$	$1\frac{1}{2}$	$1\frac{1}{2}$	$1\frac{3}{8}$	0	$\frac{1}{4}$	$\underline{\frac{1}{2}}$	0	0	0	$\frac{1}{8}$	$\frac{1}{4}$

Tableau 5 — Basic variables: $f,\ x_1,\ x_3$

Basic variables	$(\bar 4,\bar 2)$	x_2	x_4	y_2	y_1	δ_1	δ_2	δ_3	δ_4
f	84	-2	-2	10	3	$3\frac{1}{2}$	$3\frac{1}{2}$	$20\frac{1}{2}$	22
x_1	1	$\frac{2}{3}$	$\frac{1}{2}$	$-1\frac{2}{3}$	$\frac{1}{3}$	$\frac{1}{6}$	$\frac{1}{6}$	$\frac{1}{4}$	$\frac{1}{2}$
x_3	$1\frac{1}{2}$	0	$\frac{1}{4}$	$-\frac{1}{2}$	0	0	0	$\frac{1}{8}$	$\frac{1}{4}$

Tableau 6 — Basic variables: $f,\ x_2,\ y_2$

Basic variables	$(\bar 4,\bar 3)$	$(\bar 4,3,1)$	$(\bar 4,3,2)$	$(\bar 4,3,2,1)$	$(\bar 4,3,2,1)$	x_1	x_4	x_3	y_1	δ_1	δ_2	δ_3	δ_4
f	72	68	68	64	64	3	-3	-10	4	4	4	20	21
x_2	9	$8\frac{3}{4}$	$8\frac{3}{4}$	$8\frac{1}{2}$	$8\frac{1}{2}$	$1\frac{1}{2}$	2	5	$\frac{1}{2}$	$\frac{1}{4}$	$\frac{1}{4}$	1	2
y_2	3	0	3	3	3	0	$\frac{1}{2}$	2	0	0	0	$\frac{1}{4}$	$\frac{1}{2}$

Tableau 7 — Basic variables: $f,\ x_1,\ y_1$

Basic variables	$(\bar 4,3,2)$	x_2	x_4	x_3	y_1	δ_1	δ_2	δ_3	δ_4
f	54	-2	-7	-20	3	$3\frac{1}{2}$	$3\frac{1}{2}$	18	17
x_1	6	$\frac{2}{3}$	$1\frac{1}{3}$	$3\frac{1}{3}$	$\frac{1}{3}$	$\frac{1}{6}$	$\frac{1}{6}$	$\frac{2}{3}$	$1\frac{1}{3}$
y_1	3	0	$\frac{1}{2}$	1	0	0	0	$\frac{1}{4}$	$\frac{1}{2}$

subject to

(1.9) $\frac{1}{2}\delta_1 + 3x_1 + \frac{1}{2}\delta_2 + 2x_2 + 2\delta_3 + 10x_3 + \delta_4 + 4x_4 \leqq 18$,

(1.10) $\frac{1}{4}\delta_3 + 2x_3 + \frac{1}{10}\delta_4 + \frac{1}{2}x_4 \leqq 3$,

(1.11) $x_1, x_2, x_3, x_4 \geqq 0$,

          $\delta_1, \delta_2, \delta_3, \delta_4 = 0$ or 1 ,

(1.12) $x_j \geqq 0$ if $\delta_j = 1$,

$$j = 1, 2, 3, 4 .$$

          $x_j = 0$ if $\delta_j = 0$.

This is the formulation which will be used for the solution of the problem. As indicated before, the problem can be formulated as an integer problem, but this will enlarge the problem by means of the addition of the constraints of the type $x_j \leqq k_j \delta_j$, which will complicate the solution of the problem. Of course, if a computer program is available for integer programming, while no computer program can be found for the fixed-charge problem, the integer programming formulation can be useful.

We shall now describe an application of the branch-and-bound method to the problem (1.8)–(1.12). First the optimal solution of the problem without constraint (1.12) should be found, after which the constraints of (1.12) are imposed one by one.

Tableau 0 of Table 1 gives the set-up tableau for the problem. In two iterations the optimal solution for the problem in which the constraints (1.12) are disregarded is obtained, see the first solution indicated by (–) in Tableau 2. This solution does not satisfy the fixed-charge constraints (1.12) because x_3 and x_4 are nonzero while δ_3 and δ_4 are zero. It is obvious that if the solution (–) had satisfied the fixed-charge constraints the optimal solution would have been obtained.

Now the fixed-charge constraints (1.12) are successively imposed. Any of the four constraints of (1.12) can be imposed, which means that the optimal solution for $\delta_j = 0$, $x_j = 0$ and that for $\delta_j = 1$, $x_j \geqq 0$ are generated if constraint j is imposed. Let us consider imposing the first constraint. For $\delta_1 = 0$, $x_1 = 0$, the optimal solution (–) does not change; it remains as given in Tableau 2. The solution for $\delta_1 = 1$ is obtained by subtracting the elements of the column of δ_1 from the elements of the column (–); in terms of the underlying equation system, this is explained by taking the term in δ_1 to the left side of the equation system and putting $\delta_1 = 1$. The result is

$$f = 83^5/_6 \, ,$$

(1.13) $x_4 = 1^2/_3 \, ,$

$$x_3 = 1^1/_{12} \, .$$

If any of the basic variables apart from f would have been negative, a feasible and optimal solution can be obtained by using the dual method. Hence, proceeding from the optimal solution without any fixed-charge constraint, the fixed-charge constraint 1 is imposed by considering the optimal solution with $\delta_1 = 0$, $x_1 = 0$ and the optimal solution with $\delta_1 = 1$, $x_j \geq 0$. In the first case $f = 88$ and in the second case $f = 83^5/_6$. This situation is indicated by the following decision tree

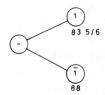

In this tree $(\bar{1})$ indicates the optimal solution with $\delta_1 = 0$ and $x_1 = 0$ and (1) the optimal solution with $\delta_1 = 1, x_1 \geq 0$.

On both solutions other fixed-charge constraints may be imposed in the same manner. In this way a decision tree may be built up, giving as its ultimate tips the solutions in which all fixed-charge constraints are imposed, if these solutions exist. The values of the objective function could be compared for these solutions and the solutions with the maximum value of the objective functions could be selected. This, of course, amounts to a complete enumeration of optimal solutions for all combinations of possibilities for the fixed-charge constraint. It should be attempted to improve upon this.

This can be done by the branch-and-bound method by not exploring all branches of the tree but only those with the maximum value of the objective function. Then the problem remains which constraint to impose at each node. As in the traveling-salesman problem, the constraint having the most discriminative power in terms of the objective function can be chosen. Hence for each fixed-charge constraint j not yet imposed, the value of f for the optimal solution with $\delta_j = 0$ and $x_j = 0$, which is indicated by $f_{\bar{j}}$, is computed and the value of f for the optimal solution with $\delta_j = 1$ and $x_j \geq 0$, which is indicated by f_j is computed. Then the constraint corresponding with

(1.14) $$\underset{j}{\text{Max}} \ |f_{\bar{j}} - f_j|$$

is first imposed.

In the following, problems and their optimal solutions will be indicated by the combinations of constraints. Thus problem $(1,\bar{2},4)$ is the problem with $\delta_1 = 1, x_1 \geqq 0, \delta_2 = 0, x_2 = 0$, and $\delta_4 = 1, x_4 \geqq 0$. The starting point is solution $(-)$ of Tableau 2. No fixed-charge constraints are imposed on the solution; we should decide which constraint to impose first. The solutions of problem $(\bar{1})$ and problem (1) were obtained above, so that $f_{\bar{1}} = 88, f_1 = 83^5/_6$ and $|f_{\bar{1}} - f_1| = 4^1/_6$. For constraint 2 we find exactly the same results in the same manner: $f_{\bar{2}} = 88, f_2 = 83^5/_6$ and $|f_{\bar{2}} - f_2| = 4^1/_6$.

Now constraint 3 should be imposed on solution $(-)$. First the case $\delta_3 = 0$ and $x_3 = 0$ is considered. Since x_3 is a basic variable with a nonzero value in solution $(-)$, it should disappear from the basis. In the dual method a negative basic variable was eliminated from the basis in such a way that the optimality in the narrow sense was preserved. In this case a positive basic variable has to be eliminated in such a way that the optimality in the narrow sense is preserved, but this case can be reduced to that of the dual method. The equation of x_3 in Tableau 2 for solution $(-)$ can be written as follows.

(1.15) $$1 = -^1/_2 x_1 - ^1/_3 x_2 + 1^1/_3 y_2 - ^1/_6 y_1 - ^1/_{12}\delta_1 - ^1/_{12}\delta_2 + x_3 .$$

Let us define $x_3^* = -x_3$. Then (1.15) can be written as

(1.16) $$-1 = ^1/_2 x_1 + ^1/_3 x_2 - 1^1/_3 y_2 + ^1/_6 y_1 + ^1/_{12}\delta_1 + ^1/_{12}\delta_2 + x_3^* .$$

The third row of Tableau 2 can be altered accordingly. The dual method may now be applied to the resulting solution, which means that we select as the new basic variable the nonbasic variable corresponding to

(1.17) $$\underset{j}{\text{Min}} \left(\frac{a_{0j}}{-a_{rj}} \ \middle| \ a_{rj} < 0 \right) .$$

The same result can be obtained if the transition from (1.15) to (1.16) does not occur by selecting the new basic variable according to

(1.18) $$\underset{j}{\text{Min}} \left(\frac{a_{0j}}{a_{rj}} \ \middle| \ a_{rj} > 0 \right) .$$

Hence in Tableau 2, y_2 is selected as the new basic variable which replaces

x_3. The result is Tableau 3. The solution of this tableau is optimal in the narrow sense, which is necessarily so if (1.18) is applied; the x_3-element in the f-row is negative but x_3 is constrained to zero. The values of basic variables are not necessarily nonnegative; if some negative values are found, the dual method is applied until a feasible and optimal solution is found. It is possible that no feasible solution can be found, in which case the branch concerned should be ignored for that node. In Tableau 3, the values of basic variables are nonnegative, so that no further iterations are necessary; hence Tableau 3 constains the solution to problem $(\bar{3})$. Hence $f_{\bar{3}} = 85\frac{1}{2}$.

The solution to problem (3) is found in Tableau 2 by subtracting the elements of the δ_3-column from those of column $(-)$, since there are no negative basic variables, no iterations of the dual method are necessary. Hence $f_3 = 66\frac{1}{2}$ and $|f_{\bar{3}} - f_3| = 19$.

The solution of problem $(\bar{4})$ is found in the same way as that of problem $(\bar{3})$. In order to find the new basic variable in Tableau 2 which replaces x_4, we have to compare

$$(1.19) \qquad \mathrm{Min}\left(\frac{2}{4}, \frac{{}^2\!/_3}{1\,{}^1\!/_3}, \frac{4\,{}^1\!/_3}{{}^2\!/_3}\right) = \frac{{}^2\!/_3}{1\,{}^1\!/_3}\,,$$

so that x_2 enters the basic replacing x_4. The resulting tableau, Tableau 4 gives the optimal solution for problem $(\bar{4})$, so that $f_{\bar{4}} = 87$. The optimal solution to problem (4) is found by subtracting in Tableau 2 the elements of column δ_4 from those of column $(-)$; the resulting solution is nonnegative so that $f_4 = 64$. Hence $|f_{\bar{4}} - f_4| = 23$.

Determining

$$(1.20) \qquad \mathrm{Max}_j\, |f_{\bar{j}} - f_j| = \mathrm{Max}\,(4\frac{1}{6}, 4\frac{1}{6}, 19, 23) = 23\,,$$

we decide that fixed-charge constraint 4 should be imposed first on solution $(-)$. The beginning of the decision tree is therefore

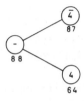

In the following the decision tree is explored along the best branches

until the top of the tree is reached, after which possible alternative branches having higher values of f than those at the top are searched; this means that we are following Variant II of the branch-and-bound method. Hence solution $(\bar{4})$ of Tableau 4 should be considered. Which of the three remaining fixed-charge constraints should first be imposed? For solution $(\bar{4})$ we determine as we did for solution $(-)$: solution $(\bar{4},\bar{1})$ is identical to solution $(\bar{4})$, so that $f_{\bar{1}} = 87$. Solution $(\bar{4},1)$ is found by subtracting the δ_1-column from column $(\bar{4})$, so that $f_1 = 83$. Hence $|f_{\bar{1}}-f_1| = 4$. Since x_2 is a basic variable in solution $(\bar{4})$, an iteration of the (modified) dual method is necessary, see Tableau 5, which gives the solution $(\bar{4},\bar{2})$. Solution $(4,2)$ is found by subtracting the δ_2-column from column $(\bar{4})$; $f_2 = 83$. Hence $|f_{\bar{2}}-f_2| = 1$. To find solution $(\bar{4},\bar{3})$, an iteration of the dual method is necessary, see Tableau 6. $f_{\bar{3}} = 72$. Solution $(\bar{4},3)$ is obtained by subtracting the f_3-column from column $(\bar{4})$; $f_3 = 65^3/_4$ and $|f_{\bar{3}}-f_3| = 6^1/_4$. Then we determine

$$(1.21) \qquad \operatorname*{Max}_{j} |f_{\bar{j}}-f_j| = \operatorname{Max}(4, 1, 6^1/_4) = 6^1/_4 \ ,$$

which means that constraint 3 should be imposed first. The decision tree is now

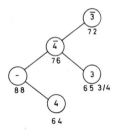

We proceed from solution $(\bar{4},\bar{3})$. The solution of problem $(\bar{4},\bar{3},\bar{1})$ is identical to that of solution $(\bar{4},\bar{3})$ so that $f_{\bar{1}} = 72$. We easily find $f_1 = 68$, so that $|f_{\bar{1}}-f_1| = 4$. The solution to problem $(\bar{4},\bar{3},\bar{2})$ is found by eliminating x_2 from the basis in Tableau 6; from Tableau 7 we have $f_{\bar{2}} = 54$. We easily find $f_2 = 68$, so that $|f_{\bar{2}}-f_2| = 14$. These are the only two constraints not yet imposed. After determining

$$(1.22) \qquad \operatorname*{Max}_{j} |f_{\bar{j}}-f_j| = \operatorname{Max}(4, 14) = 14 \ ,$$

it is decided that constraint 2 should be imposed. For the present state of the decision tree, see Figure 3, of which the two highest nodes should be ignored.

Since $68 > 54$, we proceed from solution $(\bar{4},\bar{3},2)$. Now only constraint

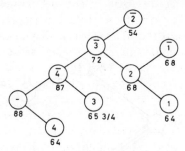

Fig. 3.

1 remains to be imposed. The solution of problem $(\overline{4},\overline{3},2,\overline{1})$ is the same as that of problem $(\overline{4},\overline{3},2)$ and the solution to problem $(\overline{4},\overline{3},2,1)$ is easily found. These solutions are entered in the decision tree of Figure 3, which is now completely described. The best solution found so far which satisfied all fixed-charge constraints is $(\overline{4},\overline{3},2,\overline{1})$ with $f = 68$.

Now other branches should be searched in order to find solutions which might be better or cutting off these branches because they lead to smaller values of f. From solution $(\overline{4},\overline{3},2,\overline{1})$, having checked before that solution $(\overline{4},\overline{3},2,1)$ has a smaller value, we go over solution $(\overline{4},\overline{3},2)$ to solution $(\overline{4},\overline{3})$ where we have a look at solution $(\overline{4},\overline{3},\overline{2})$. This solution has a value of 54, so that this solution and the solutions resulting from imposing more constraints on it (which only leads to lower values) can be ignored. Moving further down, we arrive at solution $(\overline{4})$ and then to solution $(\overline{4},3)$ with value $65^3/_4$. Since this is smaller than 68, we can ignore this solution and the solutions resulting from it by imposing more constraints.

Via solution $(-)$ we arrive at solution 4, with value 64, which is smaller than 68, so that this solution and solutions resulting from it by imposing further constraints may be ignored. Since no branches are remaining, solution $(\overline{4},\overline{3},2,\overline{1})$ with value 68 must be the optimal solution to the fixed-charge problem.

Instead of always going upwards in the decision tree, Variant II, it is also possible to branch out always at the node with the highest value of the objective function, Variant I. In this case the optimal solution is found after the top has been reached; no going down the tree afterwards is necessary. This method requires more memory space but less computations than the former approach.

Note that a large number of elements of the tableaux of Table 1 are not used at all; for instance, the columns of x_j and δ_j when $\delta_j = 0$ is imposed are

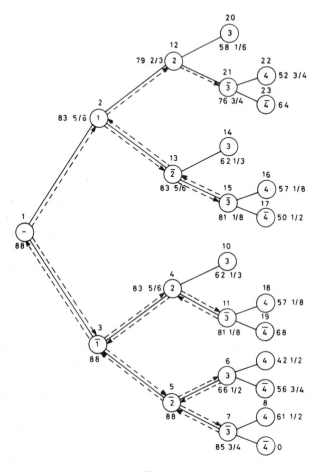

Fig. 4.

quite superfluous. In general, substantial computational savings can be obtained by only generating columns when they are necessary.

If a different rule is used for the selection of the fixed-charge constraint to be imposed on a given solution, the decision tree may be quite different. It might be thought that basing the selection of these constraints on the resulting difference of the objective function is rather elaborate computationally. Figure 4 gives the decision tree which would have been obtained if at each node the constraints are imposed in the order 1,2,3,4. The dashed lines with the arrows give the sequence in which nodes are generated; at each node it is supposed that the two nodes obtained by imposing a fixed-charge constraint are generated. From $(-)$ we go to $(\bar{1})$, then to $(\bar{2})$, then to $(\bar{3})$, and then to (4); there a solution is reached satisfying all fixed-charge constraints, with $f = 61\frac{1}{2}$. Now we go back to $(\bar{2})$ and go to (3) since it has $f = 66\frac{1}{2}$. Since the end nodes have lower values than $61\frac{1}{2}$, we go back to $(\bar{2})$, then back to $(\bar{1})$, from there we branch upwards to (2) since it has $f = 83\frac{5}{6}$, from there upwards to $(\bar{3})$ with $f = 81\frac{1}{8}$. An end node is found there with $f = 68$, so that this is the lower bound of the objective function. We go back to (2); here the upward branch (3) with $f = 62\frac{1}{3}$ is cut off since $62\frac{1}{3} < 68$. We go back to $\bar{1}$, then since the other upward branch already has been searched, back to $(-)$, then upwards to the other branch (1), then upwards to the best branch $(\bar{2})$. Here the upward branch (3) is cut off since $62\frac{1}{3} < 68$. We go upwards to $(\bar{3})$ and find that its end nodes have lower values than 68. Hence we go back from $(\bar{3})$ to $(\bar{2})$, then since the other upward branch has been cut off, back to (1), then upwards to (2). The upwards branch (3) is cut off since $58\frac{1}{6} < 68$. We go upwards to $(\bar{3})$ and find that its end nodes have lower values than 68. Now all branches of the decision tree have been cut off, so that the optimal solution of the fixed-charge problem must have been the solution with $f = 68$. This is the solution of the problem $(\bar{1},2,\bar{3},\bar{4})$.

Instead of Variant II, we could have used Variant I, always branching out from the node having the highest value of f. The sequence of nodes generated in this manner is given by the numbers above the nodes. In this case, the number of nodes generated is decreased by 2, but it is still substantial.

The number of nodes generated if the constraint sequence 1,2,3,4 is used is 25 or 23, which is more than the number of solutions to be computed for complete enumeration, which is $2^4 = 16$. Though this may not be typical, especially since only a small example was used, it illustrates the fact that branch-and-bound methods are not always efficient. It also indicates that the use of the "greatest difference of f" criterion for the selection of constraints to be imposed can be very effective.

16.2. The Zero-One Integer Problem

In the zero-one integer problem, the integer variables can only take the values zero and one, while in general integer problems the integer variables can take any nonnegative integer value (subject, of course, to any possible linear constraints). It should be noted that general integer programming problems can be formulated as zero-one problems by substituting for any integer variable x_j according to

(2.1) $x_j = z_{j1} + z_{j2} + ... + z_{jb}$, $z_{ji} = 0$ or 1 , $i = 1, ..., b$,

where b is any existing or assumed integer upper bound for x_j. However, this reformulation is not of great use; it is better to develop different, though similar methods for zero-one problems and general problems. Most integer programming problems turn out to be of the zero-one type. First a method for these problems will be explained.

In the branch-and-bound method for the zero-one integer problem, first the optimal solution is determined for the problem in which the integer constraints have been replaced by constraints of the type $0 \leqq x_j \leqq 1$. Then the zero-one constraints are successively imposed on the solution in the manner indicated before.

For a more detailed explanation the following example is used. Maximize

(2.2) $f = \frac{1}{4}x_1 + \frac{1}{2}x_2 + x_3 + 2x_4$

subject to

(2.3)
$$\frac{1}{2}x_1 + x_2 + x_3 + 2x_4 \leqq 1\frac{3}{4} ,$$
$$x_1 + x_2 + \frac{3}{10}x_3 + \frac{3}{5}x_4 \leqq 1\frac{1}{2} ,$$

(2.4) $x_1, x_2, x_3, x_4 = 0$ or 1 .

First the ordinary linear programming problem is solved in which the constraints (4) are replaced by

(2.5) $0 \leqq x_1, x_2, x_3, x_4 \leqq 1$.

Tableau 0 of Table 2 is the set-up tableau for this problem. The upper-bound constraints of (2.5) will be taken into account in an implicit way. One iteration of the simplex method yields the optimal solution, see Tableau 1.

Now the zero-one constraints should be imposed. The constraint to be imposed first can be determined according to various criteria. As in the traveling-salesman problem and the fixed-charge problem the constraint could be taken which gives the greatest difference in f for 0 or 1 of the variable concerned. A somewhat simpler rule is to take the basic integer

Table 2
Tableaux for the zero-one integer problem

Tableau	Basic variables	Values Basic Variables			x_1	x_2	x_3	x_4
0	f	0			$-\frac{1}{4}$	$-\frac{1}{2}$	-1	-2
	y_1	$1\frac{3}{4}$			$\frac{1}{2}$	1	1	2
	y_2	$1\frac{1}{2}$			1	2	$\frac{3}{10}$	$\frac{3}{5}$

Tableau	Basic variables	$x_3=1$			x_1	x_2	x_3^*	y_1
1	f	$1\frac{3}{4}$	$1\frac{3}{4}$		$\frac{1}{4}$	$\frac{1}{2}$	0	1
	x_4	$\frac{7}{8}$	$\frac{3}{8}$		$\frac{1}{4}$	$\frac{1}{2}$	$\frac{1}{2}$	$\frac{1}{2}$
	y_2	$\frac{39}{40}$	$\frac{39}{40}$		$\frac{17}{20}$	$1\frac{7}{10}$	0	$-\frac{3}{10}$

Tableau	Basic variables	$x_3=1$			x_1		x_3^*	y_1
2	f	$1\frac{3}{8}$			0		$-\frac{1}{2}$	$\frac{1}{2}$
	x_2	$\frac{3}{4}$			$\frac{1}{2}$		1	1
	y_2	$-\frac{3}{10}$			0		$-1\frac{7}{10}$	$\underline{-2}$

Tableau	Basic variables	$x_3=1$	$x_3=0$	$x_1=1$ $x_3=1$	x_1^*		x_3^*	y_2
3	f	$1\frac{3}{10}$	$\frac{3}{8}$	$1\frac{3}{10}$	0		$-3\frac{7}{40}$	$\frac{1}{4}$
	x_2	$\frac{3}{5}$	$\frac{3}{4}$	$\frac{1}{10}$	$\frac{1}{2}$		$\frac{3}{20}$	$\frac{1}{2}$
	y_1	$\frac{3}{20}$	1	$\frac{3}{20}$	0		$\frac{17}{20}$	$-\frac{1}{2}$

Tableau	Basic variables	$x_1=1$ $x_3=1$			x_1^*		x_3^*	
4	f	$1\frac{1}{4}$			$-\frac{1}{4}$		-1	
	y_2	$\frac{1}{5}$			1		$\frac{3}{10}$	
	y_1	$\frac{1}{4}$			$\frac{1}{2}$		1	

variable having the largest difference from 0 or 1. This rule is used in the following. In Tableau 1, the only basic integer variable is x_4, so that the optimal solutions for $x_4 = 0$ and for $x_4 = 1$ are considered. For $x_4 = 0$, x_4 should become nonbasic; the new basic variable is determined by

$$(2.6) \qquad \text{Min} \quad \frac{1/4}{1/4}, \frac{1/2}{1/2}, \frac{0}{1/2}, \frac{1}{1/2} = 0 .$$

Hence x_3 should replace x_4, but if this happens the value of x_3 is

$$\frac{\tfrac{7}{8}}{\tfrac{1}{2}} = 1\tfrac{3}{4} \; ,$$

which exceeds the upper bound of x_3. Hence x_3 is put equal to 1, which is done by subtracting the elements of the column of x_3 from the values of basic variables, yielding new values of basic variables. Now the third ratio in (2.6) is ruled out, so that the smaller ratio is 1, which belongs both to x_1 and x_2. Let us take x_2 as the new basic variable replacing x_4. The result is Tableau 2, in which the x_4-column is deleted since in this and in subsequent solutions x_4 should remain zero. In this solution y_3 has a negative value, so that the dual method is used to eliminate this variable from the basis. The new basic variable turns out to be y_1. In Tableau 3 the optimal solution with $x_4 = 0$ is obtained; it has $f = 1\tfrac{3}{10}$.

Now the optimal solution with $x_4 = 1$ should be determined. Hence x_4 should be increased in Tableau 1. This can be done only if there is at least one negative element in the row of x_4 (think of the optimality criterion in the simplex method). Since there is no negative element in this row, x_4 cannot be increased and any solution with $x_4 = 1$ is infeasible. The value of f for $x_4 = 1$ may then be put at $-\infty$. The decision tree is now

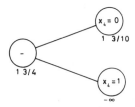

Now we should branch from the node $x_4 = 0$, the solution of which is given by Tableau 3. In this solution x_2 is the only basic integer variable, so that we should consider the optimal solutions for $x_4 = 0$, $x_2 = 0$ and $x_4 = 0$, $x_2 = 1$. For the first solution x_2 should be decreased. The new basic variable is determined according to

$$(2.7) \qquad \text{Min} \left(\frac{0}{\tfrac{1}{2}}, \frac{\tfrac{1}{4}}{\tfrac{1}{2}} \right) = 0 \; .$$

Note that for x_3 no ratio is taken, since it is put at its upper bound, so that it cannot be increased. x_1 should be the new basic variable, but if it replaces x_2, its value is $1\tfrac{1}{6}$, which exceeds 1. x_1 is put at its upper bound by subtracting the elements of its column from the values of basic variables. After this y_2 is the only nonbasic variable eligible which therefore replaces x_2 as a basic variable. This results in the solution of Tableau 4 which has $f = 1\frac{1}{4}$.

For the solution of the problem with $x_4 = 0$, $x_2 = 1$, x_2 should be increased in the first solution of Tableau 3. There is no negative element in the row of x_2, but if x_3 is decreased from its upper bound, x_2 increases. x_3 can be put at 0 again by adding the column of x_3 to that of the values of basic variables. In this way x_2 is increased from $\frac{3}{5}$ to $\frac{3}{4}$. A further increase is impossible, so that there is no feasible solution with $x_4 = 0$, $x_2 = 1$. Hence we may put $f = -\infty$ for this solution. These two branches can be entered into the decision tree, see Figure 5, in which other branches should be disregarded for a moment.

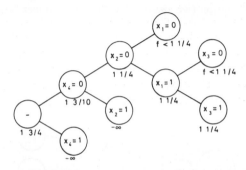

Fig. 5.

Now we should branch out from the optimal solution with $x_4 = 0$, $x_2 = 0$. Since this solution happens to satisfy the other integer constraints ($x_1 = 1$, $x_3 = 1$), other integer values for x_1 and x_3 can only decrease the objective function. The remaining part of the decision tree is therefore easily completed.

From the decision tree and Tableau 4 it is concluded that the optimal solution of the integer problem is $x_1 = 1$, $x_2 = 0$, $x_3 = 1$, $x_4 = 0$, $f = 1\frac{1}{4}$. Note that in this small problem there is no difference between "going up and coming back" which is Variant II and "branching at the node with the maximum upper bound" which is Variant I. In larger problems such a difference will usually occur.

16.3. **The General Integer Problem**

Land and Doig [12] have developed a branch and-bound method for general integer problems which will be explained with some less essential modifications in the following.

The difference with the method for zero-one integer problems is to be found in the branching. In zero-one problems only two branches can be developed at each node. In general integer problems this is no longer true, since the variable of which the integer constraint is to be imposed can take any nonnegative integer value. Let us suppose that in a certain optimal solution with no or only some integer constraints imposed, the integer variable x_j has the value $4^2/_5$. In principle the following branching may take place from this solution (we assume that there is an upper bound on x_j of 6):

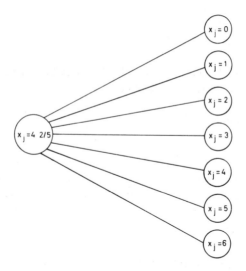

It is important to find out the relations between the values of f for the various optimal solutions. We shall prove that these are as in Figure 8, namely that f decreases or at most remains the same as x_j is decreased from $x_j = 4^2/_5$ or increased from this value.

Suppose that x_1 is the variable on which the integer constraint is imposed and that the tableau of the optimal solution without this integer constraint is

Basic variables	Values basic variables	x_3	x_4	x_5	.
f	a_{00}	a_{01}	a_{02}	a_{03}	.
$x_1(x_1^*)$	$a_{10}(0)$	a_{11}	a_{12}	a_{13}	.
x_2	a_{20}	a_{21}	a_{22}	a_{23}	.
.	.	.	.	.	.

In general, the value of x_1, a_{10} will not be an integer, but this need not be excluded. Let us define $x_1^* = x_1 - a_{10}$. If this is substituted into the equation system underlying the tableau, x_1 is replaced by x_1^* and a_{10} by 0. Let us consider an upward variation of x_1^* in such a way that the optimality of the solution, apart from the variable x_1^*, is preserved. This is done as in the dual method by introducing into the basis the variable corresponding with

$$(3.1) \qquad \min_j \left(\frac{a_{0j}}{-a_{1j}} \,\bigg|\, a_{ij} < 0 \right).$$

Let us assume that the new basic variable found in this manner is x_3, so that a_{11} is used as a pivot. The resulting tableau is

Basic variables	Values basic variables	x_1^*	x_4	x_5	.
f	a_{00}	$-a_{01}a_{11}^{-1}$	$a_{02}-a_{01}a_{11}^{-1}a_{12}$	$a_{03}-a_{01}a_{11}^{-1}a_{12}$	.
x_3	0	a_{11}^{-1}	$a_{11}^{-1}a_{12}$	$a_{11}^{-1}a_{13}$	.
x_2	a_{20}	$-a_{21}a_{11}^{-1}$	$a_{22}-a_{21}a_{11}^{-1}a_{12}$	$a_{23}-a_{21}a_{11}^{-1}a_{13}$	.
.	.	.	.	.	.

Because the new basic variable has been chosen according to (3.1) this is still an optimal solution.

In the equation system underlying the tableau the terms in x_1^* may be moved to the other side of the equation sign. The terms in x_1^* are now considered as a parametric term of the values of basic variables. The resulting tableau may be written in a general notation as follows.

| Basic variables | Values basic variables | | x_4 | x_5 | . |
	$c-t$	$\lambda-t$			
f	a_{00}^*	b_0^*	a_{01}^*	a_{02}^*	.
x_3	a_{10}^*	b_1^*	a_{11}^*	a_{12}^*	.
x_2	a_{20}^*	b_2^*	a_{21}^*	a_{22}^*	.
.	.	.	.	.	.

We have $b_0^* = a_{01}a_{11}^{-1} \leqq 0$. Now $\lambda = x_1 - a_{10}$ is parametrically increased. The leaving basic variable is selected according to

$$(3.2) \qquad \underset{i}{\mathrm{Min}} \left(\frac{a_{i0}^*}{-b_i^*} \,\middle|\, b_i^* < 0 \right) = \frac{a_{r0}^*}{-b_{r0}^*} \quad ,$$

and the new basic variable according to

$$(3.3) \qquad \underset{j}{\mathrm{Min}} \left(\frac{a_{0j}^*}{-a_{rj}^*} \,\middle|\, a_{rj}^* < 0 \right) = \frac{a_{0k}^*}{-a_{rk}^*} \quad .$$

This means that in the following iteration b_0^* is transformed into

$$(3.4) \qquad b_0^* - a_{0k}^* a_{rk}^{*-1} b_r^* \quad .$$

Since $a_{0k}^* \geqq 0$, $a_{rk}^{*-1} < 0$, and $b_r^* < 0$, the λ-term coefficient of the value of f decreases in this and in following iterations. Since $b_0^* \leqq 0$, the slope of f-curve to the right of $\hat{x}_j$ in Figure 6 must be nonpositive and never increases.

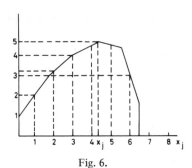

Fig. 6.

If there is no negative element a^*_{rj} in (3.3), the problem has no feasible solution for $\lambda > a^*_{r0}/-b^*_{r0}$; such a case is indicated for $x_j = 6\frac{1}{2}$ in Figure 6.

In a similar way it is proved that f is decreasing for a downward variation of x^*_1. In this case we have instead (3.1):

$$(3.5) \qquad \text{Min}\left(\frac{a_{0j}}{a_{1j}} \middle| a_{1j} > 0\right).$$

Suppose that in this case $a_{11} > 0$ and that the first column corresponds with (3.5). Then $b^*_0 = a_{01}a^{-1}_{11} \geq 0$ and the coefficient of the λ-term of the value of f is again given by (3.4), but in this case $b^*_r > 0$ so that this coefficient is nondecreasing for decreasing values of x^*_1. This implies decreasing values of f for decreasing x^*_1.

This means that when branching at a certain solution it is sufficient first to generate the optimal solution at the adjacent integer values of the variable to be constrained at integer values. Hence in the hypothetical example we would branch as follows

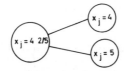

The other branches, for example $x_j = 3$ or $x_j = 6$, are not immediately generated since they will have a value of f lower than the branches of the adjacent integers or at most equal to their values. But if we now branch out from one of the two resulting branches, say $x_j = 4$, it should be remembered that the branch $x_j = 3$ exists and may have a higher value of f than a branch resulting from $x_j = 4$.

As an example for the method, the following problem is considered. Maximize

$$(3.6) \qquad f = -10x_1 + 111x_2$$

subject to

$$(3.7) \qquad \begin{aligned} -x_1 + 10x_2 &\leq 40, \\ x_1 + x_2 &\leq 20, \end{aligned}$$

Table 3
Simplex trableaux for general integer problem

Tableau	Basic variables	Values basic variables	x_1	x_2
0	y_1	40	-1	$\frac{10}{1}$
	y_2	20	1	
	f	0	10	-111
			x_1	y_1
1	x_2	4	$-\frac{1}{10}$	$\frac{1}{10}$
	y_2	16	$1\frac{1}{10}$	$-\frac{1}{10}$
	f	444	$-1\frac{1}{10}$	$11\frac{1}{10}$
			y_2	y_1
2	x_2	$5\frac{5}{11}$	$\frac{1}{11}$	$\frac{1}{11}$
	x_1	$14\frac{6}{11}$	$\frac{10}{11}$	$-\frac{1}{11}$
	f	460	1	11
			$x_1=14$	y_1
3	x_2	$5\frac{2}{5}$	$-\frac{1}{10}$	$\frac{1}{10}$
	y_2	$\frac{3}{5}$	$1\frac{1}{10}$	$-\frac{1}{10}$
	f	$459\frac{2}{5}$	$-1\frac{1}{10}$	$11\frac{1}{10}$
			y_2	$x_1=15$
4	x_2	5	1	1
	y_1	5	-10	-11
	f	405	111	121
			$x_1=13$	y_1
5	x_2	$5\frac{3}{10}$	$-\frac{1}{10}$	$\frac{1}{10}$
	y_2	$1\frac{7}{10}$	$1\frac{1}{10}$	$-\frac{1}{10}$
	f	$458\frac{3}{10}$	$-1\frac{1}{10}$	$11\frac{1}{10}$
			$x_1=14$	$x_2=5$
6	y_1	4	-1	10
	y_2	1	1	1
	f	415	10	-111

Table 3 (continued)

Tableau	Basic variables	Values basic variables	$x_1=12$	y_1
7	x_2	$5\frac{1}{5}$	$-\frac{1}{10}$	$\frac{1}{10}$
	y_2	$2\frac{4}{5}$	$1\frac{1}{10}$	$-\frac{1}{10}$
	f	$457\frac{1}{5}$	$-1\frac{1}{10}$	$11\frac{1}{10}$
			$x_1=13$	$x_2=5$
8	y_1	3	-1	10
	y_2	2	1	1
	f	425	10	-111
			$x_1=11$	y_1
9	x_2	$5\frac{1}{10}$	$-\frac{1}{10}$	$\frac{1}{10}$
	y_2	$3\frac{9}{10}$	$1\frac{1}{10}$	$-\frac{1}{10}$
	f	$456\frac{1}{10}$	$-1\frac{1}{10}$	$11\frac{1}{10}$
			$x_1=12$	$x_2=5$
10	y_1	2	-1	10
	y_2	3	1	1
	f	435	10	-111
			$x_1=10$	y_1
11	x_2	5	$-\frac{1}{10}$	$\frac{1}{10}$
	y_2	5	$1\frac{1}{10}$	$-\frac{1}{10}$
	f	455	$-1\frac{1}{10}$	$11\frac{1}{10}$
			$x_1=11$	$x_2=5$
12	y_1	1	-1	10
	y_2	4	1	1
	f	445	10	-111

(3.8) $x_1, x_2 \geqq 0$

(3.9) x_1, x_2 integer

First Variant I will be followed. Tableau 0 of Table 3 gives the set-up tableau. In two iterations of the simplex method the optimal solution for the

problem without integer constraints is found, see Tableau 2. Various criteria
for the variable to be made integer first exist. Here x_1 will be made an integer
first. Since $x_1 = 14^6/_{11}$, the solutions with $x_1 = 14$ and $x_1 = 15$ should be
considered. Using upper-bound techniques, these solutions are speedily found,
see Tableaux 3 and 4. The decision tree is now as follows

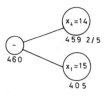

We now branch out at $x_1 = 14$ by making x_2 an integer, but at the same time
generate the other adjacent node of $x_1 = 14$, which is $x_1 = 13$. Hence we
should generate the optimal solutions for $x_1 = 14$, $x_2 = 5$, and $x_1 = 14$,
$x_2 = 6$, and $x_1 = 13$. Tableau 3 is the starting point. Two of these solutions
are found in the Tableaux 5 and 6; it turns out that the solution $x_1 = 14$,
$x_2 = 6$ is infeasible. The decision tree is now

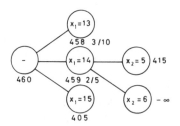

Since the node $x_1 = 13$ has the maximum value of f, it should be used for
branching out, so that the solutions for $x_1 = 13$, $x_2 = 5$ and $x_1 = 13$ and
$x_2 = 6$ should be generated. But also the adjacent node $x_1 = 12$ should be
generated. In the same way the method can be continued. Table 3 gives the
optimal solutions and Figure 7 the decision tree for the problem. The optimal
solution turns out to be $x_1 = 10$, $x_2 = 5$. Variant II for this problem is left as
an exercise.

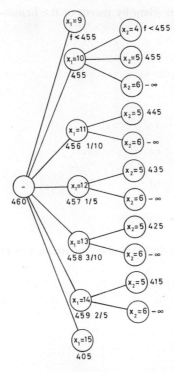

Fig. 7.

Exercises

1. Solve the following integer programming problem by means of the branch-and-bound method: Maximize

$$3x_1 + 4x_2$$

subject to

$$3x_1 + 2x_2 + x_3 = 8$$

$$x_1 + 4x_2 + x_4 = 10$$

$$x_1, x_2, x_3, x_4 \geq 0 \text{ and integer.}$$

2. Solve the following problem by means of the branch-and-bound method:
Maximize:

$$2x_1 + x_2$$

subject to

$$2x_1 + x_2 \geq 7\frac{1}{2} ,$$

$$12x_1 + 7x_2 \leq 55 ,$$

$$2\frac{1}{2}x_1 + x_2 \leq 9\frac{1}{2} ,$$

$$x_1, x_2 \geq 0 \text{ and integer} .$$

3. Solve by means of the branch-and-bound method: Minimize:

$$f = 4x_1 + 5x_2$$

subject to

$$3x_1 + x_2 \geq 2 ,$$

$$3x_1 + 2x_2 \geq 7 ,$$

$$x_1 + 4x_2 \geq 5 ,$$

$$x_1, x_2 \geq 0 \text{ and integer} .$$

4. Solve by the branch-and-bound method the T.V. distribution problem of Chapter 11 assuming that it is only possible to sell in a market after advertising expenditures have been made. The advertising expenditures for Holland, Britain, Germany and Denmark are assumed to be $3000, $5000, $4000 and $2000 per period.

BIBLIOGRAPHY

Only the literature referred to in the text and a few well-known books are included. For more complete bibliographies, see [3], [5], and [20].

[1] R.S. Beresford and M.H. Peston, A Mixed Strategy in Action, *Operations Research Quarterly,* Vol. 6 (1955), pp. 173–175.

[2] A. Charnes, Optimality and Degeneracy in Linear Programming, *Econometrica,* Vol. 20 (1952), pp. 160–170.

[3] A. Charnes and W.W. Cooper, *Management Models and Industrial Applications of Linear Programming,* Vols. I and II, New York: J. Wiley and Sons, 1961.

[4] A. Charnes, W.W. Cooper and A. Henderson, *An Introduction to Linear Programming.* New York: J. Wiley and Sons, and London: Chapman and Hall, 1953.

[5] G.B. Dantzig, *Linear Programming and Extensions.* Princeton, N.J.: Princeton University Press, 1963.

[6] L.R. Ford and D.R. Fulkerson, *Flows in Networks.* Princeton, N.J.: Princeton University Press, 1962.

[7] R.E. Gomory, An Algorithm for Integer Solutions in Linear Programming, in: *Recent Advances in Mathematical Programming,* R. Graves and P. Wolfe (eds.). New York: McGraw-Hill, 1963.

[8] G. Hadley, *Linear Programming.* Reading, Mass.: Addison-Wesley Publishing Company, 1962.

[9] G. Hadley, *Nonlinear and Dynamic Programming.* Reading, Mass.: Addison-Wesley Publishing Company, 1964.

[10] L.V. Kantorovich, *Mathematical Methods of Organizing and Planning Production.* Leningrad State University, 1969 (in Russian). Translated and reprinted in *Management Science,* Vol. 6, No. 4 (July, 1960), pp. 366–422.

[11] T.C. Koopmans (ed.), *Activity Analysis of Production and Allocation.* New York: J. Wiley and Sons, 1951.

[12] A.H. Land and A.G. Doig, An Automatic Method of Solving Discrete Programming Problems, *Econometrica,* Vol. 28 (1960), pp. 497–520.

[13] C.E. Lemke, The Dual Method of Solving the Linear Programming Problem, *Naval Research Logistics Quarterly,* Vol. 1, No. 1 (1954), pp. 36–47.

[14] J.D.C. Little, K.G. Murty, D.W. Sweeney and C. Karel, An Algorithm for the Traveling Salesman Problem, *Operations Research Quarterly,* Vol. 11 (1963), pp. 972–989.

[15] C. McMillan, Jr., *Mathematical Programming.* New York: J. Wiley and Sons, 1970.

[16] C. van de Panne and A. Whinston, The Simplex and the Dual Method for Quadratic Programming, *Operations Research Quarterly,* Vol. 15 (1964), pp. 355–388.

362 *Bibliography*

[17] C. van de Panne and A. Whinston, An alternative Interpretation of the Primal-Dual Method and Some Related Parametric Methods, *International Economic Review*, Vol. 9 (1968), pp. 87–99.

[18] C. van de Panne and A. Whinston, The Symmetric Formulation of the Simplex Method for Quadratic Programming, *Econometrica*, Vol. 37 (1969), pp. 507–527.

[19] S. Vajda, *Mathematical Programming*. Reading, Mass.: Addison-Wesley Publishing Company, 1961.

[20] H.M. Wagner, *Principles of Operations Research*. Englewood Cliffs, N.J.: Prentice-Hall, 1969.

INDEX